THE PASTORAL ELEGY

AN ANTHOLOGY

Edited with Introduction, Commentary, and Notes

BY

THOMAS PERRIN HARRISON

ENGLISH TRANSLATIONS

BY

HARRY JOSHUA LEON

1968

OCTAGON BOOKS, INC.

New York

Reprinted 1968
by special arrangement with the University of Texas Press

OCTAGON BOOKS, INC.
175 FIFTH AVENUE
NEW YORK, N. Y. 10010

LIBRARY OF CONGRESS CATALOG CARD NUMBER: 68-16774

Printed in U.S.A. by
NOBLE OFFSET PRINTERS, INC.
NEW YORK 3, N. Y.

Ægloga vndecima.

Argument.

I N this xi. Aeglogue he bewaileth the death of some maiden of
great bloud whom he calleth Dido. The personage is secret, and
to me altogether vnknowne, albeit of himselfe I often required
the same. This Aeglogne is made in imitation of Marot his
song, which he made vpon the death of Loyes the French Queene.
But farre passing his reach, and in mine opinion all other the Ae-
logues of this booke.

Thenot. Colin.

C Olin my deare, when shall it please thée sing,
  As thou were wont songes of some iouisaunce?
Thy Muse too long slombreth in sorrowing,
Lulled a sléepe through loues misgouernaunce,

Now

Spargite humum foliis, inducite fontibus umbras.

—*Virgil*

So may some gentle Muse
With lucky words favour *my* destined urn,
And as he passes turn,
And bid fair peace be to my sable shroud.

—*Milton*

PREFACE

Of the various kinds of pastoral song the elegy alone has persisted down to modern times. The Greek *Daphnis* by Theocritus is the first of the ancient shepherd dirges to claim attention; our English *Thyrsis* is possibly the last. Extensive as the compass of this book is, the poems here included set forth with fair completeness the evolution of this genre, which, after all, has remained distinct and clear cut. Although it is believed that the group of twenty-three poets is both representative and exhaustive so far as concerns the development of the elegy, the problem of selection may not always have been successfully met. Immediate acknowledgment in this regard is due the preliminary survey of the field by Professor J. H. Hanford, "The Pastoral Elegy and Milton's *Lycidas*" (*Publications of the Modern Language Association*, 1910). His estimate of the significance of individual poems has often been adopted, and his critical analysis appears frequently in the notes. Pastoral elegy as a literary type free of satiric or romantic bias ends with Milton's *Lycidas*. Hence, in great measure all Milton's predecessors are regarded by comparison, by contrast, and by direct contribution as leading the way to *Lycidas*. The intrinsic worth of a poem, its representative aspects, and the reputation of the author: these, too, have helped to narrow the problem of choice. The editor has tried to secure a balanced representation of Greek, Roman, Italian, French, and English poets without damage to the larger purpose of illustrating the tradition of pastoral elegy from its beginnings.

A single representative of the medieval elegy is considered adequate. Radbert's poem was chosen because it is both conspicuous and fully representative and because it directly influenced Petrarch, opportunity being thus provided of showing the continuity of the tradition, and more specifically, the medieval elements in the work of the great Italian humanist. The Renaissance Neo-Latinists are represented by Castiglione, whose *Alcon* seemed a logical inclusion by reason of its genuine excellence and its influence upon both Milton poems. Drummond hold a dual claim. His paraphrase of Castiglione exemplifies the poetic ideal of his school and it throws into relief the work of his great contemporary, Milton. The earlier tribute to Prince Henry, a superior performance, sufficiently evinces its Spenserian origins to warrant the omission of Fletcher, Drayton, and Browne, those other great Spenserians.

Standard texts have been adopted throughout. Those of the foreign poems, except the Greek, accompany the translations, which have been uniformly and literally executed. Most of the continental vernacular poems now appear for the first time in English translation. Individual titles of poems, when supplied by the editor, have been bracketed.

As far as possible, introductory materials have been abridged in order to avoid repetition of generally accessible facts. The work of W. W. Greg, *Pastoral Poetry and Pastoral Drama* (London, 1906), and that of E. Carrara, *La Poesia Pastorale* (Milan, 1909), are both indispensable to students of the pastoral. Of the various short surveys the best is that by Sir Edmund Chambers, introductory to *English Pastorals* (London, 1906). The introduction for the present volume roughly traces the evolution of the elegy by directing attention to the poems and poets here included. The less familiar lives of authors and the facts about their poetry precede the notes for the individual poems. A brief bibliography for each poet lists the more important books and articles which the editor has used. The notes attempt to point out the growth of the pastoral elegy through the centuries and by cross reference to demonstrate the unbroken continuity of the tradition. Parallel citations, often merely illustrative, indicate direct or indirect imitation. A useful study in this connection is that by George Norlin, "The Conventions of the Pastoral Elegy" (*American Journal of Philology*, 1911). The catalogue after the notes includes explanations of all but the most familiar mythological references and the names of persons and places included in the various poems.

The editor and translator wish especially to acknowledge the generous aid of Professor E. K. Rand of Harvard University and Professor Frederic Duncalf of The University of Texas in the difficult task of preparing both notes and translation for the medieval elegy by Radbert. For examining the completed manuscript and for their helpful suggestions the editor is grateful to Professor J. H. Hanford of Western Reserve University, and to Professor George C. Taylor of the University of North Carolina. To several colleagues and friends the editor and translator are indebted: especially to Professors A. B. Swanson and C. A. Swanson of the

Department of Romance Languages, who read and revised the translations of the vernacular poems, and to Professors J. B. Wharey and R. H. Griffith, both of whom kindly read portions of the manuscript. Thanks are owing to The Houghton Mifflin Company for permission to use the Cambridge texts of the poems by Spenser, Milton, Pope, and Shelley; and to the Macmillan Company for permission to include Arnold's *Thyrsis*. Finally, acknowledgment is due The University of Texas, a special grant from which has made possible the publication of this book.

CONTENTS

Contents

INTRODUCTION

I

THE ORIGINS OF PASTORAL ELEGY

As an artistic form pastoral elegy[1] begins with Theocritus' first idyl, the devices of which have been repeated through the ages. But the Daphnis legend is a late Greek development of the symbol under which earlier peoples mourned the withering vegetation of summer. "Under the symbols of Linus, Daphnis, or Adonis, the country people of early times lamented the decay of the fresh beauty of spring, under the burning midsummer heat. This primitive germ of serious feeling has perpetuated itself in that melancholy mood which runs throughout the pastoral poetry of all countries. From that tendency of the Greek imagination to give a human meaning to all that interested it, this dirge over the fading beauty of the early year soon assumed the form of the lament over the death of a young shepherd-poet, dear to gods and men, to the flocks, herds, and wild animals, to the rocks and mountains, among which he had lived. In the Daphnis of Theocritus, the human passion of love produces the blighting influence on the life of the shepherd which in the original myth was produced by the fierce heat of summer on the tender life of the year. A still later development of the myth appears in the lament over the extinction of youthful genius by early death."[2]

As this statement fully surveys the long course of pastoral elegy from its beginnings in primitive worship, so many of its conventions may be partly explained by reference to early myths. Hylas, Hyacinthus, Narcissus, Linus, Adonis—these personifications of the destruction of the tender life of nature came to be known as youths beloved of gods, fond of hunting and rural life, famously musical,

---

[1]From the unsuccessful efforts of Renaissance poets in England to adapt the classical elegiac distich the word *elegy* came to be loosely applied to various kinds of lyric—amorous, didactic, occasionally threnodic. The term *pastoral elegy* was apparently first used in 1595, when *Astrophel* was so described by Spenser. (See F. W. Weitzmann, "Notes on the Elizabethan *Elegie*," *Publications of the Modern Language Association*, L, 1935, 435–443.)

[2]W. Y. Sellar, *The Roman Poets of the Augustan Age*, Oxford, 1883, p. 155.

and destined to an early death. The name Linus or Ailinus, mentioned by Homer and often by Virgil as master-singer, derives from the words *ai lanu* (woe to us) which formed the burden of the Adonis and similar songs in the East. The name Adonis itself is a misnomer coming from the Semitic *Adon,* or "lord," by which the deity Tammuz was worshiped in Egypt and western Asia.[3] Roses and anemones grew from the blood of Adonis, as from Hyacinthus sprang "that sanguine flower inscribed with woe." Again, the importance of the Adonis myth, celebrated by both Theocritus and Bion, appears in a further particular: it contains the germ of the later conventional note of joy which usually concludes the pastoral elegy. "In the great Phoenician sanctuary of Astarte at Byblus," states Frazer,[4] "the death of Adonis was annually mourned, to the shrill wailing notes of the flute, with weeping, lamentation, and beating of the breast; but next day he was believed to come to life again and ascend up to heaven in the presence of his worshippers." Thus with the return of spring Adonis would come again, again join his divine mistress Aphrodite. Bion represents this joyful union as preceding the lamentation for the departed youth: "Hymenaeus quenched every torch at the doorposts and he scattered the nuptial wreath and no more did he sing 'Hymen, Hymen,' no more his own song, but 'Alas for Adonis,' he chants, even more than the bridal song."

A familiar device—unfortunately well known for its abuse—has received Ruskin's designation of "pathetic fallacy," by which both the animate and the inanimate things in nature mourn or rejoice with mankind. In Theocritus wolves, jackals, lions mourn the fate of Daphnis, his flocks bewail him; in Moschus woodland glades, all green things are called to voice their sorrow. Ultimately, the sorrow of nature for the death of humanity looks back to an earlier time when the death was that of nature, not humanity. Thus what was once the source of sorrow—the withering vegetation—becomes the mourner. Other influences contributed to assure the prominence of this aspect of elegy. First is the popularity of the Orpheus legend. Orpheus, too, was a youth who met death before his prime,

---

[3]Sir James G. Frazer, *The Golden Bough,* New York, 1929, I, 324 ff. See further the notes for Bion, *Lament for Adonis.*

[4]P. 335.

and had he not moved rocks and trees by his music? Later, the language in which the Golden Age was described, influenced as it was by that of the Hebraic prophets, was introduced by Virgil in the lines to Caesar:[5]

> Ipsi laetitia voces ad sidera iactant
> Intonsi montes; ipsae iam carmina rupes,
> Ipsa sonant arbusta: 'Deus, deus ille, Menalca.'

But Virgil is the first poet to subordinate the idea of Nature's sentience. In Eclogue 1.38–39, for example, Menalcas thus addresses Tityrus, who has left his farm and now returns:

> Ipsae te, Tityre, pinus
> Ipsi te fontes, ipsa haec arbusta vocabant.

They called him back in the sense that they depended on his care. Milton follows his master in this art, and further he so directs attention to the beauty of the things described that the literal sense is lost:

> Thee, Shepherd, thee the woods and desert caves,
> With wild thyme and the gadding vine o'ergrown,
> And all their echoes, mourn.
> The willows, and the hazel copses green,
> Shall now no more be seen
> Fanning their joyous leaves to thy soft lays.

The rôle of Nature, having its origin in man's grief for the death in Nature, reappears in the frequent contrast between the cyclic course of the seasons from death to life, on the one hand, and the finality of human death on the other. The sentiment in the well-known lines of Job (14.7–10) is found in Moschus (99–104),[6] who contrasts the perennial life of plants with the "right long sleep without end or waking" of poor mortals. And throughout the course of pastoral elegy this thought runs like a refrain. A natural outgrowth of grief itself, it remains a universal human emotion. Although it did not originate in pastoral poetry, the frequent occurrence there of this contrasting idea adds color and truth to the pastoral metaphor.

---

[5]See note for Virgil, Eclogue 5.60–64.
[6]See note for further illustrations.

II

THE CLASSICAL PASTORAL

The whole story of the origins of pastoral elegy is incompletely known, and the foregoing remarks merely touch upon its history prior to Theocritus. The two idyls which appear in this book exemplify fully the Greek genius; moreover, a study of them discloses the significant but seldom recognized fact that Theocritus anticipated his Roman disciple in the more important pastoral devices. In these Theocritus unconsciously developed the lines which the later elegy was to follow: from Idyl 1 sprang most of the conventions, from Idyl 7 the integral suggestion that the poet represent himself in his poem. The first completely represents the objective pastoral idyl, which has been defined as "a dramatic presentation of some characteristic scene in the joyous life of herdsmen. It is dramatic in that it represents the movement and speech of the actors *in propria persona*, but it has neither the action nor the unity of movement necessary to true drama."[7] The dramatic method of Theocritus was to become, in Virgil's weak imitation, the germ of the pastoral drama and masque, which flourished briefly in Renaissance Italy and England. But in Idyl 7, where the poet masquerades with his friends, the pastoral takes a new turn, for in succeeding ages personal allegory becomes all-important. Providing precedent for the introduction of the author, the Greek poem inspired the personal element in Moschus' *Lament for Bion* and later in Virgil's tenth eclogue, where the poet takes the rôle of comforter to the lovelorn Gallus. To a marked degree the evolution of pastoral elegy centers about the poet-shepherd, whose rôle increases in importance as the elegy is removed from the province of realism. In time the distinction of the elegy is measured, not primarily by the sincerity of the poet's grief in the loss of a friend, but by his mode of giving expression to his own ideas about life. Once the poet speaks *in propria persona*, inevitably he voices ideas personal and intimate to himself. This fact is evident from the first as in Idyl 7 Theocritus speaks about fellow-poets and their art.

---

[7]Martha H. Shackford, "A Definition of the Pastoral Idyll," *Publications of the Modern Language Association*, XIX (1904), 591.

With Theocritus as their guide the obscure poets of the *Lament for Adonis* and the *Lament for Bion* carried forward the tradition of pastoral elegy in several notable particulars;[8] but in them the pastoral suffers a loss of idyllic simplicity as the world of Theocritus gives way to artificiality and oriental luxurance. From this downward course the pastoral was redeemed by Virgil, whose ten eclogues are supremely important to students of the tradition, although to the casual reader they appeal less immediately than do the Greek idyls.

To his work Virgil brought a painstaking art, a transforming genius unknown to the Greeks. Virgil is among the first of the poet-scholars; his genius is like that of Spenser and Milton, its evolution traceable, like theirs, in the early poems. In this connection Professor Rand remarks:[9] "The art of constantly retouching affects the poet's mind as well as his work; he retouches his temperament; he moulds it into a more delicate and responsive instrument, until it can produce spontaneously what once was the culmination of refining toil." The later history of pastoral is the history of imitation; but pastoral writers more readily understand the imitative principle of Virgil than they share with him the subtle art of imitation, for success demands both genius and scholarship. Those students of nature who see in the eclogues little of the freshness, the spontaneity, and the realism of Theocritus may recognize, as Conington remarks,[10] that imagination is shown "in the words which embody a thought as well as in the thought which they embody." It is in this intellectual association that the eclogues abound. Virgil turned the pastoral in the direction from which it never swerved, and because he developed it to its height, later writers strove vainly to attain his excellence. As elegy soon assimilated new features, it alone of the pastoral types was free to develop and reach a new maturity. During the Middle Ages the Messianic eclogue placed Virgil with the Hebraic prophets, and when Petrarch revived the pastoral it was to Virgil that he turned. What excellence the pastoral may claim in later times is in great measure attributable to a study of Virgil. Immediately, of course,

---

[8]See pp. 260–262.

[9]*The Magical Art of Virgil*, Harvard University Press, 1931, p. 23.

[10]*P. Vergili Maronis Opera*, edited by John Conington, London, 1881, I, 14.

the tradition was kept alive by the post-Augustans, Calpurnius and Nemesian.

III

THE MEDIEVAL PASTORAL

The pastoral during the Middle Ages is a relatively obscure subject, but a good deal can be learned about it by a careful study of one fairly representative example. It is perhaps less surprising to find Virgil quoted by a churchman in the course of long scriptural commentary than to discover a genuine pastoral elegy appended to the long prose life of a departed monk. This phenomenon is presented in the *Vita* of Adalhardus, written by his disciple Paschasius Radbertus, a distinguished scholar of the ninth century. The relationship between *Vita* and *Egloga* may be accounted for by the fact that both are outgrowths of what were termed "rotuli" and "tituli." It was a monastic usage, Carrara explains,[11] "di inviar messaggeri che portassero certi 'rotuli' dove si segnavano i nomi dei morti, con qualche verso epitafico. I 'rotuli' passando di monastero in monastero si arricchivano di tali versi, che eran detti 'tituli," i quali assumevan un' apparenza di canto amebeo, essendo presso a poco sempre uniformi le querele e le espressioni di dolore. Questi imitò Radberto nell'ecloga, come nella 'Vita' avrà seguita la foggia dei 'rotuli,' scrivendo in versi ciò che prima s'era detto in prosa."

The aim of the poet, then, was to adapt to pastoral language the theme of the *Vita*, or in other words, to allegorize it; the prefatory key makes this point clear. Radbert's method derives from Virgil, whom it resembles even in the occasional inconsistency of the allegory. For example, as women, Phyllis and Galatea mourn the death of Adalhard, yet when occasion demands Galatea becomes a place, the locality of New Corbie, a monastery. Formerly she was "virgo ferox" (76) and "regio sterilis" (100), with reference to the barbarous state of Saxony before the founding of New Corbie. Now, says Phyllis of her, she is "porta poli" and "ianua vitae" (100). Such liberties are no less surprising than, for example, in Virgil's tenth eclogue, where Gallus is now a soldier, now a shepherd.

---

[11]Enrico Carrara, *La Poesia Pastorale*, Milan, 1909, p. 57.

A review of the *Egloga* discloses various extensions of the elegiac tradition. In Radbert's poem, as in the *Vita*, sorrow for the departed abbot assumes the form of an extensive contemplation of Death and execration against it, and second, an exaltation of the old man's virtues. In both respects the *Egloga* marks an advance upon the classical elegy. Virgil had sung the works of Caesar, and Nemesian had extolled the character of his subject; in the conjunction of these features Radbert's work contributes signally to the genre. Moreover, as these subjects dominate the first part of the elegy, so the consolation theme pervades the remainder of it. In the extension of this phase and in the emphasis which it bears lies Radbert's most important addition. The imagery reveals the poet's dual allegiance to Virgil's account of the godlike Caesar and the associations of the Messianic eclogue, and to the pseudo-Biblical tradition of a Christian heaven. Here as elsewhere in medieval literature the two traditions merge, and Renaissance poets bear witness to the permanence of the combination. Finally, the medieval conceptions of the earthly paradise resulted in an increasingly sensuous picture of the heavenly paradise. This phenomenon is manifest in Radbert's *Egloga;* its peculiar significance for pastoral elegy becomes clearer as one marks the influence of Radbert's poem upon Petrarch, in Eclogue 11. Ultimately the imagery of the earthly paradise is fully absorbed by the pastoral elegy, not directly through Radbert, but through Boccaccio, who borrowed extensively from Dante.

A final contribution of Radbert's poem should be noted. The religious note being pervasive in the poem, its theme sorrow for a dead abbot, inevitably the *Egloga* falls heir to the figure of shepherd and flock, a figure which in the hands of Petrarch and his followers was to find effective use in church satire. Strengthened by Christ's declaration (John, 10.11), the metaphor took firm hold and became as commonplace in homily as in pastoral.

IV

THE EARLY RENAISSANCE PASTORAL

In his attention to form as well as in his return to classic purity of language, Petrarch rescued the pastoral from the amorphous state it had reached during the Middle Ages. It emerges again as a work

of conscious art. At the same time the poet's eclogues are intimately linked with the Middle Ages. In using the pastoral for
personal religious reflections or church satire, Petrarch developed a
motive implicit in the medieval pastoral. Thus, although he did not
originate the idea, he proved to later centuries that the eclogue could
be used effectively in setting forth the religious interests of any age.

But with Petrarch, method comes before matter and is of more
actual importance. In his own words:[12] "Ex huiusce sermonis
[i.e. allegoriae] genere, poetica omnis intexta est." Allegory is not
only essential in poetry: allegory is the very substance of poetry.
"He seems to hold," says Tatham,[13] "that the more allegory a poem
has, the better its poetry, or—to put the matter personally—the
more completely a poet hides his real meaning, the higher his
merit." In accordance with this principle Petrarch wrote his
twelve eclogues, declaring with entire justice that they could be
understood only with a key. Three of the poems (1, 2, and 5)
Petrarch himself glossed; for the rest Benvenuto Rambaldi da
Imola, Donato Albanzani, and other friends provided elaborate
glosses.

Boccaccio is next in importance, and *Olympia* is eloquent of his
manner and method. Strictly speaking, the poem is not a pastoral,
but a medieval vision of the kind familiar to English readers in the
Middle English *Pearl*. The poem, written about 1361, was conceived as a memorial to Boccaccio's five-year-old daughter Violante,
dead two or three years previous. Except in the picture of Paradise,
we find only vague Virgilian reminiscence, there being little or no
similarity to Virgil's elegiac pastorals. The method is derived from
Petrarch; the materials are largely from Dante—the *Purgatorio* and
Paradiso. In Boccaccio's elaboration of the Dantean earthly and
heavenly paradise lies his most important contribution to the pastoral elegy, for both Marot and Ronsard imitate his manner and
occasionally his language.

The poem is cast in the medieval framework of the vision,
familiar in Dante and others but unique in pastoral. "È questo

---

[12]*Epistolae de Rebus Familiaribus*, edited by G. Fracassetti, Florence, 1859,
II, 83.

[13]Edward H. R. Tatham, *Francesco Petrarca His Life and Correspondence*,
London, 1926, II, 388–389.

l' unico esempio della visione, che entra nel genere bucolico," explains Carrara,[14] "ed è anche il primo esempio di poesia domestica,
per la quale non l'amata o una saggia guida ispirino pensieri di
salvezza al poeta, ma la voce giovanetta d'una figliuola. Dante
avea 'spirazione' da Beatrice; il Petrarca, da Laura; il Boccaccio,
sognante Fiammetta, era tratto a pensieri d'amore, nè la tradizione
della scuola potè mai in lui tanto da angelicare la sensuale immagine
di Maria. Ci voleva la virginale figura d'una figliuola, per questo:
e la cosa non è senza importanza."

An amazing aspect of this poem appears in Boccaccio's incongruous attempt to delineate a pastoral heaven. As Dantean imagery
is clothed in shepherd weeds, the effect becomes at times grotesque.
Christ first appears as Codrus, who delivered from Hell the Father's
flocks; but a little later He appears as a Lamb by the side of the
Virgin. Yet Boccaccio follows a well-defined tradition in describing
heaven in terms of the earthly paradise as the imagery of the
Aeneid combines with that of the *Purgatorio*. Moreover, the Biblical
figure of shepherd and flock, strongly implied in earlier elegies
such as Radbert's, gives authority to Boccaccio's audacious attempt.
In terms of the pastoral tradition the entire poem consists of elaborate consolation, a mood familiar to Boccaccio from Petrarch.

V

THE LATER RENAISSANCE PASTORAL

Boccaccio's eclogues were not printed until 1504, when Giunta
included the entire group in an anthology issued in Florence. A
more extensive edition, including the pastorals of thirty-eight poets,
was issued from the press of Oporinus (Basle, 1546). It was in
such collections that Petrarch and Boccaccio as well as later Neo-
Latin poets were read at home and abroad. The Neo-Latin movement proceeding for a time parallel with efforts in the vernacular,
some poets wrote in both languages. Among these is the Neapolitan
Sannazaro, who achieved great distinction first in his Italian
Arcadia, then late in life in his Latin Piscatory Eclogues, a new
species.

---

[14]Pp. 126–127.

Sannazaro accomplished a purpose significant for the later pastoral in restoring the Arcadia of Virgil as a setting. Arcadia became the ideal land of escape from reality, a retreat from the turmoil of actual life; and its painter so felt the gentle appeal of its unreality that throughout his work Arcadia becomes a theme in itself personal and intense, without need of narrative. "What religion or the wild revelry that found its fullest expression in the license of carnival gave to other men of his day, he sought in the construction of an ideal world as remote from his own as possible. In his 'Arcadia' he has garnered up everything that he held most dear: his first love, his mother, his friends, his loyalty to his king and his religion, Naples and his home there, his delight in the great poets of all ages, as in the beauty of rural scene and woodland and the peace and simplicity of his imaginary primitive country life, all steeped in a scholar's melancholy."[15]

Moreover, this aim the poet has pursued in accordance with the humanistic theory of poetry as imitation. Classical poets in company with the moderns have been so sedulously followed that each page of the *Arcadia* is a mosaic of paraphrase and reminiscence. Petrarch had known no Greek, and Boccaccio had turned to Virgil; here in the *Arcadia* Theocritus, Bion, Moschus, and other Greeks join company with the Romans, with Petrarch, and with Boccaccio. Thus Sannazaro achieved for poetry what Erasmus had attempted for prose, when excerpting the ancients became the fashion. And— of first importance in the study of Sannazaro's successors—the *Arcadia*, by reason of its scholarship, assumed a place equal in importance to the ancients themselves, as the romance was studied and imitated reverently by French and English pastoralists.

Later in life Sannazaro turned his attention to Latin. After his return to Naples, in 1504, the poet composed the long epic, *De Partu Virginis*, to which he devoted himself more than to a second literary project, the first of its kind—a series of five Piscatory Eclogues. These two Latin works, appearing together in 1526, attained a popularity equal to that enjoyed by the *Arcadia*. Justly, it seems, Sannazaro claimed originality in inventing the piscatory, for though mythology and even Theocritus provided suggestions, the Italian

---

[15]*London Times Literary Supplement*, September 4, 1930, p. 689.

poet established the type by composing a series of piscatories, which alone were to define the scope of the meagre genre. In these poems the setting is native and Theocritean; the method is Virgilian. Here are the traditional Virgilian types—the elegy, the lover's lament, the singing match, the panegyric. Furthermore, Sannazaro's fishermen converse in the very language of Virgil. The imitative method is identical with that of the *Arcadia,* although more restricted; and this accounts largely for the wide popularity of both works. The poems, composed at Mergellina within sight and sound of the Neapolitan bay, gave expression, then, to the scholarly side of the poet as well as to his genuine love of the scenes.

Following humanistic principles, Sannazaro established for his successors the vernacular pastoral and the new piscatory. Their task lay for the most part in writing after the fashion of Sannazaro, as the tremendous popularity of his work indicates. The future course of the elegy as of the pastoral generally is now to be more clearly marked by sheer imitation. No significant changes appear in the outlines of pastoral elegy, and hence the story of its progress resolves itself into that of the individuals who wrote in this kind.

The elegiac *Alcon,* by Baldassare Castiglione, exemplifies the best of the Neo-Latinists, who like Sannazaro in his fisherman eclogues turned directly to Virgil. While affecting the Virgilian manner in this poem, Castiglione was impelled by another motive in his choice of Latin. Like his follower John Milton, Castiglione was deeply moved in the loss of an intimate, and possibly he recognized in Latin a freer medium for the expression of his sorrow. Without exception, among pastoral elegies, it may be granted, Castiglione's *Alcon* and Milton's *Epitaphium Damonis* succeed in giving rein to the emotions while following the accepted pastoral conventions. Both poets move easily in the two worlds at the same time: the world of art and that of feeling. Though nearly half the poem *Alcon* is conventionalized from Virgil and Moschus, in the latter part the poet freely voices his sorrow without violence to pastoral conventions. *Alcon* is neither poetical exercise nor slavish imitation: preserving the best in the tradition, it is as really a product of scholarship as of genuine feeling.

Yet in the early decades of the sixteenth century there was an important place for what modern criticism calls slavish imitation, particularly in the vernacular eclogue. For his imitative pastorals the name of Luigi Alamanni is less significant in literary history than for his early employment of blank verse. Preceding the French Pléiade by half a century, Alamanni pointed the direction of their efforts. Besides two long poems, he wrote eclogues, Pindarics, odes, sonnets, hymns, and elegiacs, these latter pieces being published long before the appearance of *La Deffence*. Du Bellay knew the work of "seigneur Loys Aleman" and notes his use of blank verse, "en sa non moins docte que plaisante *Agriculture*"; and Ronsard imitated some of Alamanni's hymns. By his example Alamanni instructed the French in what classical models to follow.

The revival of pastoral as one of the classical kinds was not least among the interests of that group of Florentines who gathered at the Orti Oricellari. In his youthful contributions Alamanni was content to follow closely the footing of the Greek pastoral triad—Theocritus, Bion, and Moschus. Gradually, however, he detached himself, following other models and adapting his eclogues more freely to the contemporary subjects and conditions of his own life. Though always his work betrays the forthright craftsman, Alamanni gains importance in the fact that his pastorals were eagerly read and imitated by later poets of the century both on the Continent and in England; the very exactness of his method established his kinship with the ancients themselves.

In the year 1532, when the first volume of Alamanni's *Opere Toscane* appeared, Clément Marot issued the first collection of his poems under the title *Adolescence clémentine*. Unlike that of Alamanni, the work of Marot, great as it was in volume as in variety, belonged both to the Middle Ages and to the Renaissance. His devotion to Villon, whose works he edited, his achievements in the old verse forms—rondeaux and ballades—, stylistic and linguistic qualities: these linked Marot with a past which was soon to be discarded with the rise of the Pléiade. Yet humanism is manifest in his interest in Virgil, Ovid, the Greek Musaeus, in Petrarch and Erasmus. And that which distinguishes Marot from Alamanni, for example, is originality. Whatever he put his hand to bore the imprint of his genius, his French spirit, his homely naiveté; "en

toute idée il apercevait vite le point incisif et brillant," remarks
Héricault.[16]

Yet on the side of language, destined as it was to undergo
marked changes, Marot's work stood condemned in the eyes of the
Pléiade.   Moreover, Marot acknowledged no debt to Italy, and it
was to Italy that the poets of the Pléiade turned for inspiration.
In England both Wyatt and Surrey were indebted to Marot as well
as to Alamanni; but during what Sidney Lee terms the "inter-
regnum" in English poetry Marot's popularity waned in France,
as in England all poetry waned.   After Marot's dethronement,
Ronsard reigning in his stead, one English poet chose to adapt to
good advantage some measures and themes from the earlier poet:
in the *Visions* of Petrarch, in the linked quatrains in his sonnets,
and in two eclogues of the *Shepheardes Calender,* Edmund Spenser
owed his inspiration to Marot.

Antoine de Baïf was not only poet but reformer.   In 1567, with
the approval of the King, he founded the Academy of Music and
Poetry, and the succeeding years witnessed not only a prolific output of verse from the pen of Baïf, but his unstinting efforts towards
the reform of French verse.   Professing to abominate rhyme, Baïf
proposed the application of classical principles to French verse;
vers mesurés were to supplant rhyme and natural accentuation, and
orthography was to be simplified.   Despite the King's encourage-
ment, the movement failed, for by 1584 the Academy had ceased
to exist.   Yet the example of Baïf, as well as that of others, in
forsaking the hexameter for various metrical and stanzaic patterns,
was followed by the English Spenser.

The eclogues of Baïf, written mostly before 1560, preceded the
pastoral efforts of both Ronsard and Belleau, who praised Baïf as
their antecedent.   Of the nineteen, eleven are translations.   Theocritus is the poet's chief model, Bion and Virgil occupying second
place among the ancients; of the humanists Sannazaro (the Latin
eclogues) and Navagero are his favorites.   Five idyls of Theocritus
were translated: *Le Cyclope* (8) from Idyl 11, *Le Pastoureau* (12)
from Idyl 20, *Les Moissoneurs* (14) from Idyl 10, *Le Satyreau*

---

[16]C. d'Héricault, Biography, p. xxii (*Oeuvres Complètes de Clément Marot,*
edited by M. Pierre Jannet, Paris, 1868–72, IV).

(18) from Idyl 27, *Le Combat* (19) from Idyl 6.   Eclogue 4
(*Marmot*) combines Virgil and Theocritus; Eclogues 5 and 6,
Theocritus, Virgil, and Sannazaro; Eclogue 9 combines two Virgilian eclogues, Bion, and Ovid, each adaptation being separate and
easily distinguished.   Such is the imitative genius of Baïf. "Labeur
d'ouvrier appliqué, non d'artiste," writes Augé-Chiquet.[17] "Une seule
préoccupation obsède l'esprit de Baïf; il veut enrichir son sujet, le
charger d'ornements empruntés, accumuler les épisodes, fussent-ils
disparates. . . . Son caractère s'accommodait mal de la douceur
bucolique, son rude poing est malhabile à tenir la houlette
enrubannée. Il le reconnaît enfin et, comme il dit, voue à Pan sa
'challemie.' "

There is no need to discuss here the far-reaching importance of
Ronsard, great poet of the French Renaissance. Recognized at home
and abroad, Ronsard in pastoral was sure to claim attention. Two
poems fall within the scope of the present anthology; both illustrate
his genius in adapting classic originals. First stands the long
Bergerie, the elegiac motif of which is entitled "Angelot." This
poem reflects divers sources and succeeds in combining with the
pastoral some features of the masque. Fontainebleau is the supposed scene, and each pastoral character is matched in the French
nobility. In spite, however, of a seeming independence, Ronsard's
elegy in honor of Henry II manifests little originality, for the poem
consists of a series of paraphrases from Virgil's Eclogue 5, from
Sannazaro's Prose 5 and Eclogue 5, from Boccaccio's *Olympia*,
from Navagero's *Damon*, and from Marot's *Loyse*. Obviously, then,
imitation is Ronsard's principle; and the French poet's universal
popularity in England contributed not only to the importance of his
work but to the acceptance of this principle of composition. With
equal justice, certainly with more evidence of direct influence, this
observation applies to Ronsard's second great poem in the tradition
of pastoral elegy—*Adonis*. Its great antecedent, Bion's *Lament for
Adonis*, though not essentially pastoral, became a favorite Renaissance theme on the Continent, partly no doubt by reason of Ovid's
extensive treatment of it. Ronsard's *Adonis*, first published in

---

[17]Mathieu Augé-Chiquet, *La Vie, Les Idées et L'oeuvre de Jean-Antoine de
Baïf*, Paris, 1909, pp. 254–255.

1563, finely illustrates the Renaissance treatment of the popular pseudo-pastoral theme, and as the immediate source of Spenser's *Astrophel* it holds a special interest.

For English poetry the most important event of the year 1579 was the publication of the *Shepheardes Calender*, by Edmund Spenser. Experimental in metre, eclectic in matter, the *Calender* signally illustrates the temper of both its author and the times. Of the poet's manifold aims the most important was his desire to provide English poetry with one of the poetic kinds "wherein it faulteth": after the best continental models and criticism to write eclogues in accordance with the established types. And E. K. mentions Theocritus, Virgil, Mantuan, Petrarch, Boccaccio, Marot, and Sannazaro as those "whose foting this Authour every where followeth; yet so as few, but they be wel sented, can trace him out." In pastoral poetry the imitative principle extended even to the definition and use of the Petrarchan misnomer *aeglogue*, which E. K. boldly and scornfully defends against such malaprops as *eclogue* and *eclogai*.

In choosing Marot as model for two of the twelve eclogues, however, Spenser was not siding wholly with the doctrines of the French Pléiade, which in other matters he deeply respected. In "November" Spenser follows the language of Marot's elegy on the death of Louise of Savoy, and in the dialogue he adopts the French poet's device of linking quatrains. He set the elegy proper in a stanza of his own invention, this very originality, as Hughes points out,[18] allying him with the later French poets. Thus the matter and possibly the linked quatrains Spenser derived from Marot; his metrical inventiveness he owed to the later Frenchmen. Two new features of pastoral elegy, lacking in "November," Spenser gave place to in separate eclogues—the catalogue of flowers and church satire. In the "April" panegyric to Elizabeth, Spenser appropriately employed the flower device, which in English poetry was to find consummate expression in Milton. The church eclogues, especially "May," he devoted to satire. The flower motif was an ancient one; the satirical motif had been employed with effect by Petrarch, Mantuan, and

---

[18]M. Y. Hughes, *Virgil and Spenser*, Berkeley, California, 1929, pp. 265–271.

others. These elegiac conventions and others unite in the *Shepheardes Calender,* where in twelve poems the entire pastoral tradition is focussed. It remained for Milton to give permanence to that which is best in the pastoral within the scope of a single poem, *Lycidas.*

As concerns the history of pastoral elegy, the importance of "November" and the passages from "April" and "May" is more widely recognized than are the Sidney elegies. But a study of Milton and Shelley discloses their intimate familiarity with both the *Ruines of Time* and *Astrophel* (even two elegies by Lodowick Bryskett reflect Milton's interest in the *Astrophel* volume). Unlike the influence of the *Calender,* which shaped the general lines of later elegy and marked its scope, *Astrophel* provided verbal suggestion and a strong Platonic coloring in the consolation. Especially interesting is the contrast which Spenser's elegy presents with *Adonais,* both poets adapting the ancient Adonis theme.

Although the *Shepherd's Pipe,* by William Browne, contains perhaps better verse than can be found in any volume of William Drummond, this Scotch poet's efforts in pastoral elegy better represent the period between Spenser and Milton. A study of Drummond's extensive poetic achievements emphasizes his extreme imitative habits, which were encouraged, not so much by a desire to transform his models, as by the mediocrity of his own poetic talents. Drummond was more the scholar than the poet. "A full third of Drummond's compositions are translations or close paraphrases, and betray in no uncertain manner the imitative temper of his Muse. The rest are best described as adaptations from foreign models," writes L. E. Kastner.[19] A different opinion is held by another of Drummond's editors, W. C. Ward: "The many productions of his pen which are wholly original, afford ample proof that it was not from poverty of invention that he became a borrower. His was the full equipment of the poet, and what he took from others he had made already his own by sympathy and delight." But even this writer admits the inferiority of *Alcon,* which of course has suffered by comparison with Milton's similar *Epitaphium.*

---

[19]*The Poetical Works of William Drummond of Hawthornden,* London, 1913, I, xliii.

As the poem which gathers into its compass the entire tradition of pastoral, *Lycidas* can be rightly judged only by the laws of its kind. Yet readers of *Lycidas* are left cold less often through antipathy toward the pastoral form than through the feeling of Milton's insincerity. This impression seems the more justified in the light of the *Epitaphium Damonis,* in which emotion is more prominent than artistic purpose.

Several facts in this regard are worth noting. First, it is necessary to remember the conditions under which the poem was composed. Milton, at Horton, had been away from Cambridge for five years. The poem which he was asked to prepare was to join others in the memorial volume, *Obsequies to the Memory of Edward King* (*Lycidas* to stand last in the group of thirteen). Commemorative poems, customary on like sad occasions, were commonly known as "Tears" or "Lachrymae." Honoring a dead student and penned by his fellows, such elegies were distinctly academic. As a pastoral allegory of college life and friendship *Lycidas* was written primarily for its author's former associates. Calling to mind, hence, the best in the classical tradition familiar alike to his fellow students, Milton set out to compose a poem which, as Saintsbury remarks, might teem with "key- and catch-words which brother students might recognize, and which might awake in them, as in himself, pleasant trains of association and remembrance." In some measure this explains the highly imitative character of *Lycidas.* Looking forward, one recognizes the similar aim in *Thyrsis.* So vivid were Arnold's memories of Oxford that, as he later admitted somewhat ruefully, "not enough is said about Clough." Milton gained a more perfect balance of emphasis, but with reference to college life and friends both *Lycidas* and *Thyrsis* are academic poems.

At the time when he was called upon, Milton remembered at least two facts about Edward King: that he had written some verse at Cambridge and that he was preparing himself for church orders. Beyond these *Lycidas* yields nothing, nor does Milton name King in a letter to Diodati a month after King's death. It is highly significant that the two bits of fact which Milton knew are introduced in *Lycidas,* not as subjects in themselves for poetic eulogy, but as starting points for themes intimately personal to himself:

>   he knew
> Himself to sing, and build the lofty rhyme. . . .
> So may some gentle Muse
> With lucky words favour *my* destined urn,
> And as he passes turn,
> And bid fair peace be to my sable shroud!
> For we were nursed upon the self-same hill,
> Fed the same flock, by fountain, shade, and rill.

Apparently Milton is thinking of the analogy between King and himself. *Lycidas* is a poem about Milton and his reactions to life.

On the one hand, then, *Lycidas*, facing towards Cambridge, resembles Arnold's *Thyrsis* in its collegiate associations; on the other, it approaches *Adonais* in that both Milton and Shelley seriously concern themselves with questions arising from a contemplation of death. The personal element in pastoral elegy had increased from the beginning; neither digressive nor excrescent, it remains an inevitable product of the theme itself, even when the emotion is intense. Artistic success in elegy is more readily achieved when the poet has won complete detachment, for as it has been said, "a poet is responsible to the Muses that his works have artistic value apart from their value as an expression of his own feelings."[20] It is well, then, to recognize the completeness of Milton's detachment in *Lycidas*, his intense preoccupation with problems suggested by King's tragedy. Turning to the *Epitaphium Damonis*, one discovers Milton less concerned with artistic effects perhaps because of his inability to attain emotional detachment.

Masson expressed the almost universal opinion of the *Epitaphium Damonis* when he wrote:[21] "The poem is, beyond all question, the finest, the deepest in feeling, of all that Milton has left us in Latin, and one of the most interesting of all his poems, whether in Latin or English." But recently this has been challenged by Tillyard, who writes:[22] "Though containing perhaps the most beautiful passages, the *Epitaphium* is not the best of Milton's Latin poems. And the reason is that it reveals a troubled, disunited mind. A quite successful poem dealing with painful experience will not reveal

---

[20]W. L. Renwick, *Edmund Spenser*, London., 1925, p. 126.

[21]*The Poetical Works of John Milton*, edited by David Masson, London, 1903, I, 112.

[22]E. M. W. Tillyard, *Milton*, London, 1934, p. 99.

a troubled state of mind: it will derive its success precisely from expressing a state of mind that has found equilibrium after and in spite of sorrow." Comparison with *Lycidas* illustrates the differences arising from the separate moods in which the poems were undertaken. In the *Epitaphium* Milton's sorrow in the loss of Diodati is immediately perceptible as it is pervasive, both the Latin language and pastoral convention assisting the expression of that sorrow by veiling its intimacy.

Having chosen the pastoral as medium for his poetical tribute to his friend, inevitably Milton turned to the accepted classical models. The title itself copied from Moschus, the poet echoes other classical pastorals, of which, as in *Lycidas*, Virgil's tenth eclogue predominates. Yet as a late Neo-Latinist, Milton did not neglect his contemporaries, and from the welter of sixteenth-century Latin hexameters special reasons obtain for his remembering *Alcon*, in which Castiglione mourns the loss of an intimate. A comparison of the *Epitaphium* with William Drummond's elegy in honor of Sir Anthony Alexander, which also depends upon Castiglione's *Alcon*, discloses the difference between Milton and a poetaster, and in the *Epitaphium* a superior taste which his contemporary was incapable of conveying in verse. Whatever its models, the *Epitaphium* remains a peculiarly intimate revelation of the author, a biographical record of Milton at thirty-two.

VI

AFTERMATH

The eighteenth century marks the decline of the formal pastoral. Dominated by precise theory, the pastoral output of the time is negligible in poetic values as compared to previous achievement in this kind. Excluding individual literary taste in favor of the criteria of literary history, one finds after Milton only an aftermath. With him the continuity of the pastoral tradition ceased, partly of course because new and contrary currents of thought were in motion, but chiefly because there remained no further direction in which the pastoral could naturally expand. The interlude involving Pope, Philips, and Gay even contributed to the new romantic beginnings.

The elegies of Shelley and Arnold stand alone, testifying perhaps that this form of the pastoral contained enduring qualities independent of literary currents.

The English neo-classic pastoral in both theory and practice sprang directly from two French essays: Rapin's *Reflections on Aristotle's Poesy* (1674) and Fontenelle's *Essay on the Nature of the Eclogue* (1688). The ideas of both were incorporated by Pope in his *Discourse on Pastoral Poetry*. This treatise is invaluable in a study of Pope and his followers, for, as Professor Jones observes,[23] "Most of the criticisms that have been directed against Pope's poems are entirely beside the point, because the poems cannot be blamed for not being what they were not intended to be." It must be admitted that his pastorals follow the laws which he set down.

The famous *Discourse* comprehends rules for every feature—form, style, and content; and the pastorals of the period, varied as they were, reflect the spirit of Pope's rules and the force of his example. In its entire removal from real life the pastoral again sought, as during the Renaissance, to glorify the Golden Age and thus provide spiritual consolation for those wearied with the stress of urban life. For a little while the age was content to view only what Pope called "the best side" of country life, but soon it began to show impatience towards the polite efforts to conceal the miseries of rural folk.

The six poems of Ambrose Philips reflect a theory of the pastoral somewhat different from Pope's. An avowed disciple of Theocritus and Spenser, whose shepherd names he adopts, Philips succeeded in reproducing something of the manner of Spenser and the matter of Virgil. The ideal of the Golden Age Philips thrust aside in an ingenuous attempt to be true to the actual lives and conditions of the country. A lover of rural scenes and associations and a devoted student of the older pastorals, Philips yet understood neither country life nor the pastoral tradition; and besides, he was deficient in lyrical gifts. Consequently, with the exception of a few passages which show some personal recollection of rural imagery, the pastorals represent insipid and nerveless attempts to combine the

---

[23]Richard F. Jones, "Eclogue Types in English Poetry of the Eighteenth Century," *The Journal of English and Germanic Philology*, XXIV (1925), 38.

virtues of Spenser and Virgil. Their sentimental bias helped to earn for Philips the nickname Namby Pamby, which long clung to him in both life and letters. In view of the marked inferiority of Philips' work the judgment of his contemporaries is difficult to understand.

Pope lauded Philips' pastorals only until he discovered that other critics were similarly disposed. Not satisfied with the revenge of a letter to the *Guardian* praising Philips ironically, Pope engaged his friend John Gay to burlesque the pastorals of Philips. The result was the *Shepherd's Week* (1714), a series of six eclogues which, following the time arrangement suggested by Pope, were labeled as days of the week, Monday through Saturday, Sunday being omitted, explains Gay, "ours being supposed to be christian shepherds and to be then at church worship." Philips had attempted to nationalize the pastoral, as it were, by introducing realistic touches; Gay mistakenly believed that frankly realistic pictures of actual country folk would most effectively hold up to ridicule Philips and the Theocritean manner. Unintentionally Gay won the kind of acclaim which he had least anticipated. Despite the unnaturally ridiculous names of his characters, Gay's rural idyls more nearly approach the spirit of Theocritus than he had imagined. Finally, towards the last of the century Crabbe in the *Village* (1783) summarily put an end to the formal pastoral. Giving expression to humanitarian convictions, this poem marks the beginnings of new interests in literature. Of the pastoral types which retained their formal dress the elegy was to survive as still a means of paying poetic tribute to the dead.

In structure and detail Shelley's *Adonais* follows the beaten paths of the traditional elegy, and yet almost each line bears intimately the impress of the poet's individuality—his prejudice as well as his idealism. The question of what the success of *Adonais* owes to Shelley's choice of the pastoral machinery is unanswerable; still it is likely that without it any elegiac poem of the length of *Adonais* must become repetitive and tedious. The poem exhibits a scholarly assimilation of the great pastoral elegies both classical and modern; it was, as its author described it, "a highly wrought *piece of art*."

Like many of his contemporaries, Shelley turned first to the Greeks, whose spontaneity and informality appealed more strongly than the elegance of the Romans. The mottoes prefixed to *Adonais* point the direction of his deeper interests, and his letters are eloquent of his love of Greek learning. Among the classical elegies, Bion's *Lament for Adonis* is of first importance in a study of *Adonais*. Nor did Shelley forget Moschus' allusion to Bion's death by poison, strikingly if untruthfully like reviewers' poison; parts of both poems he had previously versified in English. Through stanza xxxvii *Adonais* betrays the marked influence of the two Greek elegies. In the remaining seventeen stanzas, which gradually effect a transition from the theme of sorrow to that of peace and immortality, the poet's inspiration is less Greek than English. And to Spenser Shelley is bound not only by Neo-Platonism and the Spenserian stanza, but by pastoral themes and imagery from *Astrophel* and "November" of the *Calender*.

The last of the great pastoral elegies, Arnold's *Thyrsis*, offers interesting affinities. As an allegory commemorating college life, the poem suggests immediately *Lycidas*, and with Milton's Latin elegy *Thyrsis* is linked through the intimacy of poet and friend. Here, it must be admitted, the analogies are virtually complete; yet Arnold's tribute to Clough was inevitably drawn into the traditional pastoral forms and conventions. As in other successful elegies, the traditional here merges with what is personal and direct in poetic thought and contributes to its fullness of expression.

In a letter to his mother, April 7, 1866, Arnold includes an interesting comment upon *Thyrsis*:[24]

"Tell him [Edward] that the diction of the poem was modelled on that of Theocritus, whom I have been much reading during the two years this poem has been forming itself, and that I meant the diction to be so artless as to be almost heedless. . . . The images are all from observation, on which point there is an excellent remark in Wordsworth's notes, collected by Miss Fenwick. The cuckoo on the wet June morning I heard in the garden at Woodford, and all those three stanzas you like are reminiscences of Woodford. . . . It is probably too *quiet* a poem for the general taste, but I think it will stand wear."

---

[24]*Letters of Matthew Arnold*, edited by George W. E. Russell, New York, 1895, I, 325.

Equally significant are the poet's confessions to J. C. Shairp, April 12, 1866:[25]

" 'Thyrsis' is a very quiet poem, but I think solid and sincere. It will not be popular, however. It had long been in my head to connect Clough with that Cumner country, and when I began I was carried irresistibly into this form; you say, truly, however, that there is much in Clough (the whole prophet side, in fact) which one cannot deal with in this way, and one has the feeling, if one reads the poem as a memorial poem, that not enough is said about Clough in it; I feel this so much that I do not send the poem to Mrs. Clough. Still Clough *had* this idyllic side, too; to deal with this suited my desire to deal again with that Cumner country: anyway, only so could I treat the matter this time."

The realistic aim being uppermost, the very cuckoo of that June morning ringing in his ears, he was carried into the manner of Theocritus, whom he had been reading. But for the most part, Arnold achieves realistic description of external nature which is as much Wordsworthian as Theocritean. *Thyrsis* depicts the Oxford countryside as seen by an Oxonian, not by one who, like Theocritus, was deeply interested in country life; and it is the most popular of Arnold's poems because of its truth of scene. Arnold's acknowledgment that the diction of the poem, modeled after Theocritus, was "so artless as to be almost heedless" suggests the direct contrast with Shelley's description of *Adonais* as "a highly wrought *piece of art*." Arnold's statement, justified in the poem, implies that he had thrown aside the formalities of the later pastoral in turning directly to the Greek manner of simplicity. But, as the personal theme demands a formal machinery, it is perhaps significant that when the poem returns to Thyrsis the pastoral figures also return.

In conclusion, it may be observed that the history of the English lyric pastoral affords only two figures who can justly claim kinship with the Greek idyl: these are Gay and Arnold. The inadvertent realism of Gay in depicting the lives of English shepherds is the nearest approach to Theocritus' pictures of Sicilian life and customs. Arnold's effects, as it has been noted, are also distinctly Greek, but on the side of external, not human, nature. Arnold's *Thyrsis* reflects a delight in nature which is tinged with sadness;

---

[25]Pp. 326–327.

of this the reader of Theocritus is often aware. Finally, a study of *Thyrsis*, its beauty and its ample sincerity, tends to confirm what was inevitable from the beginnings of pastoral elegy—that only Milton, perhaps, has in employing its artifices mastered them to the end of harmonizing emotional expression and poetic artistry.

THEOCRITUS

IDYL 1
DAPHNIS

Thyrsis. Goatherd.

Thyr. Sweet is the whispering, goatherd, of yonder murmuring pine by the springs and sweet also is your piping. After Pan you shall carry off second prize. If he chooses the horned goat, you shall get the she-goat, but if he takes the she-goat for his prize, the kid shall come to you. The flesh of the kid is delicious until you milk it.

Goat. Sweeter, shepherd, is your song than the sound of yonder water that tumbles from the rock on high. If the Muses carry off the ewe for their gift, then shall your prize be the stall-fed lamb; but if it pleases them to take the lamb, the ewe shall be yours as second prize. 10*

Thyr. Will you, by the Nymphs, will you sit down here, goatherd, on this hill slope by the tamarisks and play your pipe? I will tend your goats meanwhile.

Goat. It is not right, shepherd, for us to play the pipe at noon. We are afraid of Pan, for at this time he is tired from his hunting and rests. He is quick-tempered and there is ever fierce anger resting on his nostrils. But, Thyrsis, you were wont to sing of the woes of Daphnis and you reached great success with the pastoral 20 Muse. So come, let us sit here under the elm, opposite that Priapus and the fountain nymphs, where are the shepherd's seat and the oaks. If you will but sing as you once sang when you contended with Chromis of Libya, I will allow you three milkings of a twinner goat. Though she has her two kids, she gives two pailfuls of milk; and I'll give you also a deep bowl, coated with sweet wax, a two-handled vessel, just finished and still smelling of the chisel. Around its edge on top there winds ivy, ivy 30 sprinkled over with helichryse, and opposite twines the tendril, rejoicing in its saffron fruit. Between these is carved a woman, like some masterpiece of the gods, and she is arrayed in robe and

---

*Line numbers refer to the text of the original.

fillet. By her are two men with fine long hair, exchanging abusive words. All this does not touch her heart, but now she glances with a smile on the one man, now casts her attention to the other, while the men, now for a long time hollow-eyed with love, do but strive in vain. Next to this group are carved an old fisherman and

40 a rough cliff, on which the aged man is with effort dragging a great net for a cast, and he is like one who toils mightily. Why, you would say he was fishing with all the strength of his limbs, for the muscles all over his neck swell out so, gray-haired as he is, but his strength is like that of youth. Just a wee bit removed from this sea-worn old man is a vineyard, well laden with clusters of ripe grapes, and a little boy is guarding this, seated on a stone wall. On both sides of him are two foxes: one is prowling along the rows plundering the ripe fruit, while the other turns all her

50 cunning to the lad's wallet, vowing that she will not let him off till she makes him breakfast on dry fare. But he is weaving a lovely locust trap with stalks of asphodel, fastening them to a reed; and he is not so much concerned for his wallet or the plants as he rejoices in his weaving. And all over the bowl spreads soft acanthus. It is a marvelous sight for goatherds. The wonder of it would amaze your heart. As the price of it I gave a Calydnian boatman a goat and a big cheese loaf of white milk. Never yet has the bowl touched my lip, but it lies still unsoiled. I should

60 right gladly please you with it, if you will only oblige me by singing that charming song. Now I'm not jesting. So come on, my good fellow. You will not keep your singing for Hades that brings forgetfulness to all.

The Song of Thyrsis

Begin, dear Muses, begin the pastoral song.

Thyrsis of Aetna am I, and 'tis the sweet voice of Thyrsis. Where were you when Daphnis pined away, where were you, O Nymphs? Were you in the lovely vales of Peneus or of Pindus? You surely did not haunt the mighty stream of Anapus or the steep of Aetna or the sacred water of Acis.

70 *Begin, dear Muses, begin the pastoral song.*

For him the jackals, for him the wolves howled with grief; for him in death the lion of the forest lamented.

Begin, dear Muses, begin the pastoral song.

Many cows by his feet, many bulls, many heifers and calves sorrowed.

Begin, dear Muses, begin the pastoral song.

First came Hermes from the mountain and said, "Daphnis, who makes thee suffer thus? With whom, my good lad, art thou so much in love?"

Begin, dear Muses, begin the pastoral song.

Then came the cowherds; the shepherds and the goatherds came.   80
They all asked him what ill he was suffering. Then came Priapus and said, "Wretched Daphnis, why dost thou pine away? The maiden is roaming among all the springs, all the groves—

Begin, dear Muses, begin the pastoral song.

—searching for thee. Thou art too poor a lover and art a help-less creature. Thou wast known as a cowherd, but now thou dost act like a goatherd. When the goatherd sees the bleating nannies being covered, he weeps out his eyes that he was not born a he-goat.

Begin, dear Muses, begin the pastoral song.

So when thou seest the girls as they laugh merrily, thou weepest   90
out thine eyes because thou art not dancing among them." To these the cowherd answered not a word, but carried through his bitter love and so carried it through to the end of his doom.

Begin, Muses, begin again the pastoral song.

Now came also sweet Cypris with laughter, with laughter in her heart, but making a show of heavy wrath, and she said, "Surely, thou didst boast, Daphnis, that thou wouldst throw Love for a fall; but hast thou not rather thyself been thrown by irresistible Love?"

Begin, Muses, begin again the pastoral song.

To her Daphnis replied, "Cruel Cypris, vengeful Cypris, Cypris   100
enemy to mortals. Dost thou think that all my sun has already set? No, even in Hades Daphnis will bring grievous pain to Love.

Begin, Muses, begin again the pastoral song.

Is not the cowherd said to have won Cypris? Begone to Ida! Begone to Anchises! Oak trees and galingale are there, and the bees hum pleasantly by their hives.

Begin, Muses, begin again the pastoral song.

Charming, too, is Adonis, since he also pastures flocks and smites
hares and pursues all the wild beasts.

110

Begin, Muses, begin again the pastoral song.

Then thou shouldst go once more and set thyself before Diomed
and say, 'I am victor over the cowherd Daphnis, so do thou battle
now against me.'

Begin, Muses, begin again the pastoral song.

Ah, you wolves and jackals and bears with dens in the mountains, farewell! I, the cowherd Daphnis, shall no more be with
you in the woodland, no more in the forests and the groves. Farewell, Arethusa, and rivers that pour your fair water through
Thymbris.

Begin, Muses, begin again the pastoral song.

120

It is I, the Daphnis who tends the cows here, the Daphnis who
brings the bulls and the calves to drink.

Begin, Muses, begin again the pastoral song.

Pan, Pan, whether thou art among the lofty mountains of Lycaeus,
or art ranging about great Maenalus, come to the isle of Sicily
and leave the height of Helice and the lofty tomb of Lycaon's
son, a tomb admired even by the gods.

End, Muses, come end the pastoral song.

Come, King, and bear away this honey-breathing pipe of hard-
ened wax, a fair instrument, well curved to the lip; for I am now

130

being dragged down to Hades by Love.

End, Muses, come end the pastoral song.

Now you may bear violets, you bramble bushes; bear them, you
thistles, and let the lovely narcissus spread its foliage over the
juniper. Let all things be changed, and let the pine tree bear
pears, since Daphnis dies, and let the stag drag down the dogs
and let the screech owl from the mountains contend with nightingales."

End, Muses, come end the pastoral song.

When he had spoken thus, he ceased. Aphrodite wished to raise
him up again, but all his threads from the Fates had left him

and Daphnis went down the stream. The eddying flood washed over   140
the man loved by the Muses, the man not scorned by the Nymphs.

End, Muses, come end the pastoral song.

Now do you give me the goat and the bowl that I may do my
milking and pour a libation to the Muses. Fare you well, many
times, Muses, farewell, and I will sing you even a sweeter song
at a later time.

Goat. May your lovely mouth, Thyrsis, be filled with honey and
filled with the honeycomb, and may you eat the sweet fig of
Aegilus, for you sing better than the cicada. Here is your bowl.
Just look, friend, how fragrant it is! You'll think it was washed   150
in the springs of the Horae! Come here, Cissaetha. Now you milk
her. Stop jumping about, you goats, else the buck will be after you.

IDYL 7

THE HARVEST FESTIVAL

At one time Eucritus and I were walking to the Hales from the
city, Amyntas forming the third in our party. A harvest festival
to Deo was being celebrated by Phrasidamus and Antigenes, two
sons of Lycopeus, noble remnants, if any there be, of the good
men of a former time, descended from Clytia and Chalcon himself, who with his foot brought forth the spring of Burina by
firmly planting his knee on a rock; and by the springs poplars
and elms wove a shady grove, arching it over with tresses of green
leaves. We had not yet gone half the way nor had the tomb of   10
Brasilas come into our sight, when, thanks to the Muses, we met
a wayfarer, a fine man of Cydonia, one named Lycidas. He was
a goatherd, nor could anyone who beheld him have mistaken him,
for he distinctly looked the goatherd. On his left shoulder he
wore the tawny hide of a shaggy goat, reeking of fresh rennet,
and over his chest was fastened an old cloak with a plaited
girdle, and he carried a crooked staff of wild olive in his right
hand. Quietly smiling, he said to me with merry eyes, while   20
laughter played on his lips, "Simichidas, where are you dragging
your feet at noonday, when even the lizard is asleep in the stone
walls and the tomb-haunting larks do not stir abroad? Are you
hurrying uninvited to a feast or rushing to the wine-pressing of

some townsman? Why, under your hurrying feet every rock sings as it strikes your boots!"

I replied to him, "My dear Lycidas, everyone says that as a piper you are far outstanding among the herdsmen and the reap-
30   ers. This truly fills my heart with joy. Yet to my thinking I hope that I can equal you. Our way lies to a harvest festival. Friends of ours are holding a feast to fair-robed Demeter, mak-ing her an offering of the first yield, for the goddess has well filled their threshing floor with barley in rich measure. But come now. The way is common to us both and common is the day. Let us sing our pastoral songs. Perhaps each will bring pleasure to the other. For I too am a clear-voiced mouthpiece of the Muses and all call me best of singers. But I do not readily believe them, by Zeus, for to my thinking I do not yet surpass either that excel-
40   lent Sicelidas of Samos or Philitas in singing, but I would con-tend against them as a frog against the locusts."

I said this with a purpose. The goatherd, with a pleasant laugh, said, "I'll make you a gift of this staff, because you are a branch of Zeus, entirely fashioned in the mold of truth. Just as I greatly despise a builder who strives to build a house as high as the summit of Mount Oromedon, so do I despise those birds of the Muses who cackle against the Chian singer and toil in vain. But
50   come, let us begin at once our pastoral song, Simichidas. See now, my friend, if you like this little ditty which I lately worked out in the mountain:

The Song of Lycidas

"Ageanax will have a fair voyage to Mitylene, even when the Kids are in the west and the south wind drives the wet waves and when Orion holds his feet on the ocean, if he will but set free Lycidas, who is burned by Aphrodite, since a hot love for him consumes me. The halcyons will still the waves and the sea and the south wind and the east wind, which stirs the seaweed on the highest shore—the halcyons, which are of all birds most beloved
60   by the sea-green Nereids, of all those birds which take their prey from the sea. As Ageanax makes his voyage to Mitylene, may all be favorable to him and may he reach harbor after a happy journey. On that day I will crown my head with a wreath of dill

or of roses or even of gillyflowers, and I will draw the wine of
Ptelea from the bowl as I recline by the fire and someone shall
roast the bean on the fire. And my couch shall be elbow-deep,
thickly covered with fleabane and asphodel and curling celery.
And lying at ease, I will drink, calling Ageanax to mind in my
very cups and pressing my lips to the dregs. Two shepherds shall   70
play the pipe for me, one from Acharnae and one from Lycope,
while Tityrus shall sing close by how once Daphnis, the cowherd,
loved Xenea and how the mountain was sorely afflicted about him
and how the oaks mourned for him, the oaks that grow by the
banks of the river Himera, when he wasted away as the snow
melts beneath lofty Haemus or Athos or Rhodope or remotest
Caucasus. He shall sing also how once a broad chest received
the living goatherd through the cruel audacity of his lord and
how the flat-nosed bees came from the meadow to the sweet cedar   80
box and fed him with soft flowers because the Muse had poured sweet
nectar on his lips. O blest Comatas, a truly happy adventure didst
thou go through as thou wast enclosed within the chest and feeding on the honeycomb of bees, thou didst suffer through a year
with its seasons. I wish that thou wert numbered among those living in my day; then would I tend thy lovely goats in the mountains while listening to thy voice, and thou wouldst recline beneath
the oaks or the pines, sweetly singing, divine Comatas."

After singing thus, he ceased; whereupon I said to him, "Dear   90
Lycidas, many are the songs which the Nymphs taught me also as
I tended my herds in the mountains, excellent songs which report
has perhaps carried even to the throne of Zeus. But by far outstanding among them all is this one with which I shall begin to
reward you. So listen, for you are beloved of the Muses.

The Song of Simichidas.

"The Loves have sneezed on Simichidas. For the hapless wretch
loves Myrto as much as the goats love the springtime. Aratus,
who is most dear to me, bears within his heart a passion for a
lad. Aristis knows of this, that splendid man, far the best of men,   100
whom not even Phoebus himself would grudge to have sing with
the lyre by his tripods—he knows that Aratus is consumed in his
bones with love for a lad. I pray thee, Pan, who dost possess

the charming plain of Homole, that thou shouldst press him unsought into the dear arms of my friend, whether the lad is the dainty Philinus or some other. If thou shouldst bring this to pass, dear Pan, then may not the lads of Arcadia flog thy sides and shoulders with squills when but scanty meat is left to them. But if thou shouldst decree otherwise, then mayest thou itch and scratch thyself with thy nails all over thy body and sleep on nettles, and mayest thou be in the mountains of the Edonians in the midst of winter, betaking thyself to the river Hebrus close to the Bear; and in the summer mayest thou tend the flocks among the farthest Ethiopians under the cliff of the Blemyes, from which the Nile is seen no longer. And do you, leaving the sweet spring of Hyetis and of Byblis and leaving Oecus, the lofty home of fair-haired Dione, you Loves, that are like blushing apples, smite, I pray, with your arrows the charming Philinus; smite him, since the ill-starred lad does not pity my friend. Why, he is even softer than a ripe pear, and the women say, 'Ah, Philinus, the bloom of your beauty is fading.' Let us no more, Aratus, keep watch at his house door nor wear out our feet. Let the cock with his crowing at dawn bring painful numbness to some other. Let Molon alone, my dear friend, suffer torture at this school. But let us be at peace, and have with us some old sorceress who by spitting on us shall keep far from us all unpleasantness."

Thus I sang, and he, with a pleasant laugh, as before, handed me his shepherd's staff to be a gift of friendship from the Muses. Then turning aside to the left, he took the road to Pyxa, while Eucritus and I and our handsome Amyntas turned toward Phrasidamus' farm. There on deep beds of sweet rushes and fresh-cut vine leaves we reclined happily. High above our heads swayed many poplars and elms. The sacred stream close by gushed murmuring from the cave of the Nymphs. On the shady boughs the dusky cicadas chirped busily, while far off the tree toad uttered his cry in the dense bramble thickets. Larks and linnets sang; the turtledove sighed; yellow bees were flitting about the springs. All the air was filled with the fragrance of rich summer, the fragrance of the harvest time. There were pears at our feet, and by our sides rolled apples in profusion. The young trees were bowed toward the ground with the weight of their plums. The

four-year seal of pitch was loosened from the mouths of the
wine jars. Castalian Nymphs, who dwell on the height of Parnassus, did ever the aged Chiron set such a bowl before Heracles   150
in the rocky cave of Pholus? Was that shepherd by the Anapus,
the mighty Polyphemus, who hurled mountains at ships, lured by
such nectar as this to move his feet in dance within the sheepfolds, even such a draught as you Nymphs poured out on that
day by the altar of Demeter of the threshing floor? On her heap
of grain may I once more plant a great winnowing fan, and may
she smile as she holds sheaves and poppies in both her arms.

BION

LAMENT FOR ADONIS

I weep for Adonis; lovely Adonis is dead. Dead is lovely Adonis; the Loves join in weeping. Sleep no more, Cypris, amid crimson raiment. Awake, wretched goddess, and in sable robe smite thy bosom and say to all, "Lovely Adonis is dead."

I weep for Adonis; the Loves join in weeping.

Lovely Adonis lies in the mountains, his thigh wounded with the tusk, his white thigh with the white tusk, and brings anguish to Cypris, as he feebly breathes forth his life and his dark blood
10   drips down over his snow-white flesh and his eyes are dimmed beneath his brows and the rose flees from his lip, on which dies also the kiss which Cypris shall never more carry away. Cypris delights in his kiss though he lives no more; but Adonis knows not that she kissed him as he died.

I weep for Adonis; the Loves join in weeping.

Cruel, cruel the wound which Adonis has in his thigh, but more grievous the wound which Cytherea bears in her heart. Around this lad the faithful dogs howled, and the Nymphs of the moun-
20   tains weep, and Aphrodite, her tresses flying loose, wanders amid the woods, sorrowing, with hair unbraided, with feet unsandaled, and the thornbushes wound her as she goes and they draw her divine blood. With shrill cries she rushes through the far glens, wailing for her Assyrian lord and calling upon the lad. But around his navel the dark blood was spouting and his chest was made red with the blood from his thighs and crimson now was Adonis' breast that before was white as snow.

"Alas for Cytherea," the Loves join in weeping.

She has lost the lovely man and with him she has lost her
30   divine beauty. Lovely was the form of Cypris while Adonis lived, but her beauty died with Adonis. "Alas for Cypris," all the mountains say, and the oak trees say, "Alas for Adonis"; and the rivers wail for the sorrows of Aphrodite, and the springs in the mountains weep for Adonis. The flowers are red with pain, and Cythera through all its mountain sides, through every glen sings the piteous strain, "Alas for Cytherea; lovely Adonis is dead."

And Echo returned the cry, "Lovely Adonis is dead." For the sorrowful love of Cypris who would not have wailed "Alas"? As she saw, as she beheld the unchecked wound of Adonis, as she saw   **40** the crimson blood about his drooping thigh, stretching forth her arms, she moaned, "O stay, Adonis, ill-fated Adonis, stay, that I may possess thee for the very last time, that I may embrace thee and mingle lips with lips. Awake but a little, Adonis, and give me this last kiss; kiss me as long as a kiss may live, until from thy soul into my mouth, even into my very heart, thy breath may flow, and I may drain thy sweet love charm and drink up all thy love and treasure this kiss as I will Adonis himself, since   **50** thou, ill-starred lad, art fleeing from me. Thou art fleeing afar, Adonis, and art going into Acheron and to that hateful and savage king; yet must I live on wretchedly, for I am a goddess and cannot follow thee. Persephone, take my lord, for thou art much stronger than I and every lovely thing must descend to thee. But I am utterly forlorn and I bear unceasing anguish and I weep for my Adonis, who is dead, and I am in fear of thee. Thou art dying, my thrice-beloved, and my love has fled from me like a dream. Cytherea is widowed and desolate are the Loves in her halls. My charmed girdle has perished with thee. O why,   **60** reckless lad, didst thou go hunting? Why, being so lovely, wast thou so mad as to fight with a wild beast?" Thus wailed Cypris; the Loves join the lament: "Alas for Cytherea; lovely Adonis is dead." So many tears does the Paphian shed as Adonis sheds drops of blood; and they all turn into flowers on the ground. The blood brings forth the rose and the tears the windflower.

I weep for Adonis; lovely Adonis is dead.

Weep for thy lover no more in the woods, Cypris. No good couch for Adonis is the lonely bed of leaves. Let the dead Adonis   **70** now have thy couch, Cytherea. Though in death, he is lovely; so lovely in death, like one that sleeps. Lay him down in the soft raiment in which once he slept, in which through the night he shared sacred sleep with thee, on a bed all of gold. The bed yearns for Adonis, dismal though his fate. Cast on him wreaths and flowers. With him all things have died, even as he, and the flowers are all withered. Sprinkle him with Syrian unguents, sprinkle him with perfumes. Let all perfumes perish; Adonis, who was thy own perfume, is dead. Dainty Adonis is laid in 80 crimson robes and around him the Loves weep and lament, cutting their long hair for Adonis. One has thrown over him his arrows, one his bow, one his wing, one his quiver; and one has loosed the sandal of Adonis, and others bear water in a golden basin, and one washes his thighs, and one fans Adonis from behind with his wings.

"Alas for Cytherea," the Loves join in weeping.

Hymenaeus quenched every torch at the doorposts and he scattered the nuptial wreath and no more did he sing, "Hymen, 90 Hymen," no more his own song, but "Alas for Adonis," he chants, even more than the bridal song. The Graces weep for the son of Cinyras: "Lovely Adonis is dead," they say to one another. "Alas," they shriek far more than they cry the paeon. And the Fates weep aloud for Adonis in Hades, and they sing of him, but he heeds them not. 'Tis not that he does not desire it, but the Maiden does not release him.

Cease thy lamentations this day, Cytherea; refrain from beating thy breast. Thou must weep for him again; thou must bewail him again in another year.

MOSCHUS

LAMENT FOR BION

Sound me a mournful dirge, you glens and Dorian stream, and
weep, you rivers, for charming Bion. Grieve now, you plants, and
make lamentation now, you groves, and now, you flowers, breathe
away your fragrance with sorrowing clusters. Now turn crimson
with grief, you roses and you windflowers; now, hyacinth, utter
the sound of your letters and show a deeper "AI, AI" on your
petals. The beautiful singer is dead.

Begin, Sicilian Muses, begin the dirge.

You nightingales that lament amid the thick leaves, announce
to the Sicilian streams of Arethusa that Bion the cowherd is dead,   10
that with him music also has died and Dorian song has perished.

Begin, Sicilian Muses, begin the dirge.

Wail mournfully, Strymonian swans, by the waters, and with
notes of lamentation chant a plaintive lay, even such as old age
sings on your lips, and say to the Oeagrian maidens, say to all
the Bistonian nymphs, "The Dorian Orpheus is dead."

Begin, Sicilian Muses, begin the dirge.

He, the well-beloved of the herds, sings no more, and no more   20
does he sing sitting beneath the desolate oaks, but by Pluteus'
side he sings a chant of Lethe. The mountains are mute and the
cows that wander by the bulls are weeping and will not pasture.

Begin, Sicilian Muses, begin the dirge.

For thy swift doom, Bion, Apollo himself lamented and the
Satyrs sorrowed and the black-robed Priapi. The Pans sigh for
thy song, and the fountain nymphs sobbed in the woodland and
their waters turned to tears. Echo sobs among the rocks be-   30
cause she is silent and can no more mimic thy lips. At thy
dying the trees dropped their fruit, the flowers all withered. The
lovely milk did not flow from the sheep, nor the honey from the
hives, but it perished sorrowing in the wax; for no more must
the honey be gathered, now that thy honey has perished.

Begin, Sicilian Muses, begin the dirge.

Not so did the Siren grieve by the shores of the sea, nor so
did the Nightingale once sing among the cliffs, nor so did the
40   Swallow lament in the far mountains, nor so did Ceyx cry out
for the pain of Alcyon, nor so did the Cerylus sing in the green
waves, nor so in the eastern glens did Memnon's bird lament for
the son of Eos while flying around his grave, as they all did
sorrow for dead Bion.

Begin, Sicilian Muses, begin the dirge.

The nightingales and all the swallows which once he made glad,
which he taught to speak, sat by the tree trunks and wailed before
one another, and the others gave answer, "You birds of sorrow,
do you also mourn."

50   *Begin, Sicilian Muses, begin the dirge.*

Who will ever play on thy flute, my thrice-beloved? Who will
place his mouth on thy reeds, who would be so bold? For thy
lips and thy spirit still breathe therein and the echo of thy song
is still kept alive in those tubes. Shall I bear the pipe to Pan?
Perchance even he would fear to press his mouth thereto, lest he
come but second after thee.

Begin, Sicilian Muses, begin the dirge.

Galatea also weeps for thy song, she whom once thou didst
delight when she sat with thee by the shore of the sea; for thou
60   didst not sing like the Cyclops. From him lovely Galatea fled,
but thee she beheld more gladly than the sea spray. And now,
forgetful of the wave, she sits on the desolate sands, but still
she tends thy cows.

Begin, Sicilian Muses, begin the dirge.

Together with thee, cowherd, have perished all the gifts of
the Muses, the charming kisses of maidens, the lips of boys, and
around thy body the gloomy Loves are weeping, and Cypris yearns
for thee far more than for that kiss with which lately she kissed
70   the dying Adonis. This, most tuneful of rivers, is thy second sorrow; this, Meles, thy new sorrow. Of old, Homer died, that
sweet mouth of Calliope, and it is said that thou didst grieve for
thy lovely son with tear-filled streams, and thou didst fill all the

sea with thy voice. Now thou dost weep again for another son
and thou art pining away with a fresh grief. They were both
beloved of fountains: the one drank of the spring of Pegasus, the
other quaffed the waters of Arethusa. The one sang of the lovely
daughter of Tyndareus and the mighty son of Thetis and of
Menelaus, son of Atreus; but this poet's song was not of wars,   80
not of tears, but of Pan, and he, a cowherd, had a clear voice
and sang as he tended his herds, and he fashioned pipes and
milked the sweet heifer and taught of the kisses of boys and nurtured Love in his bosom and stirred the passion of Aphrodite.

Begin, Sicilian Muses, begin the dirge.

Every famous city, Bion, mourns thee, every town. Ascra sorrows for thee far more than for Hesiod. The Boeotian woodlands
do not yearn so for Pindar. Not for Alcaeus did charming Lesbos
grieve so, nor did the Teian city lament so much for her bard.   90
Paros yearns for thee more than for Archilochus. Rather than for
Sappho Mitylene still sighs for thy music. Thou art Theocritus
to the Syracusans. But I sing a strain of Ausonian sorrow, I no
stranger to the pastoral song, but I am heir to that Dorian Muse
which thou didst once teach to thy pupils and with which thou
didst endow me, leaving thy wealth to others, but to me the herit-
age of song.

Begin, Sicilian Muses, begin the dirge.

Alas, when the mallows perish in the garden, and the green
celery, and the luxuriant, curling dill, they later come to life   100
again and grow in another year; but we, the great, the mighty,
the wise men, when once we die, unhearing we sleep in the hollow
earth, a right long sleep without end or awaking. Even so shalt
thou be in the ground, wrapped in silence; but the Nymphs have
willed that the frog should ever keep up his song; but I would
not begrudge the Nymphs, for the song he sings is not beautiful.

Begin, Sicilian Muses, begin the dirge.

Poison came, Bion, to thy mouth; it was poison thou didst eat.
Could it have come to such lips and not have turned to sweet-   110
ness? What mortal was so brutal as to mix poison for thee or to
give it to thee at thy call? He had fled far from song.

Begin, Sicilian Muses, begin the dirge.

But Justice overtakes all men. In this my sorrow I shed tears lamenting thy fate. Were I but able, even as Orpheus descended to Tartarus, as once did Odysseus, as Alcides of old, I too should quickly have gone to the abode of Pluteus, that I might see thee, and, if thou singest to Pluteus, that I might hear what thou singest. 120 Ah, come! Sing out to the Maiden a Sicilian strain and a sweet pastoral song. She too is a Sicilian and once she sported on Aetna's shores. She knows the Dorian song. Not unrewarded will be thy lay; and as once when Orpheus played sweetly on the lyre, she granted him Eurydice's return, so will she send thee also, Bion, to the mountains. But if I too had such power with the pipe, I should myself sing before Pluteus.

VIRGIL

Menalcas. Mopsus.

Men. Now, Mopsus, since we have met, good as we both are, you at blowing into the light reeds, I at singing verses, why do we not sit down here, where the elms are blended with the hazels?

Mop. You are the older: it is fitting for me to obey you, Menalcas, whether we go beneath the shade which flutters as the zephyrs stir it or whether we choose to enter the cave. Look how the wild vine has dotted the cave with scattering clusters.

Men. In our hills only Amyntas strives against you.

Mop. He may as well strive to surpass Phoebus in singing.

Men. Begin first, Mopsus, if you have a song of passion for Phyllis   10 or praise of Alcon or abuse of Codrus. Begin. Tityrus will tend your browsing kids.

Mop. Rather will I try these verses which I wrote lately on the green bark of a beech tree and set to music, marking the alternations. Then you can go tell Amyntas to strive against me.

Menalcas. Mopsus.

Men. Cur non, Mopse, boni quoniam convenimus ambo,
Tu calamos inflare levis, ego dicere versus,
Hic corylis mixtas inter considimus ulmos?
Mop. Tu maior; tibi me est aequum parere, Menalca,
Sive sub incertas Zephyris motantibus umbras,
Sive antro potius succedimus. Aspice, ut antrum
Silvestris raris sparsit labrusca racemis.
Men. Montibus in nostris solus tibi certat Amyntas.
Mop. Quid, si idem certet Phoebum superare canendo?
Men. Incipe, Mopse, prior, si quos aut Phyllidis ignes,   10
Aut Alconis habes laudes, aut iurgia Codri.
Incipe; pascentis servabit Tityrus haedos.
Mop. Immo haec, in viridi nuper quae cortice fagi
Carmina descripsi et modulans alterna notavi,
Experiar: tu deinde iubeto ut certet Amyntas.

Men. As the pliant willow yields to the pale olive, and the lowly nard to the crimson rose beds, so much do I think Amyntas yields to you. But say no more, lad; we have come into the cave.

20 *Mop.* For Daphnis, destroyed by a cruel death, the Nymphs wept— you hazels and rivers, you bear witness to the Nymphs—when the mother clasped the piteous body of her son and called out upon the cruel gods and stars. In those days, Daphnis, none drove the pastured cattle to the cool streams, no beast drank of the river or touched a blade of grass. Daphnis, that even the Punic lions bewailed thy death, the wild mountains and the woods declare. It was Daphnis who taught men to yoke Armenian tigers to the car,

30 to lead the dancing bands of Bacchus, and to twine the pliant wands with soft foliage. As the vine adorns the trees, as the grapes adorn the vines, as the bulls adorn the herds, as the wheat adorns the fertile fields, so wert thou all the adornment of thy people. Now that the Fates have taken thee away, even Pales herself, even Apollo has left the fields. Often in the furrows to which we entrusted the large grains of barley, unfruitful darnel and sterile oats spring up. In place of the soft violet, in place of the crimson narcissus, there

Men. Lenta salix quantum pallenti cedit olivae,
Puniceis humilis quantum saliunca rosetis,
Iudicio nostro tantum tibi cedit Amyntas.
Sed tu desine plura, puer; successimus antro.
Mop. Extinctum Nymphae crudeli funere Daphnim   20
Flebant; vos coryli testes et flumina Nymphis;
Cum complexa sui corpus miserabile nati
Atque deos atque astra vocat crudelia mater.
Non ulli pastos illis egere diebus
Frigida, Daphni, boves ad flumina; nulla nec amnem
Libavit quadrupes, nec graminis attigit herbam.
Daphni, tuum Poenos etiam ingemuisse leones
Interitum montesque feri silvaeque locuntur.
Daphnis et Armenias curru subiungere tigris
Instituit, Daphnis thiasos inducere Bacchi   30
Et foliis lentas intexere mollibus hastas.
Vitis ut arboribus decori est, ut vitibus uvae,
Ut gregibus tauri, segetes ut pinguibus arvis,
Tu decus omne tuis. Postquam te fata tulerunt,
Ipsa Pales agros atque ipse reliquit Apollo.
Grandia saepe quibus mandavimus hordea sulcis,
Infelix lolium et steriles nascuntur avenae;
Pro molli viola, pro purpureo narcisso,

now rise the thistle and the bramble bush with sharp thorns. Strew
leaves on the ground, raise shade over the springs, you shepherds,   40
for Daphnis bids us pay him such honor, and build a tomb and to
the tomb add a verse: "Daphnis was I in the woodlands, known
from here even to the stars, guardian of the fair flock, myself more
fair."

Men. Your song, divine poet, is to me what sleep in the grass is to
the weary, or the quenching of thirst in the summer's heat with a
leaping stream of sweet water. Not with your pipe alone, but with
your voice also you equal your teacher. Happy lad, you shall henceforth be second after him. Still, I shall now reply with my song,   50
as best I can, and exalt your Daphnis to the stars. Daphnis shall I
raise to the stars. Daphnis loved me also.

Mop. Can there be a greater reward to me than this? Not only was
the lad himself a worthy theme for song, but Stimichon has long
since praised your songs to me.

Men. Radiant Daphnis marvels at the unfamiliar threshold of
Olympus and beneath his feet beholds the clouds and stars. Thereat
exultant joy possesses the woodlands and all the fields and Pan and
the shepherds and the maiden Dryads. The wolf plots no ambush   60

> Carduus et spinis surgit paliurus acutis.
> Spargite humum foliis, inducite fontibus umbras,   40
> Pastores; mandat fieri sibi talia Daphnis;
> Et tumulum facite, et tumulo superaddite carmen:
> Daphnis ego in silvis, hinc usque ad sidera notus,
> Formosi pecoris custos, formosior ipse.
> *Men.* Tale tuum carmen nobis, divine poeta,
> Quale sopor fessis in gramine, quale per aestum
> Dulcis aquae saliente sitim restinguere rivo.
> Nec calamis solum aequiparas, sed voce magistrum.
> Fortunate puer, tu nunc eris alter ab illo.
> Nos tamen haec quocumque modo tibi nostra vicissim   50
> Dicemus, Daphninque tuum tollemus ad astra;
> Daphnin ad astra feremus: amavit nos quoque Daphnis.
> *Mop.* An quicquam nobis tali sit munere maius?
> Et puer ipse fuit cantari dignus, et ista
> Iam pridem Stimichon laudavit carmina nobis.
> *Men.* Candidus insuetum miratur limen Olympi
> Sub pedibusque videt nubes et sidera Daphnis.
> Ergo alacris silvas et cetera rura voluptas
> Panaque pastoresque tenet Dryadasque puellas.
> Nec lupus insidias pecori, nec retia cervis   60

for the flock, nor do any snares devise guile for the stag, for kindly
Daphnis loves peace. Even the shaggy mountains rapturously hurl
their voices to the stars; now even the cliffs, even the trees shout the
song: "A god, a god is he, Menalcas!" Mayest thou be kindly
and propitious to thy people. Lo, four altars: two for thee, Daphnis,
and two altars of sacrifice for Phoebus. Two cups foaming with
fresh milk will I dedicate to thee each year, and two bowls of rich
olive oil, and cheering the feast above all with abundant Bacchus,
70   before the fire, if it is cold; in the shade, if it is harvest time, I will
pour from the goblets the new nectar of Ariusian wine. Before me
shall sing Damoetas and Aegon of Lyctus; Alphesiboeus shall mimic
the dancing Satyrs. These honors shall forever be thine, both when
we pay the yearly vows to the Nymphs and when we purify the
fields. As long the boar loves the mountain ridges, as long as the
fish loves the streams, as long as the bees feast on thyme, the cicadas
on dew, always shall thy honor, thy name, and thy praises abide.
As to Bacchus and to Ceres, so also to thee shall the farmers yearly
80   pay their vows. Thou too shalt bind them with vows.
Mop. What gifts, what reward shall I pay for such a song? Not so
great is my joy in the whistle of the rising south wind or in the

Ulla dolum meditantur; amat bonus otia Daphnis.
Ipsi laetitia voces ad sidera iactant
Intonsi montes; ipsae iam carmina rupes,
Ipsa sonant arbusta; deus, deus ille, Menalca!
Sis bonus o felixque tuis! en quattuor aras:
Ecce duas tibi, Daphni, duas altaria Phoebo.
Pocula bina novo spumantia lacte quotannis
Craterasque duo statuam tibi pinguis olivi,
Et multo in primis hilarans convivia Baccho,
Ante focum, si frigus erit, si messis, in umbra,   70
Vina novum fundam calathis Ariusia nectar.
Cantabunt mihi Damoetas et Lyctius Aegon;
Saltantis Satyros imitabitur Alphesiboeus.
Haec tibi semper erunt, et cum sollemnia vota
Reddemus Nymphis, et cum lustrabimus agros.
Dum iuga montis aper, fluvios dum piscis amabit,
Dumque thymo pascentur apes, dum rore cicadae,
Semper honos nomenque tuum laudesque manebunt.
Ut Baccho Cererique, tibi sic vota quotannis
Agricolae facient; damnabis tu quoque votis.   80
Mop. Quae tibi, quae tali reddam pro carmine dona?
Nam neque me tantum venientis sibilus austri,

beating of the wave on the shore or in the rivers that flow down amid rocky vales.

Men. First I shall reward you with this frail reed. It was this which taught me "Corydon was fired with love for fair Alexis"; it taught me also "Whose flock is this? Is it Meliboeus's?"

Mop. Do you then take this crook, which Antigenes could not get from me, though he asked me many a time, and at that time he was worthy of my love. See how fair it is with its even joints and its brass, Menalcas.

90

Nec percussa iuvant fluctu tam litora, nec quae
Saxosas inter decurrunt flumina valles.
Men. Hac te nos fragili donabimus ante cicuta.
Haec nos, "Formosum Corydon ardebat Alexim,"
Haec eadem docuit, "Cuium pecus? an Meliboei?"
Mop. At tu sume pedum, quod, me cum saepe rogaret,
Non tulit Antigenes—et erat tum dignus amari—
Formosum paribus nodis atque aere, Menalca.   90

ECLOGUE 10
GALLUS

Grant me, Arethusa, this final effort. I must sing a few verses for my Gallus, but such as Lycoris herself will read. Who would refuse verses to Gallus? So, when thou flowest beneath the Sicanian waves, may not bitter Doris mingle her waters with thine, begin; let me sing of the anxious love of Gallus, while my flat-nosed goats crop the tender shrubs. I sing to no deaf ears; the woods reecho all my words.

What groves, what glens possessed you, Naiad maidens, when

ECLOGUE 10

GALLUS

Extremum hunc, Arethusa, mihi concede laborem:
Pauca meo Gallo, sed quae legat ipsa Lycoris,
Carmina sunt dicenda: neget quis carmina Gallo?
Sic tibi, cum fluctus subterlabere Sicanos,
Doris amara suam non intermisceat undam.
Incipe; sollicitos Galli dicamus amores,
Dum tenera attondent simae virgulta capellae.
Non canimus surdis; respondent omnia silvae.
    Quae nemora, aut qui vos saltus habuere, puellae

10   Gallus was languishing with an unworthy love? It was not the
mountain ridge of Parnassus or of Pindus that delayed you, nor
even Aonian Aganippe. For him even the laurels, even the tamarisks wept, and as he lay under a lonely crag, even pine-bearing
Maenalus and the rocks of cold Lycaeus wept for him. The sheep
also stand around him—they are not ashamed of us, nor wouldst
thou be ashamed of thy flock, divine poet; even lovely Adonis
pastured sheep by the streams—and the shepherd came and the
20   plodding swineherds came; Menalcas came, dripping from the
winter's acorns. All asked, "For whom is this love of thine?"
Apollo came and said, "Gallus, why are thou so mad? Thy
beloved Lycoris has followed another amid snows and rough
camps." Also Silvanus came with the rustic adornment of his
head, shaking the flowering fennel and great lilies. Pan, the god
of Arcadia, came, and we saw him ourselves, brilliant with the
blood-hued elderberries and with vermilion. "Will there be no
end of this?" he cried. "Love cares not for such deeds; cruel
30   Love is not sated with tears nor the grasses with streams nor the
bees with clover nor the goats with leaves."

Naides, indigno cum Gallus amore peribat?   10
Nam neque Parnasi vobis iuga, nam neque Pindi
Ulla moram fecere, neque Aonie Aganippe.
Illum etiam lauri, etiam flevere myricae;
Pinifer illum etiam sola sub rupe iacentem
Maenalus et gelidi fleverunt saxa Lycaei.
Stant et oves circum;—nostri nec paenitet illas,
Nec te paeniteat pecoris, divine poeta:
Et formosus ovis ad flumina pavit Adonis—
Venit et upilio; tardi venere subulci;
Uvidus hiberna venit de glande Menalcas.   20
Omnes "Unde amor iste, rogant, tibi?" Venit Apollo:
"Galle, quid insanis?" inquit; "tua cura Lycoris
Perque nives alium perque horrida castra secuta est."
Venit et agresti capitis Silvanus honore,
Florentis ferulas et grandia lilia quassans.
Pan deus Arcadiae venit, quem vidimus ipsi
Sanguineis ebuli bacis minioque rubentem.
"Ecquis erit modus?" inquit; "Amor non talia curat;
Nec lacrimis crudelis Amor, nec gramina rivis,
Nec cytiso saturantur apes, nec fronde capellae."   30

But sadly he replied, "Still, Arcadians, you will sing of this in your mountains, you Arcadians, who alone are skilled in song. Ah, how softly then would my bones repose, if but your pipe would some day tell of my love! Would that I had been one of you, or even the keeper of your flock or the pruner of your ripened grape! If at least I had Phyllis or Amyntas or any other mad love—What if Amyntas is dusky! Violets also are dark and hyacinths are dark. Then my love would lie with me amid the willows under the clinging vine. Phyllis would gather garlands for me, Amyntas would sing. Here are cool springs, Lycoris, here are soft meadows, a grove is here; here beside you I would wear out my life with time alone. But now a mad love for savage Mars keeps me in arms in the midst of weapons and threatening foes, while you, far from your native land (let me not believe such a tale) are beholding Alpine snows, cruel maiden, and the cold Rhine, alone without me. Oh, may the cold do you no harm! May the rough ice not cut your tender feet! I will go, and those verses which I composed in the Chalcidian measure I will now attune to the pipe of the Sicilian shepherd. I am determined to choose suffering in the woods among the dens of wild beasts and

Tristis at ille: "Tamen cantabitis, Arcades," inquit,
"Montibus haec vestris: soli cantare periti
Arcades. O mihi tum quam molliter ossa quiescant,
Vestra meos olim si fistula dicat amores!
Atque utinam ex vobis unus, vestrique fuissem
Aut custos gregis, aut maturae vinitor uvae!
Certe, sive mihi Phyllis, sive esset Amyntas,
Seu quicumque furor,—quid tum, si fuscus Amyntas?
Et nigrae violae sunt et vaccinia nigra—
Mecum inter salices lenta sub vite iaceret;
Serta mihi Phyllis legeret, cantaret Amyntas.
Hic gelidi fontes, hic mollia prata, Lycori,
Hic nemus; hic ipso tecum consumerer aevo.
Nunc insanus amor duri me Martis in armis
Tela inter media atque adversos detinet hostis:
Tu procul a patria—nec sit mihi credere tantum!—
Alpinas, a dura, nives et frigora Rheni
Me sine sola vides. A, te ne frigora laedant!
A, tibi ne teneras glacies secet aspera plantas!
Ibo, et, Chalcidico quae sunt mihi condita versu
Carmina, pastoris Siculi modulabor avena.
Certum est in silvis, inter spelaea ferarum
Malle pati tenerisque meos incidere amores

to carve the tale of my love in the young trees. They will grow; you, my love, will grow with them. Meanwhile I will range over Maenalus in the company of the Nymphs or I will hunt fierce boars. No cold shall keep me from encircling the glades of Parthenius with dogs. Already I fancy that I am passing through cliffs and echoing woods. What joy to speed Cydonian shafts from Parthian bow!—As though this is a cure for my madness or that god can learn to soften at the sorrows of men. Again, I care no more for the Hamadryads, no more even for song. Withdraw from me again, you woodlands. My sufferings cannot alter that god, not even if I should drink of the Hebrus in the midst of the frost, or endure the snows of the rainy Sithonian winter, nor if, when the dying bark shrivels on the tall elm, I should drive the sheep of the Aethiopians under Cancer's star. Love is victor over all. Let me too yield to Love."

This will be enough, goddesses, for your poet to sing, while he sits and weaves a basket of pliant mallow, Pierides. You will make these verses most worthy in the eyes of Gallus, love for whom increases within me each hour, as the green alder shoots up in the early springtime. Let us rise. The shade is wont to be

Arboribus; crescent illae, crescetis, amores.
Interea mixtis lustrabo Maenala Nymphis,
Aut acris venabor apros; non me ulla vetabunt
Frigora Parthenios canibus circumdare saltus;
Iam mihi per rupes videor lucosque sonantis
Ire; libet Partho torquere Cydonia cornu
Spicula. Tamquam haec sit nostri medicina furoris,   60
Aut deus ille malis hominum mitescere discat!
Iam neque Hamadryades rursus nec carmina nobis
Ipsa placent; ipsae rursus concedite silvae.
Non illum nostri possunt mutare labores,
Nec si frigoribus mediis Hebrumque bibamus
Sithoniasque nives hiemis subeamus aquosae,
Nec si, cum moriens alta liber aret in ulmo,
Aethiopum versemus oves sub sidere Cancri.
Omnia vincit Amor; et nos cedamus Amori."
    Haec sat erit, divae, vestrum cecinisse poetam,   70
Dum sedet et gracili fiscellam texit hibisco,
Pierides; vos haec facietis maxima Gallo,
Gallo, cuius amor tantum mihi crescit in horas,
Quantum vere novo viridis se subicit alnus.

harmful to singers; harmful is the juniper's shade. Shade also injures the crops. Get along home, my well-fed goats, Hesperus is coming, get along.

> Surgamus; solet esse gravis cantantibus umbra;
> Iuniperi gravis umbra; nocent et frugibus umbrae.
> Ite domum saturae, venit Hesperus, ite capellae.

NEMESIAN

[MELIBOEUS]

Timetas. Tityrus.

Tim. While you are weaving a basket of the river rush, Tityrus,
and the fields are free from the hoarse cicadas, begin, if you know
some song composed for the slender reed. For Pan has taught you
how to blow into reeds with your lips, and propitious Apollo has
favored you with verse. Begin, while the kids crop the willows
and the cows the grass, while the dew and the mildness of the
early sun exhort you to let your flock range the green meadow.

Tit. Do you, neighbor Timetas, a youth and beloved by the gods,
urge to song these years of mine and this hoary head? Once I
composed and sang verses to the reeds, while carefree youth
sported with gay love. Now my head is white and passion has
cooled with the years. Already my pipe hangs as an offering to
rural Faunus. Now the fields resound with you. For of late victorious in song, you laughed to scorn the reeds and the discordant

ECLOGUE 1

[MELIBOEUS]

Timetas. Tityrus.

Tim. Dum fiscella tibi fluviali, Tityre, iunco
Texitur et raucis immunia rura cicadis,
Incipe, si quod habes gracili sub harundine carmen
Compositum. Nam te calamos inflare labello
Pan docuit versuque bonus tibi favit Apollo.
Incipe, dum salices haedi, dum gramina vaccae
Detondent, viridique greges permittere campo
Dum ros et primi suadet clementia solis.
Tit. Hos annos canamque comam, vicine Timeta,
Tu iuvenis carusque deis in carmina cogis?
Diximus et calamis versus cantavimus olim,
Dum secura hilares aetas ludebat amores.
Nunc album caput et veneres tepuere sub annis,
Iam mea ruricolae dependet fistula Fauno.
Te nunc rura sonant; nuper nam carmine victor

blasts of Mopsus, with myself the judge. With me aged Meliboeus
listened to you both and praised you to the skies. Now after he
has completed a life of good service, a portion of that secluded
realm, the heaven of the righteous, possesses him. Proceed, therefore, if there lives in your heart any gratitude to Meliboeus. Let
your sweet flute praise his honored shade.

Tim. It is fitting for me to obey your commands, and what you
command is welcome to me. For the old man was worthy that
Phoebus should celebrate him with song, Pan with his pipes, and
Linus and Oeagrian Orpheus with the lyre, and that they should
sound the praises of the man's many glorious deeds. But since
you demand praise from my pipe, hear the song which the cherry
tree that you see by the river holds on this theme, preserving my
verses in its carved bark.

Tit. Come, speak them. But that the pine chattering in the
wind may not disturb us, let us rather seek these elms and beeches.

Tim. Here it is pleasant to sing; for the soft meadow offers green
herbage and all the grove is silent far and wide. See how afar
the tranquil bulls are cropping the grass.

> Risisti calamos et dissona flamina Mopsi
> Iudice me. Mecum senior Meliboeus utrumque
> Audierat laudesque tuas sublime ferebat;
> Quem nunc emeritae permensum tempora vitae
> Secreti pars orbis habet mundusque piorum.
> Quare age, si qua tibi Meliboei gratia vivit,
> Dicat honoratos praedulcis tibia manes.
> *Tim.* Et parere decet iussis et grata iubentur.
> Namque fuit dignus senior, quem carmine Phoebus,
> Pan calamis, fidibus Linus aut Oeagrius Orpheus
> Concinerent totque acta viri laudesque sonarent.
> Sed quia tu nostrae laudem deposcis avenae,
> Accipe quae super haec cerasus, quam cernis ad amnem,
> Continet, inciso servans mea carmina libro.
> *Tit.* Dic age; sed nobis ne vento garrula pinus
> Obstrepat, has ulmos potius fagosque petamus.
> *Tim.* Hic cantare libet; virides nam subicit herbas
> Mollis ager lateque tacet nemus omne: quieti
> Adspice ut ecce procul decerpant gramina tauri.

All-father Sky and you Waters, source of being, and thou Earth,
mother of our bodies, and thou vital Air, receive these songs and
waft them to our Meliboeus, if it is granted to mute shades to
have feeling after death. For if sublime souls inhabit the celestial
realms and starry abodes and have their joy of heaven, do thou
give heed to our strains which even thou hast cherished in thy
kindly heart and which thou, Meliboeus, hast approved. A long
life and an old age long esteemed by all and happy years and
the last cycle of our mortal span have closed the days of an
upright life. Yet not less were our groans and tears than if
envious death had plucked the years of thy prime. Neither did
the common fate of man restrain such lamentations as these:

"Alas, Meliboeus, thou liest stilled in the chill of death by
the law of mankind, in thy hoary old age worthy of heaven and the
council of the gods. Thy breast was filled with righteous authority.
Thou wast accustomed to decide the disputes of the rustics, soothing their varied quarrels with patience. Under thee love of right,
under thee respect for justice flourished. A boundary stone marked
the disputed fields. There was a friendly dignity in thy counte-

Omniparens aether et rerum causa, liquores,
Corporis et genetrix tellus, vitalis et aer,
Accipite hos cantus atque haec nostro Meliboeo
Mittite, si sentire datur post fata quietis.
Nam si sublimes animae caelestia templa
Sidereasque colunt sedes mundoque fruuntur,
Tu nostros adverte modos, quos ipse benigno
Pectore fovisti, quos tu, Meliboee, probasti.
Longa tibi cunctisque diu spectata senectus
Felicesque anni nostrique novissimus aevi
Circulus innocuae clauserunt tempora vitae.
Nec minus hinc nobis gemitus lacrimaeque fuere
Quam si florentes mors invida carperet annos;
Nec tenuit tales communis causa querellas:
"Heu, Meliboee, iaces mortali frigore segnis
Lege hominum, caelo dignus canente senecta
Concilioque deum. Plenum tibi ponderis aequi
Pectus erat. Tu ruricolum discernere lites
Adsueras, varias patiens mulcendo querellas.
Sub te iuris amor, sub te reverentia iusti
Floruit, ambiguos signavit terminus agros.
Blanda tibi vultu gravitas et mite serena

nance, a kindly brow on thy tranquil forehead; but thy heart was kindlier than thy countenance. Thou didst encourage us to fit reeds to our lips, to join them together with wax, and didst teach us to beguile our painful cares. Not suffering our sluggish youth to become languid, thou didst often present no mean gifts to our deserving Muse. Often despite thy advanced years, lest we be reluctant to sing, thou didst gladly repeat a song with the reed of Phoebus. Happy Meliboeus, farewell! To thee rural Apollo, plucking the laurel, offers gifts of fragrant foliage. The Fauns, each according to his power, offer clusters of grapes from the vine, stalks from the harvest, and fruits from every tree. Venerable Pales offers vessels foaming with milk, the Nymphs bring honey, Flora offers varicolored garlands. This is the last tribute for the dead. The Muses offer songs, songs the Muses offer, and we tune them to the pipe. Now of thee, Meliboeus, the woodland plane tree whispers, of thee the pine. Every song which Echo repeats to the woods resounds of thee. Our herds tell of thee. Sooner will seals graze in the dry meadows and the shaggy lion live in the sea and the yew trees ooze sweet honey and, with the laws of the seasons confused, harsh winter will produce the harvest

60

70

Fronte supercilium, sed pectus mitius ore.
Tu calamos aptare labris et iungere cera
Hortatus duras docuisti fallere curas;
Nec segnem passus nobis marcere iuventam   60
Saepe dabas meritae non vilia praemia Musae.
Saepe etiam senior, ne nos cantare pigeret,
Laetus Phoebea dixisti carmen avena.
Felix o Meliboee, vale! tibi frondis odorae
Munera dat lauros carpens ruralis Apollo;
Dant Fauni, quod quisque valet, de vite racemos,
De messi culmos omnique ex arbore fruges;
Dat grandaeva Pales spumantia cymbia lacte,
Mella ferunt Nymphae, pictas dat Flora coronas:
Manibus hic supremus honos. Dant carmina Musae,   70
Carmina dant Musae, nos et modulamur avena:
Silvestris te nunc platanus, Meliboee, susurrat,
Te pinus; reboat te quicquid carminis Echo
Respondet silvae; te nostra armenta loquuntur.
Namque prius siccis phocae pascentur in arvis
Hirsutusque freto vivet leo, dulcia mella
Sudabunt taxi, confusis legibus anni

and summer the olive, sooner will autumn offer blossoms, the
80 springtime offer grapes, than my pipe, Meliboeus, will leave thy
praises unsung."

Tit. Proceed, lad, and do not abandon the song you have begun.
For so sweetly do you sing, that favoring Apollo will carry you
on and will propitiously conduct you to the imperial city. Even
here in the woodlands an assured fame has already opened for
you an auspicious path, bursting through the clouds of envy with
her wings. But now the sun is driving his horses down from the
height of the firmament, urging us to offer the river's waters to
our flocks.

> Messem tristis hiemps, aestas tractabit olivam,
> Ante dabit flores autumnus, ver dabit uvas,
> Quam taceat, Meliboee, tuas mea fistula laudes."   80
> *Tit.* Perge, puer, coeptumque tibi ne desere carmen.
> Nam sic dulce sonas, ut te placatus Apollo
> Provehat et felix dominam perducat in urbem.
> Iamque hic in silvis praesens tibi fama benignum
> Stravit iter, rumpens livoris nubila pennis.
> Sed iam sol demittit equos de culmine mundi,
> Flumineos suadens gregibus praebere liquores.

RADBERT

ECLOGUE BY TWO NUNS

An eclogue by two nuns uttered in one dirge of praise. These nuns Adalhard is praised for having cherished as though the one were given as the church in wedlock to him in place of Christ; whereas the other he begot by the same in accordance with monastic discipline, miraculously balancing them. Also it is undoubtedly to be understood that one of these is called Galatea on account of the radiance of her countenance, and that the other in turn he consecrated under the name of Phyllis by reason of her love of charity.

Galatea. Phyllis.

Gal. 'Wail, men, I beseech you, with me for the father in a pious wail, and let everyone of advanced age implore indulgence. Bedew the earth with tears and deck with flowers the field, at the obsequies of the father; therefore let all things drip with tears. With the aid of the tongue let hearts so emit lamentations that on every side even the stars may re-echo the moaning. Let the rustic Roman and the Latin tongue celebrate him, and together with them let the Saxon also speak, with wailing in place of song. Do ye all turn hither, as that great poet sang: "Build a tomb and to the tomb add a verse." Bear the blessed limbs of the old man

EGLOGA DUARUM SANCTIMONIALIUM

Egloga duarum sanctimonialium uno favoris planctu conplosa. Quas Adalhardus velud unam sibi in coniugium vice Christi ecclesiam enutrisse; aliam vero ex eadem secundum monasticam disciplinam miro libramine admodum genuisse peroratur. Quarum quoque unam propter candorem vultus Galatheam vocari, porro aliam propter amorem caritatis Fillidis nomine consecrasse taxatum iri non ambigitur.

Galathea. Fillis

Gal. 'Plangite, queso, viri, mecum pie plangite patrem,
Omnis et inploret veniam provectior aetas.
Spargite humum lacrimis, conponite floribus arvam
Patris ad excubias; hinc fletibus omnia sudent.
Officio linguae prodant sic corda vagitus,
Ut passim resonent etiam simul astra mugitum.
Rustica concelebret Romana Latinaque lingua,
Saxo quibus pariter plangens pro carmine dicat.
Vertite huc cuncti, cecinit quam maximus ille:
"Et tumulum facite et tumulo superaddite carmen."

10

to the renowned spot, even of him who labored to reveal to us
the glowing veins. At his obsequies with the mixed band let the
clergy sing in alternate voices these divine poems. Let the shepherds proclaim in verses that he was great, the keeper of a fair
flock, himself more fair, and let the crowd echo in answer: "O
God, beloved Creator, grant favor to thy servant; the realm of
Paradise do we beseech for him and pray: have compassion upon
the old man, have compassion upon thy servants, for assuredly
thou dost know how worthy he was of compassion." Then, I beg,
let heartfelt love and pain and groans resound; then let boys vie
in virtue, old men for renown.'

Phyl. 'Who, pray, would not wail that a man exalted beyond the
stars is reduced to ashes, that he is enclosed in such hard marble,
that he, the fame of whose merit speeds through the earth among
all peoples, even the race of kings, is food for worms? Alas,
what now shall we do, wretchedly faced by death? We weep,
we groan, but we have no power to call him back. So then he
is called: he is gone; he hears not those who love him. Our
bosoms are rent, our bowels are torn with sorrow; neither to the
tears nor to the lamentations of the mourners does he hearken.

Membra beata senis celebri conferte locello,
Qui nobis studuit venas aperire calentes.
Huius ad exequias clerus cum mixta caterva
Vocibus alternis divina poemata narrent:
Pastores, fuerit quod magnus, versibus edant,
Formosi pecoris custos formosior ipse,
Vulgus et econtra resonet: "Deus, alme creator,
Da veniam famulo: paradysi regna precamur,
Et petimus: miserere seni, miserere tuorum;
Tu quam dignus erat misereri, denique nosti."   20
Hinc, rogo, cordis amorque dolor gemitusque resultet,
Hinc pueri virtute, senes de nomine certent.'
Fill. 'Quis, rogo, non plangat hominem super astra levatum
In cineres redigi, quam duro marmore tegi?
Cuius in orbe volat virtutum fama per omnes,
Prosapies augustorum est quod vermibus esca?
Heu, quid hinc facimus miseri sub morte locati?
Ploramus, gemimus, sed nec revocare valemus.
Ergo vocatur: abest; sed nec exaudit amantes.
Pectora rumpuntur, lacerantur viscera luctu;   30
Ille nec exaudit lacrimas nec threna dolentum.

Because we are in torment, our hearts are torn with confusion, grief assails our spirits, nor does unhearing death give heed. Now do we preserve the dusty earth of the body, but that illustrious man translated to the stars rejoices in the choir. Hence I desire that with vigor you men and lads and maidens shall wail; with a devout heart let flow the salty fountains, in order that, because our sad origin has brought what all of us must suffer—and such alone has been of yore the nature of those before us—we should all together feel the same suffering of mind. Let sorrow, weeping, and tears at once smite the air; henceforth let a single lamentation flow through the lips of monks.'

Gal. 'I beg that you, Corbie, being older, consign the old man to the tomb; thereafter I, the younger, bereft of such a protector, will compose for alternate voices a lament instead of a song. And when you, a happy mother, bore me, a happy daughter, by one sire, you called me then by your name, saying: "O comely I, you shall be my second self for all future time." Rejoicing, thrice blessed, he established me with his own hands, offering many prophesies with saving words. For as then the demon was raging and his iniquitous power and the worship of his shrine

40

50

Et quia torquemur, laceramur corde tumultu,
Luctus adest animis nec mors surdissima curat.
Pulveream servamus hinc de corpore glebam,
Clarus at ille choro laetatur ad astra relatus.
Unde velim virtute, viri puerique puellae,
Plangite, corde pio salsos producite fontes,
Ut, quia tristis origo dedit quod patimur omnes—
Atque una ex antiquo est haec natura priorum—
Una sit et cunctis etiam conpassio mentis.   40
Mesticiae, fletus, lacrimae simul aethera pulsent;
Hinc inde unus in ora fluat fletus monachorum.'
Gal. 'Oro senem senior tumulo, Corbeia, condas;
Porro minor ego mox tali viduata patrono
Vocibus alternis gemitum pro carmine pangam.
Quam dudum generans felix felicem mater ab uno
Atque tuo vocitans pridem de nomine faris:
"O formosa ego, tu mihi nunc eris alter in evum."
Quam fundavit ovans manibus ter ille beatus
Plura salutiferis tribuens oracula verbis.   50
Nam quo tunc demon seviebat, iniqua potestas

had polluted all the land, he overthrew the altars and consecrated the sheepfolds of the flocks of Christ. Then cutting out far and wide from the very bottom the roots of the grove, he founded there a sacred monastery filled with monks.'

Phyl. 'O too happy I, what sorrows I am forced to undergo! Although through divine gift, rich boons are heaped upon thee, first on soil of Amiens, while thou seemest to have merited to lead the flock of Corbie, most sacred shepherd, the Saxon land also recognized thee as its father, that thou mightst bring back doubled the talents entrusted to thee by God. But thou, faithless death, with thy poisons, knowest not how to spare anyone, nor even ourselves; neither dost thou give heed to gifts. Thou knowest not how to love men nor to preserve our founders. For all men thou remainest the one lot of the irrevocable hour. By death hast thou torn away suddenly that blessed one from us, one whom all together with complaining voices we weep, groan, bewail, lament, love: but thou knowest not how, O pitiless death, pitying to take pity upon the pitiful. Alas, the sorrow of it! lo, so enviously thou drawest in all men with thee, so that of all the life we have lived hitherto thou mightst swallow everything.'

Et cultus fani totam fedaverat arvam,
Vertit aras, pecudum sacravit ovilia Christi.
Funditus inde procul luci radice recisa,
Sancta locavit ibi monachis caenobia plena'.
Fill. 'O felix nimium, quos cogor inire dolores!
Munere divino quamvis comulentur opima
Ambianense prius, qui dum meruisse videris
Corbeio preesse gregi, sanctissime pastor,
Te patrem esse novit etiam Saxonica cespis,
Ut commissa deo duplicata talenta reportes.
Sed tu, mors male fida venenis, parcere nescis
Ulli nec nobis; nec tu quoque munera curas.
Nescis amare viros, nescis servare patronos.
Omnibus una manes sors inrevocabilis horae.
Quae nobis stimplo rapuisti morte beatum
Illum, quem pariter querelosis vocibus omnes
Plangimus ac gemimus, flemus, lacrimamus, amamus:
Sed nescis, misera, miseris miserans misereri.
Proh dolor, ecce trahis omnes sic invida tecum,
Ut, quicquid iam viximus actenus, omnia sorbas'.

Gal. Then the reverend sister, the youngest of us, said: 'O how gentle of word and kindly was the master! Why hast thou so suddenly left us in our great weakness? Now in death thou wilt ever be happy through the ages; but I, a savage virgin, bloody from many wars, am dripping with a rainy fountain of tears after thy death, and amid a mighty groaning I beat my guilty breasts; hence do I wash with salt drops my blotched face, so that however black I may be with blotches and dark with poisons, now with a snowy countenance blent with the color of roses shall I become fair, shall I be radiant. I shall blaze and yet be wet, and all too happy in thee I shall weep in season as long as the last mournful span of my life abides.'

Phyl. Then also spoke the mother, after whose name she was called: 'You will never surpass me with tears nor with lamentations, nor in re-echoing graceful songs, nor in uttering vows. Therefore I desire that you mix the honey; let me make adornment with flowers; do you also pluck wan violets, while I gather lilies and cover over the mound with sweetest herbs. Since he was worthy of such tribute, who himself provided us with many

> *Gal.* Tum veneranda soror, nostrum parvissima, dixit:
> 'O verbo quam mitis erat blandusque magister.
> Cur nos tam subito liquisti valde tenellos?
> Tu siquidem moreris semper per saecula felix,
> Sed ego, virgo ferox, multis sanguinea bellis
> Ymbrifero post te lacrimarum fonte madesco
> Atque sub ingenti gemitu rea pectora tundo;
> Hinc faciem guttis diluo salsis maculosam,
> Quamvis nigra meis maculis sim et fusca venenis,   80
> Ut niveo vultu respersa colore rosarum
> Flavescam, niteam, flagrem simul atque madescam
> Atque, tui nimium felix, in tempore plangam,
> Quamdiu maneat flebilis pars ultima vitae'.
> *Fill.* Tum quoque mater ait, cuius de nomine dicta:
> 'Non me tu lacrimis vinces aut fletibus umquam,
> Non cantus resonare leves, non pandere vota.
> Unde velim: tu misce favos, ego floribus ornem;
> Tu quoque pallentes violas, ego lilia carpam
> Et superaspergam tumulum quam suavibus herbis;   90
> Hic quoniam condignus erat muneribus istis,
> Dilicias nobis qui multas prestitit ipse

delights and wholly painted you with the crimson blood of Christ. This the prophet Isaiah had already predicted of yore: Behold now the sacred trees of glory come clapping their hands; and here exult the myrtle, the fir-tree, and the pine; here flourish the vine and the grape and the glistening olive besides, and like paradise and the garden of delight are you nurtured with flowing waters from the height of heaven. You who had been a barren region, a descent to Avernus, now stand open, having become the portal of heaven and the gate of life. Nor does the former treachery of death avail to equal so swift a course, wherewith now already with soaring head you touch the glorious and lofty stars of the heavens and in your splendor you wax exceeding bright in the world. And soon no former nurse of monks can be more fruitful than you beneath the four corners of the sky. Therefore, sister, I beg you to utter lament instead of song because the father had completed scarce eighty years and not yet had your breasts chanced to flow with milk. Lo, suddenly he died and the pitcher of the fountain has been broken.'

Both Together. 'Counsellor of his country, he was filled with the wisdom of Christ.'

Et totam roseo te pinxit sanguine Christi.
Esaias vatis quod iam predixerat olim:
Sancta tibi hinc veniunt plaudentia ligna decoris,
Exultant inibi myrtus, abies sive pinus,
Vitis et uva, nitens etiam pinguescit oliva,
Ac tamquam paradysus et hortus diliciarum
Inriguis nutriris aquis de vertice caeli.
Quae fueras regio sterelis, descensus Averni,   100
Porta poli iam facta pates sive ianua vitae.
Nec valet equiperare prior perfidia mortis
Tam celerem cursum, quo nunc gloriosa
Iam caput excelsa caelorum sidera tangis
Atque nitore tuo nimium splendescis in orbe,
Vel citius qua nulla prior nutrix monachorum
Cardine sub quadro poterit fecundior esse.
Unde, soror, facias planctum pro carmine, posco,
Octoginta pater quod vix compleverat annos
Et necdum tua forte manarunt ubera lacte.   110
En subito periit vel fracta est idria fontis.'
Micton. 'Consilium patriae, Christi sapientia plenus.'

Gal. 'Alas, mother,' then said the daughter, leaning on God, 'Why should you desire to renew such great sorrow by telling it, or to recall the day than which none more cruel ever was or can now be or can ever be in the future? In the death of our founder this day has at once taken from us every glory of life, cutting short the promises of his virtues. Alas, how piteous are we, we who live away from him, for we are laid low by an exceedingly evil lot, we   120 who have been unable to fare to heaven, placed by his side; for I have deemed it better to die with him than to live.'
Phyl. 'Therefore, you people, whom the water of Christ has cleansed, bring forth flowing streams from your innermost heart, and let us wail the fate of my virgin spouse, a man prudent, sober, chaste, full of charity, mild, humble, also just and kindly, noble and upright, than whom no man was more wise, in whose speech sparkled the wisdom of Christ, there was revealed a springing   130 fountain of life, a doctrine of salvation. Distinguished in character, filled with the teaching of the virtues, gentle, peaceful, merciful and exceeding modest—these, I would have you know, were the estates of his right, of these the bridal gifts of my dowry are redolent. Therefore my blessed love for him grows even as

Gal. 'A mater,' subnixa deo tum filia dixit,
'Quid tantos renovare velis narrando dolores
Aut memorare diei, qua nec sevior ulla
Vel fuit, esse potest poteritque aut esse futura?
Quae simul abstraxit nobis pereunte patrono
Omne decus vitae virtutum vota recidens.
Heu nos quam miseri, absentes qui vivimus illo,
Quod sumus in nimium depressi sorte maligna,   120
Qui pariter caelum nequivimus ire locati;
Cum quo namque mori melius quam vivere duxi.'
Fill. 'Quapropter, populi, Christi quos abluit unda,
Flumineos latices producite pectoris imo
Virgineumque meum plangamus sorte maritum,
Prudentem, sobrium, castum, caritate repletum,
Mansuetum, humilem nec non iustum atque benignum,
Nobilitate probum, quo nec sapientior ullus;
Cuius in eloquio micuit sapientia Christi,
Fons patuit saliens vitae, doctrina salutis.   130
Moribus insignis, virtutum dogmate plenus,
Mitis, pacificus, clemens et valde modestus—
Ista fuere sui, velim cognoscas, praedia iuris,
Ista meae redolent viritim sponsalia dotis.
Unde beatus amor tantum mihi crescit in illo,

in the new-born spring the world increases with flowers.   But all
the more for this has sorrow followed me through the hours,
because my insatiable ardor for him blazes exceedingly and because
henceforth there can be no remedy for my grief, if I am not
140   permitted at least to celebrate that sacred name.'

Gal. Thereat Galatea exceeding happy asserts: 'Begin at last to
lay aside such grievous plaints. The Muses marvel perchance at
such rites and their songs in amazement have left their melodies.
All things—even the stones—grieve with your lamentations. Oh,
if,' she says, 'there might be a return of his love in order that we
who are overwhelmed with such waves of tears for him may at
length be revived by the breath of his sweetness. May we some
150   day with joined hands fare to the citadel, to the chambers of that
kingdom whither he has long been summoning us. Let us feed
eternally in celestial fields, into which the happy old man Menalcas
has deserved to enter, even he who has taken with him our
affections afar and draws after him sighs from our very heart-
strings.'

Phyl. 'Indeed the rights of prayer are bound to reach yonder,

Quantum vere novo se mundus floribus auget.
Sed proinde magis luctus successit in horis,
Quod nimium fraglet in eo insaciabilis ardor
Et quod nulla mei sit abhinc medicina doloris,
Si non vel liceat mihi sanctum pangere nomen.'   140
Gal. Ad quod quam nimium felix Galathea fatetur:
'Incipe sollicitos tales iam ponere questus.
Forte mirantur enim tanto pro funere Musae
Et stupefacta suos liquerunt carmina melos.
Omnia congemuere tuis—et saxes—threnis.
O si,' inquit, 'veniat tunc ille recursus amoris,
Quae tantis in eo lacrimarum cogimur undis,
Ut tandem renovemur eius dulcedinis austu.
Interdum manibus iunctis pergamus ad arcem,
Ad thalamos regni, quo dudum nos vocat idem.   150
Ethereis pascamur eo quam perpete campis,
Quo meruit senior felix intrare Menalcha,
Qui nostros secum quam longe duxit amores
Et trahit e nostris post se suspiria fibris.'
Fill. 'Illo etenim voti debentur iura coire,

although here midway before us is the sad tomb. But if stead-
fastly we seek, we knock, we inquire, I say there is no doubt that
after death we shall come to the city in which reign piety, goodness,
peace, light, plenty; there gleam happiness, fruition, rest, and joys;   **160**
there every good shines, sweet concord caresses; glory, praise, and
honor gush from one fountain; life everlasting rejoices, the pastures
of virtue flourish; angelic flocks give thanks, heavenly places are
green; rewards at last are made sure with unfailing gifts, for God
is ever near in person; rich rewards are disclosed among companies
of the apostles and the patriarchs. There breathes a pleasant
fragrance sweeter than any herbs; mossy plots lie open with the
splendid martyr band. The city of the prophets is fragrant with   **170**
the breath of sweetness; the bright ranks wax golden with virgin
bloom; there do all enjoy pious pleasures on every side, and all
re-echo singing with one heart, with mellifluous voice, each singing
in this wise.'

Gal. 'Leave off any more, my mother,' the sister Galatea then said;
'haply shall we sing these things better after we have seen them,

Quamquam adeo nobis media est via triste sepulchrum.
Sed si constanter petimus, pulsamus, quaerimus, inquam,
Post cineres quin, haud dubium, veniamus ad urbem,
Qua pietas, bonitas, pax, lux, opulentia regnant;
Laetitiae, fructus, requies et gaudia fulgent;   160
Omne bonum renitet, dulcis concordia mulcet;
Gloria, laus et honor uno de fonte manatur;
Vita perennis ovat, virtutum pascua florent;
Angelicae gratulantur oves, caelestia vernant;
Premia perpetuis firmantur denique donis,
Quod deus semper adest presens, reserantur opima
Inter apostolicas patriarcharumque cohortes;
Spirat odor quam dulcis suavior omnibus herbis;
Martyrio splendente choro muscosa patescunt;
Castra prophetarum redolent dulcedinis austu;   170
Candida virgineo flavescunt agmina flore;
Omnia concelebrant inibi pia gaudia passim
Et resonant omnes una de corde canentes
Mellifluas voces in talia carmina quisque.'
Gal. 'Desine plura,' soror tum, 'mater,' ait Galathea,
'Ista quidem inspecta melius tum forte canemus,

when rejoicing heaven shall also be our happy lot. Meanwhile gather flowers of the fields and lilies, until the joyous chorus of alleluias echoes about us. Strew the way with violets, the field with blossoms of virtue, adorn the path with roses, scatter lilies in the streets.'

180

> Cum paradysus ovans nobis quoque sorte virebit.
> Actenus agrorum flores et lilia carpe,
> Donec alleluiatica circum gaudia stridant.
> Sparge viam violis, virtutum floribus arvam,
> Pinge rosis callem, plateis lilia sterne.'

180

PETRARCH

ARGUS

Ideus. Pythias. Silvius.

Id. Already the golden sun was facing the west, and was driving
his steeds to accomplish his downward journey with easy course;
nor in many generations had any day witnessed such deep quiet
in the groves: here and there the sated flocks were lying, and a
gentle sleep possessed the shepherds; some were binding smooth
sticks, some were weaving leafy garlands while singing, some were
fashioning pliant reeds. Then a black cloud obscured glittering
Phoebus, and night rushing suddenly arrived before its expected
time; the air was roughened with fearful hail; in rivalry stormed 10
wind and rain, and thunder descended from the riven clouds. A
towering cypress, torn from its roots by the crash of the heavens,
tumbled down and shook both hills and fields, once the favorite of
the sun, the devoted care of the now buried sun; nor yet did the
love of the sun avail to ward off the fatal disaster, and harsh fate

ECLOGUE 2

ARGUS

Ideus. Phitias. Silvius.

Id. Aureus occasum iam sol spectabat, equosque
Pronum iter urgebat facili transmittere cursu;
Nec nemorum tantam per secula multa quietem
Viderat ulla dies: passim saturata iacebant
Armenta et lenis pastores somnus habebat;
Pars teretes baculos, pars nectere serta canendo
Frondea, pars agiles calamos; tum fusca nitentem
Obduxit Phebum nubes, precepsque repente
Ante expectatum nox affuit; horruit ether
Grandine terribili; certatim ventus et imber 10
Sevire et fractis descendere fulmina nimbis.
Altior, ethereo penitus convulsa fragore,
Corruit et colles concussit et arva cupressus,
Solis amor quondam, solis pia cura sepulti;
Nec tamen evaluit fatalem avertere luctum
Solis amor, vicitque pium fors dura favorem.

laid low his cherished favorite. Alas, Phoebus, too foreseeing a prophet wast thou then: "Some day to itself, some day to others, this tree will be a cause for tears," thou saidst. Terrified by the crash of its mighty downfall, soon the crowd of shepherds fled, all that had sat carefree under that shade through the long day. Some made for the mountains, some for the threshold of their safe hut, some hid their heads in caves and the gaping earth. Silvius and Pythias perchance sought out with hurrying step the same cliff, and both in their terror found concealment in twin caverns, groaning not a little. Later, when the clouds thinned and the force of the storm was broken for a while, and when the rumblings of the wearied sky were stilled, weeping Pythias began: "Gracious Jupiter, if our sin has deserved this, if the rustic piety of the shepherds is decayed, be indulgent to our woodlands, we pray! Have pity upon the innocent flock, and in more propitious mood, gather together the scattered goats; let the udders once marked by thy tender lips move thee, unless perchance the nectar of the starry court has brought thee forgetfulness of that milk. Verily thy nurse was of the flock!" With such words of complaint he fell silent, and with his hand he beat his breast and his face.

Prescius, heu! nimium vates tum, Phebe, fuisti:
"Dum sibi dumque aliis erit hec lacrimabilis arbor,"
Dixisti. Ingentis strepitu tremefacta ruine
Pastorum mox turba fugit, quecumque sub illa
Per longum secura diem consederat umbra;
Pars repetit montes, tuguri pars limina fidi,
Pars specubus terreque caput submittit hianti.
Silvius et Phitias scopulum fortassis eundem
Precipiti petiere gradu, geminisque cavernis
Occuluere animas trepidi, nec pauca gementes.
Post, ubi laxatis tempestas fracta parumper
Nubibus et celi siluerunt murmura fessi
Incipit illacrimans Phitias: "O Iupiter alme,
Si scelus hoc nostrum meruit, si rustica sordet
Pastorum pietas, silvis ignosce, precamur;
Innocui miserere gregis, meliorque capellas
Collige dispersas; teneris signata labellis
Ubera te moveant, nisi forte oblivia lactis
Illius astrigere nectar tibi suggerit aule:
De grege nempe fuit nutrix tua!" Talia questus,
Subticuit, pectusque manu percussit et ora.

When Silvius heard the lamentation from his part of the cliff (for they could not discern each other in person, being separated by the small obstruction of a projecting rock and by a leafy branch), agitated in mind he thus replied, restraining a groan: "Pythias, Pythias, I confess that long since I noticed that the stars were threatening, after I observed the flaming rays of Mars, and Saturn lingering in the rainy sign, and Jove blocked, and Venus looking obliquely, and after I marked the alien whistlings of the winds. Did we not see from afar the clouds rising from the marshy, reeking mire and driven into our heavens? Did we not see the fleeing cranes, the foul gulls by the shores? Or the ravens and the wandering coots? Did we not see the gloomy stars and Phoebe vanishing wrapped in cloud; then the many signs of a rising storm which once the elders of the woodland foretold? Yet we must bear it. Such is the life of man, Pythias; so savage fortune alternates joy with sorrow. Let the world go on by its ancient rule; let our experience of life profit us. Wherever the wretched flock falls to ruin, it is glorious to stand."

40

50

> Silvius, audita rupis de parte querela,
> (Nam neque se coram cernebant, obice parvo
> Pretente silicis ramoque comante dirempti)
> Concussa sic mente refert, gemitumque coercens:
> "O Phitia, Phitia; fateor, sic astra minari
> Iampridem adverti, postquam flamantia Martis
> Lumina, et imbrifera Saturnum in parte morantem,
> Obsessumque Iovem, et Venerem transversa tuentem,
> Sibila ventorum postquam peregrina notavi.
> Nonne procul nebulas, limo exalante palustri,
> Surgere et in nostrum delatas vidimus axem?
> Nonne grues profugas, turpesque ad litora mergos?
> Num corvos, fulicasque vagas, num sidera mesta
> Vidimus et nimbo velatam abscedere Pheben,
> Tum que multa olim nascentis signa procelle
> Silvicole cecinere senes? Sed ferre necesse est.
> Hec est vita hominum, Phitia; sic leta dolendis
> Alternat fortuna ferox. Eat ordine mundus
> Antiquo; nobis rerum experientia prosit:
> Quo grex cumque miser ruerit, consistere pulcrum est."

40

50

"Silvius, above all dear to me and ever greatest," answered
60 Pythias, "at your counsel I shall dry my eyes. If only you have
some solace for bitter loss, let timely forgetfulness lighten our
grievous disasters."

"Rather," said he, "is it your task to share with me those songs
that you have stored away. Daphnis was once sung by shepherds,
and now great Argus will rightly be sung by you. Why by you,
and not by us both, Pythias? Are you also minded now to voice a
song of Argus? You are too prone to hide everything. Begin;
perhaps I shall follow, unless your voice should deter me," said
Silvius.

With a loud voice the other interrupted his sighs:

Pyth. Argus, honor of the world! Argus, sorrow of the deserted
70 wood! Was devouring death permitted this license with thy sacred
body? Did earth dare this? Has the dark earth covered thee, who
already wast alone the watcher of starry Olympus? Whither is
departed our benefactor, whither the glory of our age? Who will
long beforehand foretell the storms from the heavens? Who, I
wonder, will with his voice touch wild beasts and oaks and stones?
Or who will pass away in sweet song the long night? Who will
affright the wild boars? Who will lay snares for the deer? Who

"Care michi in primis et semper maxime Silvi,"
Respondit Phitias, "oculos, te consule, tergam;
Tu modo, si quod habes damni solamen acerbi,   60
Tempestiva graves relevent oblivia casus."
"Imo," ait ille, "tuum est que condita carmina servas
Mecum partiri: Daphnis pastoribus olim,
Et tibi nunc ingens merito cantabitur Argus.
Quid tibi, non nobis, Phitias? num te quoque carmen
Argeum vocitare libet? Nimis omnia celas.
Incipe; forte sequar, nisi vox tua terreat," inquit
Silvius. Ille alta fregit suspiria voce:
Phit. Arge, decus rerum! Silve dolor, Arge, relicte!
Hoc licuit rapide sacro de corpore morti?   70
Hoc ausa est tellus? Te, qui stellantis Olimpi
Iam solus spectator eras, humus obruit atra?
Quo favor, et nostri rediit quo gloria secli?
Quis tempestates prenoscet ab ethere longe?
Quis michi voce feras quercusque et saxa movebit,
Aut longam dulci traducet carmine noctem?
Quis terrebit apros? Quis tendet retia dammis?

will catch birds with lime? Ah, who will care for the wretched
sheep, dipping them in the river? Who will duly sing the rites of
Cybele and humbled Phoebus serving on the grassy pasture of **80**
Admetus? Of whom will the sheepstealer in the night be afraid?
Whom will the docile she-goats under the high rock know, whom
the vigilant, faithful dogs, whom his sweet mistress? Who, I ask,
will hold the solemn games on the shores, reviving the neglected
contest of ancestral custom? From whom will those in doubt
receive counsel, and the dwellers of the woodland far and wide
receive divine oracles? Who in time of stress will furnish aid to
suppliants? Argus, once most lovely, the Dryads' love and sorrow,
what will the wood, what will the cave, what will the hills without **90**
thee? And after thee shall anyone either desire or be able to live?
Believe it, shepherds, it is death to live after Argus. Now you will see
the pools already drying up all around, the lakes, the springs, the
very sea. Changed will be the breath of the wind, changed the color
in the herbage, changed the fragrance of the flowers. Neither will
fruits retain their wonted flavors, nor meadows their foliage, nor
rivers their waters, nor sheep their fleece, nor the field its rich ears
of wheat. For he alone with his glance (nor are we in error) was

Quis visco captabit aves? Quis, flumine mergens,
Ah! miseras curabit oves? Quis sacra Cibeles,
Atque humilem, Admeti famulantem in gramine, Phebum 80
Rite canet? Quem nocturnus trepidabit abactor?
Quem noscent dociles alta sub rupe capelle?
Quem vigiles fidique canes? Quem dulcis amica?
Quis michi solennes statuet per litora ludos,
Insuetam patrio renovans ex more palestram?
A quo consilium dubii, divinaque late
Silvestres responsa ferent? Quis tempore in arcto
Suplicibus prestabit opem? Pulcherrime quondam
Arge, amor ac luctus Driadum, quid silva, quid antrum,
Quid sine te colles? Et post te vivere quisquam 90
Aut volet, aut poterit? Pastores, credite, mors est
Vivere post Argum. Iam nunc arescere circum
Stagna, lacus, fontes, ipsumque videbitis equor;
Spiritus alter erit ventis, color alter in herbis,
Floribus alter odor; solitos nec poma sapores
Servabunt, nec prata comas, nec flumina limphas,
Vellera nec pecudes, nec opimas campus aristas.
Omnia namque oculis unus (nec fallimur) ille

100 wont to gladden all things and to make them fruitful. Under his leadership the woodland was always safe; peace was on his brow; with a word he banished the clouds. He has departed; a changed fortune disquiets his people.

Sil. You bring forth my tears; and no more is life sweet to me after Argus. But we shall yield to our star of life.

Pyth. You are departing! I observe it; but not without a song, Silvius. If you desire to go, sing; go afterwards, review your own sorrows.

Sil. King of shepherds was Argus, who possessed a hundred Lyncean eyes, a hundred attentive ears with their senses, a hundred limbs, 110 a hundred hands, a hundred arms. Yet he had but one tongue, with which he could move crags and beasts, and tear from the earth the deep-rooted ash trees. Long since distinguished was he in the woodlands, famous in all the pastures, everywhere sung by fair maidens, pasturing a thousand snow-white flocks in a thousand nooks. After he became wearied with the groves and the long toil, he has departed, never to return; with winged course he flies forth through trackless ways to the mountains. Thence from the highest summit he looks down, and beholds our cares and our

Letificare suis et fecundare solebat.
Illo silva fuit semper sub principe tuta;   100
Pax inerat fronti, purgabat nubila verbo.
Ille abiit; fortuna suos mutata fatigat.
Sil. Extorques lacrimas; nec iam michi vivere dulce est
Post Argum. Sed vivaci parebimus astro.
Phit. Effugis! Agnosco. Nusquam sine carmine, Silvi.
Si libet ire, cane; post i, tua damna recense.
Sil. Pastorum rex Argus erat, cui lumina centum
Lincea, cui centum vigiles cum sensibus aures,
Centum artus, centumque manus, centumque lacerti,
Lingua sed una fuit, cum qua rupesque ferasque   110
Flecteret et fixas terre divelleret ornos.
Ille diu clarus silvis, perque omnia notus
Pascua, formosis cantatus ubique puellis,
Mille greges niveos pascens per mille recessus.
Postquam pertesum est nemorum longique laboris,
Irrediturus abit, volucrique per avia saltu
Evolat in montes. Illinc de vertice summo
Despicit et nostras curas nostrosque tumultus,

confusion, and how great is the distress of the wood that once he
ruled.   He speaks with Jove and to him entrusts the bereaved fold.   120
Argus, farewell!   Brief the delay, we shall all follow thee.

Id. With these words they depart; Pythias bends his way to the
fields of his native Sulmo; the other seeks his Etruscan woods.   I
alone with my grief remained on the sorrowful shore.

> Regnateque videt quanta est angustia silve;
> Alloquiturque Iovem et viduum commendat ovile.   120
> Arge, vale! Nos te cuncti, mora parva, sequemur.
> *Id.* His dictis, abeunt; patrii Sulmonis ad arva
> Contendit Phitias, silvas petit alter Etruscas;
> Solus ego afflicto merens in litore mansi.

ECLOGUE 11

GALATEA

Niobe. Fusca. Fulgida.

Nio. Lead the way, sister, to the tomb and to the stones of the cold
sepulchre.
Fus. Why do you seek food for tears?   Sister, what do you desire?
Nio. A groan is great comfort for deep sorrow, and sighs, lamentations relieve the afflicted heart.   A confined sorrow consumes the
soul; open grief is the best medicine for a saddened breast.   Would
that my feelings had ever been the same as now!   Never would
numbness turn this heart to stone; hurtful it was to keep silent in

ECLOGUE 11

GALATEA

Niobe. Fusca. Fulgida.

> *Nio.* Duc, soror, ad tumulum gelidique ad saxa sepulcri.
> *Fus.* Quid lacrimis alimenta petis? Germana, quid optas?
> *Nio.* Est gemitus magni solamen grande doloris,
> Afflictamque animam relevant suspiria, questus.
> Enecat arctatus mentem dolor; optima mesti
> Pectoris est medicina palam lugere. Fuisset
> Idem animus semper! Nunquam hec precordia torpor
> Verteret in silicem; nocuit tacuisse dolenti.

my grief. But let that be; now that I am eager to weep, lead me where there is abundance of weeping.

10 *Fus.* Make your way hither, where you will see the necks of oxen bound with knotty muzzles, and the frequent watching of dogs beneath the narrow threshold, and the yellow Molossians near the doors. That place confines the cause of your sorrow. Now look before you: here has been laid Galatea, than whom Nature has created nothing more lovely on earth, unless our love has utterly deceived us. Here lay down that which oppresses you; clasp the tomb; plant kisses upon the stones; speak words to the still shade. *Nio.* Alas, too narrow the abode, too narrow the abode for such beauty! Is this now, Galatea, thy dwelling? Perceiving thy

20 radiance, the sun was amazed, and having avowed his equal and then having avowed his superior, astounded he plunged himself belated into the waves. Is this now, Galatea, thy dwelling? Do you stars stand in the sky? Dost thou, Boötes, sport on the sinking wain? Dost thou, Jupiter, with tranquil aspect traverse the arched expanse of the sky? Dost thou yet advance, chilly old man with the scythe, and thou, Orion armed? Moon, dost thou complete thy wonted phases, and thou, fleet messenger of the gods; and thou, Venus, who wilt change thy name in turn? Here thou liest all

> Mitto autem; cupidam modo duc ubi copia flendi.
> *Fus.* Carpe iter hac, qua nodosis innexa capistris   10
> Colla boum, crebrasque canum sub limine parvo
> Videris excubias, gilvosque ad claustra molossos.
> Ille locus tua damna tegit, iamque aspice contra:
> Hic Galathea sita est, qua nil natura creavit
> Pulcrius in terris, nisi nos amor usque fefellit.
> Depone hic quodcunque premit; complectere bustum;
> Oscula fer saxis; umbre dic verba silenti.
> *Nio.* Heu nimis arcta domus, tanto domus arcta decori!
> Hec sedes Galathea tibi est? Quam fulgere cernens,
> Sol stupuit, fassusque parem, fassusque subinde   20
> Maiorem, attonitus serum sese abdidit undis.
> Hec sedes, Galathea, tibi? Vos sidera celo
> Statis? In occiduo ludis temone, Boote?
> Jupiter, ore poli lustras convexa sereno?
> Is gelidus cum falce senex, armatus Orion?
> Luna, vices peragis solitas, volucerque deorum
> Interpres, nomenque Venus positura vicissim?

pale, Galatea, already dust and ashes, already nothing! Unless perchance thy spirit lives on the celestial height and thence serenely beholds thy weeping friends. Nought dost thou answer me, thou other half of my soul, and likewise the best half? Lend me your right hands at my prayer, if there is still any faith in the world or if there still survives any ancient piety. Alas! By what means, my sister, shall I now roll back the formidable stone? I will rush into her arms, I will plant kisses on her; and this precious body will I bear away at my bosom with fainting effort, and closely pressing it to me I will carry it into the shrine and lay it in the secret sanctuaries of the gods. Everlasting honors will I add, which the world may celebrate; I will add bands of maidens and venerable rites and fitting ceremonials for a goddess. There shall be no lack of torch or hymns, sounding far and wide a woman's praises. Alas, too hard for me is the stone, a heavy and unmoving weight. I fail under the burden, sister, and with my effort I am spent.

Fus. Rise, sister, rise; forbear to defile your sacred body with a corpse. Let the present content you; in vain would you long for what is past; safe is forgetfulness in one who loves. Truly, yesterday cannot be brought back by any art; death removes cares, death loosens all ties.

> Hic pallens, Galathea, iaces; iam terra cinisque,
> Iam nichil! Etherea nisi forsan spiritus arce
> Vivit, et inde videt flentes tranquillus amicas.
> Nil michi respondes, anime pars altera nostre,
> Optima pars eadem? Dextras adhibete precanti,
> Siqua fides mundo est, pietas seu prisca superstes.
> Heu! Lapidem infestum, qua nunc, soror, arte revolvam?
> Irruam in amplexus, figam oscula; dulce cadaver
> Hoc referam moribunda sinu fotumque sacellis
> Inferam et archanis divum penetralibus abdam.
> Addam perpetuos celebret quos mundus honores;
> Virgineos addam cetus, ritusque verendos
> Et sua sacra dee; nec fax nec carmina deerunt,
> Femineas longe lateque sonantia laudes.
> Heu michi predurum lapidem, grave pondus inersque!
> Deficio sub fasce, soror, nitensque fatisco.
> *Fus.* Surge, soror, surge; sacrumque cadavere corpus
> Commaculare cave. Placeant presentia; frustra
> Preteritum expectes; tuta est oblivio amanti.
> Nempe hesterna dies ulla nequit arte reverti;
> Mors adimit curas, mors omnia vincla resolvit.

Nio. Enough now of weeping, death has shattered our loves. Would that death had equally shattered our sorrows! I hoped; for its fulfillment was nigh; alas, it betrayed me.

Fus. I live, but unhappily, and I am preserved for every sorrow. Soft! Behold, sad Fulgida is approaching in the path to the left and with silent brow chides your complaints.

Ful. Why, you wretched and blind in spirit, why do you so deeply mourn mortal destinies? Why do you weep, Niobe? Rather, begin to learn how to endure whatever life harsh fate has afforded and will afford. Me, too, love doth afflict, and I am moved by sorrow for my dear ones. But what could you do? Futile the weapons you would press against the goad; better is patience for those crushed down; of itself the mind makes many things lighter by endurance. Why do you groan? Galatea was destined to die; hereafter she will be immortal. To pine over one's own loss is not love; to mourn another's happy lot is envy. How much has departed from us we all know, and how much has departed from an ungrateful world; but we endure it. Do you cease and look up to her that holds a better fate and pray for heaven when you have left the earth.

Nio. Iam satis est fletum, nostros mors fregit amores.
Fregissetque utinam nostros mors equa labores!
Speravi; prope nam steterat; miseramque fefellit.
Fus. Vivo, sed infelix, et luctus servor in omnes.
Parcius! En levo tristis tibi Fulgida calle
Advenit, et tacita castigat fronte querelas.
Ful. Quid, misere ceceque animi, mortalia fletis
Tam graviter? Quid fles, Niobe? Quin incipe vitam
Scire pati, quamcunque dedit sors dura dabitque.
Et me torquet amor, desiderioque meorum
Permoveor. Sed quid facias? Arma irrita calces
Adversus stimulum; melior patientia pressis;
Multa sibi facit ipse animus leviora ferendo.
Quid gemitis? Moritura fuit Galathea; deinceps
Immortalis erit. Proprio tabescere damno
Non amor. Alterius sortem lugere secundam
Invidia est. Quantum nobis decesserit, omnes
Scimus, et ingrato quantum decesserit orbi;
Sed ferimus. Vos desinite, ac meliora tenentem
Suspicite, et celum terris optate relictis.

Fus. Nonsense! With what wings can earthly creatures attain heaven?

Ful. With heavenly wings; so the earth, so the stars claim their own. 70

Fus. This superstition is common, indeed, but we approve only that which is certain.

Ful. Fusca, you inhabit the lowest places; we occupy the heights, and the site of heaven and earth we view from on high.

Nio. Leave off these ancient obscurities and inexplicable truth, and give over the entire dispute to those who are to come. Fulgida, do you rather (for you know the rural Muses) speak for the tomb an epitaph, which a later age may read.

Ful. Here the fairest Galatea has left her body; and liberated she now frequents the heavens and the royal mansions of the Thunderer 80 and the choirs and banquets of those on high. Death has touched her rosy limbs, death has touched her white neck, her cheeks, and her star-bright eyes, and in the dark earth it has buried her tranquil countenance. Should anyone cherish things mortal or hope here firmly to plant his steps? Of what avail birth or probity? Of what avail riches, or beauty, or youth? Of what avail a comely aspect? Of what avail great glory of name? All these were hers;

Fus. Fabula! Quis alis celum terrestria prendent?
Ful. Ethereis; sic terra suum, sic astra reposcunt. 70
Fus. Credulitas vulgata quidem; nos certa probamus.
Ful. Fusca, locis imis habitas; nos summa tenemus,
Et celi terreque situm speculamur ab alto.
Nio. Ambages veteres et inenodabile verum
Mittite, et integram venturis tradite litem.
Fulgida, quin potius (Musas nam noscis agrestes)
Dic titulum busto, relegat quem serior etas.
Ful. Hic liquit Galathea suum pulcherrima corpus;
Libera iamque polos et regia tecta Tonantis
Ipsa quidem superumque choros mensasque frequentat. 80
Mors roseos artus, mors candida colla genasque
Sidereosque oculos tetigit, voltusque serenos
Obscura demersit humo. Mortalia quisquam
Diligat, aut speret stabiles hic figere plantas?
Quid genus, aut probitas? Quid opes? Quid forma? Quid etas?
Quidve decens cultus? Quid gloria nominis ingens?
Omnia contigerant; manus abstulit omnia mortis.

all has the hand of death taken away. Naked, returning to her home, she fled from the beloved prison.

Nio. Naked not at all is she whom glory clothes, a garment ever more brilliant and fresh in hue with the long years. Every woman through the ages who is pleasing in countenance and in mind, in song or in speech, and who is desirous to please, will bear her before her eyes. We, as long as this life breath shall remain with our wretched body and compel us to live, even among the shades below and the misty streams of Lethe, we shall bear her as the pattern of virtue and the model of beauty within our heart in ever-mindful devotion. Only then will thy name depart from our breast, Galatea, when the stars shall flee their proper abodes, when bees shall abandon their zeal for honey, doves their nests, the turtle his mate, the wolf his prey, goats the arbute-bushes, a guarded woman her wiles, the slave his falsehoods.

Nuda, domum repetens, e carcere fugit amato.
Nio. Nuda quidem minime, quam gloria vestit, amictus
Clarior assidue longisque recentior annis.
Hanc quecunque sibi vultuque animoque per evum
Aut cantu aut sermone placens cupiensque placere,
Deferet ante oculos; hanc nos, dum spiritus iste
Artubus herebit miseris et vivere coget;
Hanc, vel apud Manes nebulosaque flumina Lethes,
Exemplarque pudicitie formamque decoris
Corde sub hoc semper memori pietate feremus.
Tum nostro, Galathea, tuum de pectore nomen
Exibit, fugient propriis cum sedibus astra,
Mellis apes studium linquent, nidosque columbe,
Coniugium turtur, predam lupus, arbuta capre,
Custodita dolos mulier, mendacia servus.

BOCCACCIO

(From a Letter to Martino da Signa)

The fourteenth eclogue is called Olympia from the Greek "olympos," which means "splendidum" (brilliant) or "lucidum" (shining) in Latin, and thence the sky is called Olympus. The reason for assigning the name Olympia to this eclogue is that there is considerable talk therein about the character of the celestial region. The speakers are four: Silvius, Camalus, Terapon, and Olympia. By Silvius I mean myself, whom I name so because I had the first idea of this eclogue in a certain forest. The Greek "Camalos" means "hebes" (dull) or "torpens" (sluggish) in Latin, because therein the character of a sluggish slave is indicated. "Terapon": I do not indicate the meaning of this because I do not remember it without referring again to the book from which I took the material about the others. So please pardon me; you know that the memory of men is faulty, especially that of old men. By Olympia I mean my little daughter who died some time ago at that age at which we believe that those dying become citizens of heaven. Therefore instead of Violante, her name while she lived, I call her after her death "celestial," that is, "Olympia."

Silvius. Camalus. Terapon. Olympia.

Sil. Unless I am in error, lads, I think the sacred rural gods are rejoicing and the whole wood is filled with the song of birds.

Quartadecima egloga Olympia dicitur ab "olympos" grece, quod "splendidum" seu "lucidum" latine sonat, et inde "celum" dicitur "Olympus"; et ideo huic egloge hoc nomen Olympia attributum est, quoniam in ea plurimum de qualitate celestis regionis habeatur sermo. Collocutores quatuor sunt, Silvius, Camalus, Terapon et Olympia. Pro Silvio me ipsum intelligo, quem sic nuncupo, eo quod in silva quadam huius egloge primam cogitationem habuerim. "Camalos" grece, latine sonat "hebes" vel "torpens," eo quod in eo demonstrentur mores torpentis servi. "Terapon" huius significatum non pono, quia non memini, nisi iterum revisam librum ex quo de ceteris sumpsi, et ideo ignoscas: scis hominum memoriam labilem esse, et potissime senum. Pro Olympia intelligo parvulam filiam meam olim mortuam ea in etate in qua morientes celestes effici cives credimus: et ideo, ex Violante dum viveret, mortuam "celestem" idest "Olympiam" voco.

Silvius. Camalus. Terapon. Olympia.

Sil. Sentio, ni fallor, pueri, pia numina ruris
Letari et cantu volucrum nemus omne repleri.

Lycos runs back and forth with friendly barking; what he has seen
I know not: with his tail he bespeaks a friend. Go, then; already
with the darkness is blent bright day, long heralded; seek out what
it is, what our Lycos has seen there, and report what you find.

Cam. While unable to compose his wretched breast in slumber,
alas, sorrowfully reclining upon the soft turf, Silvius gives orders
10   and he desires his lads to wander through the terrifying shadows
of night, weary though they are from the long labor of the day.

Sil. Camalus, when the Ebro will provide the earth with the first
torches of night, when Delia will lead the chariot of her brother to
the west, when the deer will bring down the lion, then the servant
will obey his master without a murmur. Terapon, do you loose
the bolts of our shelter; banish fear; find out, I pray you, what
the dog has seen.

Ter. Hasten, come, get up, old man! Already a fire is attacking
the ancient oaks and masters the night with its glare; the whole
20   wood is burning, already the blazing flame is licking at the house,
and terrified at the approach of the light, I have hastily returned
within. The fire is already licking at the house.

> Itque reditque Lycos blando cum murmure; quidnam
> Viderit ignoro: cauda testatur amicum.
> Ite igitur, iam clara dies diffunditur umbris,
> Precantata diu; quid sit perquirite, quidve
> Viderit inde Lycos noster, compertaque ferte.
> *Cam.* Dum nequit in somnum miserum componere pectus,
> Imperat ex molli recubans, heu! cespite mestus
> Silvius, et noctis pavidas lustrare tenebras   10
> Vult pueros, longo fessos in luce labore.
> *Sil.* Camale, dum primos terris prestabit Hyberus
> Nocturnos ignes, currus dum Delia fratris
> Ducet ad occasum, dum sternet cerva leones,
> Obsequium prestabit hero sine murmure servus.
> O Terapon, stabuli tu solve repagula nostri;
> Pone metum: videas catulus quid viderit, oro.
> *Ter.* Festina, fac, surge, senex! Iam corripit ignis
> Iam veteres quercus et noctem lumine vincit;
> Uritur omne nemus, fervens iam flamma penates   20
> Lambit, et occursu lucis perterritus intra
> Festinus redii. Lambit iam flamma penates!

Sil. Revered Pan, god of shepherds, aid us, I pray; and you lads, resist the flames with water. But hold on for a little, Terapon, stop a moment. What is this? What do I see? Am I in my right mind? Do I dream perchance? No, I do not. Assuredly that is a light, not flame or fire. Do you not see the leaves luxuriant, and the hazels verdant in the midst of the light, and the beeches on every side whole and untouched? Why, no disturbing heat even burns us.   30
Ter. If you look skyward the stars declare night, but in the wood a kindly light indicates day. What great marvel is afforded us?
Sil. Thus does nature vary her normal course, unfolding day and night blent on earth; neither Phoebe's lamp nor the sun's rays do I behold! Do you not perceive an unwonted fragrance in the wood, as if perchance Mother Nature had made of this a Sabaean grove? What fresh flowers has the night brought forth there? What songs besides do I hear? All this declares that celestial beings haunt these regions and these pastures.
Olym. Hail, our precious glory, best father, hail! Fear not, I am   40
your child. Why do you turn away your eyes?
Sil. I know not whether I am awake, I confess, or whether I am beholding dreams, for before me is the voice of my daughter and her

> *Sil.* Pastorum venerande deus Pan, deprecor, assis;
> Et vos, o pueri, flammis occurrite lymphis.
> Siste parum, Terapon, paulum consiste. Quid istud?
> Quid video? Sanusne satis sum? dormio forsan?
> Non facio! Lux ista quidem, non flamma vel ignis.
> Nonne vides letas frondes corilosque virentes
> Luminis in medio, validas ac undique fagos
> Intactas? Imo nec nos malus ardor adurit.   30
> *Ter.* Si spectes celo, testantur sydera noctem:
> In silvis lux alma diem. Quid grande paratur?
> *Sil.* Sic natura vices variat, noctemque diemque
> Explicuit mixtos terris; nec lumina Phebe
> Nec solis radios cerno! Non sentis odores
> Insolitos silvis, nemus hoc si forte Sabeum
> Fecisset natura parens? Quos inde recentes
> Nox peperit flores? quos insuper audio cantus?
> Hec superos ambire locos et pascua signant.
> *Olym.* Salve, dulce decus nostrum, pater optime, salve!   40
> Ne timeas, sum nata tibi. Quid lumina flectis?
> *Sil.* Nescio num vigilem, fateor, seu somnia cernam,
> Nam coram genite voces et dulcis ymago

sweet form stands there surely: I fear I am deceived, for oft in the darkness the gods delude dull mortals. Let us seek our doors.

Olym. Silvius, why do you doubt? Or do you believe Olympia would deceive her father and would show herself to the light without the gods' consent? Hither have I come to take away your sorrowing tears.

Sil. I know you: love deceives me not, nor dreams. O my too, too
50   dearly beloved, the sole hope of your father, what god has kept you, daughter? Fusca reported that while I sought the Chalcidian hills and the wide Vesuvian pastures, you were torn from us and were hidden in the sacred bosom of Cybele and could not be seen thereafter; believing this and wretchedly grieving, my daughter, amid the high mountains, the deep shades, and the sequestered woodlands, I mourned for you and wept long for you and oft called your name. But if I am worthy, do you disclose, I beseech you, in what haunts has so long a time kept you? Say, through whose gift is your white
60   vestment, woven with yellow gold? What light not seen before now gleams in your eyes? Who are your companions? How wondrous tall you have become in a short time: to me, daughter, you seem ripe for a husband.

> Stant equidem: timeo falli, quia sepe per umbras
> Illusere dii stolidos. Nos claustra petamus.
> *Olym.* Silvi, quid dubitas? an credis Olympia patrem
> Ludat et in lucem sese sine numine divum
> Prebeat? Huc veni lacrimas demptura dolentes.
> *Sil.* Agnosco: nec fallit amor, nec somnia fallunt.
> O nimium dilecta michi, spes unica patris,   50
> Quis te, nata, deus tenuit? Te Fusca ferebat,
> Calcidicos colles et pascua lata Vesevi
> Dum petii, raptam nobis Cibelisque sacrato
> Absconsam gremio, nec post hec posse videri;
> Quod credens merensque miser, mea virgo, per altos
> Te montes umbrasque graves saltusque remotos
> Ingemui flevique diu multumque vocavi.
> Sed tu, si mereor, resera quibus, obsecro, lustris
> Te tenuit tam longa dies? Dic, munere cuius
> Intertexta auro vestis tibi candida flavo?   60
> Que tibi lux oculis olim non visa refulget?
> Qui comites? Mirum quam grandis facta diebus
> In paucis: matura viro michi, nata, videris!

Olym. The garments which you, revered father, gave to me the Berecynthian mother holds in her vast bosom; but these vestments, this form, and this glittering countenance the Virgin gave me, and with her have I been. But look whether you have ever beheld these companions of mine: it will delight you to see them.

Sil. In truth I do not remember having seen them: not even Narcissus, I say, was more lovely than these, nor such indeed was   70
Daphnis, the glad hope of the dryads, nor fair Alexis.

Olym. Do you not know your own Marius and Julius, and my precious sisters, and their lovely features? They are your fair children.

Sil. Their appearance prevented me from recognizing my sons' well-known cheeks, darkened as they are with a downy beard. Now join hands and come that I may offer you my embraces and glad kisses, and may satisfy my soul! What praises shall I sing to thee, Pan, to thee, Silvanus? Lads, lay bare the palaestra and celebrate the games of your fathers. Let gifts for the victors be hung from the sacred beeches, and make ready the bowls foaming with wine;   80
sing of glad Lyaeus and deck the Lares with wreaths; let altars rise of grassy turf; slay to Trivia a white sheep, and likewise offer a

> *Olym.* Exuvias quas ipse michi, venerande, dedisti,
> Ingenti gremio servat Berecinthia mater;
> Has vestes formamque dedit faciemque coruscam
> Parthenos, secumque fui. Sed respice nunquid
> Videris hos usquam comites: vidisse iuvabit.
> *Sil.* Non memini vidisse quidem: nec pulchrior, inquam,
> His Narcissus erat, non talis denique Daphnis   70
> Qui dryadum spes leta fuit, non pulcher Alexis.
> *Olym.* Non Marium Iuliumque tuos dulcesque sorores
> Noscis, et egregios vultus? Tua pulchra propago est.
> *Sil.* Abstulit effigies notas lanugine malas
> Umbratas vidisse meis. Iam iungite dextras,
> Amplexusque meos ac oscula leta venite
> Ut prestem, satiemque animam! Quas, Pan, tibi laudes,
> Quas, Silvane, canam? Pueri, nudate palestras
> Et ludos agitote patrum. Stent munera fagis
> Victorum suspensa sacris, paterasque parate   80
> Spumantes vino, letum cantate Lyeum
> Et sertis ornate lares; altaria surgant

dark sheep to sacred Night; bring reed pipes for the boys, Terapon, bring garlands for the maidens.

Olym. We have reed pipes, Silvius, we have fit garlands, and if you have such great desire to prepare a holiday, we shall sing notes unknown in these woods.

Sil. Why, the wood is still; now silent flows the Arno, and all the field is still: and you, lads, be also still.

90

Olym. Eternal we live through the merits and divinity of Codrus, who lately, sent from high Olympus into the womb of the Virgin, brought back the Golden Age to earth; enduring the vile abuse of shepherds, nailed upon a cedar, he willingly yielded the victory to death.

Eternal we live through the merits and divinity of Codrus.

So with his glorious blood he washed away the ancient uncleanness, the diseases, and old sores of the infected flock: then seeking the vales of Pluto, he broke through the barriers and led back to the sun-light the flocks and herds of our fathers.

100

Eternal we live through the merits and divinity of Codrus.

Thence, Death overthrown, he opened the fragrant fields of Elysium,

Cespite gramineo; Trivie mactate bidentem
Candidulam, Noctique pie sic cedite fulvam;
Fer calamos pueris, Terapon, fer serta puellis.
Olym. Sunt, Silvi, calami, sunt serta decentia nobis,
Et, si tanta tibi cura est deducere festum,
Ignotos silvis modulos cantabimus istis.
Sil. Imo, silva silet, tacitus nunc defluit Arnus
Et silet omnis ager: pueri, vos atque silete.   90
Olym. Vivimus eternum meritis et numine Codri,
Aurea qui nuper, celso dismissus Olympo
Parthenu in gremium, revocavit secula terris;
Turpia pastorum passus convitia, cedro
Affixus, leto concessit sponte triumphum.
  Vivimus eternum meritis et numine Codri.
Sic priscas sordes, morbos scabiemque vetustam
Infecti pecoris preclaro sanguine lavit:
Hincque petens valles Plutarci septa refrinxit,
In solem retrahens pecudes armentaque patrum.   100
  Vivimus eternum meritis et numine Codri.
Morte hinc prostrata, campos reservavit odoros

he led the sacred flock to gardens flowing with honey, a victor refulgent with laurel and with oak, and gave us eternally our wished homes.

Eternal we live through the merits and divinity of Codrus.

At the last every sheep shall resume its cast-off fleece; he himself, coming a second time, shall divide the goats from the sheep: these he shall leave to wild beasts, those he shall establish in eternal homes and in after times he shall enclose them in a new   **110** heaven.

Eternal we live through the merits and divinity of Codrus.

Sil. Do you perceive how foolish we are to think that Latin shepherds sing with their pipes, marring the time of their voices! I have seen Maenalian youths along the slopes of Lycaeus, and the Thracian bard, wont to entice the crags with song, yet I cannot grant any one of these so skilled that I may count him the peer of my children. What throats! what voice! what harmony this was! finally, what melody in the pipes! Truly neither Queen Calliope, guardian of the vocal grove, nor even the god who presides in the   **120** Gorgonian cave can equal them. The oaks bent their tops, and the dainty nymphs made their silent return to the light, wolves and dogs

Elysii, sacrumque gregem deduxit in ortos
Mellifluos victor lauro quercuque refulgens,
Optandasque dedit nobis per secula sedes.
   Vivimus eternum meritis et numine Codri.
Exuvias in fine sibi pecus omne resummet;
Ipse, iterum veniens, capros distinguet ab agnis,
Hosque feris linquet, componet sedibus illos
Perpetuis celoque novo post tempora claudet.   110
   Vivimus eternum meritis et numine Codri.
Sil. Sentis, quam stulti Latios cantare putamus
Pastores calamis, perdentes tempora vocum!
Menalios vidi iuvenes per dorsa Lycei,
Treitium et vatem solitum deducere cautes
Carmine, nec quenquam possum concedere tanti,
Ut similem natis faciam. Que guctura! que vox!
Quis concentus erat! stipulis quis denique flatus!
Non equidem nemoris custos regina canori
Caliopes, non ipse deus qui presidet antro   120
Gorgoneo equiparet. Flexere cacumina quercus,
Et tenues nymphe tacitos petiere regressus

remained hushed. Besides, youths, did you perceive the divine sense of this hymn? Never did Tityrus of yore sing me such themes, nor the elder Parrhasian Mopsus in the sunny woods: it is all sacred and memorable. Let snowy doves—my care—be given to the maids, but to the boys stout bows which Ischirus once gave.

130   *Olym.* Let your things be; nothing mortal is borne to those rich shores which we inhabit; the eternal rejects the mortal.

Sil. What shores, my daughter, do you speak of? what shores, I pray? Yonder house will shelter us all, and the green herbage offer us quiet sleep, and the turf a table beneath the ilex; and this crystal stream will bountifully supply our cups; soft chestnuts and fresh fruits this rustic wood will bear for us, the fecund flock tender kids and cheese besides. What shores, then, do you seek?

Olym. Have I not told you, dear father, that the Berecynthian

140   mother keeps in her bosom the garments which you gave me? I am not she that I was when I lived as a little child with you, for I have joined the number of the gods; fair Olympus awaits me and my companions; we must turn our steps towards our homeland. Live in happiness, dearest father!

In lucem, mansere lupi catulique tacentes.
Preterea, o iuvenes, sensistis carminis huius
Celestes sensus? Nunquam michi Tytirus olim
Cantavit similes, senior nec Mopsus apricis
Parrasius silvis: sanctum et memorabile totum est.
Virginibus nivee dentur, mea cura, columbe,
Ast pueris fortes dederat quos Yschiros arcus.
Olym. Sint tua; nil fertur quod sit mortale per oras   130
Quas dites colimus; renuunt eterna caducum.
Sil. Quas oras, mea nata, refers? quas, deprecor, oras?
Nos omnes teget illa domus, somnosque quietos
Herba dabit viridis cespesque sub ylice mensam;
Vitreus is large prestabit pocula rivus;
Castaneas mites et poma recentia nobis
Rustica silva feret, teneros grex fertilis edos
Lacque simul pressum. Quas ergo exquiritis oras?
Olym. Non tibi, care pater, dixi, Berecinthia mater
Exuvias gremio servet quas ipse dedisti?   140
Non sum que fueram, dum tecum parvula vixi,
Nam numero sum iuncta deum; me pulcher Olympus
Expectat comitesque meos; stat vertere gressus
In patriam; tu vive, pater dulcissime, felix!

Sil. Alas! I shall die with weeping, daughter, if you leave me thus unhappy.

Olym. Banish your grief, I pray; do you expect now to break the bonds of fate with your tears?   All of us who are created in the woodlands are born to death: I have done what you too, Silvius, will later do.   Vex not the eternal years of the gods with envy, I   **150** pray; believe that peace is to be yours after death, and render devout praises to heaven that in dying I fled death and the toils of the woodlands.   I am separated but for a time; afterwards you shall surely behold me, and joyfully lead with me endless years.

Sil. With tears I shall pour out my eyes and my wretched old age. Alas! after troubled fortunes, in what wood shall I seek you who have fled, twice torn by force from our shores?

Olym. I am returning to Elysium, to which you shall some day ascend.

Sil. Of Elysium, I recall, Minciades once would sing to the reed,   **160** with which none was ever more skilled; is the Elysium he sings of yours?   It will please me to know.

Olym. He did, surely, through force of his genius perceive some of its grandeur and in part the aspect of the place; but small part

> *Sil.* Heu! moriar lacrimans, miserum, si, nata, relinquis.
> *Olym.* Pone, precor, luctus; credisne refringere fatum
> Nunc lacrimis? Omnes silvis quotcunque creati
> Nascimur in mortem: feci quod tu quoque, Silvi,
> Post facies. Noli, queso, lacerare deorum
> Invidia eternos annos; tibi crede quietem   **150**
> Post funus, laudesque pias michi reddito celo,
> Quod moriens fugi mortem nemorumque labores.
> Separor ad tempus; post hec me quippe videbis,
> Perpetuosque trahes mecum feliciter annos.
> *Sil.* In lacrimis oculos fundam tristemque senectam.
> Heu! quibus in silvis post anxia fata requiram
> Te profugam, ex nostris bis raptam viribus oris?
> *Olym.* Elysium repeto, quod tu scansurus es olim.
> *Sil.* Elysium, memini, quondam cantare solebat
> Minciades stipula, qua nemo doctior usquam;   **160**
> Estne, quod ille canit, vestrum? Didicisse iuvabit.
> *Olym.* Senserat ille quidem vi mentis grandia quedam,
> Ac in parte loci faciem: sed pauca canebat,

thereof did he sing if you could but see how many, how lovely the things which the Elysium of the righteous holds, the most delightsome abode of us gods.

Sil. What mountains does that place occupy? in what shores is it set? That which Minciades did not see or of his own will left untold do you tell us. To listen has right oft been a grateful relief from labor: perchance the power to see it will come.

170 *Olym.* In a secluded spot is a mountain inaccessible to the weary flock, bright with perpetual light, in which Phoebus first rises from the depths of the earth; on its topmost peak rests a wood, lifting towards the stars lofty palms and likewise glad laurels and never-fading cedars, and olives of Pallas, dear to beloved peace. Who can next describe the manifold flowers, who the fragrance which the soft breeze wafts there, who the streams like silver, bedewing all around with wondrous flood, trailing their winding courses with

180 soft murmur now here now there amid the trees? Golden apples the place bears surpassing those of the Hesperides; there are birds speckled with gold; goats there are with golden horns, and gentle does, and lambs, besides, their snowy fleeces ruddy with bright

Si videas quam multa tenet, quam pulchra piorum
Elysium sedesque deum gratissima nostrum.
Sil. Quos tenet iste locus montes? quibus insitus oris?
Que non Minciades vidit seu sponte reliquit,
Da nobis. Audire fuit persepe laborum
Utile solamen: veniet mens forte videndi.
Olym. Est in secessu pecori mons invius egro,   170
Lumine perpetuo clarus, quo primus ab imis
Insurgit terris Phebus, cui vertice summo
Silva sedet palmas tollens ad sydera celsas
Et letas pariter lauros cedrosque perennes,
Palladis ac oleas optate pacis amicas.
Quis queat hinc varios flores, quis posset odores
Quos lenis fert aura loco, quis dicere rivos
Argento similes mira scaturigine circum
Omnia rorantes, lepido cum murmure flexus
Arbustis mixtos nunc hinc nunc inde trahentes?   180
Hesperidum potiora locus fert aurea poma;
Sunt auro volucres picte, sunt cornubus aureis
Capreoli et mites damme, sunt insuper agne
Velleribus niveis claro rutilantibus auro,

gold; there are cows and bulls, also, and fat heifers, all glorious
with gold, and gentle lions and gentle griffins, their manes radiant
with gold. We have a sun of gold and a moon of silver, and
greater stars shine there than for you. There a perpetual spring is 190
sullied with no rain winds, a tempered air pervades the joyous
regions. Thence are banished earthly mist and night and discord.
There no death awaits the flocks nor sickly age, and heavy cares are
absent and wasting disease and pain; everyone's desires are fulfilled
of their own accord. What more can I tell? With sweet music
the balmy air resounds.

Sil. Wondrous is your tale; and I deem sacred that wood which
you describe and the abode of the gods. But who, pray, is lord of
it? And tell me, my daughter, of your companions and the manners
of the place.

Olym. Here on a high, grassy mound sits aged Archesilas; he keeps 200
the flocks and rules the orbs; if perchance you should wish to
describe his features, in vain will be your effort: this the mind
cannot grasp. Glad is he, exceeding fair and all serene, and in his
bosom lies a white Lamb, from whom comes food pleasing to the

> Suntque boves taurique simul pinguesque iuvence,
> Insignes omnes auro, mitesque leones
> Crinibus et mites gryphes radiantibus auro.
> Aureus est nobis sol ac argentea luna,
> Et maiora quidem quam vobis sydera fulgent.
> Ver ibi perpetuum nullis offenditur austris, 190
> Letaque temperies loca possidet. Exulat inde
> Terrestris nebula et nox et discordia rerum.
> Mors ibi nulla manet gregibus, non egra senectus,
> Atque graves absunt cure maciesque dolorque;
> Sponte sua veniunt cunctis optata. Quid ultra?
> Dulcisono resonat cantu mitissimus aer.
> *Sil.* Mira refers; sanctamque puto sedemque deorum
> Quam memoras silvam. Sed quisnam presidet illi?
> Et comites, mea nata, refer ritusque locorum.
> *Olym.* Hac in gramineo summo sedet aggere grandis 200
> Archesilas, servatque greges et temperat orbes;
> Cuius enim si forte velis describere vultus,
> In cassum facies: nequeunt comprendere mentes.
> Est alacer pulcherque nimis totusque serenus,
> Huius et in gremio iacet agnus candidus, ex quo

sylvan folk, and we feed thereon; thence has come our salvation and life to those reborn. From them both alike there springs a fire such that you would think it a marvel; such light does it shed upon all things: the sad it comforts and it purges the light of the mind, it provides counsel to the wretched, and the strength of the falling it renews, and sweet love it sheds in their hearts. There stands an aged band of satyrs suppliant on each side; all in white, crowned with chaplets of roses, it sounds the praises of the Lamb with harp and voice. Behind is the purple order of venerable men, I say, and the brows of all are bound with verdant laurel. These have praised the true God with pipes at the cross-roads, and with brave soul have overcome cruel hardships. After these is a snowy-white band, with lilies encircling their brows; joined to this stand we, your fair band of children. After these there follows the renowned rank of saffron color, and blazing in great splendor it sings with resounding voice God's praises and serves the King; among these Asylas with serene countenance was singing when, these woods removed, I was first taken upon the mountain.

Sil. Did then, I implore you, our Asylas ascend the mount? Worthy was he, for he was gentle and an eminent pattern of the ancient

Silvicolis gratus cibus est, et vescimur illo;
Inde salus venit nobis et vita renatis.
Ex his ambobus pariter sic evolat ignis,
Ut mirum credas; hoc lumen ad omnia confert:
Solatur mestos et mentis lumina purgat,
Consilium miseris prestat viresque cadentum
Instaurat, dulcesque animis infundit amores.
Stat satyrum longeva cohors hinc undique supplex,
Omnis cana quidem roseis ornata coronis,
Et cytharis agni laudes et carmine cantat.
Purpureus post ordo virum venerabilis, inquam,
Et viridi cunctis cinguntur tempora lauro.
Hi cecinere Deum stipulis per compita verum,
Et forti sevos animo vicere labores.
Agmen adest niveum post hos, cui lilia frontes
Circumdant; huic iuncta cohors tua pulchra manemus
Natorum. Crocei sequitur post ordo coloris
Inclitus, et magno fulgens splendore sonora
Voce deum laudes cantat regique ministrat;
Quos inter placido vultu cantabat Asylas,
Cum silvis assumpta prius sum monte levatis.
Sil. Ergo, precor, noster montem conscendit Asylas?
Emeruit, nam mitis erat fideique vetuste

faith: may God grant that I see him again! But speak, did he   230
know you, I pray, as you approached the height?

Olym. Why, rejoicing indeed he cast his arms about my neck, and
after he gave me glad embraces and printed a hundred kisses on my
brow, with many accompanying him he spoke: 'Have you come,
dearest offspring of my Silvius! "De Libano sponsa veni" now
let us sing and the sacred hymns and, my granddaughter, honor the
Mother of man' and leading me, he placed me with bended knees
where the fair Virgin was seated. Gladly she received her hand-
maid in her arms, and devoutly she spoke: 'My daughter, behold,
you shall join our pious bands, and enjoy eternal wedlock with   240
your spouse, and be ever known as Olympia in heaven, as you
were Violante on earth' and she arrayed me in the garments which
you see. If I should tell you with what songs the forest then rang,
what verses the lyric shepherd's pipe produced, scarcely will you
believe; the song filled the entire hollow of the mount, and such a
fire flashed that you would say all was being consumed in flames,
and rose blossoms fell through all the air.

Sil. Tell us further, we beg, who is the Virgin?

    Preclarum specimen: faciat Deus ipse revisam!
    Sed dic, tene, precor, novit dum culmen adires?   230
    Olym. Imo equidem applaudens iniecit brachia collo,
    Et postquam amplexus letos ac oscula centum
    Impressit fronti, multis comitantibus, inquit:
    'Venisti, o nostri soboles carissima Silvi!
    "De Libano" nunc "sponsa veni" sacrosque hymeneos
    Cantemus, matremque viri, mea neptis, honora,'
    Meque trahens, genibus flexis, quo pulchra sedebat
    Parthenos, posuit. Leta hec suscepit in ulnis
    Ancillam, dixitque pie: 'Mea filia, nostris
    Ecce choris iungere piis sponsique frueris   240
    Eternis thalamis, et semper Olympia celo,
    Que fueras terris Violantes, inclita fies,'
    Inque dedit vestes quas cernis. Si tibi narrem
    Quos cantus tunc silva dedit, quos fistula versus
    Pastoris lyrici, credes vix; omne per antrum
    Insonuit carmen montis, tantusque refulsit
    Ignis, ut exuri dixisses omnia flammis,
    Et totum rosei cecidere per aera flores.
    Sil. Que sit Parthenos nobis superadde, precamur.

250 *Olym.* The gracious mother of Jove is she and daughter of the
Son, the resplendent glory of the gods, the adornment of heaven,
knowing no night, the celestial star, the sure hope of safety for
shepherds, watcher over flocks, the wished rest from toils. Fauns
and nymphs worship her, great Apollo extols her with praises on
the lyre and acknowledges her as his Queen; adored, seated upon
the ancient Father's throne, on the right hand of the Son, she shines
with such splendor that, being most comely, she makes glad with
her countenance the forest, mountain, hills, and heavens, and about
260 her fly white bands of swans, and as mother they greet her, proclaiming her the spouse and daughter of eternal light.

Sil. And what do you do, children, while the swans with their
throats utter praise?

Olym. We children cull flowers and, fashioning garlands, bind our
unshorn hair, and in glad dances we wander through woods, springs,
and sounding streams, and playing amid the herbage, with high
voices we sing the merited honors of the serene Virgin and likewise
the praises of the Son. Who can recount the wood's delights, who
270 with words reveal them? No one. He must needs like birds put

Olym. Alma Iovis genitrix hec est et filia nati,	250
Splendens aula deum, celi decus, inscia noctis,	
Ethereum sydus, pastorum certa salutis	
Spes custosque gregum requiesque optata laborum.	
Hanc fauni nympheque colunt, hanc grandis Apollo	
Laudibus extollit cythara dominamque fatetur;	
Que residens solio patris veneranda vetusti	
A dextris geniti tanto splendore refulget,	
Ut facie silvam montem collesque polosque	
Letificet formosa nimis, cui candida circum	
Agmina cignorum volitant matremque salutant,	260
Luminis eterni sponsam genitamque cientes.	
Sil. Et vos quid, pueri, plaudunt dum gucture cigni?	
Olym. Nos pueri legimus flores factisque corollis	
Cingimus intonsos crines letisque choreis	
Ambimus silvam fontes rivosque sonoros,	
Et mediis herbis ludentes vocibus altis	
Parthenu placide meritos cantamus honores	
Et geniti laudes pariter. Quis gaudia silve	
Enumerare queat, quis verbis pandere? Nemo.	
Induat ut volucres pennas quibus alta volatu	270

on wings with which in flight to seek those lofty realms and behold them: all else is vain.

Sil. This is truly to be wished: but what Daedalus is there anywhere who will give me nimble wings and bind them to my shoulders and show me the easy way and teach me flight?

Olym. Feed your brother's hunger, give draughts of milk to the weary, minister to those in bondage and clothe the naked, raise up the fallen while you may, and let your cave be opened to the stranger; such services shall provide you with an eagle's fleet wings, and with God showing the way, you shall fly aloft.

Sil. Whither are you going? Whither, daughter, do you flee, and 280 do you leave your wretched father overwhelmed in tears? Alas! she has vanished into the heavenly breezes and has drawn with her the fragrance which she brought. With tears shall I go to death and drag out my old age. You, lads, drive the calves to pasture: Lucifer rises and now the sun is sent forth from the midst of the shadows.

> Expetat et videat, opus est: sunt cetera frustra.
> *Sil.* Sunt optanda quidem: sed quis michi Dedalus usquam
> Qui tribuat pennas agiles nectatque lacertis,
> Ostendatque viam facilem doceatque volatum?
> *Olym.* Pasce famem fratris, lactis da pocula fessis,
> Assis detentis et nudos contege, lapsos
> Erige, dum possis, pateatque forensibus antrum:
> Hec aquile volucres prestabunt munera pennas,
> Atque Deo monstrante viam volitabis in altum.
> *Sil.* Quo tendis? quo, nata, fugis, miserumque parentem   280
> Implicitum linquis lacrimis? Heu! cessit in auras
> Ethereas, traxitque simul quos duxit odores.
> In mortem lacrimis ibo ducamque senectam.
> Vos, pueri, vitulos in pascua pellite: surgit
> Lucifer et mediis iam sol emittitur umbris.

. . . Here, discovered by ten cowherds, who were dancing in a ring
around the revered tomb of the shepherd Androgeo in the manner
in which the lascivious Satyrs are often wont to dance in the woods
at midnight while waiting for the beloved Nymphs to come forth
from the neighboring streams, we set ourselves to join with them
in performing the sad office. One of these, more worthy than the
others, stood in the middle of their dance near the high tomb on
an altar newly fashioned of green herbage; and here, according to
the ancient custom, sprinkling thereon two vessels of new milk, two
of sacred blood, and two of very fine, rich wine, and an abundant
supply of most dainty flowers of varied hues, and harmonizing his
10   voice in sweet and plaintive mood to the music of the shepherd's
pipe and the castanets, he sang copiously the praises of the entombed
shepherd:

"Rejoice, rejoice, Androgeo, and if it is granted peaceful souls
to hear after death, listen to our words; and these solemn honors,
which now thy fellow ploughmen are rendering to thee, wherever

. . . Ove ritrovati da diece vacchari che intorno al venerando sepolchro del
pastore Androgeo in cerchio danzavano, a guisa che sogliono sovente y lascivi
Satyri per le selve la mecza notte saltare aspectando che da li vicini fiumi
eschano le amate Nymphe, ne pusimo con loro insieme ad celebrare il mesto
officio. De' quali un più che gli altri degnio stava in meczo del ballo presso
a l'alto sepolchro in un altare nuovamente fatto di verde erbe; et quivi,
secondo lo anticho costume, spargendo duo vasi di novo latte, duo di sacro
sangue e duo di fumoso et nobillisimo vino, et copia habondevole di fiori
tenerissimi et di diversi colori, et accordandosi con suave et pietoso modo
10   al suono de la sampogna et di nacchari, cantava distesamente le lode del
sepolto pastore: "Godi, godi, Androgeo, et se doppo la morte ale quiete
anime è concesso il sentire, ascolta le parole nostre; e y sollenni honori, y
quali hora y tuoi bifolci ti rendono, ovunche felicemente dimori, benegno

thou dwellest in blessedness, receive and accept with benison.
Surely I do believe that thy gracious soul is now hovering about
these woods and sees and hears exactly that which we are doing in
its memory today above the new burial. If this is really true, then
how can it be that at such calling thou dost make us no reply?
Ah, thou wast wont with the sweet sound of thy pipe to brighten
all our grove with delightful harmony. How art thou now, enclosed
in a small space, constrained to lie amid cold stones in eternal   20
silence? With thy sweet words thou wouldst always bring peace to
the disputes of the quarreling shepherds; how has thou now, in
departing, left them exceedingly irresolute and unhappy? Noble
father and master of all our band, where shall we find thy peer?
Whose teaching shall we follow? Under whose instruction shall
we henceforth live securely? Surely, I do not know who will hereafter be our trusted guide in times of doubt. Thou wise shepherd,
when shall our woods ever see thee again? When in these
mountains shall men again love justice, righteousness in life, and
reverence for the gods? These qualities all flourished so nobly
under thy wings, that perhaps never at any other time did revered
Boundary mark off the disputed fields more justly than in thy time.   30
Alas, who will now sing of the Nymphs in our woods? Who will
hereafter give us trusty counsel in our adversities, and gratifying

prendi et accepta. Certo yo creggio che la tua gratiosa anima vada ora
intorno ad queste selve volando, et veda et senta puntualmente cziò che per noi
ogie in sua ricordatione si fa sovra la nuova sepultura. La qual cosa se è
pur vera, or come può egli essere che ad tanto chiamare non ne risponda?
Deh tu solevi col dolce suono dela tua sampogna tucto il nostro boscho di
delectevole armonia fare lieto; come ora, in picciol luogho rinchiuso, tra
freddi sassi sey constructo di giacere in eterno silencio? Tu con le tue parole   20
dulcissime sempre repacificavi le questioni de' litiganti pastori: come ora li
hay, partendoti, lasciati dubiosi et scontenti oltra modo? O nobile padre
et maestro di tucto il nuostro stuolo, ove pari ad te il troveremo? y cuy
admaestramenti seguiremo noi? sotto cui disciplina viveremo ormay securi?
Certo, yo non so chi ne sia per lo inanci fidata guida nei dubiosi casi. O
discreto pastore, quando mai più le nostre selve ti vedranno? quando per
questi monti fia may amata la iusticia, la drictezza del vivere et la riverenza
degli Dii? Le quale cose tucte sì nobelmente socto le tue ale fiorivano; per
maniera che forse may in nessun tempo il riverendo Termine segniò più   30
egualmente li ambigui campi che nel tuo. Oymè, chi nei nostri boschi omay
canterà le Nymphe? chi ne darà più nele nostre adversità fedele conseglio,

comfort and delight in our times of sadness, as thou wouldst do, by
often singing sweetest verses on the banks of the flowing rivers?
Alas, our herds without thy pipe can scarcely feed on the green
meadows, yet while thou didst live, at the sound thereof they were
wont to chew the grasses so sweetly under the delightful shade of
the cool ilexes. Alas, at thy departing, all our gods departed together with thee from these fields; and every time thereafter that
we have tried to sow the shining grain, instead of grain we reaped
the wretched darnel with sterile oats in the dreary woods; and in
40 place of violets and other flowers there issued forth brambles with
sharp and poisonous thorns in our fields. Therefore, shepherds,
throw grasses and leafy boughs on the ground and cover the cool
fountains with shady branches, because our Androgeo desires that
this be done in his honor. Happy Androgeo, farewell, farewell for
evermore. Behold, woodland Apollo, all in festive garb, is coming
to thy tomb to adorn thee with his fragrant garlands; and likewise
the Fauns with garlanded horns and laden with sylvan gifts are
bringing thee each what he can, ears of grain from the field, clusters
of grapes from the vines with all the vine leaves, and ripe fruits from
every tree; vying with these, the neighboring Nymphs, formerly
50 so loved and revered by thee, all come now with the whitest baskets,

et nele mesticie piacevole conforto et dilecto, come tu facevi cantando sovente
per le rive de' correnti fiumi dolcissimi versi? Oymè, che appena y nostry
armenti sanno senza la tua sampogna pascere per li verdi prati; li quali
mentre vivesti solevano sì dolcemente al suono di quella ruminare le herbe
socto le piacevole ombre dele fresche elcine. Oymè, che nel tuo dipartire
si partirono insieme con teco da questi campi tucti li nostri Dii; et quante
volte dopo havemo facta pruova di seminare il candido frumento, tante invece
di quello havemo ricolto lo infelice loglio con le sterile avene per li sconsolati
40 boschi; et in luogo di viole et d'altri fiori sono usciti pruni con spine
acutissime et velenose per le nostre campagne. Per la qual cosa, pastori,
gittate erbe et frondi per terra, et de ombrosi rami coprite y freschi fonti,
peroche così vuole che in suo honore si facza il nostro Androgeo. O felice
Androgeo, addio, eternamente addio. Eccho che il pastorale Apollo tucto
festivo ne viene al tuo sepolchro per adornarti con le sue odorate corone;
e y Fauni similmente con le ingirlandate corna et carichi di silvestri duoni,
quel che ciaschun può ti portano, de' campi le spiche, degli arbosti y racemi
con tucti i pampini, et de ognie albero maturi fructi; ad invidia dei quali
le convicine Nymphe, da te tanto adietro amate et reverite, vengono ora tucte
50 con canistri bianchissimi, pieni di fiori et di pomi odoriferi, ad renderti y

full of flowers and fragrant fruits, to return to thee the honors they
have received; and what is greater, and than which no more everlasting gift can be offered to the buried ashes, the Muses offer thee
verses: verses the Muses offer thee, and we with our pipes sing of
thee and always will sing, as long as the herds pasture in these
groves; and these pines and these oaks and these plane trees, which
stand around thee, shall whisper thy name as long as the world
endures; and the bulls together with all the rustic flocks shall in
every season show reverence to thy shade, and loudly lowing they
shall call thee through the echoing woodlands. So, from now on,
thou shalt ever be in the number of our gods, and as to Bacchus and
to sacred Ceres, so also to thy altars shall we offer due sacrifices,   60
at the fire if it is cold, in the cool shadows, if it is hot. And sooner
will the poisonous yew trees sweat the sweetest honey and the sweet
flowers will make their honey bitter, sooner will the grain be reaped
in winter and we shall pick the black olives in summer, ere in these
regions thy fame will be silenced."

These words ended, he suddenly began to play on a sweet bagpipe
which hung behind his back; at the melody of which, Ergasto, with
tears still in his eyes, opened his lips to sing as follows:

ricevuti honori; et quel che magiore è, et del quale più eterno duono ale
sepolte ceneri dare non si può, le Muse ti donano versi: versi ti donano le
Muse, et noy con le nostre sampogne ti cantamo et canteremo sempre, mentre
gli armenti pasceranno per questi boschi, et questi pyni et questi cerri et
questi piatani che d'intorno ti stanno, mentre il mondo serà, susurreranno il
nome tuo; e y tori parimente con tucte le paesane torme in ognie stagione
faranno riverenza ala tua ombra, et con alte voci mugiendo ti chiamaranno
per li respondenti selve. Tal che da ora innanci serai sempre nel numero de'
nostri Dii, et sicome a Baccho et ala sancta Cerere, cossì anchora ad toy
altari y debiti sacrificii, si serrà freddo, faremo al fuogho; si caldo, ale   60
fresche ombre. Et prima y velenosi tassi suderanno mele dulcissimo e y
dolci fiori il farranno amaro, prima de inverno si mecterranno le biade et de
estate coglieremo le nere olive, che may per queste contrate si taccia la fama
tua." Queste parole finite, subitamente prese ad sonare una suave cornamusa,
che dopo le spalle li pendea; ala melodia dela quale, Ergasto, quasi co le
lacrime in su gli occhi, così aperse le labra ad cantare.

ECLOGUE 5

ERGASTO OVER THE TOMB

Thou blessed and beautiful soul, that, released from thy bonds, hast risen naked to the heavenly cloisters, where thou mayest take delight, joined with thy star; and happy there, disdaining our thoughts, thou dost show thyself like a beautiful sun among the most
10 radiant spirits, and under thy feet thou dost behold the wandering stars, and amid pure fountains and sacred myrtles thou dost pasture celestial flocks and from there dost scorn earthly cares.

Other mountains, other plains, other woods and streams thou beholdest in heaven, and fresher flowers and other Fauns and Silvani in sweet places of summer's warmth, following the Nymphs
20 in happier loves. Such, amid fragrant odors, sweetly singing in the shade, between Daphnis and Meliboeus sits our Androgeo and fills the heavens with rare sweetness, blending the elements with

ECLOGUE 5

ERGASTO SOVRA LA SEPULTURA

Alma beata et bella,
  Che da' ligami sciolta
  Nuda salisti ney superni chiostri,
  Ove con la tua stella
  Ti godi insieme accolta;
  Et lieta ivi, schernendo y pensier nostri,
  Quasi un bel sol ti mostri
  Tra li più chiari spirti,
  Et sotto le tue piante
  Vedi le stelle errante,   **10**
  Et tra pure fontane et sacri mirti
  Pasci celesti greggi,
  Et le mundane cure indi dispreggi.
Altri monti, altri piani,
  Altri boschecti et rivi
  Vedi nel cielo et più novelli fiori,
  Altri Fauni et Silvani
  Per luoghi dolci estivi
  Seguir le Nymphe in più felici amori.
  Tal fra suavi odori   **20**
  Dolce cantando all' ombra
  Tra Daphni et Melibeo
  Siede il nostro Androgeo,
  Et di rara dolcezza il cielo ingombra,
  Temprando gli elementi

the sound of new, unwonted accents.

As is the vine to the elm and to the herds the bull, and the swaying grain to the happy fields, so wast thou the glory and pinnacle of our band. Ah, cruel Death, and who could ever escape, if with your flames you burn the loftiest summits? Who will ever see in the world a shepherd so joyous, one that singing among us such sweet measures may cover the grove with foliage and raise shade of fair branches over the waters?

The sacred goddesses wept for thy piteous death, the rivers know of it, and the caves and the beech trees; the green banks wept, and the pale and withered grasses, and for many days the sun did not show his rays, nor did the wild beasts appear in any field, nor did the flocks go out among the mountains, nor did they taste of grasses or of springs. Such sorrow did thy bitter fate bring to all, that in the light and in the dark, the wood resounded with "Androgeo, Androgeo."

30

40

50

Col suon di novi inusitati accenti.
Quale la vite al'olmo,
    Et agli armenti il toro,
    Et l'ondeggiante biade ay lieti campi,
    Tale la gloria e 'l colmo
    Fustù del nostro choro.
    Ay cruda morte, et chi fia che ne scampi,
    Se con tue fiamme avampi
    Le più elevate cime?
    Chi vedrà may nel mondo
    Pastor tanto giocondo,
    Che cantando fra noy sì dolci rime
    Sparga il boscho di fronde,
    Et di bei rami induca ombra su l'onde?
Pianser le sante Dive
    La tua spietata morte:
    I fiumi il sanno e le spelunch' e y faggi;
    Pianser le verdi rive,
    L'herbe pallide et smorte,
    E'l sol più giorni non mostrò suoi raggi,
    Nè gli animal selvaggi
    Usciron in algun prato,
    Nè greggi andar per monti,
    Nè gustaro herbe o fonti:
    Tanto dolse ad ciaschun l'acerbo fato;
    Tal che al chiaro et al foscho
    Androgeo Androgeo sonava il boscho.

30

40

50

Then thou shalt always see fresh garlands at thy sacred tomb, and the offerings of ploughmen, so that in every season, like a strange dove, thou shalt flit over the lips of the shepherds; nor 60 will there ever come a time when thy fair name will be extinguished, as long as there will be snakes in the thornbushes and fishes in the streams. Nor shalt thou live only on my weary tongue, but through many shepherds in a thousand other pipes and a thousand verses.

If there lives among you any spirit of love, you thick, leafy oaks, spread your shade over these quiet buried bones.

> Dunche fresche corone
>   Ala tua sacra tomba
>   Et voti di bifolci ognor vedray,
>   Tal che in ognie stagione,
>   Quasi nuova colomba,
>   Per bocche de' pastor volando andray;
>   Nè verrà tempo may
>   Che 'l tuo bel nome extingua,   60
>   Mentre serpenti in dumi
>   Serranno et pesci in fiumi.
>   Nè sol vivray nela mia stanca lingua,
>   Ma per pastor diversi
>   In mille altre sampogne et mille versi.
> Se spirto algun d'amor vive fra voy,
>   Quercie frondose et folte,
>   Fate ombra alle quiete ossa sepolte.

ECLOGUE 11

[MAMILLIA]

ERGASTO ALONE

Since that charming style and sweet song may no more be hoped for in this wood,

Once more, Muses, begin your lament.

ECLOGUE 11

[MAMILLIA]

ERGASTO SOLO

> Poi che 'l soave stile e 'l dolce canto
>   Sperar non lice più per questo bosco,
>   Ricominciate, o Muse, il vostro pianto.

Weep, sacred hill, so shady and dark; and you hollow caves and dusky grottoes, come howling to weep with us. Weep, beech trees and rugged mountain oaks, and with weeping relate to these rocks our lamentable, harsh fate. Lament, you rivers, bare and bereft of 10 all sweetness; and you fountains and streams, check your course and halt your steps. And you that live hidden among the woods, gloomy Echo, reply to my words and write on the tree trunks that which I speak. Weep, you vales, abandoned and desolate; and you Earth, on your mantle paint the lilies dark and black the violets. Skilled Egeria and Theban Manto has Death with sudden fury 20 taken from us.

Once more, Muses, begin your lament.

And if you, o shore, have at any time hearkened to human emotions, I pray you now to accompany the sorrowing pipe turned to lamentation. You grasses and flowers, which at one time were lofty and great kings in the world and now in harsh fate lie amid the rivers

> Piangi, colle sacrato, opaco et fosco;
>   Et voi, cave spelunche et grotte oscure,
>   Ululando venite ad pianger nosco.
> Piangete, faggi e quercie alpestre et dure,
>   Et piangendo narrate ad questi sassi
>   Le nostre lacrimose aspre venture.
> Lacrimate voi, fiumi ignudi et cassi   10
>   D'ogni dolcezza; et voi, fontane et rivi,
>   Fermate il corso et ritenete i passi.
> Et tu, che fra le selve occolta vivi,
>   Echo mesta, rispondi ale parole,
>   Et quant'io parlo per li tronchi scrivi.
> Piangete, valli abandonate et sole;
>   Et tu, terra, depingi nel tuo manto
>   I gigli oscuri et nere le viole.
> La dotta Egeria et la Thebana Manto
>   Con subito furor Morte n'ha tolta.   20
>   Ricominciate, Muse, il vostro pianto.
> Et se tu, riva, udisti alcuna volta
>   Humani affetti, hor prego che accompagni
>   La dolente sampogna ad pianger volta.
> O herbe, o fior, ch'un tempo excelsi et magni
>   Re foste al mondo et hor per aspra sorte
>   Giacete per li fiumi et per li stagni,

30   and pools, come all with me to pray Death that he should, if it
can be, end my sorrows, and that he become wearied of my loud
cries.   Weep, Hyacinth, for your lovely spoils, and redoubling
your ancient laments, depict my sorrows in your leaves.   And you
blessed shores and sunny slopes, remind Narcissus of his grief, if
ever you were friendly to my prayers.   No more let grass or flowers
become green in the field, no more on rose or amaranth let that
40   lovely, bright, charming, gracious hue be discerned.   Alas, who can
hope any more for glory or praise?   Dead is faith, dead is firm
judgment.

Once more, Muses, begin your lament.

And while with sighs I cry out in vain, little birds, so amorous and
gay, come forth, I pray, from your loved nest.   Philomel, renew-
ing each year your ancient woes and with sweet accents making
yourself heard by the woods and the caves; and if it is true,
50   Progne, that still you lament and that your senses were not taken
from you with your shape, but that still you grieve and repent for

Venite tutti meco ad pregar Morte,
    Che, se esser può, finisca le mie doglie,
    Et gli rincresca il mio gridar sì forte.   30
Piangi, Hyacintho, le tue belle spoglie,
    Et radoppiando le querele antiche,
    Descrivi i miei dolori in le tue foglie.
Et voi, liti beati et piagge apriche,
    Ricordate ad Narcisso il suo dolore,
    Se giamai foste di miei preghi amiche.
Non verdeggi per campi herba nè fiore,
    Nè si scerna più in rosa o in amaranto
    Quel bel vivo leggiadro almo colore.
Lasso, chi può sperar più gloria o vanto?   40
    Morta è la fe', morto è 'l giudicio fido.
    Ricominciate, Muse, il vostro pianto.
Et mentre sospirando indarno io grido,
    Voi, ucelletti inamorati et gai,
    Uscite, prego, da l'amato nido.
O Philomena, che gli antichi guai
    Rinovi ogni anno, et con soavi accenti
    Da selve et da spelunche udir ti fai;
Et se tu, Progne, è ver ch'or ti lamenti,
    Ne con la forma ti fur tolti i sensi,
    Ma del tuo fallo anchor ti lagni et penti;   50

your crime; leave off, I pray, your intense cries, and until I become hoarse with my speaking, let neither of you tell or think of her own evil lot.

Ah, the thorns dry up, and then when they have had a brief space to recover their former strength, each returns and grows in its own place; but with us, when once Heaven overpowers us, neither wind nor sun nor rain or spring avails to restore us to our earthly shell. **60** And the sun, ever fleeing from morn till eve, leads on our days and our lives in his course, and he returns even as he was before. Happy was Orpheus who, before his final hour, to recover her for whom he wept so sorely, went safely there where men since fear to go. He conquered Megaera, he conquered Rhadamanthus, he stirred to pity the King of that cruel realm.

Once more, Muses, begin your lament.

Oh why, alas, with the sound of the curved wood, is it not granted **70** to me to blend notes so sad as to secure me the boon of my dearly beloved? Even if my rhymes are less known than those of Orpheus,

> Lasciate, prego, i vostri gridi intensi,
>   Et, finchè io nel mio dir diventi roco,
>   Nessuna del suo mal ragione o pensi.
> Ai, ai, seccan le spine, et poi che un poco
>   Son state ad ricoprar l'antica forza,
>   Ciascuna torna e nasce al proprio loco;
> Ma noi poi che una volta il Ciel ne sforza,
>   Vento nè sol nè pioggia o primavera
>   Basta ad tornarne in la terrena scorza.   60
> E 'l sol, fuggendo anchor da mane ad sera,
>   Ne mena i giorni e 'l viver nostro inseme,
>   Et lui ritorna pur come prima era.
> Felice Orpheo che, inanzi l'hore extreme,
>   Per ricoprar colei che pianse tanto,
>   Sicuro andò dove più andar si teme.
> Vinse Megera, vinse Rhadamanto,
>   Ad pietà mosse il Re del crudo regno.
>   Ricominciate, Muse, il vostro pianto.
> Hor perchè, lasso, al suon del curvo legno   70
>   Temprar non lice ad me sì meste note,
>   Ch'impetri gratia del mio caro pegno?
> Et se le rime mie non son sì note
>   Come quelle d'Orpheo, pur la pietade

surely pity ought to make them sweet and reverent in heaven. But if, in scorn of our human state, she should refuse to come, I should be happy indeed to find the paths closed to my departure. What vain desire, what a restless state is mine! I know, indeed, that with herb and enchantment I cannot change the immortal decree. Surely that shining gate of ivory can give over to slumber my countenance and my speech.

Once more, Muses, begin your lament.

But it cannot restore or give me her who left me blind without her light, nor take away from heaven a star so rare. But do you, noble, fortunate river, summon your Nymphs to your sacred depths and renew your ancient, gracious custom. You made the fair Siren known in all the world with so proud a tomb. That was your first sorrow, this your second. Grant that she find another trumpet to sing of her, so that men shall always hear that name which resounds of itself. So may your fair current never be disordered by rains, aid in some measure my crude style so that pity may temper it; not

Dovrebbe farle in ciel dolci et devote.
Ma se, schernendo nostra humanitade,
  Lei schifasse il venir, sarei ben lieto
  Di trovar all'uscir chiuse le strade.
O desir vano, o mio stato inquieto!
  Et so pur che con erba o con incanto
  Mutar non posso l'immortal decreto.
Ben può quel nitido uscio d'elephanto
  Mandarmi in sogno il volto et la favella.
  Ricominciate, Muse, il vostro pianto.
Ma ristorar non può, nè darmi quella
  Che cieco mi lasciò senza il suo lume,
  Ne torre al ciel sì peregrina stella.
Ma tu, ben nato aventuroso Fiume,
  Convoca le tue Nymphe al sacro fondo,
  Et rinova il tuo antico almo costume.
Tu la bella Sirena in tutto il mondo
  Facesti nota con sì altera tomba.
  Quel fu 'l primo dolor, quest' è 'l secondo.
Fa che costei ritrove un'altra tromba
  Che di lei cante, acciochè s'oda sempre
  Il nome che da se stesso rimbomba.
Et, se per pioggia mai non si distempre
  Il tuo bel corso, aita in qualche parte
  Il rozzo stil, sì che pietade il tempre.

that it may be worthy to inscribe on pages, but that here among   100
these beech trees it may but abide, so filled with love, wanting in
every artifice, so that on these rough, wild trunks the other shepherds
who will come here may read of noble character and of deeds
honorable and wise; and then increasing every hour from year to
year, her memory may remain in the woods and mountains, as long
as there will be grasses on the earth and stars in the sky. Beasts,
birds, caves, trees, and springs, men and gods will extol that lofty   110
and holy name in verses proud and graceful. And since at the end
I must rise somewhat, forsaking the rough pastoral style,

Once more, Muses, begin your lament.

No more do I produce a sound dull and mean, but one so clear and
beautiful that it may be heard from heaven by that proud, noble,
gentle spirit. May this spirit with its radiance reach even to here,
may it extend me aid and while I speak, descend often in pity to   120
behold me. And if thy state is such that the tongue fails to describe
it, let thy spirit excuse me before itself and teach me the way to

    Non che sia degno da notarsi in charte,   100
      Ma che sol reste qui tra questi faggi
      Così colmo d'amor, privo d'ogn'arte;
    Acciochè in questi tronchi aspri et selvaggi
      Leggan gli altri pastor che qui verranno
      I bei costumi e gli atti honesti et saggi;
    Et poi crescendo ogni hor più di anno in anno,
      Memoria sia di lei fra selve et monti,
      Mentre herbe in terra et stelle in ciel saranno.
    Fiere, ucelli, spelunche, alberi et fonti,
      Huomini et dei quel nome excelso et santo   110
      Exalteran con versi alteri et conti.
    Et perchè al fine alzar conviemmi alquanto,
      Lassando il pastoral ruvido stile,
      Ricominciate, Muse, il vostro pianto.
    Non fa per me più suono oscuro et vile,
      Ma chiaro et bello, che dal ciel l'intenda
      Quella altera ben nata alma gentile.
    Ella coi raggi suoi fin qui si stenda,
      Ella aita mi porga, et mentre io parlo
      Spesso ad vedermi per pietà discenda.   120
    Et se 'l tuo stato è tal che ad dimostrarlo
      La lingua manche, ad se stessa mi scuse,
      Et m'insegne la via d'in charte ornarlo.

honor thee in my pages. But there shall yet come a time when the gracious Muses will be in honor and these mists and shadows will be utterly removed from the eyes of mortals. Then it will surely behoove each one to purge himself of these mundane and near-sighted thoughts and to fill his heart with secure hopes. Then I
130   know my verses will appear unpolished and obscure, but I hope that they will be praised at least by the shepherds in these woods. And many that now are not esteemed will then see their names depicted in vermilion and yellow flowers in the midst of the fields; and the fountains and the rivers in the valleys murmuring will repeat that which I now sing, with clear and sparkling crystals.
140   And the trees that I now consecrate and plant here will reply whistling to the wind.

Bring an end, Muses, to your lament.

Happy the shepherds who, desiring to attain to such heights, have put on their wings, though it be not in our power to know when. But thou, a soul fair and immortal beyond all others, that perhaps dost hear me from heaven and prove me to be equal to thy

> Ma tempo anchor verrà che l'alme Muse
>   Saranno in pregio, et queste nebbie et ombre
>   Dagli occhi dè mortai fien tutte excluse.
> Allhor pur converrà ch'ogniuno sgombre
>   Da se questi pensier terreni et loschi,
>   Et di salde speranze il cor s'ingombre.
> Ove so che parranno incolti et foschi   130
>   I versi miei, ma spero che lodati
>   Saran pur da'pastori in questi boschi.
> Et molti che hoggi qui non son pregiati
>   Vedranno allhor di fior vermigli et gialli
>   Descritti i nomi lor per mezzo i prati;
> Et le fontane e i fiumi per le valli
>   Mormorando diran quel ch'ora io canto,
>   Con rilucenti et liquidi crystalli.
> E gli alberi ch'or qui consacro et pianto
>   Risponderanno al vento sibilando.   140
>   Ponete fine, o Muse, al vostro pianto.
> Fortunati i pastor che, desiando
>   Di venir in tal grado, han poste l'ale;
>   Benchè nostro non sia saper il quando.
> Ma tu più ch'altra bella et immortale
>   Anima, che dal ciel forse m'ascolti
>   Et mi dimostri al tuo bel choro eguale,

fair choir, obtain from these thick, shading laurels the boon that
with their ever green foliage they may cover both of us here   150
entombed. And to the sweet sound of sparkling waters let the
singing of birds still be joined, that the spot may abound in every
charm. Then, if my life is indeed prolonged so that, as I desire, I
may be able to do thee honor (and may Heaven not sever me from
this wish), I hope that over thee that harsh, eternal, unwaking sleep
will not have the power to keep thee enclosed in so narrow a
trench; if only my verses can promise so much.   160

> Impetra ad questi lauri ombrosi et folti
>   Gratia, che con lor sempre verdi fronde
>   Possan qui ricoprirne ambo sepolti.   150
> Ed al soave suon di lucide onde
>   Il cantar degli ucelli anchor si aggiunga,
>   Acciochè il luogo d'ogni gratia abonde.
> Ove, se 'l viver mio pur si prolunga
>   Tanto che, com'io bramo, ornar ti possa
>   (Et da tal voglia il Ciel non mi disgiunga),
> Spero che sovra te non havrà possa
>   Quel duro eterno inexcitabil sonno
>   D'haverti chiusa in così poca fossa:
> Se tanto i versi miei prometter ponno.   160

PISCATORY ECLOGUE 1
[PHYLLIS]

Lycidas. Mycon.

Lyc. I was wondering, Mycon, as recently I ranged the neighboring
shores waiting for the swift tunny at their feeding places, why the
raven strangely made such a din, why the dripping coots, sheltered
here and there amid the crags and caves, filled the sad rocks with

PISCATORY ECLOGUE 1
[PHYLLIS]
Lycidas. Mycon.

Lyc. Mirabar, vicina, Mycon, per litora nuper
Dum vagor exspectoque leves ad pabula thynnos,
Quid tantum insuetus streperet mihi corvus et udae
Per scopulos passim fulicae perque antra repostae

lamentable cries, while no more did the curving dolphin leap from
the sea nor lead his wonted bands as always amid the waves. Lo,
the day had come on which I had laid dear Phyllis in the earth and
at her grave wept over her devoted shade, oh wretched am I; and
yet I do not after this leave off my sad existence, nor does even
cruel Pylemon hesitate to offer solace.

Myc. Surely that was why as I wandered here and yon all night,
roaming every side of Posilipo and skirting fishy Nisida in my swift
boat, the querulous sea gulls uttered a strangely mournful cry. It
was Phyllis who was summoning them to the shades below, it was
Phyllis (if we may believe it) called them to mourn, Lycidas, and
to offer sacred tribute at her tomb.

Lyc. Alas, dear Mycon, what a solemn procession (now that I recall
it) what hands, what features did I mark with these eyes; with these
eyes, I say, what rites did I witness, heart-broken; nor yet did cruel
sorrow drive me to the cliffs, to the rocks, nor did the violence of
the flame consume me on the same pyre, nor did at least some god
drown me in the sea.

Myc. Lycidas, Lycidas, do you not think that she has had a happier
fate than as if she had entered the smoky cave of Lycotas or the hut

Tristia flebilibus complerent saxa querelis,
Cum jam nec curvus resiliret ab aequore delphin
Nec solitos de more choros induceret undis.
Ecce dies aderat caram qua Phyllida terrae
Condidimus tumuloque pias deflevimus umbras,
Ah miseri; et posthac nec tristes linquimus auras
Nec dubitat saevus solatia ferre Pylemon.
Myc. Scilicet id fuerat tota quod nocte vaganti
Huc illuc, dum Pausilypi latus omne pererro
Piscosamque lego celeri Nesida phaselo,
Nescio quid queruli gemerent lacrimabile mergi.
Phyllis ad inferias, Phyllis (si credimus) illos
Ad gemitum, o Lycida, tumulique ad sacra vocabat.
Lyc. Eheu, care Mycon, qualis spectacula pompae
(Nunc recolo) quas ipse manus quaeve ora notavi
His oculis; his, inquam, oculis quae funera vidi
Infelix; nec me tandem dolor improbus egit
In scopulos, in saxa, rogove absumpsit eodem
Ignea vis, vel saltem aliquis deus aequore mersit.
Myc. O Lycida, Lycida, nonne hoc felicius illi
Evenisse putas quam si fumosa Lycotae

of shaggy Amyntas, and were now, alas, hunting vile bait for the
hook or mending the broken fish-baskets with slender withe? But
if you know some song to mourn a former flame, to bear witness to 30
shades and ashes loved of yore, begin, while the beach stretches out
its soft sands before you and the mad waves have stilled their
uproar.

Lyc. Rather these hastily prepared verses which I recently composed to those ashes as I gazed out from the end of the harbor over
the curving shores and paid honor to the stones of her snow-white
tomb, these will I begin; do you with your hands strew over her
tomb the cone-bearing cypress and cover the mound with green
myrtle.

Myc. Behold, we have brought you moss from the azure sea; behold,
purple shells and also corals gathered from all the deep and torn 40
with effort from the lowest rocks. Do you now begin the solemn
chant; begin, while Milcon, the lad from Baia, lays out his nets
in the sun and coils his dripping lines.

Lyc. What rocks, goddesses, what caves, daughters of Nereus, do
you reveal to me? What herbs from some hidden shore, what
grasses fraught with magic juices wilt thou, Father Glaucus, now

> Antra vel hirsuti tegetem subiisset Amyntae,
> Et nunc heu viles hamo sibi quaereret escas
> Aut tenui laceras sarciret vimine nassas?
> Sed tu, si quid habes veteres quod lugeat ignes,
> Quod manes cineresque diu testetur amatos,   30
> Incipe, quandoquidem molles tibi litus harenas
> Sternit et insani posuerunt murmura fluctus.
> *Lyc.* Immo haec quae cineri nuper properata parabam
> Carmina, ab extremo cum jam cava litora portu
> Prospicerem et nivei venerarer saxa sepulcri,
> Incipiam; tu coniferas ad busta cupressus
> Sparge manu et viridi tumulum super intege myrto.
> *Myc.* En tibi caerulei muscum aequoris, en tibi conchas
> Purpureas, nec non toto quaesita profundo
> Et vix ex imis evulsa corallia saxis   40
> Afferimus; tu sollemnes nunc incipe cantus.
> Incipe, dum ad solem Baianus retia Milcon
> Explicat et madidos componit in orbe rudentes.
> *Lyc.* Quos mihi nunc, Divae, scopulos, quae panditis antra,
> Nereides? Quas tu secreti litoris herbas,
> Glauce pater, quae monstriferis mihi gramina sucis

show me; so that I, leaving the earth behind, ah, a wretched creature, becoming a new dweller of the watery seas, may follow thee
50   with changed body amid the floods, and strike the foaming marble
of the waves with twofold tail?   For why should I, alas, miserably
wish for life on an earth lonely without Phyllis?   Or what happiness should I imagine, now that I am bereft of my light?   Or what
should I hope for here?   Why should I now tarry longer in unhappiness in order that, stretched out on this vile seaweed, I might see
only dried shrubs and abandoned shores and cast my words upon a
thankless tomb?   Is this, forsooth, the wedlock, these the happy
nuptials that I am to celebrate?   Is it thus that Venus grants me
the joys of the wished nuptial torch?   Is it thus that Lucina brings
60   us doubts and fears?   Who, who has torn thee from me, sweetest
Phyllis, Phyllis, once the peace and only hope of my life, now
grief rather and eternal sorrow deep within my breast?   It was not
permitted me to join with thee in sleep that I longed for nor to
pluck the sweet gifts of early youth or together with thee to prolong
life to its last years.   Now (who would believe it?) this stone keeps
thee and to me thou art nowhere; nowhere on earth is Phyllis, but
her memory and her shade delude my wretched nights through

Ostendes nunc, Glauce, quibus tellure relicta,
Ah miser, et liquidi factus novus incola ponti
Te sequar in medios mutato corpore fluctus
Et feriam bifida spumantia marmora cauda?   50
Nam quid ego heu solis vitam sine Phyllide terris
Exoptem miser?   Aut quidnam rapta mihi luce
Dulce putem?   Quidve hic sperem?   Quid jam morer ultra
Infelix?   An ut hac vili projectus in alga
Arentes tantum frutices desertaque cernam
Litora et ingrato iactem mea verba sepulcro?
Scilicet hos thalamos, hos felices hymenaeos
Concelebrem?   Sic speratae mihi gaudia taedae
Dat Venus?   Ambiguos sic dat Lucina timores?
Quis mihi, quis tete rapuit, dulcissima Phylli,   60
Phylli meae quondam requies spesque unica vitae,
Nunc dolor aeternusque imo sub pectore luctus?
Non licuit tecum optatos coniungere somnos
Dulcia nec primae decerpere dona iuventae
Aut simul extremos vitam producere in annos.
Nunc te (quis credat?) lapis hic habet et mihi nusquam es;
Nusquam terrarum Phyllis, sed fabula et umbrae

fearful dreams. Wretched that I am, in what clime, pray, shall I
seek thee? Or where shall I follow thee? Once because of thee 70
I found pleasure in the earth and its peoples and its happy cities
with their walls; but now I desire only to traverse the bounds of
the unmeasured deep and to wander wildly through the stormy
waves, mingling with throngs of Tritons and among the sea monsters
of the rocks and among formless seals with unsightly body, so that
I may nevermore see the land. Now, thou earth that I have lived
on for so many years; ye peoples and cities, farewell; ye beloved
shores, farewell; then farewell, too, thou best loved Phyllis. We
shall rear for thee, we shall rear seven altars facing the watery
surges, and yearly according to custom we shall offer in sacrifice 80
for thee seven monsters of the mighty deep, shaggy sea calves, and
for thee oyster shells shall hang in seven wreaths, blent with purple
shells and white pebbles. Here for thee Nisaee and Cymodoce with
unbound golden locks and gentle Palaemon with his devoted mother
and Panope and Galatea, guardian of the Sicilian deep, shall join
in their solemn dances and shall utter chants which once Proteus,
bard with divine spirit, taught them when he wept for the death of

Frustrantur miseras per dira insomnia noctes.
Me miserum, qua te tandem regione requiram?
Quave sequar? Per te quondam mihi terra placebat 70
Et populi laetaeque suis cum moenibus urbes;
Nunc juvat immensi fines lustrare profundi
Perque procellosas errare licentius undas
Tritonum immixtum turbis scopulosaque cete
Inter et informes horrenti corpore phocas,
Quo numquam terras videam. Jam jam illa tot annis
Culta mihi tellus, populique urbesque valete,
Litora cara valete, vale simul optima Phylli.
Nos tibi, nos liquidis septem pro fluctibus aras
Ponemus septemque tibi de more quotannis 80
Monstra maris magni vitulos mactabimus hirtos,
Et tibi septenis pendebunt ostrea sertis,
Ostrea muricibus variata albisque lapillis.
Hic tibi Nisaee et flavos resoluta capillos
Cymodoce mitisque pia cum matre Palaemon
Et Panope et Siculi custos Galatea profundi
Sollemnes nectent choreas et carmina dicent
Quae Proteus quondam divino pectore vates
Edocuit, magni cum funera fleret Achillis

90 mighty Achilles and comforted the bitter grief of Thetis. But thou, whether thou dost blissfully dwell in the lofty heavens, or now amid Elysian shades and the revered company of Lethe thou dost pursue the fishes in limpid pools, or dost gather with lovely finger never-fading flowers, narcissus, crocus, and long-lived amaranth, and dost blend the delicate seaweed with pale violets, look down upon us and graciously come to us; ever shalt thou be goddess of waters, ever a glad token for fishermen. To thee, as to the Nymphs,
100 to Nereus, to golden-haired Amphitrite, shall the victorious boats pour out libations. Meanwhile accept this my last song for thy tomb, a song which, as he binds his line to a slender reed, the fisherman may scan and from the high cliff heave a sigh: "In the bosom of the beloved Siren Phyllis lies, and thou, Sebeto, dost rise happy in a double tomb."

Myc. Sweet is the sound of your songs, Lycidas, nor would I rather hear the laments of halcyons or on the damp grassy bank near the water listen to the sweet, plaintive notes of swans. But (so
110 may neighboring Megaria ever afford an abundance of shellfish and adjacent Mergellina yield for you oysters and sea urchins of

Et Thetidis luctus consolaretur amaros. 90
At tu, sive altum felix colis aethera, seu jam
Elysios inter manes coetusque verendos
Lethaeos sequeris per stagna liquentia pisces,
Seu legis aeternos formoso pollice flores,
Narcissumque crocumque et vivaces amaranthos,
Et violis teneras misces pallentibus algas,
Aspice nos mitisque veni; tu numen aquarum
Semper eris, semper laetum piscantibus omen.
Ut Nymphis Nereoque, ut flavicomae Amphitritae,
Sic tibi victrices fundent libamina cymbae. 100
Interea tumulo supremum hoc accipe carmen,
Carmen quod, tenui dum nectit arundine linum,
Piscator legat et scopulo suspiret ab alto:
IN. GREMIO. PHYLLIS. RECVBAT. SIRENIS. AMATAE.
CONSVRGIS. GEMINO. FELIX. SEBETHE. SEPULCRO.
Myc. Dulce sonant, Lycida, tua carmina, nec mihi malim
Alcyonum lamenta aut udo in gramine ripae
Propter aquam dulces cycnorum audire querelas.
Sed tu (sic faciles vicina Megaria semper
Sufficiat conchas, sic proxima Mergilline 110
Ostrea saxosaeque ferat tibi rupis echinos)

the rocky cliffs) since night still postpones her dark shadows and
the sun has not yet traversed all the sky, do you begin again and
repeat your song for me; repeated songs have charm.

Lyc. Do not compel me in my sorrow, Mycon, do not so; enough
have my eyes, enough now have my exhausted cheeks dripped tears;
see, grief has closed up my parched throat and shakes my innermost breast with sobs, and my weakened voice forsakes my panting
breath. Yet at another time I shall sing this for you, and more
and perhaps better songs, if the Muse will attend my singing.   120
Rather some day hereafter to be viewed by sailing ships under the
broad rock of either Procida or Misenum, I shall inscribe these
verses and I shall trace huge letters of green which the passing
sailor may scan from the deep and say: "Lycidas, Lycidas made
these verses." But since your companions shouting all over the
beach await you and require your strength for the nets, come now,
let us get up. I shall remain by this tomb; do you go to your
fellows, for it is time to seek the bait and now your baskets float   130
empty without their burden.

> Quandoquidem nox obscuras jam distulit umbras
> Necdum permensus caelum Sol, incipe rursus
> Atque itera mihi carmen; habent iterata leporem.
> *Lyc.* Ne miserum, ne coge, Mycon; sat lumina, sat jam
> Exhaustae maduere genae; dolor (aspice) siccas
> Obduxit fauces quatit et singultibus imum
> Pectus, anhelantemque animam vox aegra relinquit.
> Et tamen haec alias tibi nos et plura canemus,
> Fortasse et meliora, aderit si Musa canenti.   120
> Quin et veliferis olim haec spectanda carinis,
> Seu Prochytae, seu Miseni sub rupe patenti,
> Inscribam grandesque notas ferrugine ducam
> Praeteriens quas nauta mari percurrat ab alto
> Et dicat: "Lycidas, Lycidas haec carmina fecit."
> Sed quoniam socii passim per litus ovantes
> Exspectant poscuntque tuas ad retia vires,
> Eia age jam surgamus. Ego haec ad busta sedebo;
> Tu socios invise, escas nam quaerere tempus
> Et tibi nunc vacuae fluitant sine pondere nassae.   130

CASTIGLIONE

ALCON

For Alcon taken away by the fates in the first flower of his youth, the meadows' ornament and lovers' comfort, whom so often the Fauns and Dryads heard sing, whom so often Pan, so often Apollo admired; for Alcon the shepherds wept. Above all, beloved Iolas, his sad face bathed in flowing tears, called to the cruel heavens and the cruel stars. Like Philomel, who in the darkness bemoans her lost brood, or like the turtle dove bereft of his mate and companion
10 that a cruel shepherd has spied incautious from afar and with sharp reed has brought down from a lofty oak; resting neither on the verdant bough nor on the glad turf, nor drinking the sweet water of the glassy stream, but with his sighs proclaiming only his lost love, he feebly fills the high groves with mournful complaints. Not a day found wretched Iolas without a tear, neither when the sun rises nor when it plunges into the waves; he gave no thought to pasturing the flocks or the sleek bulls or after feeding to drive
20 them to the rivers to drink; nor did he take care to shut in folds the

ALCON

Ereptum fatis primo sub flore juventae,
Alconem nemorum decus, et solatia amantum,
Quem toties Fauni et Dryades sensere canentem,
Quem toties Pan est, toties miratus Apollo,
Flebant pastores; ante omnes carus Iolas,
Tristia perfundens lacrimis manantibus ora,
Crudeles Superos, crudeliaque astra vocabat.
Ut gemit amissos foetus Philomela sub umbris,
Aut qualis socia viduatus compare turtur,
Quam procul incautam quercu speculatus ab alta   10
Immitis calamo pastor dejecit acuto:
Non viridi sedit ramo, non gramine laeto,
Non vitrei dulcem libavit fluminis undam,
Sed gemitu amissos tantum testatus amores,
Languidulus moestis complet nemora alta querelis.
Nulla dies miserum lacrimis sine vidit Iolam,
Nec cum Sol oritur, nec cum se condit in undas:
Non illi pecudes, non pingues pascere tauros
Cura erat, aut pastos ad flumina ducere potum,
Haedorumve gregem aut vitulos includere septis: 20

flock of kids or the bullocks; only amid the woods or on the solitary
shore, alone with his despair and forgetting to yield to the late
night, in vain he poured forth these words to the cliffs and sands
unhearing:

"Alcon, beloved of the Muses and of Apollo, Alcon, the half of
my soul, Alcon, thou chief part of my heart and source of my
grief, destined to keep undrying tears in these eyes, what god or
what hapless chance has torn thee from me? Does, then, the harsh-
ness of cruel fate carry away all that is best? Is, then, some divinity
unkind only to the good? The reaper does not gather before its   30
time the young wheat, the rude husbandman does not pluck the unripe
fruit: but savage death has plunged thee in black Avernus before
thy time, and has laid greedy hands upon thy springing years.
Alas, ill-starred youth! with thee has perished the solace of the fields,
with thee Love and the Graces, and our joys. Their tresses have
fallen from the trees, the woods are spoiled of their glory and
deny to shepherds their accustomed shade. The meadows have lost
their splendor, shriveling with dying grasses; dried are the springs,
the rivers are dry. The sterile fields deny their promised yield,   40
and evil rust has devoured the growing wheat. Dismal squalor

> Tantum inter silvas, aut solo in littore secum
> Perditus, et serae oblitus decedere nocti,
> Rupibus haec frustra et surdis jactabat arenis:
>   "Alcon deliciae Musarum et Apollinis, Alcon
> Pars animae, cordis pars Alcon maxima nostri,
> Et dolor, his lacrimas oculis habiture perennes,
> Quis Deus, aut quis te casus miser abstulit? ergo
> Optima quaeque rapit duri inclementia fati?
> Ergo bonis tantum est aliquod male numen amicum?
> Non metit ante diem lactentes messor aristas,   30
> Immatura rudis non carpit poma colonus:
> At fera te ante diem mors nigro immersit Averno,
> Injecitque manus rapidas crescentibus annis.
> Heu miserande puer! Tecum solatia ruris,
> Tecum Amor et Charites periere, et gaudia nostra.
> Arboribus cecidere comae, spoliataque honore est
> Silva suo, solitasque negat pastoribus umbras.
> Prata suum amisere decus, morientibus herbis
> Arida; sunt sicci fontes, et flumina sicca.
> Infoecunda carent promissis frugibus arva,   40
> Et mala crescentes rubigo exedit aristas.

possesses the herds and the masters of the herds: the unfed wolf
rages in the stalls, and savagely tearing lambs from the udder,
rends both them and their hapless mothers, and even amid the dogs
fearlessly carries his booty away from the shepherds.   Naught but
mournful are the sounds of woodlands, pastures, and rivers, and
the flowing springs wept thy sad rites, the flowing springs, woods,
pastures, and rivers. Alas, ill-starred youth! Thy death moves the
gods. Through the groves the farmers beheld the wood nymphs
weeping, and Pan and Silvanus and the little goat-footed Satyrs.
Yet no longer by tears or by lamentation are the impious fates
moved, nor does Death unhearing hearken to my cries.

50

"Cut down by the plow the grasses die in their fields, then again
spring up from the green sod; but the Fates join not together
again the threads once they are broken. Behold, the declining sun
now sinking in the heavens is setting, and as it dies, kindles the
stars in the sky; still, when it has bathed its chariot in the western
waves, it will again revisit the lands with orient light. But
when once we have bathed in the black waters of cruel death and
the door of that relentless realm has been shut, no way leads ever

60

Squalor tristis habet pecudes, pecudumque magistros:
Impastus stabulis saevit lupus, ubere raptos
Dilaniatque ferus miseris cum matribus agnos;
Perque canes praedam impavidus pastoribus aufert.
Nil nisi triste sonant et silvae, et pascua, et amnes,
Et liquidi fontes tua tristia funera flerunt,
Et liquidi fontes, et silvae, et pascua, et amnes.
Heu miserande puer! Tangunt tua funera Divos.
Per nemora agricolae flentes videre Napeas,   50
Panaque, Silvanumque, et capripedes Satyriscos.
Sed neque jam lacrimis aut questu fata moventur
Impia, nec nostras audit Mors surda querelas.
    "Vomeribus succisa suis moriuntur in arvis
Gramina, deinde iterum viridi de cespite surgunt;
Rupta semel non deinde annectunt stamina Parcae.
Adspice, decedens jam Sol declivis Olympo
Occidit, et moriens accendit sidera coelo;
Sed tamen occiduo cum laverit aequore currus,
Idem iterum terras orienti luce reviset.   60
Ast ubi nigra semel durae nos flumina mortis
Lavere, et clausa est immitis janua regni;

to the upper light, everlasting sleep overwhelms our eyes, and enshrouds us in bitter darkness. Then vainly tears, fruitless vows, and prayers pour forth; and vows, tears, and prayers the storm-wind bears away. Alas, ill-starred youth, stolen away by envious fates. I shall behold thee no more surrounded by the crowd of shepherds victoriously contend with swift arrow or with javelin, or 70 overcome thy fellows in strenuous wrestling. No more shall I, lying at ease in the soft shade with thee, escape the hot sun of a long summer day; nor will thy pipe again soothe the neighboring hills, nor the shadowy vales re-echo with thy cunning songs. Not thy Lycoris, her name so often inscribed on the bark, and my flame Galatea, no more will they both hear us two sing of our mad love. For we two have lived together from our tender years until now, we have borne together cold and heat, nights and days, and our herds were pastured together with common toil. These my fields 80 were thine as well: we lived as one. Then why since thou art gone has life been left to me?

"Alas, in an evil hour the anger of the gods parted me from my native shores, that I might not close the dying eyes of my friend

Nulla unquam ad Superos ducit via, lumina somnus
Urget perpetuus, tenebrisque involvit amaris:
Tunc lacrimae incassum, tunc irrita vota, precesque
Funduntur, fert vota Notus, lacrimasque, precesque.
Heu miserande puer, fatis surrepte malignis!
Non ego te posthac pastorum adstante corona
Victorem adspiciam volucri certare sagitta,
Aut jaculo, aut dura socios superare palaestra.   70
Non tecum posthac molli resupinus in umbra
Effugiam longos aestivo tempore soles;
Non tua vicinos mulcebit fistula montes,
Docta nec umbrosae resonabunt carmina valles:
Non tua corticibus toties inscripta Lycoris,
Atque ignis Galatea meus, non jam simul ambos
Audierint ambae nostros cantare furores.
Nos etenim a teneris simul usque huc viximus annis,
Frigora pertulimusque aestus, noctesque, diesque,
Communique simul sunt pasta armenta labore.   80
Rura mea haec tecum communia: viximus una;
Te moriente igitur cur nam mihi vita relicta est?
    "Heu male me ira Deum patriis abduxit ab oris!
Ne manibus premerem morientia lumina amici,

with my hands nor with my mouth catch the last breath of his spirit even as it departed into the air and the kisses from his icy lips! Leucippus, thee do I envy; to thee in thy sorrow good Alcon as he died rendered his last charges, and on thy face he looked with failing eye.   Thou it was that laid his cold limbs on the mournful bier, thy tears were shed over his grave and cruel tomb: whence after fit weeping and due obsequies, thou, a happy companion, hast followed Alcon even to the world of shades, and didst not endure an aimless life without thy friend; and now, walking gladly in the shade of Elysium, thou enjoyest the companionship of precious Alcon and shalt enjoy him for aye.   And some good shepherd perhaps has laid thy bones in the selfsame grave with him on the edge of a flowering bank, revering the shades of both with pious honor, and has shed the same tears on both.   But I neither poured forth sad tears at his death nor did I render just dues to my hapless friend.   But rather, unaware of his cruel lot and misfortune, in vain was I fondly fashioning idle dreams:

" 'I shall dwell in these glorious fields; then my Alcon will come hither, leaving the hills and the unfriendly rocks, the pestilential

Aut abeuntis adhuc supremum animae halitum in auras
Exciperem ore meo, gelidis atque oscula labris.
Invideo, Leucippe, tibi; suprema dolenti
Deficiens mandata bonus tibi praebuit Alcon,
Spectavitque tuos morienti lumine vultus:
Frigida tu moesto imposuisti membra feretro,   90
Sparsisti et lacrimis bustum, ingratumque sepulchrum:
Inde ubi defletum satis est, et justa peracta,
Alconem ad manes felix comes usque secutus,
Amisso vitam socio non passus inertem es;
Et nunc Elysia laetus spatiaris in umbra,
Alcone et frueris dulci, aeternumque frueris.
Atque aliquis forsan pastor pius ossa sepulchro
Uno eodemque simul florentis margine ripae,
Amborum sacro manes veneratus honore,
Composuit, lacrimasque ambobus fudit easdem.   100
Ast ego nec tristes lacrimas in funere fudi,
Debita nec misero persolvi justa sodali.
Quin etiam, sortis durae ignarusque malorum,
Vana mihi incassum fingebam somnia demens:
" 'Haec ego rura colam celeberrima; tum meus Alcon
Huc veniet linquens colles, et inhospita saxa,

waves, and herbs reeking with venom, and he will visit these soft
meadows and wholesome streams. I shall run to meet him from
afar; I shall be the first to know my friend as he comes; I shall be   **110**
the first to smother him with loving embraces; our new joys will
force out tears of happiness. Thus at last we shall happily enjoy
long wished discourse, and we shall delight in telling over in turn
the heavy sorrows and the hardships once passed, and in hearing
them again. Then as we speak, we shall gradually resume our old
loves, and amid pastoral delights, and the sweet repose of country
life, we shall pass our lives in untroubled peace. These fields Ceres
loves, Bacchus these hillsides, Apollo these pastures; Pales herself
affords grass for the flock, milk for the lambs. In these mountains   **120**
often the dainty nymphs were wont to pursue wild beasts at will,
and often to pursue their dances. Here the Tiber, imbued with the
hallowed glories of that ancient people, laves venerable ruins,
towering monuments. Here are woodland shades, here springs,
here cool vales, here the shepherd Corydon once sang his beautiful
Alexis. Then come, thou dearly loved youth: the pastures and
streams await thee, for thee the Nymphs are now weaving garlands

Infectasque undas, et pabula dira veneno,
Molliaque inviset prata haec, fluviosque salubres.
Occurram longe, et venientem primus amicum
Agnoscam; primus caris complexibus ora   110
Impediam; excutient hilares nova gaudia fletus.
Sic tandem optato laeti sermone fruemur,
Aerumnasque graves, olim et transacta vicissim
Damna referre simul, rursusque audire juvabit:
Tum veteres sensim fando repetemus amores,
Deliciasque inter pastorum, et dulcia ruris
Otia, securae peragemus tempora vitae.
Haec amat arva Ceres, juga Bacchus, pascua Apollo;
Ipsa Pales herbas pecori, lac sufficit agnis.
Montibus his passim tenerae assuevere Napeae   120
Saepe feras agitare, et saepe agitare choreas.
Hic redolens sacros primaevae gentis honores
Perluit antiquas Tiberis decora alta ruinas.
Hic umbrae nemorum, hic fontes, hic frigida Tempe,
Formosum hic pastor Corydon cantavit Alexin.
Ergo ades, o dilecte puer: te pascua et amnes
Expectant, tibi jam contexunt florea serta,

of flowers, and on thy coming reveal their joy, and the colorful
earth brings forth fresh flowers for thee.'

130   "Such visions I, wretched man, did fashion, led by a vain hope
and not knowing that every crime is permitted the Fates and death.
But since my deluded prayers have passed away upon the light
winds, and it was not allowed me to see the living features of
Alcon, to hear and return living words, hither at least, even hither
may his shade hasten, winging through the void with soft flight,
and with compassion at last for my grief receive my tears and
sighs, breathed from the depth of my heart, and the lamentations
to which these hollow caves respond. I with my own hands shall
140   raise an empty tomb here on this bank of the Anio, solace for my
grief, and I shall place pious incense on the altars, and I shall
invoke his shade. You boys, join me in scattering fragrant flowers:
narcissus and roses, and the sweetly blushing hyacinth, and produce
thick shade with ivy and laurel. Nor let there be wanting branches
of cassia, and cinnamon blended with amomum, so that the wind
breathing upon them may spread their sweet fragrance. Alcon
deeply loved me, and he was worthy of my love, and worthy of

Adventuque tuo testantur gaudia Nymphae,
Summittitque novos tellus tibi daedala flores.'
    "Haec ego fingebam miser ab spe ductus inani,   130
Nescius omne nefas morti fatisque licere.
At postquam frustrata leves abiere per auras
Vota mea, et vivos Alconis cernere vultus
Non licuit, vivasque audire et reddere voces,
Huc saltem, o saltem umbra levi per inania lapsu
Advolet, et nostros tandem miserata dolores
Accipiat lacrimas, imo et suspiria corde
Eruta, quasque cava haec responsant antra querelas.
Ipse meis manibus ripa hac Anienis inanem
Constituam tumulum, nostri solatia luctus,   140
Atque addam pia thura focis, manesque ciebo.
Vos mecum o pueri beneolentes spargite flores,
Narcissum, atque rosas, et suave rubentem hyacinthum,
Atque umbras hedera lauroque inducite opacas.
Nec desint casiae, permixtaque cinnama amomo,
Excitet ut dulces aspirans ventus odores.
Nos Alcon dilexit multum, et dignus amari
Ipse fuit nobis, et tali dignus honore.

such tribute. Meantime, the Nymphs will interweave violets with
amaranth, and upon the tomb will strew flowers and garlands, and   150
with downcast mien they will inscribe upon the tomb this mournful
verse: 'Since the wicked fates stole Alcon away, rough mountains
are weeping, and day has been overcast with dark night; the white
has turned to black, and the sweet to bitter.' "

> Interea violas intertexent amaranthis,
> Et tumulo spargent flores et serta Napaeae,   150
> Et tumulo moestae inscribent miserabile carmen:
> 'Alconem postquam rapuerunt impia fata,
> Collacrimant duri montes, et consitus atra est
> Nocte dies; sunt candida nigra, et dulcia amara.' "

ALAMANNI

ECLOGUE 1
[COSMO]

Thyrsis. Meliboeus.

Thyr. Sweet is the piercing note of the tall pines contending with the winds, and yet no less sweet than that do I deem your pipe; such that next to the gods everyone among us shepherds grants the highest praise to you.

Mel. Sweet, shepherd, is the murmur of the water which trickles from the high cliff and drops below, but far sweeter is the sound
10 of your notes; such that next to the Muses, the fair Tuscan land offers wholly to you its praise and renown.

Thyr. Pray, if you are not averse to rest here with me, bring forth your pipe, and in this spot, adorned with myrtle and crimson flowers and roses, gladden with music the surrounding fields, while I shall in silence tend the flocks.

Mel. Thyrsis, do not ask of me that at noonday I break with my pipe the sweet slumbers of our god Pan, who in the verdant meadows

ECLOGUE 1
[COSMO]

Tirsi. Melibeo.

Tir. Dolce è l' acuto suon degli alti pini
Contrastanti coi venti, e dolce ancora
Non men di quel la tua zampogna estimo;
Tal che dopo agli Dei fra noi pastori
La prima lode a te ciascun consente.
Mel. Dolce è, pastore, il mormorar dell' onda
Che d' alta pietra stilla e in basso scende,
Ma vie più dolce il suon delle tue voci;
Tal che dopo le Muse, il pregio e 'l nome
Tutto a te porta il bel paese tósco.   10
Tir. Deh, se posar qui meco or non ti aggreva,
Trai la zampogna fuori, e in questo loco
Cui mirto adorna, e fior vermigli e rose,
Fa col suon liete le campagne intorno,
Ed io tacendo avrò cura alle greggi.
Mel. Tirsi, non mi pregar che al mezzogiorno
Con la zampogna io rompa i dolci sonni
A Pan dio nostro, che nei verdi campi

refreshes his body wearied in the chase. Ah, his wrath is too much   20
to be feared! But you, who can with your singing, no less than
Orpheus, move the forests and the mountains and make the rivers
stay, and tame the savage wolves among the herds, and with no less
skill than our Tuscan Aiolle can gladden the vales with your voice
and your music—than even our Tuscan Aiolle, in whom Florence
discovers whatever harmony, whatever art comes from Terpsichore
among us mortals—pray, with lowered voice (as indeed the other   30
day you sang at Damoetas's) sing the wretched fate of Cosmo, the
honor of us shepherds, the man whom all Tuscany still worships
and weeps for. In return for this boon I am keeping for your
reward a white goat which suckles two young like herself and each
day fills some two pails with milk. I am keeping for you besides a
rich vase adorned with fragrant juniper, and around its outside
wind ivy and green acanthus. Within, artistically engraved with   40
hand of skill are spring, summer, autumn, and winter. Here is
seen the peasant who cuts the useless branches from the low vine

Ristora il corpo affaticato in caccia.
Ah troppo l' ira sua temer si deve.   20
Ma tu che col cantar non men d' Orfeo
Fai gir le selve, i monti, e stare i fiumi,
E i feri lupi infra gli armenti acqueti,
Nè men sai far che 'l nostro tósco Aiolle
Con la voce e col suon le valli liete;
Che il nostro tósco Aiolle, in cui Fiorenza
Scorge quanta armonia, quant' arte mai
Da Tersicore vien fra noi mortali;
Deh, con più bassa voce il miser fato
(Siccome pur l' altr' ier festi a Dameta)   30
Narra di Cosmo, onor di noi pastori,
Che ancor Toscana tutta adora e piange.
Ed io 'n cambio di ciò ti serbo in dono
Una candida capra che due figli
Simiglianti a sè nutre, e ciascun giorno
Di latte quasi due vasetti colma.
Serboti appresso un ricco vaso ornato
D' odorato ginepro, il qual di fuore
Edera intorno cinge e 'l verde acanto.
Dentro per dotta man con arte sculte   40
Son primavera, estate, autunno e verno.
Ivi appare il villan che all' umil vite

and tames the high boughs of the trees and imposes new laws on them. Beyond, under the hot sky, he is seen with curved scythe in his hand intently harvesting the fruit of his wearisome, heavy labors. Rejoicing in the new wine, bathed and stained therein, he offers to kindly Bacchus sacrifices and gifts. Then when the conquered sun yields to ice and winds, in greater content he sits with his little family around the fire, and the curved plough and the other tools, dulled with long use, he sharpens and files for the sweet new times to come. And only except for power of speech, anyone would say it was the work of nature and not of human skill. This then shall be yours if you will but favor us with that sweet singing, whereof one should not be miserly, since before long death comes and makes us all mute and deaf.

Thyr. Since your request with your precious gifts forces me to recall our affliction,

> *Begin, you Muses, the mournful song.*

Where were all the Graces and the Virtues at that time? Where were you, Muses, at that time, when the bright soul of divine Cosmo

Taglia le inutil braccia, e gli alti rami
Degli arbor doma, e nuove leggi impone.
Più oltre al caldo ciel si vede intento
Con torta falce in man raccorre il frutto
Delle fatiche sue noiose e grevi.
Lieto del nuovo vin, bagnato e tinto
Porge al buon Bacco sagrifici e doni.
Poi che il Sol vinto a' ghiacci e venti cede,
Più contento s' asside al foco intorno
Con la sua famigliuola, e il torto aratro
E gli altri ferri dal lungo uso stanchi
Pei nuovi tempi dolci aguzza e lima:
E fuor solo il parlar, ciascun direbbe
Di natura opra, e non d' umane ingegno.
Questo adunque fia tuo, s' or ne concedi
Quel soave cantar, del quale avaro
Esser non si potria, perciò che in breve
Vien poscia morte, e noi fa muti e sordi.
Tir. Poi che a rinnovellar quel che n' ancide
Mi sforza il tuo pregar coi cari doni,
Date principio, o Muse, al tristo canto.
Ov' eran tutte allor Grazie e Virtuti?
Ove voi, Muse, allor che la chiara alma
Del divin Cosmo al sommo ciel salío?

ascended to highest heaven? Not then were you on the cool banks
of his limpid Arno, and not among the verdant hills of his flowered
nest, but rather were you so far away at that time that your aid was   70
too late to rescue from death your dearly beloved.

   Begin, you Muses, the mournful song.

The flocks wept, alas, the herds wept, the birds wept, the wild
beasts, the rocks, and the herbs; the sun hid; the sky, before so
bright and joyous, now sorrowful and dark, turned into rain.

   Begin, you Muses, the mournful song.

Apollo came down to us from his Parnassus and weeping said:
"Ah wretched Cosmo, whither art thou now departing? Who robs   80
the world of thee? Where is the fair speech, where the sweet song,
where the other skills and rare virtues, which once I placed in thee
as in their rightful home?"

   Begin, you Muses, the mournful song.

Then came Pan with a thousand other shepherds, mournful in
countenance, and said to himself: "Oh, alas, how death now de-
prives us of that high hope that sustained us, with regard to youth-

> Non già non già lungo le fresche rive
> Del suo chiaro Arno, e non fra i verdi colli
> Del suo fiorito nido, anzi lontane
> Foste allor sì, che tardo fu il soccorso   70
> Di tôrre a morte quel cui tanto amaste.
> Date principio, o Muse, al tristo canto.
> Pianser le greggi, ohimè, pianser gli armenti,
> Pianser gli augei, le fere, i sassi e l' erbe;
> Il Sol si ascose, il ciel pria chiaro e lieto
> Doglioso e fosco si converse in pioggia.
> Date principio, o Muse, al tristo canto.
> Discese Apollo a noi dal suo Parnaso
> E piangendo dicea: "Deh, miser Cosmo,
> Dov' or ten vai? chi di te il mondo spoglia?   80
> Dov' è il bel dir? dove il cantar soave?
> Dove l' altre scienze e virtù rare
> Che in te pur già quasi in suo albergo posi?"
> Date principio, o Muse, al tristo canto.
> Pan venne poi con mille altri pastori
> Doglioso in vista, e dicea seco: "Ahi lasso!
> Com' or morte ne toe quell' alta spene
> Che ne notria del giovinetto Cosmo?

90 ful Cosmo! How many times I said: 'Through him the fair Tuscan land shall one day become so famous that it will rob Sicily and Arcadia of their renown!' Ah, with what good cause do the herds weep and the flocks, for if he were living, perhaps neither plundering shepherds nor savage wolves would come to devour their milk and their young."

Begin, you Muses, the mournful song.

100 After these at last came she who turns the world, and we call her Fortune. Clothing her heart, which was really happy, in false sorrow, she said: "Ah, who takes thee from us, who forces thee before thy time to this final pass?"

Begin, you Muses, the mournful song.

He, who for a long space had been silent and calm, overwhelmed in a moment with becoming wrath, now broke his silence with these words: "Treacherous Fortune, deceitful goddess, that dost ever turn and trouble this blind world! Well thou knowest whether thou art the cause that I have become such as this.

Begin, you Muses, the mournful song.

> Quante volte diss' io: per costui fia
> Sì chiaro un giorno il bel paese tósco   90
> Che a Sicilia ed Arcadia il pregio involi?'
> Ahi quanto con ragion piangon gli armenti,
> Quanto le greggi, chè vivendo ei forse
> Nè rapaci pastor, nè feri lupi
> Verrían per divorarsi il latte e i figli."
> Date principio, Muse, al tristo canto.
> Dopo costoro alfin poi venne quella
> Che volge il mondo, e noi chiamiam Fortuna.
> Questa chiudendo il cor che lieto avea
> Con dolor falso disse: "Ahi chi ten toglie,   100
> Chi ti spinge anzi tempo al passo estremo?"
> Date principio, Muse, al tristo canto.
> Ei per lunga stagion tacito e queto
> Vinto in un punto d' un leggiadro sdegno,
> Ruppe il silenzio suo con queste voci:
> "O perfida Fortuna, o dea fallace
> Che il cieco mondo ognor convolgi e turbi,
> Sai ben se a tua cagion son fatto tale.
> Date principio, Muse, al tristo canto.

"Well I know through proof how thou dost raise the guilty up to   110
heaven, while trampling the good, and with what art thou dost
always confuse every honorable undertaking.

Begin, you Muses, the mournful song.

"But if I depart from this present life with less glory and praise
than I could wish, let my excuse therefor be the brief time assigned
to my fated thread by the wicked, greedy Fates, and may I be
vindicated by my beloved friends to whom I so often disclosed my
every thought.   Ah! the unjust and perverse laws of thy realm, that   120
I must bear the hurt while the fault is another's!   But be my fate
what it may; for I hope even this day to rise to heaven, if good will
in us, when the power is taken from us, be reckoned as virtue.

Begin, you Muses, the mournful song.

"You forests, you hills, you verdant, sunny slopes, you sweet
fields, you woods, to which I revealed with song the wounds of love,
alas that I now must leave!   Remain in peace.

Conclude now, you Muses, the mournful song.   130

"Ben so per pruova come al ciel sollevi   110
    I rei, calcando i buoni, e con quant' arte
    Disturbi sempre ogni onorata impresa.
Date principio, Muse, al tristo canto.
    "Ma s' io mi parto con men gloria e pregio
    Ch' io non vorrei d' esta presente vita
    Di ciò mi scuse il breve tempo dato
    Al fil fatal dall' empie avare Parche,
    E gli altri miei diletti amici, a cui
    Mostrai sì spesso ogni pensiero aperto.
    Ahi! del tuo regno leggi inique e torte,   120
    Ch' io porto il danno, ed è la colpa altrui.
    Ma di me sia che può, ch' al ciel salire
    Spero oggi ancor, se il buon volere in noi,
    Sendo tolto il poter, virtù s' estima.
Date principio, o Muse, al tristo canto.
    "O selve, o colli, o verdi piagge apriche,
    O soavi campagne, o boschi, a cui
    Cantando apersi l' amorose piaghe,
    Lasso, ch' io parto omai, restate in pace.
Date omai fine, o Muse, al tristo canto.   130

"You bright fountains and thou fair stream of Arno, that dost bathe and divide the nest where I was born, alas that I now must leave! Remain in peace.

Conclude now, you Muses, the mournful song.

"Remain here in peace, my precious friends, and do not grieve; only sometimes let some memory of me and of our noble thoughts and of our rare and lofty purposes, cut off by death, come back to 140   your hearts. And do thou also remain in peace, fair Elisa." As thus he spoke, from its terrestrial veil his soul released itself and soared naked to heaven, where it joyously abides and leaves us here in sorrow.

Conclude now, you Muses, the mournful song.

Now give me the white goat and the rich vase so that I may devoutly render sacrifices and prayers to the nine gracious Sisters. Holy Muses, to you do I many times incline my knees and my 150   spirit, and soon I hope to invoke you again with sweeter song.

> "Voi chiari fonti, e tu bel fiume d' Arno
>   Che bagni e parti il nido ov' io son nato,
>   Lasso, ch' io parto omai, restate in pace.
> Date omai fine, o Muse, al tristo canto.
>   "Voi qui restate in pace, o dolci amici,
>   Nè vi dolete, e sol di me talora
>   E de' santi pensier, degli alti e rari
>   Disegni nostri che interrompe morte
>   Qualche memoria ne' cor vostri torni.
>   E tu resta anco in pace, o bella Elisa."   140
>   Così dicendo dal terrestre velo
>   Si sciolse l' alma, e nuda al ciel salío
>   U' lieta stassi, e noi qui lascia in doglia.
> Date omai fine, o Muse, al tristo canto.
>   Tu la candida capra, e il ricco vaso
>   Dammi or sì che alle nove alme Sorelle
>   Renda divoto sagrifici e preci.
>   O sante Muse, a voi più volte inchino
>   Le ginocchia e la mente, e in breve spero
>   Chiamarvi ancor con più soave canto.   150

Mel. Such sweetness and light as ever the world possessed does the sound of your notes afford us; so let henceforth Philomela and Progne be silent, or whatever other bird may weep with greater art. Now take the rewards promised for your singing.

> *Mel.* Quanto ebbe il mondo mai di dolce e chiaro,
> Tanto ne porge il suon delle tue note;
> Sicchè omai taccia e Filomela e Progne
> O s' altro augel più dottamente piange.
> Prendi ora i premi al tuo cantar promessi.

ECLOGUE 2

[COSMO]

Leave, Nymphs, the cool grassy depths of liquid crystal and the limpid rivers that bathe the Tuscan fields round about. Seek, alas, a more sorrowful abode, that will invite you to mourn for the wretched fate of your Cosmo. You mountains, you slopes, you hills, receive no tranquil breezes within you. You lovely grasses and you once joyous trees, in sadness now cast off your blossoms and your verdure. Let the roses be pale and do you, Hyacinthus, 10 inscribe within your bosom a double sorrow, for dead is he that once brought beauty to the world.

Weep now for evermore, you Tuscan sisters.

ECLOGUE 2

[COSMO]

> Lasciate, o Ninfe, i freschi erbosi fondi
> De' liquidi cristalli, e i chiari fiumi
> Che intorno bagnan le campagne tosche.
> Cercate, ahi lasse! un piu doglioso albergo
> Che v' inviti a doler del miser fato
> Del vostro Cosmo: o monti, a piagge, o colli,
> Non ricevete in voi venti sereni.
> Voi vaghe erbette, e voi già liete piante,
> Omai triste spogliate i fiori e 'l verde.
> Pallide sian le rose, e tu, Iacinto, 10
> Descrivi entro al tuo sen doppio dolore,
> Poi che morto è chi fea già il mondo adorno.
> Piangete sempre omai, sorelle tosche.

You white swans, still weeping, as you are wont sweetly to do when near to death, say to the sands, to the rocks, to the fishes, to the waves, that no more will they hear the clear notes as they were wont, since through harsh death the new Tuscan Orpheus is taken from the world.

20   *Weep now for evermore, you Tuscan sisters.*

He who ever lived so sweet and dear to all the shepherds must no more sound his pipe, or under shady branches sweeten with song all the surrounding air. Mute stands the world, and the flock and herds flee with weeping from the clear waters and the grass.

Weep now for evermore, you Tuscan sisters.

At thy departing, gracious shepherd, fair Apollo wept, and the
30   Satyrs and the Silvani, and Pan more than any other poured forth his grief to us. The clear fountains and the cool rivulets are watering the vales and the meadows with their tears, so that where they are, it truly seems winter unending. Wretched Echo within her hollowed rocks weeps in silence, since she hopes no more to

Candidi cigni, e voi piangenti ancora
Come presso al morir dolce solete,
Dite all' arene, ai sassi, ai pesci, all' onde
Che più non sentiran le chiare note
Come solíen, poichè nel mondo è spento
Per morte acerba il nuovo tosco Orfeo.
Piangete sempre omai, sorelle tosche.   20
Quel che a tutt' i pastor sì dolce e caro
Mai sempre visse, più sonar non deve
La sua zampogna, o sotto ombrosi rami
Col suo canto addolcir l' aër d' intorno.
Muto sta il mondo, e le greggi e gli armenti
Fuggon piangendo le chiare acque e l' erba.
Piangete sempre omai, sorelle tosche.
Pianto ha la tua partenza, almo pastore,
Il biondo Apollo, i Satiri, i Silvani,
E Pan viepiù d' ogni altro a noi si dolse.   30
Le chiare fonti e i freschi ruscelletti
Rigan di pianto sì le valli e i prati
Che ben sembra, ove son, perpetuo il verno.
La misera Eco entro a' cavati sassi
Tacendo piange, poi che più non spera

return the last sound of thy words. The trees drop their fruits unripe from their lofty boughs; the flowers stand drooping. From the tender sheep no white milk drips into the vessels, no more does the greedy bee gather the sweet honey in his secret chambers, for as his most illustrious shepherd is dead, he feeds only on the bitter and shuns the sweet.

Weep now for evermore, you Tuscan sisters.

Not so mournfully on the desolate shores of the sandy seas does the dolphin weep for his dead mate, nor from the lofty roofs does Progne call with such grief for her children, nor does Philomela moan with such anguish for her foolish faith amid woods and vales, nor does Ceyx grieve so for Halcyone along the beloved banks, as all do now weep, calling on wretched Cosmo.

Weep now for evermore, you Tuscan sisters.

What shepherd so illustrious does the Tuscan land possess, what one so gifted as to dare set his mouth to thy pipe so that it, shy of

Render l' ultimo suon delle tue voci.
Gli arbor lascian cader dagli alti rami
I pomi acerbi, i fior languendo stanno.
Non dalle pecorelle il bianco latte
Nei vasi stilla, non più l' ape avara   40
Aduna il dolce mêl ne' chiusi alberghi;
Che morto essendo il suo pastor più chiaro,
Sol si pasce d' amaro e il dolce ha schivo.
Piangete sempre omai, sorelle tosche.
Non sì doglioso nei deserti lidi
Degli arenosi mar piange il delfino
La morta sposa, non per gli alti tetti
Chiama con tal dolor Progne i suoi figli,
Non Filomela con tal duol si lagna
Del folle creder suo per boschi e valli,   50
Non tanto d' Alcion si duol Ceice
Lungo le rive amate, quanto ognora
Piangon tutti chiamando il miser Cosmo.
Piangete sempre omai, sorelle tosche.
Qual sì chiaro pastore ha 'l terren tosco,
Qual tanto ornato, che por bocca ardisca
Alla zampogna tua sì ch' ella schiva

60 every other successor, may not shrink back, saying: "Ah, too noble were the breaths which gave me voice! Ah me, too skilled was the hand which made my song varied and joyous! Touch me not, for henceforth I desire to be ever widowed and mute with my first lord."

Weep now for evermore, you Tuscan sisters.

Galatea, who, leaving the salt waves of the sea, came many times joyfully to the banks of the Arno to listen to thee, now sighs and weeps, and reproaches death that, stealing thee from the world, he
70 yet preserves in life the savage Cyclops for her greater pain; whence, forgetting her sweet abode in the clear waters, on the bare sands she vents her grief and feeds herself only with calling for thee.

Weep now for evermore, you Tuscan sisters.

Together with thee, supreme shepherd, are stilled those sweet verses in lofty, ornate style, by which every noble heart was made so joyful. Sad and mournful the little Cupids, with their torches
80 quenched, their arrows and their bows broken, stand around thee, and scattering roses and flowers they often invoke thy revered spirit.

> D' ogni altro successor non fugga indietro,
> Dicendo: "Ah troppo nobil fur gli spirti
> Che mi dier voce, ohimè, troppo fu dotta   60
> La man che 'l mio cantar fea vario e lieto:
> Non mi toccar, chè omai vedova e muta
> Col mio primo signor voglio esser sempre?"
> Piangete sempre omai, sorelle tosche.
> La bella Galatea, che le salse onde
> Del mar lasciando in su le rive d' Arno
> Lieta più volte ad ascoltar ti venne,
> Sospira e piange, e con la morte duolsi
> Che, furandoti al mondo, il fer Ciclopo
> Per sua doglia maggior riserba in vita,   70
> Onde obliando il dolce suo soggiorno
> Delle chiare acque, in sulle ignude arene
> Solo in te richiamar si sfoga e pasce.
> Piangete sempre omai, sorelle tosche.
> Teco, o sommo pastor, son muti insieme
> Quei dolci versi in alto stile ornato
> Onde ogni cor gentil sì lieto andava.
> Tristi e dogliosi i pargoletti amori,
> Spente le faci, e gli strai tronchi e gli archi,
> Ti stan dintorno, e gli onorati spirti   80
> Spargendo rose e fior chiaman sovente.

Venus, bestowing on her precious poet kisses more sweet and tears more bitter than ever she bestowed on dead, beloved Adonis, now weeps for the fate of us mortals.

Weep now for evermore, you Tuscan sisters.

Far more than all others the Tuscan river, wherever it flows, laments and grieves over its heavy loss, saying: "Oh, alas! truly with good cause did I weep when that great divine light was **90** quenched, that lofty and sacred ancient son of mine, undutifully opposed to me at one time, he who with style so skilled and rare sang of heaven and the abyss and the places where the soul is purified to travel to a better haven. Again with good cause more than another I wept for him who wept for Laura and with rimes so sweet gave forth in song the thoughts of love, the ardent flames, with which all the world today resounds, and not alone these banks **100** of mine, which neighbor here. And not long thereafter together with beloved Elsa, I wept long for my dearly cherished friend, master of lofty utterance, who with fluent speech once composed his long laments for Fiammetta, and the charming discourses of

> Vener porgendo al caro suo poeta
> Baci più dolci e lagrime più amare
> Che mai porgesse al morto amato Adone,
> Piange or la condizion di noi mortali.
> Piangete sempre omai, sorelle tosche.
> Vie più di tutti gli altri il tósco fiume
> Ovunque passa sì lamenta e duole
> Del grave danno suo, dicendo: "Ahi lasso!
> Ben piansi io con ragion, quando s' estinse   90
> Quel gran lume divin, quell' alto e sacro
> Mio figlio antico, a me contrario un tempo
> Contra 'l dover; che in stil sì dotto e raro
> Cantò il cielo, e l' abisso, e i luoghi dove
> Si purga l' alma a gire a miglior porto.
> Ben con ragione ancor più d' altro piansi
> Chi Laura pianse, e che in sì dolci rime
> Gli amorosi pensier, le fiamme ardenti
> Sfogò cantando, ond' oggi suona il mondo
> Non pur le rive mie quinci vicine;   100
> Nè molto poi con l' amata Elsa insieme
> Gran tempo piansi il mio diletto amico,
> Maestro d' alto dir, che i lunghi pianti
> Già di Fiammetta in parlar sciolto stese,

110 the ten days, so splendid and beautiful that they will never see the night. But alas, never with such sorrowing voices, with such burning sighs did I weep for anyone as for my Cosmo,—ah me!—whose pipe, though youthful, had brought me no less renown than the already hoary lyre of the others. Hence, twofold grief the mere thought brings me, alas, of what the world hoped for in him."

Weep now for evermore, you Tuscan sisters.

120 The joyous roses, the fresh and green grasses, the violets, the crimson and the dark-hued flowers do indeed have a frail and fleeting life. But the sweet breezes, the kindly suns, and the waters restore their breath to them, so that from year to year they return more lovely than ever with each new April. But alas, no virtue, kingly power, or treasure could restore to us this gracious light, for when death comes, it brings us winter unending and carries off the happier times. An eternal slumber, revered Cosmo, thou must sleep beneath the earth, while elsewhere thou receivest the victory and the palm of thy good deeds.

E i dolci ragionar dei dieci giorni
Sì chiari e bei che non vedran mai notte.
Ma, lasso, ancor con sì dogliose voci
Con sì caldi sospir non piansi alcuno,
Quanto il mio Cosmo, ohimè, la cui zampogna
Pur giovinetta non m' avea men pregio   110
Dato, che l' altrui già canuta cetra:
Poi doppio duol mi reca il pensar solo
Quel che, lasso! di lui sperava il mondo."
Piangete sempre omai, sorelle tosche.
Le liete rose, le fresch' erbe e verdi,
Le violette, i fior vermigli e i persi
Bene han la vita lor caduca e frale.
Ma l' aure dolci, i Sol benigni e l' acque
Rendon gli spirti lor, che d' anno in anno
Tornan più che mai belli al nuovo aprile.   120
Ma, lassi, non virtù, regni, o tesoro
A noi render potrian quest' alma luce,
Chè quando morte vien, perpetuo il verno
Reca, e i tempi miglior si porta via.
Eterno sonno dèi, Cosmo onorato,
Dormir sotterra, mentre in altra parte
Hai del tuo bene oprar vittoria e palma.

Weep now for evermore, you Tuscan sisters.

Ah, could I but like good, Thracian Orpheus, like the fierce Tirynthian, and the wise Ulysses descend yonder, where thou art 130 in the dusky realms! For by relating to fair Proserpina and to great Pluto how the world is now saddened by thy departure, perhaps I could fill them with such pity that thou mightst yet return. But if thy sweet song and charming verses, with which in life thou didst bring such joy to others, have touched the divine ears down yonder, vain would be my hope, for so precious is the boon which I should ask that even pity herself, not to say another, would become 140 greedy and harsh thereat. So then, my sorrowful thoughts, without other hope of ever again beholding him unless death comes to cut off my heavy and weary years, let us give vent to grief with tearful song, always calling him who does not answer.

Weep now for evermore, you Tuscan sisters.

Piangete sempre omai, sorelle tosche.
    Deh! potess' io come il buon tracio Orfeo
    Come il fero Tirintio, e il saggio Ulisse,   130
    Scender là dove sei nei regni oscuri.
    Chè a Proserpina bella e al gran Plutone
    Narrando quanto il mondo oggi s' attrista
    Della partenza tua, forse pietosi
    Gli farei tal, che torneresti ancora.
    Ma se il soave canto e i dolci versi,
    Onde vivendo altrui sì lieto festi,
    Tocche han laggiù le sante orecchie, vano
    Fora 'l sperar, chè tanto è caro il dono
    Ch' io chiederei, che pur pietade stessa   140
    Ne diverria, non ch' altri, avara e cruda.
    Dunque, o tristi pensier, senz' altra spene
    Di rivederlo mai se non vien morte
    Che tronchi gli anni miei gravosi e stanchi,
    Sfoghiamo il duol con lagrimoso canto
    Lui chiamando ad ognor che non risponde.
Piangete sempre omai, sorelle tosche.

MAROT

LAMENTATION FOR MADAME LOUISE OF SAVOY, MOTHER OF THE KING, IN THE FORM OF AN ECLOGUE

Thenot. Colin.

Then. In this fair valley there are excellent delights, a clear brook murmuring near the shade, grass to one's heart's content, winds not too strong, then you, Colin, who are so passionately fond of singing. I do not desire to lessen the reverence due to Pan; but if you should accompany him to the fields he would sooner receive gain therefrom than harm: he would instruct you and you would teach him. As for songs, you would employ thereat such great art if it came to a contest, that if you would gain nothing over Pan, Pan could lay claim to nothing over you. If he wins for his prize a fine tender cheese, you will win a vessel of curdled milk; or if he prefers to take the milk, to you the cheese will be awarded.

10

DE MADAME LOYSE DE SAVOYE, MERE DU ROY, EN FORME D'EGLOGUE.

Thenot. Colin.

The. En ce beau val sont plaisirs excellens,
Un cler ruisseau bruyant près de l'umbrage,
L'herbe à souhait, les ventz non violens,
Puis toy, Colin, qui de chanter fais rage.
    A Pan ne veulx rabaisser son hommage;
Mais quand aux champs tu l'accompagnerois,
Plus tost prouffit en auroit que dommage:
Il t'apprendroit, et tu l'enseignerois.
    Quant à chansons, tu y besongnerois
De si grand art, s'on venoit à contendre,
Que quand sur Pan rien tu ne gaignerois,
Pan dessus toy rien ne pourroit pretendre.
  S'il gaigne en prix un beau fourmage tendre,
Tu gaigneras un pot de laict caillé;
Ou si le laict il ayme plus cher prendre,
A toy sera le fourmage baillé.

10

Col. Shepherd Thenot, I marvel at your songs, and I revel in them even more than in listening to the sprightly linnet or to the water   20 that falls murmuring from a mountain. If Calliope wins over you in the morning, you will gain the spoils against her in the evening, or if it happens that so noble a rival wins over you in the evening, you will conquer in the morning. Now I pray you, while my dog keeps good watch and I pasture both our flocks, sing a little of Catin, describing her fair rustic garb.

Then. The nightingale is the mistress of song; before her it behooves   30 the woodpecker to be silent; so also, while I am in a place where you may be, I will keep silent my varied reeds. But if you will sing ten times ten verses, lamenting the shepherdess Louise, you shall have quinces, six yellow and six green, of the finest fragrance since the day of Moses. And if your verses are of as fine quality as the last ones that you composed of Isabeau, you shall have not the thing which I have promised, but what is far more and better   40

> *Col.* Berger Thenot, je suis esmerveillé
> De tes chansons, et plus fort je m'y baigne
> Qu' à escouter le linot esveillé,
> Ou l'eau qui bruyt tombant d'une montaigne.   20
>   Si au matin Calliope te gaigne,
> Contre elle au soir obtiendras le butin;
> Ou s'il advient que tant noble compaigne
> Te gaigne au soir, tu vaincras au matin.
>   Or je te pry, tandis que mon mastin
> Fera bon guet, et que je feray paistre
> Noz deux troupeaux, chante un peu de Catin,
> En deschiffrant son bel habit champestre.
> *The.* Le rossignol de chanter est le maistre:
> Taire convient devant luy les pivers;   30
> Aussi, estant là où tu pourras estre,
> Taire feray mes chalumeaux divers.
>   Mais si tu veulx chanter dix foys dix vers,
> En deplorant la bergere Loyse,
> Des coingz auras six jaunes et six vertz,
> Des mieulx sentans qu'on veit depuis Moyse.
>   Et si tes vers sont d'aussi bonne mise
> Que les derniers que tu feis d'Ysabeau,
> Tu n'auras pas la chose qu'ay promise,
> Ains beaucoup plus, et meilleur et plus beau.   40

and finer. You shall have from me a double pipe, made by the hands of Raffy of Lyons, which I got with difficulty in exchange for a kid from good shepherd Michau, whom you know. I have never yet played on it but once, and I preserve it as dear as life; still you shall have it, and gladly, by doing what I ask you.

50   *Col.* You ask of me the thing I desire to do; come now, my verses, sing mournful songs, since death has carried off Louise, who kept our fields so fresh. So we are unhappy now, more bewildered at her fatal absence than the lambs when they do not find about them the mother who cares for them. Let us weep, shepherds, Nature gives us the right; let us weep for the mother of the great shepherd of this place; let us weep for the mother of excellent Margot, let us

60   weep for the mother of ourselves as well. Great shepherd, how much sorrow is yours. Nor do I know whether you or your mother renders me more saddened with grief.

> *Sing, my verses, sing bitter grief.*

De moy auras un double chalumeau,
Faict de la main de Raffy Lyonnois,
Lequel à peine ay eu pour un chevreau
Du bon pasteur Michau, que tu congnois.
   Jamays encor n'en sonnay qu'une foys,
Et si le garde aussi cher que la vie;
Si l'auras tu de bon cueur toutesfoys,
Faisant cela à quoy je te convie.
Col. Tu me requiers de ce dont j'ay envie:
Sus donc, mes vers, chantez chantz douloureux,   50
Puis que la mort a Loyse ravie,
Qui tant tenoit noz courtilz vigoureux.
   Or sommes nous maintenant malheureux,
Plus estonnez de sa mortelle absence
Que les aigneaulx à l'heure qu'entour eulx
Ne trouvent pas la mere qui les pense.
   Pleurons, bergers, Nature nous dispense:
Pleurons la mere au grand berger d'icy;
Pleurons la mere à Margot d'excellence,
Pleurons la mere à nous autres aussi.   60
   O grand pasteur, que tu as de soucy!
Ne sçay lequel, de toy ou de ta mere,
Me rend le plus de tristesse noircy;
Chantez, mes vers, chantez douleur amere.

When Louise in her thriving abode managed her excellent household with discretion, every shepherd, however rich a father he might be, chose a place for his daughter there. Sometimes Louise would see fit to have them all sit under a great elm and being in their midst, she would say to them: "Daughters, I must inform you on one point. It is not everything to have a charming figure, lands, flocks, a father rich and powerful; you must take care lest vice disfigure by long idleness the bloom of your life. Do not encourage indolence, for this is worse among young shepherdesses than among the sheep is that big ravening wolf which always comes at evening to these thickets. So then be alert to work; may God pardon good Roger: he always said that among good housewives indolence found no place." Thus spoke the mother of the great shepherd, and at her word the shepherd girls worked: one planted herbs in a garden; another tended pigeons and turtledoves; another worked new things with the needle; another then made garlands of flowers. But now

70

80

90

Lorsque Loyse en sa loge prospere
Son beau mesnage en bon sens conduisoit,
Chascun pasteur, tant fust il riche pere,
Lieu là dedans pour sa fille eslisoit.
 Aucunesfoys Loyse s'advisoit
Les faire seoir toutes soubz un grand orme,
Et, elle estant au milieu, leur disoit:
"Filles, il fault que d'un poinct vous informe.
 Ce n'est pas tout qu'avoir plaisante forme,
Bordes, troupeaulx, riche pere et puissant:
Il faut preveoir que vice ne difforme
Par long repos vostre age fleurissant.
 Oysiveté n'allez point nourrissant,
Car elle est pire entre jeunes bergeres
Qu'entre brebis ce grand loup ravissant
Qui vient au soir tousjours en ces fougeres.
 A travailler soyez doncques legeres;
Que Dieu pardoint au bon homme Roger:
Tousjours disoit que chez les mesnageres
Oysiveté ne trouvoit à loger."
 Ainsi disoit la mere au grand berger,
Et à son dict travailloient pastourelles:
L'une plantoit herbes en un verger,
L'autre paissoit colombz et tourterelles.
 L'autre à l'aiguille ouvroit choses nouvelles,
L'autre en après faisoit chappeaulx de fleurs.

70

80

90

the lovely ones do nothing more, but they only shed streams of tears and weep. They have changed their dances into lamentations, the blue to brown, the bright green to tan, and their lovely hues to vile colors.

Sing, my verses, sing sorrow decreed.

As soon as death had dealt this great blow, all the rustic pleasures were stilled; the little breezes then breathed no more, but the strong winds are still sighing thereat. Leaves and fruits blew from the trees; the bright sun gave no more warmth; the meadows stripped off their green mantle; the dark sky shed tears thereat. The great shepherd broke his pipe, desiring to concern himself only with weeping; whereat his flock that heard him lament left off grazing and took to bleating. And when Margot heard all revealed, her tender heart was not able to keep her eyes from dropping tears; so with her weeping she made a thousand weep. Then the earth became bare and feeble; many brooks went completely dry, the sea was

Or maintenant ne font plus rien les belles,
Sinon ruysseaux de larmes et de pleurs.
    Converty ont leurs danses en douleurs,
Le bleu en brun, le vert gay en tanné,
Et leurs beaulx tainctz en mauvaises couleurs.
Chantez, mes vers, chantez dueil ordonné.
    Dès que la mort ce grand coup eut donné,
Tous les plaisirs champestres s'assoupirent;
Les petis ventz alors n'ont allené,
Mais les forts ventz encores en souspirent.
    Fueilles et fruictz des arbres abbatirent;
Le cler soleil chaleur plus ne rendit;
Du manteau vert les prez se devestirent;
Le ciel obscur larmes en respandit.
    Le grand pasteur sa musette fendit,
Ne voulant plus que de pleurs se mesler,
Dont son trouppeau, qui plaindre l'entendit,
Laissa le paistre et se print a besler.
    Et quand Margot ouyt tout reveler,
Son gentil cueur ne fut assez habile
Pour garder l'oeil de larmes distiller,
Ains de ses pleurs en feit bien pleurer mille.
    Terre en ce temps devint nue et debile;
Plusieurs ruysseaux tous à sec demourerent;

disturbed and far from tranquil, and the young dolphins wept
thereat.   Hinds and stags stopped in bewilderment, beasts of prey
and beasts of the pasture, every animal grieved for Louise, excepting
the ill-natured wolves.   So grave indeed was the wound and this   120
disaster so full of unhappiness that the fair lily took on a black
hue, and the flocks wore black fleeces.   In the withered tree
Philomena complains, the swallow utters piteous and piercing cries,
the turtledove moans and shows like sorrow, and I am in accord
with their songs.   You free shepherds, treading on free grass, what
have you to say of this?   What sorrow, what distress is it to see   130
the blossoms of all our fields wither?

Sing, my verses, sing: "Farewell, all joy."

Nymphs and gods came by night in great distress to see her and
said to her: "Alas! dost thou sleep here, mistress of the shepherds,
or can it be that Death has placed thee in his toils?   Alas, the color

> La mer en fut troublée et mal tranquille,
> Et les Daulphins bien jeunes y pleurerent.
>   Biches et cerfz estonnez s'arresterent;
> Bestes de proye et bestes de pasture,
> Tous animaulx Loyse regretterent,
> Excepté loups de mauvaise nature.   120
>   Tant en effect griefve fut la poincture,
> Et de malheur l'advanture si pleine,
> Que le beau lys en print noire taincture,
> Et les troupeaux en portent noire laine.
>   Sur l'arbre sec s'en complainct Philomene;
> L'aronde en faict cris piteux et trenchans;
> La tourterelle en gemit et en meine
> Semblable dueil, et j'accorde à leurs chants.
>   O francs bergers sur franche herbe marchans,
> Qu'en dictes vous?   Quel dueil, quel ennuy est ce   130
> De voir secher la fleur de tous noz champs?
> Chantez, mes vers, chantez: "Adieu liesse."
>   Nymphes et dieux de nuict en grand' destresse
> La vindrent veoir, et luy dirent: "Helas!
> Dors tu icy, des bergers la maistresse,
> Ou si c'est Mort qui t'a mise en ses lacs?
>   Las! ta couleur (telle comme tu l'as)

that thou hast convinces us that thou art lying dead. Oh, churlish
140 Death, never did you meddle but to carry off that which is fine!
So much wisdom she held within her head; so well she knew to
love the fields of France; so well she knew to restore the roses to
the lily; so well she knew to sow good herbs; so well she knew to
maintain in safety all the cattle of all the region; so well she knew
to fence in and enclose her fold, that no one ever saw the wolves
enter there. So many times she displayed her wisdom against the
150 dark and rainy season, that France has not in a long while found
such a shepherdess in the report of its oldest men. Farewell,
Louise, farewell amid tears, farewell that body which adorns the
earth." Thus saying, nymphs and gods depart.

> *Sing, my verses, sing grief once more.*

There is naught here below that does not know of this death:
Cognac cuffs himself on his wan bosom; Romorantin recalls to
160 memory the loss; Anjou hangs his head; Angoulême does the

> Nous juge bien que morte tu reposes.
> Ha! Mort fascheuse! onques ne te meslas
> Que de ravir les excellentes choses!   **140**
>   Tant eust au chef de sagesses encloses,
> Tant bien sçavoit le clos de France aymer,
> Tant bien y sceut au lys rendre les roses,
> Tant bien y sceut bonnes herbes semer.
>   Tant bien sçavoit en seurté confermer
> Tout le bestail de toute la contrée;
> Tant bien sçavoit son parc clorre et fermer,
> Qu'on n'a point veu les loups y faire entrée.
>   Tant a de foys sa prudence monstrée
> Contre le temps obscur et pluvieux,   **150**
> Que France n'a (long temps a) rencontrée
> Telle bergere, au rapport des plus vieulx.
>   Adieu, Loyse, adieu en larmes d'yeulx;
> Adieu le corps qui la terre decore."
> En ce disant s'en vont nymphes et dieux.
> Chantez, mes vers, chantez douleur encore.
>   Rien n'est ça bas qui ceste mort ignore:
> Congnac s'en coingne en sa poictrine blesme;
> Romorantin la perte rememore;
> Anjou faict jou, Angoulesme est de mesme.   **160**

same; Amboise imbibes extreme bitterness; Maine gives voice to a lamenting sound; poor Touvre, watering Angoulême, has its bed all bereft of trout. And over its water day and night sing the white swans, with which it is all covered, foretelling in their song who does them harm, that Death through death holds his door open to them. What are you doing in this green forest, Fauns, Silvani? 170 I believe you are sleeping there! Awake, awake, to mourn for this loss, or if you sleep, dream of it as you sleep. Dream of Death, dream of the wrong it does; do not sleep without dreaming of that evil one; then on waking, relate to me all that you have dreamt, that I may sing of it.

Why is it that one sees the withering grass return to life when the summer comes, while the person who falls into the tomb, great though he be, nevermore returns? Ah, when the other day (I now 180 recall it) I heard the rook cry so loudly in an oak, "'Tis strange (I said then) if some disaster will not soon come on this kingdom."

> Amboyse en boyt une amertume extreme;
> Le Maine en mene un lamentable bruit;
> La povre Touvre, arrousant Angoulesme,
> A son pavé de truites tout destruict.
>   Et sur son eau chantent de jour et nuict
> Les cignes blancs, dont toute elle est couverte,
> Pronostiquans en leur chant qui leur nuit,
> Que Mort par mort leur tient sa porte ouverte.
>   Que faictes vous en ceste forest verte,
> Faunes, Sylvains? Je croy que dormez là!   170
> Veillez, veillez, pour plorer ceste perte,
> Ou, si dormez, en dormant songez la.
>   Songez la Mort, songez le tort qu'elle a:
> Ne dormez point sans songer la meschante;
> Puis au resveil comptez moy tout cela
> Qu'aurez songé, affin que je lo chante.
>   D'où vient cela qu'on veoit l'herbe sechante
> Retourner vive alors que l'esté vient,
> Et la personne au tumbeau trebuschante,
> Tant grande soit, jamais plus ne revient?   180
>   Ha! quand j'ouy l'autrehier (il me souvient)
> Si fort crier la corneille en un chesne,
> "C'est un grand cas (dy je lors) s'il n'advient
> Quelque meschef bien tost en cestuy regne."

So also the raven told me on an ash tree; so the star with the long tail told me; whereat I gave the rein to my sighs, for such sorrow I think I have never had.

Sing, my verses, fresh sorrow conceived.

190   No, rather, be silent; there has been enough lamenting. She has been received in the Elysian fields, beyond the labors of this distressful world. There where she is nothing has lost its bloom; never do the day and its pleasures die there; never dies the richly colored green, nor those with whom they live within that place. For every ambrosial fragrance flourishes there, and they have neither two nor three seasons, but only spring, and never do they mourn

200   for loss of friends, as we do. In those fair fields and natural mansions Louise lives, without fear, suffering or discomfort, and we below, full of human reasons, are grieved (it seems) at her joy. There she sees naught that can in any way displease her; there she eats fruit of inestimable price; there she drinks that which appeases

Autant m'en dit le corbeau sur un fresne;
Autant m'en dit l'estoille à la grand' queue;
Dont je laschay a mes souspirs la resne,
Car tel' douleur ne pense avoir onc eue.
    Chantez, mes vers, fresche douleur conceue.
Non, taisez vous, c'est assez deploré: 190
Elle est aux champs Elisiens receue,
Hors des travaulx de ce monde esploré.
    Là où elle est n'y a rien defloré;
Jamais le jour et les plaisirs n'y meurent;
Jamais n'y meurt le vert bien coloré,
Ne ceulx avec qui là dedans demeurent.
    Car toute odeur ambrosienne y fleurent,
Et n'ont jamais ne deux ne trois saisons,
Mais un printemps, et jamais ilz ne pleurent
Perte d'amys, ainsi que nous faisons.   200
    En ces beaulx champs et nayfves maisons
Loyse vit, sans peur, peine ou mesaise;
Et nous ça bas, pleins d'humaines raisons,
Sommes marrys (ce semble) de son aise.
    Là ne veoit rien qui en rien luy desplaise;
Là mange fruict d'inestimable prix;
Là boyt liqueur qui toute soif appaise;

every thirst; there she will know a thousand noble souls. Every
pleasant animal is found there, and a thousand birds give immortal   210
joy, and among them about the place flies her parrot, which departed
before her. There she beholds a radiance such that to behold it we
should wish to die. So then, since she has such eternal joy,

>   *Cease, my verses, cease to be distressed.*

Have no care for your mountains and pines; come to France, you
Nymphs of Savoy, to do honor to her who through her glory made   220
great her country and her path. She was of Savoy; well I knew it
and so do you. Come then, that before dying your eye may here
behold where she was placed after a happy end. Let each one bring
in her arms a basket filled with herbs and flowers from the place of
her birth, to scatter them upon her smooth marble tomb, the finest
that we have knowledge of. Bear bouquets that are full
blown: laurel, ivy, and glorious white lilies, green rosemary,   230
abundant roses, yellow marigold, and golden crowfoot, coxcombs

> Là congnoistra mille nobles esprits.
>> Tous animaulx playsans y sont compris,
> Et mille oyseaulx y font joye immortelle,   210
> Entre lesquelz vole par le pourpris
> Son papegay, qui partit avant elle.
>> Là elle veoit une lumiere telle
> Que pour la veoir mourir devrions vouloir.
> Puis qu'elle a donc tant de joye eternelle,
> Cessez, mes vers, cessez de vous douloir.
>> Mettez voz montz et pins en nonchaloir,
> Venez en France, ô Nymphes de Savoye,
> Pour faire honneur à celle qui valoir
> Feit par son loz son pays et sa voye.   220
>> Savoysienne estoit, bien le sçavoye,
> Si faictes vous; venez donques, affin
> Qu'avant mourir vostre oeil par deça voye
> Là où fut mise après heureuse fin.
>> Portez au bras chascune plein coffin
> D'herbes et fleurs du lieu de sa naissance,
> Pour les semer dessus son marbre fin,
> Le mieulx pourveu dont ayons congnoissance.
>> Portez rameaulx parvenuz à croissance:
> Laurier, lyerre et lys blancs honorez,   230
> Romarin vert, roses en abondance,
> Jaune soucie et bassinetz dorez,

colored purple, lovely lavender, carnations of bright hue, white hawthorns, blue hawthorns, and every flower of great natural beauty. Let each one be mindful to bring them; then throw them upon the tomb very thickly, and do not forget many olive branches, for she was the shepherdess of peace, one who knew to arrange perfect harmony between shepherds, at a time when over the world men tried to overcome one another with blows of the pruning knife, the sheephook, and the sling. Come, god Pan, come more quickly than the swallow; leave thy sheepfolds, abandoning Arcadia; cease to sing of fair-haired Syrinx; approach and put thyself in my place, to extol with better grace her with whom I am concerned: not, surely, that I am wearied of speaking of her, but thou art wrong not to grieve for her.

Now you, Thenot, who have begun to weep on hearing me speak of that very fine woman, hand over to me the promised pipe, to the end that I may sound it in conclusion and with its sound may offer

240

250

Passeveloux de pourpre colorez,
Lavende franche, oeilletz de couleur vive,
Aubepins blancs, aubepins azurez,
Et toutes fleurs de grand' beauté nayfve.
        Chascune soit d'en porter attentive,
Puis sur la tumbe en jectez bien espais,
Et n'oubliez force branches d'olive,
Car elle estoit la bergere de paix,   240
        Laquelle sceut dresser accords parfaicts
Entre bergers, alors que par le monde
Taschoient l'un l'autre à se rendre deffaicts,
A coup de goy, de houlette et de funde.
        Vien, le dieu Pan, vien plus tost que l'aronde
Pars de tes parcs, d'Arcadie desplace,
Cesse à chanter de Syringue la blonde,
Approche toy et te mets en ma place,
        Pour exalter avec meilleure grace
Celle de qui je me suis entremys: 250
Non (pour certain) que d'en parler me lasse,
Mais tu as tort que tu ne la gemys.
        Et toy, Thenot, qui à plourer t'es mys
En m'escoutant parler de la trèsbonne,
Delivre moy le chalumeau promys,
A celle fin qu'en concluant la sonne,
        Et que du son rende graces, et donne

thanks and give praise to the gods of the high mountains and the plains, so loudly that this valley may re-echo thereat.

Cease, my verses, cease here your lamentations.   260

Then. Free shepherd, how full are your verses of great sweetness and of great sadness! The song pleases me and you compel my heart to grieve more than is its wont. When all is said, Melpomene inspires your sweet style to sing with sadness. Besides, there is no heart (though it were the heart of an anvil) that this theme did not cause to sorrow. Therefore, Colin, without flattery or vain praise, you deserve not only the good flute, but one ought to present you a   270 wreath of green laurel for things so well said. Up, big bulls, and you, little sheep, go to your shelter, you have grazed enough; besides, the sun is sinking into these low borders, and the night is coming on the other side.

<blockquote>
Louenge aux dieux des haults montz et des plains,
Si haultement que ce val en resonne:
Cessez, mes vers, cessez icy voz plaincts.   260
The. O franc pasteur, combien tes vers sont pleins
De grand' doulceur et de grand' amertume!
Le chant me plaist, et mon cueur tu contrains
A se douloir plus qu'il n'a de coustume.
    Quand tout est dict, Melpomené allume
Ton stile doulx à tristement chanter;
Oultre il n'est cueur (et fust ce un cueur d'enclume)
Que ce propos ne feit bien lamenter.
    Parquoy (Colin) sans flater ne venter,
Non seulement le bon flageol merites,   270
Ains devroit on chapeau te presenter
De vert laurier, pour choses tant bien dictes.
    Sus, grans toreaux, et vous, brebis petites,
Allez au tect, assez avez brousté;
Puis le soleil tombe en ces bas limites,
Et la nuict vient devers l'autre costé.
</blockquote>

BAIF

Maidens who love the verdant banks and the coolness of the shadows near the sound of the waters, you who do not disdain, fair-eyed Nymphs, our rustic songs in these rustic places, aid my rustic voice. I desire to sing to Brinon a song which his Sidere may some time deign to read, a song of my Brinon that one day his Sidere may not read without heaving a sigh of love. No one, Nymphs, follows you more reverently than he worshiped the steps of your sacred dance. It is for him, Naiads, that I wish to pray you. Would you deny your gifts to Brinon? Maidens, begin: (so may the mad band of goatish satyrs not violate your flower; if you dance, may they not disturb your sport, and if you rest, may they not take you by surprise). Maidens, begin. Wherever you touch, maidens, wherever you place your hands all things are lovely. Sing with me. Let us recall the love of melancholy Brinon in this

ECLOGUE 2

BRINON

Pvcelles, qui aimez les verdoyans riuages,
Et pres du bruit des eaus la fraicheur des ombrages,
Vous qui ne dedaignez, ô Nymphes aux beaux yeux,
Nos champestres chansons par ces champestres lieux:
Aidez ma voix champestre. A Brinon je veu dire
Vn chant que sa Sidere vne fois daigne lire,
Vn chant de mon Brinon, que sa Sidere vn jour
Ne lise sans jetter quelque soupir d'amour.
Nul, Nymphes, ne vous suit en plus grand'reuerence
Qu'il adoroit les pas de vostre sainte dance:
C'est pour luy que ie veu, Naiades, vous prier:
Voudriez vous à Brinon vos presans dénïer?
Pucelles, commencez; (ainsi la bande fole
Des Satyres bouquins vostre fleur ne viole:
Si vous dancez, ainsi ne trouble vos ébas,
Et si vous reposez, ne vous surprenne pas).
Pucelles, commencez; où vous touchez, pucelles,
Où vous mettez la main toutes choses sont belles:
Chantez auecques moy: de Brinon langoureux
Recordon les amours en ce chant amoureux,

amorous song. Meanwhile in these thickets my flat-nosed goats will feed on the sprouts of the young branches. I sing to no deaf ears. This vale and this wood already are holding themselves prepared to reply to my voice.

Nymphs, what distant mountain, what shady forest, what river, what cliff, what hollow cave kept you when Brinon, utterly distraught with love, stretched on the grass, sobbed out his soul? Was it the laurels with which Helicon is green, or the water which gently 30
billows in fair Permessus, or the beloved grotto of the Aonian cliff or the horned summit of the Parnassian mount? For then you were not on the banks of the Seine, where the lover, pining with the distress of love, lay piteously and kindled pity in every thing, save the heart of her whom he loved. Even the junipers and even the thorn bushes wept for his misfortune. The silvery waves, which before flowed clear in the streams, swelled with their tears and 40
troubled their waters.

All run up from the fields: the cattle, astonished at seeing themselves without their master, surround him in utter sadness.

> Tandis par ces halliers mes cheures camusettes
> Brouteront les jettons des branches nouuelletes.
> Ie ne chante à des sourds. Ce valon & ce bois
> Desia se tiennent prests pour respondre à ma voix.
>   Nymphes, quel mont lointain, quelle forest ombreuse,
> Quel fleuue, quel rocher, quelle cauerne creuse
> Vous detint, quand Brinon d'amour tout éperdu
> Son ame sanglotoit dessus l'herbe étendu?
> Estoyent ce les loriers dont Helicon verdoye,
> Ou l'eau qui doucement au beau Permesse ondoye,   30
> Ou l'antre desiré du roc Aonien,
> Ou le sommet cornu du mont Parnassien?
> Car vous n'estiez alors sur les riues de Seine,
> Où l'amant languissant de l'amoureuse peine
> Couché piteusement, toute chose allumoit
> De pitié, fors le coeur de celle qu'il aimoit.
> Mesmes les Geneuriers, & mesmes les Espines
> Plourerent son malheur: les ondes argentines,
> Qui nettes parauant couloyent par les ruisseaux,
> Et crurent de leurs pleurs, & troublerent leurs eaus.   40
> Tout y acourt des chams: le bestail, qui s'étonne
> De se voir sans pasteur, tout triste l'enuironne.

Shepherds and shepherd boys were not lacking there, these with plodding pace, those with swift step, coming from all around. And each asked of him: "Whence, Brinon, does this great weakness come on you?" Louiset runs up, still quite wet from having watched all night against wolves, Louiset, the shepherd, who fash-

50 ioned the excellent nature of Brinon with excellent nourishment, training his childhood. If only his great knowledge had had some power against the fire of love!

All the gods who take care of and guard over the fields come from every side. Mercury does not delay, but flies there first of all, with head winged and heels winged. "Whence comes this mischance upon you?" said he. "With what distress, with what ailment, wretched Brinon, is your soul bewildered? What has become of your games when you bestowed the prize upon him that

60 sang best among those of good skill?" Faunus did not fail to come, tossing on his head a nodding crest of great silvery lilies and of flowering broom. Pales came on a sudden with pouch at side and sheep-hook in her hand. Pomona also came: a wreath of fruit cast a

Bergers & Pastoureaux là ne faillirent pas,
Ceux cy d'vn train pesant, ceux là d'vn viste pas,
Venans des enuirons: & chacun luy demande:
"Mais d'où te vient, Brinon, ceste langueur si grande?"
Louïset y acourt encores tout mouïllé
D'auoir contre les loups toute la nuit veillé,
Louïset le berger qui la bonne nature
De Brinon façonna de bonne norriture,   50
Son enfance instruisant: Si tout le grand sçauoir
Contre le feu d'Amour eust eu quelque pouuoir.
    Tous les Dieux qui des chams ont le soin & la garde
Viennent de toutes pars: Mercure point ne tarde,
Mais tout premier y volle, ayant aislé son chef,
Et ses talons aislez: "Doù te vient ce meschef?
(Dit-il) de quel ennuy, de quelle maladie,
Miserable Brinon, as-tu l'ame étourdie?
Où sont perdus tes jeux quand tu pendois le pris
A qui chantoit le mieux d'entre les bons espris?"   60
Faune n'y faillit pas, secouant sur la teste
De grans Lis argentez vne branlante creste
Et de Genests fleuris. Palês y vint soudain
La panetiere au flanc, la houlette en la main.
Aussi Pomone y vint: vn chapeau de fruitage

pleasant shadow over her brow. There, crowned with laurel, was pastoral Apollo, the good healing God, who would have cured his illness, if the illness that he had could have been healed either with enchantments or with the juice of roots. But he who formerly could **70** not even heal himself near Amphrysus, he, a god, wished to die. Pan came from Maenalus. A garland of pine covers his hair and encircles his brow. The skin of a lynx was stretched over his back; his flute of seven pipes hung from his neck. Pan came from Maenalus and we saw his cheek all stained with mulberries and he made the grimace which he customarily makes since the time when he sounded the first reeds which Pallas gave him. "Who, **80** Brinon," said he, "drives you to such madness? Where are all your flocks, where is their pasture? Knowing that you have utterly abandoned your care of them, most of them have strayed far away without a guide. Will you not give pause to your tears and sobs? Why, will you not henceforth do anything other than weep and pine? Love at all this, Love, fierce Love, has no concern. We do

Luy tendoit sur le front vn gracieux ombrage.
Là couuert de Lorier Apollon pastoral,
Le bon Dieu medecin, qui eust gueri son mal,
Si le mal qu'il auoit eust receu medecine,
Ou par enchantements, ou par just de racine: **70**
Mais luy-mesme jadis qui ne s'en put guerir
Pres d'Amphryse, luy Dieu souhetta de mourir.
Pan de Menale y vint: de Pin vne couronne
Affuble ses cheueux, & son front enuironne:
La peau d'vn Louceruier sur son dos s'estandoit,
Sa fluste à sept tuyaux de son col luy pendoit:
Pan de Menale y vint: & nous vîmes sa jouë
De Meures toute peinte, & si faisoit la mouë
Qu'il fait accoustumé depuis qu'il entonna
Les premiers chalumeaux que Pallas luy donna. **80**
   "Qui te pousse, Brinon (dit-il), en telle rage?
Où sont tous tes troupeaux? où est leur pasturage?
Sçachans que tu en as du tout quitté le soin,
Sans guide la plus part sont escartez au loin.
A tes pleurs & sanglots ne veux tu mettre pose?
Et quoy? ne feras-tu desormais autre chose
Que de pleindre & languir? Amour de tout cecy,
Amour, le fier Amour, ne prend aucun soucy.

90 not see the goats ever sated with leaves, nor the greedy bees with fragrant thyme, nor the flowers with sweet dew in the month of May; nor is cruel Love ever sated with tears. Sidere, while you languish for her, Sidere, the object of your love, wherever her pleasure calls her, caring little for you, runs over the clear waters, through the flowery meadows, under the cool trees."

"Alas, what shall I do? alas," said Brinon, regaining his breath with much difficulty amid dismal sobs, "Ah, cruel Sidere! Ah,
100 Sidere with heart of iron, that are pleased to see me in so cruel a hell! Ah, what shall I do, alas? I am minded, becoming a hunter, to run in the chase so that my suffering may pass away. I am minded, suddenly rushing into the woods, with horn at neck, to excite the barking of the dogs stirred against the springing beast. It seems to me already, I imagine in my thoughts that through stones, through thickets, spear in hand I am piercing the wild boars.
110 There is no mountain so stony, no grove so dense, no river so deep,

On ne voit point souler ny les cheures de fueilles,
Ny de Thym odorant les auares Abeilles,   90
Ny de douce rosee au mois de May les fleurs,
Ny le cruel Amour ne se soule de pleurs.
Sidere, cepandant que tu languis pour elle,
Sidere, ton soucy, où son plaisir l'appelle,
Peu soigneuse de toy, court sus les claires eaux
Par les prez bien-fleuris sous les frais arbrisseaux."
      "Las! que feray-ie, helas! (dit Brinon, à grand'peine
Parmy tristes sanglots recouurant son aleine)
Ha, Sidere cruelle! Ha, Sidere de fer,
Qui te plaist de me voir en ce cruel enfer!   100
Las, que feray-ie, helas! il me plaist à la chasse
Fait veneur, courir tant que ma douleur s'en passe:
Il me plaist tout soudain brossant dedans les bois,
Ayant la trompe au col, animer les abbois
Des chiens bien ameutez sur la beste élancee.
Il me semble deja, ie fein en ma pensee
Qu'à trauers les cailloux, atrauers les halliers
L'épieu dedans le poing i'enferre les Sangliers:
Il n'est mont si pierreux ny si tofu bocage,
Ny fleuue si profond, ny si facheux passage,   110

no passage so difficult, that I cannot nimbly pass through. Alas, as though Love could by these labors be some day softened! As though because of the suffering that a man may take, Love, that cruel god, could become more gentle! Alas, what then shall I do? Far away beyond the sea, right far away I desire to go to wear away my life. I desire to go right far away to some barbarous land, that no greedy mariner has ever approached. In that desolate land, at least removed from everything, I will weep for my misfortune in greater freedom. Shall I go to that land beneath the frozen north wind where the earth is always whitened with snow, where the icy Ocean can support chariots upon his broad back without bending under the weight? Shall I go to those sands, where the parched plains extend remotely far beneath the torrid sun of the south, where the black Ethiopians protect themselves against the nearby sun by digging subterranean dwellings? What shall I say in my misfortune? However far I may travel, Love will not leave me. Everywhere, even amid the ice of the North and the extreme heat of the South, wherever I go, my misfortune will follow me.

       120

       130

> Que dispos ie ne passe: Helas, quasi qu'Amour
> Se peust par ces trauaux adoucir quelque iour!
> Quasi que pour le mal qu'vn homme sçache prendre
> Amour, ce dieu cruel, plus doux se puisse rendre!
> Las, que feray-ie donc? Bien loin outre la mer
> Ie veux aller bien loin mon âge consumer:
> Ie veux aller bien loin en vn païs barbare,
> Où iamais n'aborda nul nautonnier auare:
> En ce païs desert pour le moins écarté,
> Ie pleindray mon malheur en plus grand' liberté.
>   Sous la Bize gelee en ce païs iray-je
> Où la terre est tousiours blanchissante de neige?
> Où l'Ocean glacé dessus son large dos
> Sans flechir sous le faix soustient les charïots?
> M'en iray-je aux sablons, où les plaines bruslees
> Loin sous le chaud Midy s'estendent reculees?
> Où du Soleil voisin les Ethiopes noirs
> Se deffendent, creusans des souterrains manoirs?
> Que dy-je, malheureux? Pour chemin que je face
> Amour ne me lairra: par tout, & dans la glace
> Du Nort, & du Midy dans l'extreme chaleur,
> Par tout où que j'iray me suiura mon malheur.

       120

       130

One can well flee the heat, one can well flee the cold, one can change one's land; but Love, ever harsh, Love follows us everywhere. Everything bows and bends low beneath Love. Against Love we shall win no victory. After so much misfortune I may await one blessing. Meanwhile with my loves let us carve these oak trees upon their tender bark. They will grow each day; each day you, my loves, shall grow with them."

140

Goddesses, it is enough. Here your poet alone sang these verses, while on the grass under this leafy oak he wove a basket of osier twigs to give to his beloved. Muses, make my rime agreeable to Francine, just as her beauties make her lovable to me together with her virtues, since her sweet love grows from day to day within my heart as much as the young poplar planted beneath the running water in the new season increases visibly. Let us rise; it is night, my little flock, now refreshed. The sun has set; up, return to your shelter.

150

On fuit bien la chaleur, on fuit bien la froidure,
On change de païs: mais Amour tousiours dure,
Amour nous suit par tout. Tout ploye & se met bas
Sous Amour: contre Amour nous ne gagnerons pas.
Apres tant de malheur vn bien il faut attendre:
Tandis de mes Amours sus leur escorce tendre
Grauon ces Chesneteaux: ils croistront tous les iours,
Tous les iours auec eux vous croistrez mes amours."   140
    Deesses, il suffist: icy vostre Poëte
Seul a chanté ces vers, tandis que sus l'herbette
Sous ce Chesne fueillu de vergettes d'osier
Pour donner à s'amie il laçoit vn pannier.
Muses, faites ma rime à Francine agreable,
Autant que ses beautez me la rendent aimable
Auecques ses vertus, puisque sa douce amour
Autant dedans mon coeur s'accroist de jour en jour,
Que le jeune Peuplier planté sus l'eau courante
En la saison nouuelle à vuë d'oeil augmente.   150
    Leuon-nous, il est nuit, petit troupeau refet,
Le Soleil est couché, sus retournez au tet.

RONSARD

ECLOGUE 1
ANGELOT

When good Henriot through cruel destiny ended his journey before the coming of night, our flocks, foreseeing some future danger, pined in the fields without drinking or eating; and bleating and crying and cowering to the earth, they lay as though struck by the clap of thunder. All things here below wept in distress. The sun beclouded himself in order not to behold this death, and with rusty crape hid his fair head, detesting the earth so fruitful of evil.

The Nymphs lamented him with piteous voice, the caves wept for him, the rocks and the woods. You know it, forests, who in the groves saw even the wolves and the savage lions mourning for him. This was the Henriot who, filled with prosperity, restored to honor the worship of the banished gods, and while showing himself the perfect exemplar of the arts, raised military glory to the sky.

10

ECLOGUE 1
ANGELOT

Quand le bon Henriot par fiere destinée
Auant la nuict venuë accomplist sa iournée,
Nos troupeaux preuoyans quelque futur danger
Languissoient par les champs sans boire ny manger:
Et beslans & crians & tapis contre terre
Cisoient comme frappez de l'esclat du tonnerre.
Toutes choses ça bas pleuroient en desconfort:
Le Soleil s'en-nua pour ne voir telle mort,
Et d'vn crespe rouillé cacha sa teste blonde,
Abominant la terre en vices si feconde.
    Les Nymphes l'ont gemy d'vne piteuse vois,
Les Antres l'ont pleuré, les rochers & les bois:
Vous le sçauez, forests, qui vistes és bocages
Les loups mesme le plaindre, & les Lions sauuages.
    Ce fut ce Henriot qui remply de bon-heur
Remist des Dieux banis le seruice en honneur,
Et se monstrant des arts le parfait exemplaire,
Esleua iusqu'au ciel la gloire militaire.

10

20   Even as the vine is the glory of an elm, and the glory of the vine is the new grape, and the glory of the flocks is the he-goat which leads them, and as the ears of grain are the glory of the field, and as the ripe fruits are the glory of the orchards, so was Henriot the glory of the shepherds.

How many times since his cruel death has our plowshare split the fields with yearly toil, but instead of good grain ears, they have produced only darnel, corn cockles, and useless poppies!

30   The grasses at his death lost their greenness, the roses and the lilies took on a black hue, the fair marguerite assumed a sad color, and the carnation inscribed its woe upon its leaf.

Shepherds, in his honor strew the ground with flowers, shade the streams with vine branches and ivy, and of grassy turf, green in every season, build his tomb and engrave thereon these verses: "The soul that in virtue never had its equal left its cloak here in going to its repose: oaks, spread shade over the royal tomb, and,

40   Manna, fall from heaven upon his bones."

> Tout ainsi que la vigne est l'honneur d'vn ormeau,
> Et l'honneur de la vigne est le raisin nouueau,   20
> Et l'honneur des troupeaux est le Bouc qui les meine,
> Et comme les espics sont l'honneur de la plaine,
> Et comme les fruicts meurs sont l'honneur des vergers,
> Ainsi ce Henriot fust l'honneur des Bergers.
>   Quantesfois nostre soc depuis sa mort cruelle
> A fendu les guerets d'vne peine annuelle!
> Qui n'ont rendu sinon en lieu de bons espics
> Qu' Yuraie, qu'Aubifoin, que Ponceaux inutils!
>   Les herbes par sa mort perdirent leur verdure,
> Les roses & les lis prindrent noire teinture,   30
> La belle Marguerite en prist triste couleur,
> Et l'oeillet sur sa fueille escriuit son malheur.
>   Pasteurs, en sa faueur semez de fleurs la terre,
> Ombragez les ruisseaux de pampres & de lierre
> Et de gazons herbus en toute saison verts
> Dressez luy son sepulcre & y grauez ces vers:
>
> "L'ame qui n'eut iamais en vertu son egale,
> Icy laissa son voile allant à son repos:
> Chesnes faites ombrage à la tombe Royale,
> Et vous Manne du ciel tombez dessus ses os."   40

Shepherd Henriot, instead of living on an earth full of fear, of deceit and of war, thou livest up yonder in Heaven, where better than before thou beholdest beneath thy feet the stars and the wind, thou beholdest beneath thy feet the stars and the clouds, thou beholdest the air and the sea and the known lands, like a perfect Angel released from care and from the mortal burden which torments us here.

Fair royal spirit, most exalted in Heaven, that dost scorn us and   50
our thoughts and those worldly attractions which ever after a brief pleasure make us feel a very long repentance. Even as a fair Sun amid the fair souls, surrounded by lightnings, rays, and flames, thou art radiant in Heaven and far from every fear, now an Angel, thou dost laugh at this deceitful world.

Where thou art, the springtime never loses its verdure, storms do not exist there, nor heat nor cold, but a pure and clear air, and the sun at evening does not, as here, allow himself to sink into the sea.   60

<blockquote>

O Berger Henriot, en lieu de viure en terre
Toute pleine de peur, de fraudes & de guerre,
Tu vis là haut au Ciel, où mieux que parauant
Tu vois dessous tes pieds les astres & le vent,
Tu vois dessous tes pieds les astres & les nues,
Tu vois l'air & la mer & les terres cognues,
Comme vn Ange parfait deslié du soucy
Et du fardeau mortel qui nous tourmente icy.

O belle ame royale au Ciel la plus haussée,
Qui te mocques de nous & de nostre pensée,   50
Et des appas mondains qui tousiours font sentir
Apres vn court plaisir vn tres-long repentir.

Ainsi qu'vn beau Soleil entre les belles ames
Enuironné d'esclairs, de rayons & de flames
Tu reluis dans le Ciel, & loin de toute peur
Fait Ange, tu te ris de ce monde trompeur.

Où tu es, le Printemps ne perd point sa verdure,
L'orage n'y est point, le chaud ny la froidure,
Mais vn air pur & net, & le Soleil au soir
Comme icy ne se laisse en la marine choir.   60

</blockquote>

Thou beholdest other forests, thou beholdest other shores, other higher rocks, other greener groves, other grassier meadows, and thou pasturest thy flock with other fairer flowers that never die.

Therefore our forests, our grasses and our plains, our brooks and our meadows, our flowers and our fountains, recalling thee, murmur in every place that good Henriot is now a God.

70 Be propitious to our vows. I will build thee a fair temple of ivory and of marble on the bank of the Loire, where in the month of April, when the days are long and new, I will have contests between the shepherd boys, in leaping, in wrestling on the fresh grass, while there hangs on the nearest pine the prize of a pipe.

There shall be thy Janot, who shall sing thy deeds, thy wars, thy battles, thy enemies defeated, and all that thy hand of invincible power dared, in order to raise up again the sheephook of France.

80 Now farewell, great Shepherd. As long as men shall see the waters maintain the fish and the wind the birds, we shall love thy name, and through this green bower, from age to following age thy renown shall live.

> Tu vois autres forests, tu vois autres riuages,
> Autres plus hauts rochers, autres plus verds bocages,
> Autres prez plus herbus, & ton troupeau tu pais
> D'autres plus belles fleurs qui ne meurent iamais.
>
> Et pource nos forests, nos herbes & nos plaines,
> Nos ruisseaux & nos prez, nos fleurs & nos fontaines
> Se souuenant de toy, murmurent en tout lieu
> Que le bon Henriot est maintenant vn Dieu.
>
> Sois propice à nos voeux: ie te feray d'yuoire
> Et de marbre vn beau temple au riuage de Loire   70
> Où sur le mois d'Auril aux iours longs & nouueaux
> Ie feray des combats entre les Pastoureaux
> A sauter, à luter sur l'herbe nouuellete,
> Pendant au prochain Pin le prix d'vne musette.
>
> Là sera ton Ianot qui chantera tes faits,
> Tes guerres, tes combats, tes ennemis desfaits,
> Et tout se que ta main d'inuincible puissance
> Oza pour redresser la houlette de France.
>
> Or adieu grand Berger: tant qu'on verra les eaux
> Soustenir les poissons, & le vent les oiseaux,   80
> Nous aimerons ton nom, & par ceste ramée
> D'âge en âge suiuant viura ta renommée.

Every year in thy name we shall build altars, green with turf, and as to the Aegipans, the Fauns, and the Satyrs, we shall bear sacrifice to thee. Thy Perrot shall first sing the service in a long white robe and crowned with cypress, and with the sound of the horn we will make known thy honors to the forests, that thy praise, repeated every year, may not change through the years, proving **90** stronger than death, flourishing at all times in these great forests as flowers in the springtime.

> Nous ferons en ton nom des autels tous les ans
> Verds de gazons de terre, & comme aux Egipans,
> Aux Faunes, aux Satyrs, te ferons sacrifice:
> Ton Perrot le premier chantera le seruice
> En long sourpelis blanc, couronné de cyprés,
> Et au son du cornet nous ferons aux forests
> Apprendre tes honneurs, afin que ta loüange
> Redite tous les ans, par les ans ne se change, **90**
> Plus forte que la mort, fleurissante en tout temps
> Par ces grandes forests comme fleurs au Printemps.

ADONIS

Fictes, who are not unappreciative of the children of the Muse, if your public charge does not occupy you with your labors, come read of the joy and the misfortune of Venus, for a pleasure is ever mixed with pain.

Love, desiring one day to take revenge on his mother, selected from his quiver his bitterest arrow; then shooting it at her, he buried it in her heart, and fastened in her heart the love of Adonis, Adonis, both shepherd and huntsman in one, who in his perfect **10**

ADONIS.

> Fictes, qui n'es point feint aux enfans de la Muse,
> Si ta charge publique au trauail ne t'amuse,
> Vien lire de Venus le bien & le malheur:
> Car tousiours vn plaisir est meslé de douleur.
> Amour voulant vn iour se venger de sa mere,
> Esleut de son carquois la fleche plus amere:
> Puis la tirant contre elle, au coeur la luy cacha,
> Et l'amour d'Adonis au coeur luy attacha.
> Adonis & berger & chasseur tout ensemble,
> Qui en beauté parfaite aux Images resemble: **10**

beauty resembles the statues. His lovely eyes sparkled like a brilliant star, that Tethys has long concealed within her robe; then bringing forth from the wave a living spark, she adorns all the sky with a new brilliance. A slight, downy beard covered his chin, thin, fine, curly, blonder than the velvet which grows on quinces, or the fine silk that in the springtime covers a caterpillar's back.

20 His lips rivaled the roses, which one sees in a garden opening wide at the rise of morn, and which a young maiden gathers in her lap before their lovely hue is faded by the heat. In brief, this young shepherd is quite young and quite beautiful; he seems a flowery meadow which the new spring and the sweet dew nourish in verdure, where flowers expand in a thousand hues. Indeed, it is Love himself! Venus could not have chosen a lover more lovable on whom to set her desire.

30 This fair goddess in frenzied love is concerned no more for herself nor for anything at all; she scorns Heaven and the honors of the gods; her bouquets, arranged with skillful art, are held in scorn, and such great love overwhelms her that she has lost her

Ses beaux yeux rayonnoyent comme un Astre estoilë
Que Tethys en sa robe a long temps recelé,
Puis tirant hors de l'onde vne viue etincelle,
Embellist tout le Ciel d'vne clairté nouuelle.
    Vn petit poil follet luy couuroit le menton,
Gresle, prime, frisé, plus blond que le cotton
Qui croist desur les coings, ou la soye subtile
Qui couure au renouueau le dos d'vne chenille:
Ses léures combattoyent les roses, qu'au iardin
On voit espanouyr au leuer du matin,   20
Qu'vne ieune pucelle en son giron amasse
Auant que leur beau teint par le chaud ne s'efface.
Bref ce ieune Pasteur est tout ieune & tout beau,
Il semble vn pré fleury que le Printemps nouueau
Et la douce rosée en sa verdeur nourrissent,
Où de mille couleurs les fleurs s'espanouïssent:
C'est luy-mesmes Amour! Venus n'eust sceu choisir
Vn amant plus aimable à mettre son desir.
    Ceste belle Déesse en amour furieuse,
De soy-mesme n'est plus ny de rien soucieuse,   30
Le Ciel elle mesprise, & les honneurs des Dieux:
Ses bouquets agencez d'vn art ingenieux
Luy viennent à mespris, & tant Amour la donte

care for Eryx and for Amathus.   Her swans, her doves, who were
wont to bear her to the venerable throne on which Jupiter sits, far
from her feed on the grass and filled with sadness lament in piteous
song their mistress, whom a shepherd, a child, torments without
rest, and with the shaft of love poisons her bones.   She thinks of   40
naught but of that fair mouth, of his eyes in which the Archer
prepares to do her battle, of his fair golden hair; and pining with
distress forgets herself and thinks only of him, of him who holds
the key to her sweet thought and makes her joyous or angry at his
will.   Never does she leave him, whether the sun spurring his
steeds issues from his bed, or at hottest noon, or at the hour when
he guides his car into the Ocean and lets down its reins.   50

At break of day they are inside a hut; inside a cave they tarry
at noon; in the evening they lie in the pleasant shade of an acorn-
bearing oak or of a mossy bank, stretched out upon the grass, where
in a hundred thousand ways the mother of the Loves practices her

>   Qu'elle a perdu le soin d'Eryce & d'Amathonte:
>   Ses Cygnes, ses Pigeons qui souloyent la porter
>   Au throne venerable où se sied Iupiter,
>   Loin d'elle paissent l'herbe, & remplis de tristesse,
>   D'vn pitoyable chant lamentent leur maistresse,
>   Qu'vn Pasteur, qu'vn enfant tourmente sans repos,
>   Et du trait amoureux enuenime ses os.   40
>   Elle ne pense en rien qu'en ceste belle bouche,
>   Qu'en ses yeux où l'Archer luy dresse l'escarmouche,
>   Qu'en ses beaux cheueux d'or, & languissant d'ennuy
>   Soy-mesme s'oubliant ne pense plus qu'en luy,
>   Qu'en luy qui tient la clef de sa douce pensée,
>   Et la rend comme il veut ioyeuse & courroucée:
>   Iamais ne l'abandonne, ou soit que le Soleil
>   En piquant ses cheuaux sorte de son resueil,
>   Soit au plus chaud midi, soit à l'heure qu'il guide
>   Son char en l'Ocean, & luy baisse la bride.   50
>   Dedans vne Cabane ils sont au poinct du iour,
>   Ils font dedans vn antre à midi leur seiour,
>   Au soir ils sont couchez sous le plaisant ombrage
>   Ou d'vn chesne glandeux, ou d'vn moussu riuage,
>   Estendus dessus l'herbe, où en cent mille tours
>   La mere des Amours exerce ses amours.

loves. In a hundred thousand ways she embraces him and kisses him over and over. Feeling in his soul a like spark, he sounds his pipe and to please her does not cease to sing of their delightful passions. As she hears him she keeps changing her expression; at times on her back she reclines languidly in his lap, and at times looks at him and often with a kiss interrupts his songs which are lost in the wind.

She knows his dogs, names them and calls them; she bears his horn at her neck, a new huntress, the stout javelin in her hand, and with snares and stretched nets she encircles the mid-part of the forests. She knows the names of his cattle and of the ram who in place of the shepherd leads the sheep to pasture on the plain, bravely preceding the flock with great strides, like a colonel advancing before his troops.

Exceedingly happy child! So fair Cytherea, the mother of the Loves, desires to please you alone! All alone with you she desires to shear the sheep and with her white hand to press their udders, and while kissing you to lead the cattle to pasture, to fashion

En cent mille façons l'embrasse & le rebaise:
Luy qui sent en son ame vne pareille braise,
Entonne sa Musette, & pour la contenter,
Leurs plaisantes ardeurs ne cesse de chanter.
  Elle tient en l'oyant contenance diuerse,
Tantost en son giron languist à la renuerse,
Et tantost le regarde, & d'vn baiser souuent
Entre-rompt ses chansons qui se perdent au vent.
  Elle cognoist ses chiens, les nomme & les appelle:
Porte la trompe au col, chasseresse nouuelle,
En main le fort espieu, & encerne de rets
Et de filets tendus le milieu des forests:
Sçait le nom de ses boeufs, & du belier qui meine
Paistre en lieu du berger les brebis en la plaine,
Deuançant brauement le troupeau d'vn grand pas,
Ainsi qu'vn Colonnel deuance ses soldas.
  O bien-heureux enfant! donc la belle Cythere,
La mere des Amours à toy seul veut complaire!
Seulette auecques toy veut tondre les brebis,
Et de sa blanche main leur pressurer le Pis:
Et te baisant mener les boeufs en pasturage,

baskets and make cheese, and at evening to carry back cuddled in
her lap a lamb which its mother had left in the fields. If she 80
can but always keep her mouth upon your lips, she does not fear
the odor of your vile-smelling goats, and hanging on your neck,
she does not refuse to pass the night on the bare ground at your
side, on the soft carpet of the dewy grass, embracing you in the
midst of your bleating sheep and of your great bulls that until
break of day make love to the heifers even as you do to her.

The god Mars meanwhile is consumed with vexation; he calls
himself wretched and would wish to see himself a mortal man in 90
order to die of grief. He is in despair that a hunter of the woodland should be preferred to him. Jealous and maddened he clasps
his great shield, shaking in his spite the mountains of Thrace; his
heart filled with anger and his eyes with moisture could not endure
a shepherd as rival.

Now one day Adonis was returning from the chase, panting
and exhausted from tracking down a great stag; he had cut the
sinew of its right ham and victorious was bringing home the head 100

Esclisser des paniers, & faire du froumage,
Et rapporter au soir en son giron troussé
Vn Aigneau que sa mere aux champs auoit laissé. 80
    Pourueu qu'elle ait tousiours sa bouche sur tes léures,
Elle ne craint l'odeur de tes puantes Chéures:
Et pendue à ton col, ne veut point refuser
La nuict desur la dure à tes flancs reposer,
Desur le mol tapis des herbes rousoyantes,
T'embrassant au milieu de tes brebis bellantes,
Et de tes grans taureaux qui iusqu'au poinct du iour
Font (comme tu luy fais) aux genices l'amour.
    Le Dieu Mars ce-pendant de regret se consomme,
S'appelle miserable, & se voudroit voir homme 90
Pour mourir de douleur: il est desesperé,
Qu'vn Veneur bocager soit à luy preferé!
    Ialoux & furieux sa grande targe embrasse:
De sa pique esbranlant les montaignes de Thrace,
Son coeur plein de colere, & ses yeux de moiteur,
Ne pouuoyent endurer pour riual vn pasteur.
    Or vn iour Adonis retournoit de la chasse
Pantois & las de suiure vn grand Cerf à la trace,
Auquel du iarret dextre auoit coupé le nerf,
Et veinqueur rapportoit la teste du grand Cerf. 100

of the great stag. "Beloved," said Venus, "if by chance in the woods you encounter a beast that is armed by nature, whether with claws or with teeth, I beg you, do not follow it, out of fear that your valor may bring me distress. Hunt nimble deer, kids, and goats, and the frightened hearts of conies and of hares. Leave in peace wild boars, tigers, and bears, and do not attack lions either with nets or in pursuit. Trust me, my dear, the other kind of hunt is better. Against the bold boldness is not safe. If you should die, alas, I should die of sorrow. For I could not, alas, live after your death." Thus said Venus, but the soft breaths of the wind carried away her words without avail.

It was the dead of night and weary men had their eyes pressed on the soft feather pillows closed in sleep, which the low river of Styx distils upon our eyelids. Already the stars of heaven were in mid-circuit; the heavenly Cowherd who revolves about the Bear was sinking; all that lives in the waves, that lives by the rocks, in the deep forests, fishes, snakes, lions troubled with toil, now forgetting

110

120

> "Ami (disoit Venus) si tu cours d'auenture
> Vne beste aux forests qui s'arme de nature,
> Soit d'ongles soit de dents, ie te pri' ne la suy,
> De peur que ta valeur ne cause mon ennuy:
> Chasse les Daims legers, les Cheureux & les Chéures,
> Et les coeurs effroyez des Connils & des Liéures:
> Laisse en paix les Sangliers, les Tigres & les Ours,
> Et n'assaux les Lions aux toiles ny aux cours:
> Croy moy, mon cher ami, l'autre chasse est meilleure:
> Contre l'audacieux l'audace n'est pas seure.   110
> Si tu mourois, helas! de regret ie mourrois:
> Car viure apres ta mort, helas! ie ne pourrois."
> Ainsi disoit Venus: mais les haleines molles
> Des vents ont sans effet emporté ses parolles.
> Il estoit nuict fermée, & les hommes lassez,
> Dessus la plume oisiue auoyent les yeux pressez,
> Enfermez du sommeil, que la basse riuiere
> De Styx fait distiler desur nostre paupiere.
> Ia les Astres au Ciel faisoyent leur demi-tour:
> Le celeste Bouuier qui se roule à l'entour   120
> De l'Ourse, estoit panché: tout se qui vit és ondes,
> Qui vit par les rochers, dans les forests profondes,
> Poissons, Serpens, Lions, du labeur trauaillez,
> Oublians le souci du somme estoyent sillez.

their cares, had their eyes closed in sleep. Mars alone lies awake
in Heaven; filled with frenzy, rage, fury, anger, and jealousy, he
receives sleep in neither eyes nor breast, but lies awake on his bed
without reason or plan. He turns now on one side, now on the
other, over and over again. He laments, he sighs, calls Venus   **130**
ungrateful, and burning with anger, armed head to foot, he darts
up from his bed, and as frenzy carries him abruptly, he goes to
awaken Diana and speaks in this fashion: "My sister, on whom
my happiness and my help depend, I embrace your knees as my
last refuge. Nymph, whom the chase and virtuous exercise in
wandering through the woods have kept far removed from vice,
whom the horned Fauns, the goatish satyrs fear, whenever you   **140**
wear your buskins in the hunt and your congenial band of a hundred comrade Nymphs surrounds you amid wood and mountains;
if you recall the day when outrageous Orion desired to do you
violence, that time when I courageously with ax in hand made him
drop his prey, so that in place of your body he had only your
garment; so now, Sister, return the favor to your brother in his

     Vn seul Mars veille au Ciel, qui plein de frenaisie,
De rage, de fureur, d'ire, & de ialousie,
Ny d'yeux ny d'estomac ne reçoit le sommeil,
Mais veille dans le lict, sans raison ny conseil:
Tantost sur vn costé, & tantost il se vire
Sur l'autre, coup sus coup: il lamente, il souspire: 130
Nomme Venus ingrate, & bruslant de despit
Armé de teste en pied s'eslance de son lit:
Et comme la fureur brusquement le transporte,
Va resueiller Diane, & dit en ceste sorte:
    "Ma Soeur, de qui depend mon bien & mon secours,
I'embrasse tes genoux pour mon dernier recours:
O Nymphe que la chasse & l'honneste exercice,
Parmi les bois errante, ont esloigné du vice:
Que les Faunes cornus, les Satyres bouquins
Craignent, lors qu'en chassant tu as tes brodequins,   140
Et que l'egal troupeau de cent Nymphes compagnes
Enuironnent tes flancs par bois & par montagnes:
S'il te souuient du iour qu'Orion outrageux
Te voulut violer, lors que moy courageux
Ayant la hache au poing, luy fis lascher la prise,
Si qu'en lieu de ton corps n'eut rien que la chemise:
Toy Soeur rens la pareille à ton frere au besoin:

need. One should take care of one's kin in time of danger. You
150   know how Venus, who alone used to hold the key of my life, has
departed from me to follow a shepherd lad, a hunter, a child. The
rest I keep silent. Shame prevents me from telling you how such
a goddess debases herself so miserably with a mere shepherd. I
should not have believed it, if I had not with my own eyes seen her
in the midst of her sport, kissing the lad, their arms entwined, all
naked, whereat the fever of indignation came over my heart. I
160   should surely have killed him, but with no such mean blood do I
wish to soil my hand which knows only to despoil kings of life,
and I do not wish that any glory secured by me through the death
of a shepherd be read of in any history. This youngster plans to
go hunting in the wood tomorrow with his javelin in his hand,
without dogs, in order to show his tender mistress that he is as
full of prowess as he is a handsome lad. To avenge me drive
before his eyes a savage boar, worthy of a Meleager. Enclose
within its tusks slaughter and the thunderbolt, that it may throw
170   him pale to earth in the midst of the dust, calling in vain on his

On doit de ses parens au danger auoir soin.
    "Tu sçais comment Venus qui souloit de ma vie
Tenir seule la clef, de moy s'est departie   150
Pour suiure vn pastoureau, vn veneur, vn enfant.
Du reste ie me tais: la honte me defend
De te conter comment vne telle Deesse
Dessous vn Bergerot si vilement s'abaisse.
    "Ie ne l'eusse pas creu, si de mes propres yeux
Ne l'eusse regardée au milieu de ses jeux,
Baisant le Iouuenceau bras à bras toute nuë,
Dont de despit au coeur la fiéure m'est venuë.
Ie l'eusse bien tué: mais ie ne veux souiller
Ma main en si bas sang, qui ne sçait despouiller   160
Que les Rois de la vie, & ne veux que ma gloire
Par la mort d'vn Pasteur se lise en vne histoire.
    "Ce ieune Damoiseau delibere demain
Aller chasser au bois l'espieu dedans la main,
Sans chiens: pour faire voir à sa tendre maitresse
Qu'autant qu'il est beau fils, qu'il est plein de prouesse.
    "Pour me venger, eslance au deuant de ses yeux,
Digne d'vn Meleagre, vn Sanglier furieux:
Enferme entre ses dents les meurtres & la foudre,
Que palle il le terrasse au milieu de la poudre,   170

lady to aid him, and so my love may be avenged through his death." Thus spoke this god and she, gratifying her brother, with a nod of her head, granted his request.

Scarcely had the sun bewigged himself with rays, when he grasps his javelin and runs through the forests. From bush to bush he comes and returns, and never stops idly in any one place. He looks this way, he looks that way, he hunted long and long he went   180 without finding any prey, until finally he meets with a boar, the disaster of his first test. Its eyes were of fire, and its angry back bristled with rough, cross-grained hair. Foaming, it roared, as in the valleys the descending snows roar and foam, in the winter, when the torrents roll downhill and do so much harm to the husbandman and the grain. He held himself firm on his feet to pierce the beast, and to plant the javelin in the spot where the head joins   190 the neck. The boar, startled, draws back to one side, then charging forward, he thrust his tusks obliquely into his groin, and stretched him all pale and cold upon the plain.

> Appellant pour-neant sa dame à son confort,
> Afin que mon amour se venge par sa mort."
>   Ainsi disoit ce Dieu: & elle de sa teste
> Fauorisant son frere accorda sa requeste.
>   A peine le Soleil se perruquoit de raiz,
> Qu'il empoigne l'espieu, & court par les forests:
> De buisson en buisson il reuient & retourne,
> Et iamais en vn lieu paresseux ne seiourne.
>   Il regarde deça, il regarde delà,
> Il chassa longuement, & longuement alla   180
> Sans trouuer nulle proye: à la parfin il treuue
> Vn Sanglier, le malheur de sa premiere preuue.
>   Ses yeux estoient de feu, & son dos courroussé
> De poil gros & rebours se tenoit herissé:
> Escumeux il bruyoit, comme par les vallées
> Font bruit en escumant les neiges deuallées,
> L'hyuer, quand les torrens se roulent contre-val,
> Et font au laboureur & aux bleds tant de mal.
>   Il se tint ferme en pied pour enferrer la beste,
> Et luy planter l'espieu à l'endroit où la teste   190
> Se ioint auec le col: le Sanglier estonné
> Se recule à costé, puis de front retourné,
> De trauers luy poussa ses Defenses en l'haine,
> Et tout palle & tout froid l'estendit sur la plaine.

At the cry of her beloved the poor loving goddess came, and she became all cold, even more than cold marble. She swooned; then recovering, she strikes the tender flesh of her bare bosom, plucks **200** out her hair, witnesses of her misfortune and with filthy dung degrades her head. Holding at her bosom the beloved remains, she warms them with her sighs, wets them with her tears; she laments, weeps, cries out, and heavy with sorrow, gazing on the dead man, she made her lamentation thus: "So then, my precious beloved, after so many delights, so many pleasures received, so many sweet caresses, after having called thee my heart and all my blessing, must I now in embracing thee embrace nothing more than a nothingness, thee whom Death, envious of thy loveliness, has **210** forced to bathe thy eyes in the Stygian wave. Alas, if thou hadst obeyed me, thou wouldst not have attacked one stronger than thyself. In time of need thou didst forget my counsel. The rose flees thy lips and thy kiss lives no more around thy mouth. Yet I touch it, I kiss it though dead, and thou canst not feel either my kiss or myself, my tears or my sorrows.

> Au cry de son amy la pauure amante vint,
> Qui plus qu'vn marbre froid toute froide deuint:
> Elle s'esuanouyt, puis estant reuenuë
> Frappe la tendre chair de sa poitrine nuë,
> S'arrache les cheueux, tesmoins de son mechef,
> Et de vilain fumier des-honore son chef.   200
>
> Tenant en son giron l'amoureuse despouille,
> L'eschaufe de soupirs, de ses larmes la mouille,
> Lamente, pleure, crie, & grosse de soucy,
> En regardant le mort, faisoit sa plainte ainsi:
>
> "Donque, ma chere vie, apres tant de delices,
> Tant de plaisirs receus, tant de douces blandices,
> Apres t'auoir nommé mon coeur & tout mon bien,
> Faut-il qu'en t'embrassant ie n'embrasse plus rien
> Qu'vn rien, à qui la mort des beautez enuieuse
> A fait baigner les yeux en l'onde Stygieuse!   210
>
> Las! si tu m'eusses creu, tu n'eusses assailly
> Vn plus fort: au besoin mon conseil t'a failly.
> La Rose fuit ta léure, & au tour de ta bouche
> Ne vit plus ton baiser: toutefois ie la touche,
> Morte ie la rebaise, & sentir tu ne puis
> Ny mon baiser ny moy, mes pleurs ny mes ennuis.

Alas, poor Adonis; all the Loves weep for thee.
In thy death, Adonis, all delights die.

Thy kiss was pleasing to me not only when in life thou didst kiss   220
my mouth as I kissed thee; but as I kiss thee in death, my dismal
grief is yet eased a little with a vain pleasure, because I make thee
warm and I cannot keep from kissing thee often and from looking
at thee.

Alas, poor Adonis; all the Loves weep for thee.
At thy grievous death all delights die.

Adonis, speak to me and come to comfort me; kiss me farewell
before thou dost depart. O the beautiful beloved face, O the
pleasant light of those eyes which sweetly held me captive, O the   230
curly hair, O the loving speech, O the memory of a happiness
which is too painful to me, O the pleasant beauty, O the early
youth, which though mortal have won possession of a goddess!
Alas, ye are no more and I grieve at what I am and that death has
no power over me.

> Helas pauure Adonis, tous les Amours te pleurent:
> Par ta mort Adonis, toutes delices meurent!
> Ton baiser seulement ne m'estoit pas plaisant,
> Quand viuant tu baisois ma bouche en te baisant: 220
> Mais en te baisant mort, encor ma triste peine
> Se soulage vn petit d'vne liesse vaine:
> Pource ie te reschaufe, & ne puis me garder
> De te baiser souuent, & de te regarder.
>   Helas pauure Adonis, tous les Amours te pleurent:
> Par ta fascheuse mort toutes delices meurent!
> Adonis parle à moy, & me viens consoler,
> Baise moy pour adieu auant que t'en-aller.
>   O belle face aimée, ô plaisante lumiere
> Des yeux qui me tenoient doucement prisonniere!   230
> O cheueux crespelus, ô deuis amoureux,
> O souuenir du bien qui m'est trop douloureux,
> O plaisante beauté, ô premiere ieunesse,
> Qui mortelle auez pris le corps d'vne Deesse!
> Làs! vous n'estes plus rien, & ie me deuls dequoy
> Ie suis, & que la mort n'a puissance sur moy.

Alas, poor Adonis; all the Loves weep for thee.
At thy dying all delights die with thy death.

240   Alas, with thy death my beauty has died, my color is faded, even
as in summer the flowers fade. For thee alone was I beautiful, and
for thee only did I wish to seem so. I am widowed now and I wish
to bear neither rings on my fingers nor gold in my hair, and I wish
that for evermore (so does sorrow destroy me) the mother of
Love should be garbed in black. I wish that my girdle be adorned
with black, and that I bear no more a mirror in my hand.

Alas, poor Adonis; all the Loves weep for thee.
250   *At thy death, poor Adonis, all delights die.*

Along with me the woods lament thy dying, the waters go weeping
for thee, Echo is not silent, but within her rocks redoubling her
feigned voice, through pity for me is repeating my lament. Every
fair white flower has taken a red hue, and nothing lives in the
fields but lives in grief.

Alas, poor Adonis; all the Loves weep for thee,
For with thy death all delights die.

Helas pauure Adonis, tous les Amours te pleurent:
Toy mourant, par ta mort toutes delices meurent!
Làs! auecques ta mort est morte ma beauté,
Ma couleur est ternie, ainsi comme en esté   240
Se ternissent les fleurs: pour toy seul i'estois belle,
Et pour toy seulement ie voulois sembler telle.

    Ie suis maintenant veufue, & porter ie ne veux
Ny des bagues aux doigts, ny l'or en mes cheueux,
Et si veux pour iamais (tant la douleur me tue)
Que la mere d'Amour de noir soit reuestue:
Ie veux que mon Ceston soit acoustré de noir,
Et que plus ie ne porte en la main de miroir.

    Helas pauure Adonis, tous les Amours te pleurent:
Toy mort pauure Adonis, toutes delices meurent!   250
Les bois auecques moy lamentent ton trespas,
Les eaux te vont pleurant, Echo ne s'en taist pas,
Qui dedans ses rochers redoublant sa voix feinte,
Ayant pitié de moy, va resonnant ma pleinte!
Toute belle fleur blanche a pris rouge couleur,
Et rien ne vit aux champs qui ne viue en douleur.

    Helas pauure Adonis, tous les Amours te pleurent:
Car auecques ta mort toutes delices meurent!

Alas, alas, thou art dead, thou art dead, Adonis! Thou dost leave   260
in my heart sorrows unending. My pleasures, my frolics languish
with thy death, and as I do not die, my sorrows never end. Frenzied
in soul, shrieking with loud voice, I desire to roam disheveled
through the woods, with naked feet, with naked bosom; I wish to
let my breast be scratched by every rough thorn; I wish the
thistles to tear my skin. Madly I wish to climb to the topmost
height of this nearby cliff and with mad intent hurl myself into   270
the wave head downward, to relate to the fishes and to the streams
the wrong which Fate has done me through thy grievous death.

> *Alas, poor Adonis; all the Loves weep for thee.*
> *All beauty and the graces die at thy death.*

Love has power no more; Death has power far greater, since he
takes to himself the delights of the gods. You dogs of his who
weep at the feet of your master, you whom he used to call and know
by name; you nets and snares and unsure javelin, say to your master   280

Las, helas tu es mort, tu es mort Adonis!
Tu me laisses au coeur des regrets infinis: 260
Mes plaisirs, mes esbats auec ta mort languissent,
Et pour ne mourir point mes douleurs ne finissent.
  Furieuse d'esprit, criant à haute vois,
Ie veux escheuellée errer parmy les bois,
Pieds nuds, estomac nud: ie veux que ma poitrine
Se laisse esgrafiner à toute dure espine,
Ie veux que les chardons me deschirent la peau.
Folle ie veux grimper sur le haut du coupeau
De ce prochain rocher, & folle de pensée
Me ietter dedans l'onde à teste renuersée,   270
Pour conter aux poissons & aux fleuues le tort
Que la Parque m'a fait par ta fascheuse mort.
  Helas pauure Adonis, tous les Amours te pleurent!
Les beautez par ta mort & les Charites meurent!
L'Amour ne vaut plus rien, la mort vaut beaucoup mieux,
Puis qu'elle prend à soy les delices des Dieux.
  Vous ses Chiens qui plorez aux pieds de vostre maistre,
Que par nom il souloit appeller & cognoistre:
Vous toiles & filets, & vous mal-seur espieu,
Dites à vostre maistre vn eternel adieu,   280

an eternal farewell, and run into the forests to tell the Dryads that fair Adonis' pleasant glances, which burned them with love, are dead and that also the mother of the Loves is dead of sorrow.

Alas, poor Adonis; all the Loves weep for thee.
At thy dying all delights die with thy death.

You, my yoked doves, that often through the air draw my chariot as swift as the wind, rise up into the sky and relate to the clouds that my joys have become a dream which vanishes and loses itself vainly as soon as our eye is opened by the day, or as the flowing wave, or as the smoke, when blown by the wind, is scattered, fading away in coils. You swans, who were yoked to my coach, I give you freedom, fly in liberty. Fly amid the meadows and tell the little flowers that Venus has shed as many tears as Adonis has shed drops of blood. With his blood the fair flower of the rose has painted its hue crimson, and with the tender crystal of my tiny tears the blossoms of the winter cherry have become white. And

290

300

Et courez és forests raconter aux Dryades,
Que du bel Adonis les plaisantes oeillades,
Que les bruloient d'amour, sont mortes, & qu'aussi
La mere des amours est morte de souci.
  Helas pauure Adonis, tous les Amours te pleurent:
Toy mourant, par ta mort toutes delices meurent!
Vous mes Pigeons couplez, qui parmy l'air souuent
Trainez mon chariot aussi tost que le vent,
Montez dedans le ciel, & racontez aux nuës,
Que mes liesses sont vn songe deuenuës,   290
Lequel s'esuanouist, & sans effect se pert
Aussi tost que nostre oeil par le iour est ouuert,
Ou comme l'onde coule, ou comme la fumée
Se perd du vent souflée en replis consommée.
   Vous Cygnes qui estiez à mon Coche attelez,
Ie vous donne franchise, en liberté volez:
Volez parmy les prez, & contez aux fleurettes
Que Venus a versé autant de larmelettes
Que de sang Adonis: du sang la belle fleur
De la Rose vermeille a portrait sa couleur,   300
Et du tendre crystal de mes larmes menues
Les fleurs des Coquerets blanches sont devenues.

you faithful sisters, my Graces, who weep for my misfortune and like myself remain in tears, go, leave me to myself, go, my sweet comrades, go and tell the deafest mountains, that I embrace my beloved, dead in my bosom, who does not appear like one dead, but like a man asleep, whom slumber is only just beginning to touch. Say to them that his body cannot be anointed with fragrant   310
odors: my fragrant odors, my perfumes are spilled out on the ground. Venus feels nothing more; all my sports are lost, my dances have ended, my sweetest pleasures are turned at his death to bitter sadness, my laughter to sorrow, my joy to unhappiness, and nothing lives in me save grief itself.

> *Alas, poor Adonis; all the Loves weep for thee,*
> *For with thy death all delights die.*

Cut your hair, my children, my Loves, and scatter the hairs over   320
the dead man. Shatter into fragments your quivers and your bows, quench your torches, and break into a thousand pieces all your arrows. Come about me and weep loudly and while weeping perform the rites of the dead. Let one of you with lovely fingers

Et vous fideles Soeurs mes Graces, qui plorez
Mon mal, & comme moy en larmes demeurez,
Allez, laissez moy seule, allez douces compagnes,
Allez & racontez aux plus sourdes montagnes,
Que mort en mon giron i'embrasse mon amy,
Qui ne resemble vn mort, mais vn homme endormy
Qu'encores le sommeil ne commence qu'à poindre.
Dites leur que d'odeurs son corps ne se peut oindre: 310
Mes odeurs, mes parfums sont à terre espandus,
Venus ne sent plus rien, tous mes ieux sont perdus,
Mes danses ont pris fin, mes plus douces liesses
Se tournent par sa mort en ameres tristesses,
Mon ris en desconfort, mon plaisir en malheur,
Et rien ne vit en moy que la mesme douleur.

Helàs pauure Adonis, tous les Amours te pleurent:
Car auecques ta mort toutes delices meurent!

Tondez vous mes enfans, mes Amours, & iettez
Vos cheueux sur le mort: par pieces esclattez   320
Vos carquois & vos arcs, esteignez vos flameches,
Et en mille morceaux brisez toutes vos fleches:
Venez autour de moy, & vous lamentez fort,
Et faites en plorant les obseques du mort.

close his eyelids, let one lift up his head, and let another fan him
from behind with his wing, and let one bring water in a golden
basin to wash his skin.

Alas, poor Adonis; all the Loves weep for thee.
At thy grievous death all delights die.

My thrice well beloved, raise thy eyes for but a little, drive for
but a little the sleep of oblivion from thy head in order that my
grief may come to thy ear, and that I may once more place my lips
upon thine, embracing thee in my bosom for the last time. For
thou art going, Adonis, down yonder into the lower world. For
the last farewell, kiss me, I implore thee. As long as thy kiss still
has life, kiss me in farewell. Thy breath will come into my mouth,
and thence will descend into my heart, then to the very bottom of
my soul, that from age to age I may preserve within my breast this
potion of love, which while kissing thy lips I shall drink in one
long draught. Sucking it in I shall drink it and then I shall send
it to put it in place of thee in the depths of my bosom; for
henceforth Proserpine will have joy of thee."

330

340

> Que l'vn, de ses beaus doits, luy serre la paupiere,
> L'vn souslieue sa teste, & l'autre par derriere
> L'esuente de son aile, & l'vn porte de l'eau
> Dans vn bassin doré, pour nettoyer sa peau.
>
>   Helas pauure Adonis, tous les Amours te pleurent: 330
> Par ta fascheuse mort toutes delices meurent!
> O trois fois bien-aimé, esleue vn peu tes yeux,
> Chasse vn peu de ton chef le somme obliuieux,
> Afin que ma douleur à ton oreille vienne,
> Et que ie mette encor ma léure sur la tienne,
> T'embrassant en mon sein pour la derniere fois:
> Car là bas aux enfers Adonis tu t'en-vois!
> Pour le dernier adieu baise moy ie te prie:
> Autant que ton baiser encores a de vie,
> Baise moy pour adieu: ton haleine viendra
> Dans ma bouche, & de là dans le coeur descendra,   340
> Puis iusqu'au fond de l'ame, à fin que d'âge en âge
> Ie conserue en mon sein cest amoureux bruuage,
> Qu'en tes léures baisant d'vn long trait ie boiray:
> Humant ie le boiray, & puis ie l'enuoiray
> Pour le mettre en ta place au fond de ma poitrine:
> Car de toy desormais iouïra Proserpine."

Thus spoke Venus, and moving her lips to the lips of the dead, weeping she sought the last traces of the soul and sucked them into herself so as to serve them as an eternal tomb. She bathed them   350 with her tears and with loud cries filled the rocks, the banks, and the woods; she scratched her cheeks and, seized with frenzy, tore her hair and struck her face repeatedly. He, turning his eyes towards heaven, uttered a sigh; then overcome by death he lets himself sink numbly without force and without strength into the arms of the fair one, even as one sees a candle fade away without its wax.

Soon as she saw him dead, Love in another direction carried away her sorrow swifter than wind, so that she who was but now   360 so smitten with Adonis, forgot him to love an Anchises, a Phrygian shepherd, who with stooping form pastured his cattle in the grassy meadows of Xanthus.

Such are and shall ever be the loves of women, who at the beginning are hotter than flames, and are all sighs, but in the end such love resembles the flowers of April that live no longer than a day.

> Ainsi disoit Venus, qui sa léure approchant
> Sur les léures du mort, pleurante alloit cherchant
> Les reliques de l'ame, & les humoit en elle,
> Afin de leur seruir d'vne tombe eternelle: 350
> Les baignoit de ses pleurs, & d'vne haute vois
> Remplissoit les rochers les riues & les bois,
> S'esgratignoit la iouë, & attainte de rage
> Se rompoit les cheueux, & plomboit son visage.
>
> Luy tournant vers le ciel les yeux, fist vn souspir,
> Puis pressé de la mort il se laisse assoupir
> Sans force & sans vigueur dans le bras de la belle,
> Ainsi qu'on voit faillir sans cire vne chandelle.
>
> Si tost qu'ell' le vit mort, Amour d'autre costé,
> Luy a plustost que vent son regret emporté,   360
> Si qu'elle qui estoit n'agueres tant esprise
> D'Adonis, l'oublia pour aimer vn Anchise,
> Vn Pasteur Phrygien, qui par les prez herbeux
> De Xanthe recourbé faisoit paistre ses boeufs.
>
> Telles sont & seront les amitiez des femmes,
> Qui au commencement sont plus chaudes que flames,
> Ce ne sont que souspirs, mais en fin telle amour
> Resemble aux fleurs d'Auril qui ne viuent qu'vn iour.

EDMUND SPENSER

NOVEMBER

AEGLOGA UNDECIMA

[DIDO]

Argument

In this xi. æglogue he bewayleth the death of some mayden of greate bloud, whom he calleth Dido. The personage is secrete, and to me altogether unknowne, albe of him selfe I often required the same. This Æglogue is made in imitation of Marot his song, which he made upon the death of Loys the Frenche Queene: but farre passing his reache, and in myne opinion all other the Eglogues of this booke.

Thenot. Colin.

The. Colin, my deare, when shall it please thee sing,
As thou were wont, songs of some jouisaunce?
Thy Muse to long slombreth in sorrowing,
Lulled a sleepe through loves misgovernaunce:
Now somewhat sing whose endles sovenaunce
Emong the shepeheards swaines may aye remaine,
Whether thee list thy loved lasse advaunce,
Or honor Pan with hymnes of higher vaine.
Col. Thenot, now nis the time of merimake,
Nor Pan to herye, nor with love to playe: 10
Sike myrth in May is meetest for to make,
Or summer shade, under the cocked haye.
But nowe sadde winter welked hath the day,
And Phoebus, weary of his yerely taske,
Ystabled hath his steedes in lowlye laye,
And taken up his ynne in Fishes haske.
Thilke sollein season sadder plight doth aske,
And loatheth sike delightes as thou doest prayse:
The mornefull Muse in myrth now list ne maske,
As shee was wont in youngth and sommer dayes.   20

But if thou algate lust light virelayes,
And looser songs of love, to underfong,
Who but thy selfe deserves sike Poetes prayse?
Relieve thy oaten pypes that sleepen long.
The. The nightingale is sovereigne of song,
Before him sits the titmose silent bee:
And I, unfitte to thrust in skilfull thronge,
Should Colin make judge of my fooleree.
Nay, better learne of hem that learned bee,
And han be watered at the Muses well: 30
The kindlye dewe drops from the higher tree,
And wets the little plants that lowly dwell.
But if sadde winters wrathe, and season chill,
Accorde not with thy Muses meriment,
To sadder times thou mayst attune thy quill,
And sing of sorrowe and deathes dreeriment:
For deade is Dido, dead, alas! and drent,
Dido, the greate shepehearde his daughter sheene:
The fayrest may she was that ever went,
Her like shee has not left behinde I weene.   40
And if thou wilt bewayle my wofull tene,
I shall thee give yond cosset for thy payne:
And if thy rymes as rownd and rufull bene
As those that did thy Rosalind complayne,
Much greater gyfts for guerdon thou shalt gayne
Then kidde or cosset, which I thee bynempt.
Then up, I say, thou jolly shepeheard swayne,
Let not my small demaund be so contempt.
Col. Thenot, to that I choose thou doest me tempt:
But ah! to well I wote my humble vaine,   50
And howe my rymes bene rugged and unkempt:
Yet, as I conne, my conning I will strayne.

Up, then, Melpomene, thou mournefulst Muse of nyne!
Such cause of mourning never hadst afore:
Up, grieslie ghostes! and up my rufull ryme!
Matter of myrth now shalt thou have no more:
For dead shee is that myrth thee made of yore.

Dido, my deare, alas! is dead,
Dead, and lyeth wrapt in lead:
O heavie herse!   60
Let streaming teares be poured out in store:
O carefull verse!

Shepheards, that by your flocks on Kentish downes abyde,
Waile ye this wofull waste of Natures warke:
Waile we the wight whose presence was our pryde:
Waile we the wight whose absence is our carke.
The sonne of all the world is dimme and darke:
The earth now lacks her wonted light,
And all we dwell in deadly night:
O heavie herse!   70
Breake we our pypes, that shrild as lowde as larke:
O carefull verse!

Why doe we longer live, (ah, why live we so long?)
Whose better dayes death hath shut up in woe?
The fayrest floure our gyrlond all emong
Is faded quite, and into dust ygoe.
Sing now, ye shepheards daughters, sing no moe
The songs that Colin made in her prayse,
But into weeping turne your wanton layes:
O heavie herse!   80
Now is time to die. Nay, time was long ygoe:
O carefull verse!

Whence is it that the flouret of the field, doth fade,
And lyeth buryed long in winters bale:
Yet soone as spring his mantle doth displaye,
It floureth fresh, as it should never fayle?
But thing on earth that is of most availe,
As vertues braunch and beauties budde,
Reliven not for any good.
O heavie herse!   90
The braunch once dead, the budde eke needes must quaile:
O carefull verse!

She, while she was, (that was, a woful word to sayne!)
For beauties prayse and plesaunce had no pere:

So well she couth the shepherds entertayne
With cakes and cracknells and such country chere.
Ne would she scorne the simple shepheards swaine,
  For she would cal hem often heame,
  And give hem curds and clouted creame.
  O heavie herse!   100
Als Colin Cloute she would not once disdayne.
  O carefull verse!

But nowe sike happy cheere is turnd to heavie chaunce,
Such pleasaunce now displast by dolors dint:
All musick sleepes where Death doth leade the daunce,
And shepherds wonted solace is extinct.
The blew in black, the greene in gray, is tinct;
  The gaudie girlonds deck her grave,
  The faded flowres her corse embrave.
  O heavie herse!   110
Morne nowe, my Muse, now morne with teares besprint.
  O carefull verse!

O thou greate shepheard, Lobbin, how great is thy griefe!
Where bene the nosegayes that she dight for thee?
The colourd chaplets, wrought with a chiefe,
The knotted rushringes, and gilte rosemaree?
For shee deemed nothing too deere for thee.
  Ah! they bene all yclad in clay,
  One bitter blast blewe all away.
  O heavie herse!   120
Thereof nought remaynes but the memoree.
  O carefull verse!

Ay me! that dreerie Death should strike so mortall stroke,
That can undoe Dame Natures kindly course:
The faded lockes fall from the loftie oke,
The flouds do gaspe, for dryed is theyr sourse,
And flouds of teares flowe in theyr stead perforse.
  The mantled medowes mourne,
  Theyr sondry colours tourne.
  O heavie herse!   130

The heavens doe melt in teares without remorse.
    O carefull verse!

The feeble flocks in field refuse their former foode,
And hang theyr heads, as they would learne to weepe:
The beastes in forest wayle as they were woode,
Except the wolves, that chase the wandring sheepe,
Now she is gon that safely did hem keepe.
    The turtle, on the bared braunch,
    Laments the wound that Death did launch.
    O heavie herse!   140
And Philomele her song with teares doth steepe.
    O carefull verse!

The water nymphs, that wont with her to sing and daunce,
And for her girlond olive braunches beare,
Now balefull boughes of cypres doen advaunce:
The Muses, that were wont greene bayes to weare,
Now bringen bitter eldre braunches seare:
    The Fatall Sisters eke repent
    Her vitall threde so soone was spent.
    O heavie herse!   150
Morne now, my Muse, now morne with heavie cheare.
    O carefull verse!

O trustlesse state of earthly things, and slipper hope
Of mortal men, that swincke and sweate for nought,
And shooting wide, doe misse the marked scope:
Now have I learnd, (a lesson derely bought)
That nys on earth assuraunce to be sought:
    For what might be in earthlie mould,
    That did her buried body hould.
    O heavie herse!   160
Yet saw I on the beare when it was brought.
    O carefull verse!

But maugre Death, and dreaded sisters deadly spight,
And gates of Hel, and fyrie furies forse,
She hath the bonds broke of eternall night,
Her soule unbodied of the burdenous corpse.

Why then weepes Lobbin so without remorse?
  O Lobb: thy losse no longer lament;
  Dido nis dead, but into heaven hent.
  O happye herse!   170
Cease now, my Muse, now cease thy sorrowes sourse:
  O joyfull verse!

Why wayle we then? why weary we the gods with playnts,
As if some evill were to her betight?
She raignes a goddesse now emong the saintes,
That whilome was the saynt of shepheards light:
And is enstalled nowe in heavens hight.
  I see thee, blessed soule, I see,
  Walke in Elisian fieldes so free.
  O happy herse!   180
Might I once come to thee! O that I might!
  O joyfull verse!

Unwise and wretched men, to weete whats good or ill,
Wee deeme of death as doome of ill desert:
But knewe we, fooles, what it us bringes until,
Dye would we dayly, once it to expert.
No daunger there the shepheard can astert:
  Fayre fieldes and pleasaunt layes there bene,
  The fieldes ay fresh, the grasse ay greene:
  O happy herse!   190
Make hast, ye shepheards, thether to revert:
  O joyfull verse!

Dido is gone afore (whose turne shall be the next?)
There lives shee with the blessed gods in blisse,
There drincks she nectar with ambrosia mixt,
And joyes enjoyes that mortall men doe misse.
The honor now of highest gods she is,
  That whilome was poore shepheards pryde,
  While here on earth she did abyde.
  O happy herse!   200
Ceasse now, my song, my woe now wasted is.
  O joyfull verse!

The. Ay, francke shepheard, how bene thy verses meint
With doolful pleasaunce, so as I ne wotte
Whether rejoyce or weepe for great constrainte!
Thyne be the cossette, well hast thow it gotte.
Up, Colin, up, ynough thou morned hast:
Now gynnes to mizzle, hye we homeward fast.

COLINS EMBLEME.

La mort ny mord.

GLOSS BY E. K. [EDWARD KIRKE]

Jouisaunce, myrth.

Sovenaunce, remembraunce.

Herie, honour.

Welked, shortned, or empayred. As the moone being in the waine is sayde of Lidgate to welk.

In lowly lay, according to the season of the moneth November, when the sonne draweth low in the south toward his tropick or returne.

In Fishes haske. The sonne reigneth, that is, in the signe Pisces all November. A *haske* is a wicker pad, wherein they use to cary fish.

Virelaies, a light kind of song.

Bee watred. For it is a saying of poetes, that they have dronk of the Muses well Castalias, whereof was before sufficiently sayd.

Dreriment, dreery and heavy cheere.

The great shepheard is some man of high degree, and not, as some vainely suppose, God Pan. The person both of the shephearde and of Dido is unknowen, and closely buried in the authors conceipt. But out of doubt I am, that it is not Rosalind, as some imagin: for he speaketh soone after of her also.

Shene, fayre and shining.

May, for mayde.

Tene, sorrow.

Guerdon, reward.

Bynempt, bequethed.

Cosset, a lambe brought up without the dam.

Unkempt, incompti; not comed, that is, rude and unhansome.

Melpomene, the sadde and waylefull Muse, used of poets in honor of tragedies: as saith Virgile,

'Melpomene tragico proclamat maesta boatu.'

Up griesly gosts, the maner of tragicall poetes, to call for helpe of furies and damned ghostes: so is Hecuba of Euripides, and Tantalus brought in of Seneca; and the rest of the rest.

Herse is the solemne obsequie in funeralles.

Wast of, decay of so beautifull a peece.

Carke, care.

Ah why, an elegant epanorthosis, as also soone after: *nay, time was long ago.*

Flouret, a diminutive for a little floure. This is a notable and sententious comparison '*A minore ad majus.*'

Reliven not, live not againe, sc. not in theyr earthly bodies: for in heaven they enjoy their due reward.

The braunch. He meaneth Dido, who being, as it were, the mayne braunch now withered, the buddes, that is, beautie (as he sayd afore) can no more flourish.

With cakes, fit for shepheards bankets.

Heame, for home: after the northerne pronouncing.

Tinct, deyed or stayned.

The gaudie. The meaning is, that the things which were the ornaments of her lyfe are made the honor of her funerall, as is used in burialls.

Lobbin, the name of a shepherd, which seemeth to have bene the lover and deere frende of Dido.

Rushrings, agreeable for such base gyftes.

Faded lockes, dryed leaves. As if Nature her selfe bewayled the death of the mayde.

Sourse, spring.

Mantled medowes, for the sondry flowres are like a mantle or coverlet wrought with many colours.

Philomele, the nightingale: whome the poetes faine once to have bene a ladye of great beauty, till, being ravished by hir sisters husbande, she desired to be turned into a byrd of her name. Whose complaintes be very well set forth of Maister George Gaskin, a wittie gentleman, and the very chefe of our late rymers, who, and if some partes of learning wanted not (albee it is well knowen he altogyther wanted not learning) no doubt would have attayned to the excellencye of those famous poets. For gifts of wit and naturall promptnesse appeare in hym aboundantly.

Cypresse, used of the old paynims in the furnishing of their funerall pompe, and properly the signe of all sorow and heavinesse.

The fatall sisters, Clotho, Lachesis, and Atropos, daughters of Herebus and the Nighte, whom the poetes fayne to spinne the life of man, as it were a long threde, which they drawe out in length, till his fatal howre and timely death be come; but if by other casualtie his dayes be abridged, then one of them, that is, Atropos, is sayde to have cut the threde in twain. Hereof commeth a common verse.

'Clotho colum bajulat, Lachesis trahit, Atropos occat.'

O trustlesse, a gallant exclamation, moralized with great wisedom, and passionate wyth great affection.

Beare, a frame, wheron they use to lay the dead corse.

Furies, of poetes be feyned to be three, Persephone, Alecto, and Megera, which are sayd to be the authours of all evill and mischiefe.

Eternall night is death or darknesse of hell.

Betight, happened.

I see, a lively icon or representation, as if he saw her in heaven present.

Elysian fieldes be devised of poetes to be a place of pleasure like Paradise, where the happye soules doe rest in peace and eternal happynesse.

Dye would, the very expresse saying of Plato in Phaedone.

Astert, befall unwares.

Nectar and ambrosia be feigned to be the drink and foode of the gods: ambrosia they liken to manna in scripture, and nectar to be white like creme, whereof is a proper tale of Hebe, that spilt a cup of it, and stayned the heavens, as yet appeareth. But I have already discoursed that at large in my Commentarye upon the *Dreames* of the same authour.

Meynt, mingled.

EMBLEME.

Which is as much to say as, *death biteth not.* For although by course of nature we be borne to dye, and being ripened with age, as with a timely harvest, we must be gathered in time, or els of our

selves we fall like rotted ripe fruite fro the tree: yet death is not
to be counted for evill, nor (as the poete sayd a little before) as
doome of ill desert. For though the trespasse of the first man
brought death into the world, as the guerdon of sinne, yet being
overcome by the death of one that dyed for al, it is now made
(as Chaucer sayth) the grene path way to life. So that it agreeth
well with that was sayd, that Death byteth not (that is) hurteth not
at all.

ASTROPHEL

A PASTORALL ELEGIE UPON THE DEATH OF THE MOST NOBLE AND
VALOROUS KNIGHT, SIR PHILIP SIDNEY
DEDICATED

TO THE MOST BEAUTIFULL AND VERTUOUS LADIE,
THE COUNTESSE OF ESSEX

Shepheards, that wont on pipes of oaten reed
Oft times to plaine your loves concealed smart,
And with your piteous layes have learnd to breed
Compassion in a countrey lasses hart,
Hearken, ye gentle shepheards, to my song,
And place my dolefull plaint your plaints emong.

To you alone I sing this mournfull verse,
The mournfulst verse that ever man heard tell;
To you, whose softened hearts it may empierse
With dolours dart for death of Astrophel:
To you I sing, and to none other wight,
For well I wot my rymes bene rudely dight.

Yet as they been, if any nycer wit
Shall hap to heare, or covet them to read,
Thinke he, that such are for such ones most fit,
Made not to please the living but the dead.
And if in him found pity ever place,
Let him be moov'd to pity such a case.

A gentle shepheard borne in Arcady,
Of gentlest race that ever shepheard bore,
About the grassie bancks of Haemony
Did keepe his sheep, his litle stock and store.
Full carefully he kept them day and night,
In fairest fields; and Astrophel he hight.

Young Astrophel, the pride of shepheards praise,
Young Astrophel, the rusticke lasses love,
Far passing all the pastors of his daies,
In all that seemly shepheard might behove: 10
In one thing onely fayling of the best,
That he was not so happie as the rest.

For from the time that first the nymph, his mother,
Him forth did bring, and taught her lambs to feed,
A sclender swaine, excelling far each other
In comely shape, like her that did him breed,
He grew up fast in goodnesse and in grace,
And doubly faire wox both in mynd and face.

Which daily more and more he did augment,
With gentle usage and demeanure myld,   20
That all mens hearts with secret ravishment
He stole away, and weetingly beguyld.
Ne Spight it selfe, that all good things doth spill,
Found ought in him that she could say was ill.

His sports were faire, his joyance innocent,
Sweet without sowre, and honny without gall,
And he himselfe seemd made for meriment,
Merily masking both in bowre and hall:
There was no pleasure nor delightfull play,
When Astrophel so ever was away.   30

For he could pipe, and daunce, and caroll sweet,
Emongst the shepheards in their shearing feast;
As somers larke that with her song doth greet
The dawning day forth comming from the East.
And layes of love he also could compose:
Thrise happie she whom he to praise did chose.

Full many maydens often did him woo
Them to vouchsafe emongst his rimes to name,
Or make for them, as he was wont to doo
For her that did his heart with love inflame.   40
For which they promised to dight for him
Gay chapelets of flowers and gyrlonds trim.

And many a nymph both of the wood and brooke,
Soone as his oaten pipe began to shrill,
Both christall wells and shadie groves forsooke,
To heare the charmes of his enchanting skill;
And brought him presents, flowers if it were prime,
Or mellow fruit if it were harvest time.

But he for none of them did care a whit,
(Yet wood gods for them often sighed sore,)   50
Ne for their gifts, unworthie of his wit,
Yet not unworthie of the countries store.
For one alone he cared, for one he sight,
His lifes desire, and his deare loves delight.

Stella the faire, the fairest star in skie,
As faire as Venus or the fairest faire,
(A fairer star saw never living eie,)
Shot her sharp pointed beames through purest aire.
Her he did love, her he alone did honor,
His thoughts, his rimes, his songs were all upon her.   60

To her he vowd the service of his daies,
On her he spent the riches of his wit:
For her he made hymnes of immortall praise,
Of onely her he sung, he thought, he writ.
Her, and but her, of love he worthie deemed;
For all the rest but litle he esteemed.

Ne her with ydle words alone he wowed,
And verses vaine, (yet verses are not vaine)
But with brave deeds, to her sole service vowed,
And bold atchievements, her did entertaine.   70
For both in deeds and words he nourtred was,
Both wise and hardie (too hardie, alas!)

In wrestling nimble, and in renning swift,
In shooting steddie, and in swimming strong:
Well made to strike, to throw, to leape, to lift,
And all the sports that shepheards are emong:
In every one he vanquisht every one,
He vanquisht all, and vanquisht was of none.

Besides, in hunting such felicitie,
Or rather infelicitie, he found,   80
That every field and forest far away
He sought, where salvage beasts do most abound.
No beast so salvage, but he could it kill:
No chace so hard, but he therein had skill.

Such skill, matcht with such courage as he had,
Did prick him foorth with proud desire of praise,
To seek abroad, of daunger nought y'drad,
His mistresse name, and his owne fame, to raise.
What need perill to be sought abroad,
Since round about us it doth make abroad?   90

It fortuned, as he that perilous game
In forreine soyle pursued far away,
Into a forest wide and waste he came,
Where store he heard to be of salvage pray.
So wide a forest and so waste as this,
Nor famous Ardeyn, nor fowle Arlo, is.

There his welwoven toyles and subtil traines
He laid the brutish nation to enwrap:
So well he wrought with practise and with paines,
That he of them great troups did soone entrap.   100
Full happie man (misweening much) was hee,
So rich a spoile within his power to see.

Eftsoones, all heedlesse of his dearest hale,
Full greedily into the heard he thrust,
To slaughter them, and worke their finall bale,
Least that his toyle should of their troups be brust.
Wide wounds emongst them many one he made,
Now with his sharp borespear, now with his blade.

His care was all how he them all might kill,
That none might scape (so partiall unto none):   110
Ill mynd, so much to mynd anothers ill,
As to become unmyndfull of his owne:
But pardon that unto the cruell skies,
That from himselfe to them withdrew his eies.

So as he rag'd emongst that beastly rout,
A cruell beast of most accursed brood
Upon him turnd (despeyre makes cowards stout)
And, with fell tooth accustomed to blood,
Launched his thigh with so mischievous might,
That it both bone and muscles ryved quight.   120

So deadly was the dint and deep the wound,
And so huge streames of blood thereout did flow,
That he endured not the direfull stound,
But on the cold deare earth himselfe did throw.
The whiles the captive heard his nets did rend,
And having none to let, to wood did wend.

Ah! where were ye this while, his shepheard peares,
To whom alive was nought so deare as hee?
And ye, faire mayds, the matches of his yeares,
Which in his grace did boast you most to bee?   130
Ah! where were ye, when he of you had need,
To stop his wound, that wondrously did bleed?

Ah, wretched boy, the shape of dreryhead,
And sad ensample of mans suddein end!
Full litle faileth but thou shalt be dead,
Unpitied, unplaynd, of foe or frend;
Whilest none is nigh, thine eylids up to close,
And kisse thy lips like faded leaves of rose.

A sort of shepheards, sewing of the chace,
As they the forest raunged on a day,   140
By fate or fortune came unto the place,
Where as the lucklesse boy yet bleeding lay;
Yet bleeding lay, and yet would still have bled,
Had not good hap those shepheards thether led.

They stopt his wound (too late to stop it was)
And in their armes then softly did him reare:
Tho (as he wild) unto his loved lasse,
His dearest love, him dolefully did beare.
The dolefulst beare that ever man did see
Was Astrophel, but dearest unto mee.   150

She, when she saw her love in such a plight,
With crudled blood and filthie gore deformed,
That wont to be with flowers and gyrlonds dight,
And her deare favours dearly well adorned,
Her face, the fairest face that eye mote see,
She likewise did deforme like him to bee.

Her yellow locks, that shone so bright and long,
As sunny beames in fairest somers day,
She fiersly tore, and with outragious wrong
From her red cheeks the roses rent away,   160
And her faire brest, the threasury of joy,
She spoyld thereof, and filled with annoy.

His palled face, impictured with death,
She bathed oft with teares and dried oft:
And with sweet kisses suckt the wasting breath
Out of his lips like lillies pale and soft:
And oft she cald to him, who answerd nought,
But onely by his lookes did tell his thought.

The rest of her impatient regret,
And piteous mone the which she for him made,   170
No toong can tell, nor any forth can set,
But he whose heart like sorrow did invade.
At last when paine his vitall powres had spent,
His wasted life her weary lodge forwent.

Which when she saw, she staied not a whit,
But after him did make untimely haste:
Forthwith her ghost out of her corps did flit,
And followed her make like turtle chaste;
To prove that death their hearts cannot divide,
Which living were in love so firmly tide.   180

The gods, which all things see, this same beheld,
And pittying this paire of lovers trew,
Transformed them, there lying on the field,
Into one flowre that is both red and blew:
It first growes red, and then to blew doth fade,
Like Astrophel, which thereinto was made.

And in the midst thereof a star appeares,
As fairly formd as any star in skyes,
Resembling Stella in her freshest yeares,
Forth darting beames of beautie from her eyes;   190
And all the day it standeth full of deow,
Which is the teares that from her eyes did flow.

That hearbe, of some, Starlight is cald by name,
Of others Penthia, though not so well:
But thou, where ever thou doest finde the same,
From this day forth do call it Astrophel:
And when so ever thou it up doest take,
Do pluck it softly for that shepheards sake.

Hereof when tydings far abroad did passe,
The shepheards all which loved him full deare,   200
And sure full deare of all he loved was,
Did thether flock to see what they did heare.
And when that pitteous spectacle they vewed,
The same with bitter teares they all bedewed.

And every one did make exceeding mone,
With inward anguish and great griefe opprest:
And every one did weep and waile and mone,
And meanes deviz'd to shew his sorrow best:
That from that houre since first on grassie greene
Shepheards kept sheep, was not like mourning seen.   210

But first his sister, that Clorinda hight,
The gentlest shepheardesse that lives this day,
And most resembling both in shape and spright
Her brother deare, began this dolefull lay.
Which, least I marre the sweetnesse of the vearse,
In sort as she it sung I will rehearse.

[THE LAY OF CLORINDA]

Ay me! to whom shall I my case complaine,
That may compassion my impatient griefe?
Or where shall I unfold my inward paine,
That my enriven heart may find reliefe?
Shall I unto the heavenly powres it show?
Or unto earthly men that dwell below?

To heavens?   Ah! they, alas! the authors were,
And workers of my unremedied wo:
For they foresee what to us happens here,
And they foresaw, yet suffred this be so.   10
From them comes good, from them comes also il;
That which they made, who can them warne to spill?

To men?   Ah! they, alas! like wretched bee,
And subject to the heavens ordinance:
Bound to abide what ever they decree,
Their best redresse is their best sufferance.
How then can they, like wretched, comfort mee,
The which no lesse need comforted to bee?

Then to my selfe will I my sorrow mourne,
Sith none alive like sorrowfull remaines: 20
And to my selfe my plaints shall back retourne,
To pay their usury with doubled paines.
The woods, the hills, the rivers shall resound
The mournfull accent of my sorrowes ground.

Woods, hills, and rivers now are desolate,
Sith he is gone the which them all did grace:
And all the fields do waile their widow state,
Sith death their fairest flowre did late deface.
The fairest flowre in field that ever grew
Was Astrophel; that was, we all may rew.   30

What cruell hand of cursed foe unknowne
Hath cropt the stalke which bore so faire a flowre?
Untimely cropt, before it well were growne,
And cleane defaced in untimely howre.
Great losse to all that ever him did see,
Great losse to all, but greatest losse to mee!

Breake now your gyrlonds, O ye shepheards lasses,
Sith the faire flowre which them adornd is gon:
The flowre which them adornd is gone to ashes;
Never againe let lasse put gyrlond on.   40
In stead of gyrlond, weare sad cypres nowe,
And bitter elder, broken from the bowe.

Ne ever sing the love-layes which he made;
Who ever made such layes of love as hee?
Ne ever read the riddles which he sayd
Unto your selves, to make you mery glee.
Your mery glee is now laid all abed,
Your mery maker now, alasse! is dead.

Death, the devourer of all worlds delight,
Hath robbed you and reft fro me my joy: 50
Both you and me and all the world he quight
Hath robd of joyance, and left sad annoy.
Joy of the world and shepheards pride was hee:
Shepheards, hope never like againe to see.

Oh Death! that hast us of such riches reft,
Tell us at least, what hast thou with it done?
What is become of him whose flowre here left
Is but the shadow of his likenesse gone?
Scarse like the shadow of that which he was,
Nought like, but that he like a shade did pas.   60

But that immortall spirit, which was deckt
With all the dowries of celestiall grace,
By soveraine choyce from th' hevenly quires select,
And lineally deriv'd from angels race,
O! what is now of it become, aread.
Ay me! can so divine a thing be dead?

Ah, no! it is not dead, ne can it die,
But lives for aie in blisfull Paradise:
Where like a new-borne babe it soft doth lie,
In bed of lillies wrapt in tender wise,   70
And compast all about with roses sweet,
And daintie violets from head to feet.

There thousand birds, all of celestiall brood,
To him do sweetly caroll day and night;
And with straunge notes, of him well understood,
Lull him a sleep in angelick delight;
Whilest in sweet dreame to him presented bee
Immortall beauties, which no eye may see.

But he them sees, and takes exceeding pleasure
Of their divine aspects, appearing plaine,   80
And kindling love in him above all measure,
Sweet love, still joyous, never feeling paine.
For what so goodly forme he there doth see,
He may enjoy from jealous rancor free.

There liveth he in everlasting blis,
Sweet spirit, never fearing more to die:
No dreading harme from any foes of his,
Ne fearing salvage beasts more crueltie.
Whilest we here, wretches, waile his private lack,
And with vaine vowes do often call him back.   90

But live thou there, still happie, happie spirit,
And give us leave thee here thus to lament:
Not thee that doest thy heavens joy inherit,
But our owne selves that here in dole are drent.
Thus do we weep and waile, and wear our eies,
Mourning in others our owne miseries.

WILLIAM DRUMMOND

TEARS ON THE DEATH OF MOELIADES

O Heavens! then is it true that thou art gone,
And left this woful isle her loss to moan,
Moeliades, bright day-star of the west,
A comet, blazing terror to the east;
And neither that thy spright so heavenly wise,
Nor body, though of earth, more pure than skies,
Nor royal stem, nor thy sweet tender age,
Of adamantine Fates could quench the rage?
O fading hopes! O short-while-lasting joy
Of earth-born man, which one hour can destroy!   10
Then even of virtue's spoils death trophies rears,
As if he gloried most in many tears.
Forc'd by grim Destines, Heavens neglect our cries,
Stars seem set only to act tragedies
And let them do their worst, since thou are gone,
Raise whom they list to thrones, enthron'd dethrone;
Stain princely bowers with blood, and, even to Gange,
In cypress sad glad Hymen's torches change.
Ah! thou hast left to live, and in the time
When scarce thou blossom'd in thy pleasant prime: 20
So falls by northern blast a virgin rose,
At half that doth her bashful bosom close;
So a sweet flourish languishing decays,
That late did blush when kiss'd by Phoebus' rays;
So Phoebus mounting the meridian's height,
Choked by pale Phoebe, faints unto our sight;
Astonish'd nature sullen stands to see
The life of all this All so chang'd to be;
In gloomy gowns the stars about deplore,
The sea with murmuring mountains beats the shore,   30
Black darkness reels o'er all, in thousand showers
The weeping air on earth her sorrow pours,
That, in a palsy, quakes to find so soon
Her lover set, and night burst forth ere noon.

If Heaven, alas! ordain'd thee young to die,
Why was it not where thou thy might did'st try,
And to the hopeful world at least set forth
Some little spark of thine expected worth?
Moeliades, O that by Ister's streams,
Amongst shrill-sounding trumpets, flaming gleams   40
Of warm encrimson'd swords, and cannons' roar,
Balls thick as rain pour'd by the Caspian shore,
Amongst crush'd lances, ringing helms, and shields,
Dismember'd bodies ravishing the fields,
In Turkish blood made red like Mars's star,
Thou ended hadst thy life, and Christian war!
Or, as brave Bourbon, thou hadst made old Rome,
Queen of the world, thy triumph's place and tomb!
So heaven's fair face, to the unborn which reads,
A book had been of thine illustrious deeds;   50
So to their nephews aged sires had told
The high exploits performed by thee of old;
Towns raz'd, and rais'd, victorious, vanquish'd bands,
Fierce tyrants flying, foil'd, kill'd by thy hands;
And in dear arras virgins fair had wrought
The bays and trophies to thy country brought;
While some new Homer, imping pens to fame,
Deaf Nilus' dwellers had made hear thy name.
That thou didst not attain those honours' spheres,
It was not want of worth, O no, but years.   60
A youth more brave pale Troy with trembling walls
Did never see, nor she whose name appalls
Both Titan's golden bowers, for bloody fights
Must'ring on Mars's field such Mars-like knights.
The heavens had brought thee to the highest height
Of wit and courage, showing all their might
When they thee fram'd: ay me! that what is brave
On earth, they as their own so soon should crave!
Moeliades sweet courtly nymphs deplore,
From Thule to Hydaspes' pearly shore.   70
    When Forth thy nurse, Forth where thou first didst pass
Thy tender days (who smil'd oft on her glass

To see thee gaze), meand'ring with her streams,
Heard thou hadst left this round, from Phoebus' beams
She sought to fly, but forced to return
By neighbour brooks, she gave herself to mourn;
And as she rush'd her Cyclades among,
She seem'd to plain that Heaven had done her wrong.
With a hoarse plaint, Clyde down her steepy rocks,
And Tweed through her green mountains clad with flocks,   80
Did wound the ocean, murmuring thy death;
The ocean that roar'd about the earth,
And it to Mauritanian Atlas told,
Who shrunk through grief, and down his white hairs roll'd
Huge streams of tears, that changed were in floods,
With which he drown'd the neighbour plains and woods.
The lesser brooks, as they did bubbling go,
Did keep a consort unto public woe;
The shepherds left their flocks with downcast eyes,
Disdaining to look up to angry skies;   90
Some broke their pipes, and some in sweet-sad lays
Made senseless things amazed at thy praise.
His reed Alexis hung upon a tree,
And with his tears made Doven great to be.
Moeliades sweet courtly nymphs deplore,
From Thule to Hydaspes' pearly shore.
   Chaste maids which haunt fair Aganippe's well,
And you in Tempe's sacred shade who dwell,
Let fall your harps, cease tunes of joy to sing,
Dishevelled make all Parnassus ring   100
With anthems sad; thy music, Phoebus, turn
In doleful plaints, whilst joy itself doth mourn:
Dead is thy darling who decor'd thy bays,
Who oft was wont to cherish thy sweet lays,
And to a trumpet raise thine amorous style,
That floating Delos envy might this isle.
You Acidalian archers break your bows,
Your brandons quench, with tears blot beauty's snows,
And bid your weeping mother yet again
A second Adon's death, nay Mars's plain.   110

His eyes once were your darts, nay, even his name,
Wherever heard, did every heart inflame:
Tagus did court his love with golden streams,
Rhine with his towns, fair Seine with all she claims.
But ah! poor lovers, death did them betray,
And, not suspected, made their hopes his prey.
Tagus bewails his loss with golden streams,
Rhine with his towns, fair Seine with all she claims.
Moeliades sweet courtly nymphs deplore,
From Thule to Hydaspes' pearly shore.   120
    Delicious meads, whose chequer'd plain forth brings
White, golden, azure flowers, which once were kings,
In mourning black their shining colours dye,
Bow down their heads, whilst sighing zephyrs fly.
Queen of the fields, whose blush makes blush the morn,
Sweet rose, a prince's death in purple mourn;
O hyacinths, for aye your AI keep still,
Nay, with more marks of woe your leaves now fill;
And you, O flower of Helen's tears first born,
Into those liquid pearls again you turn;   130
Your green locks, forests, cut; in weeping myrrhs,
The deadly cypress, and ink-dropping firs,
Your palms and myrtles change; from shadows dark,
Wing'd syrens, wail; and you, sad echoes, mark
The lamentable accents of their moan,
And plain that brave Moeliades is gone.
Stay, sky, thy turning course, and now become
A stately arch unto the earth, his tomb;
Over which aye the wat'ry Iris keep,
And sad Electra's sisters which still weep.   140
Moeliades sweet courtly nymphs deplore,
From Thule to Hydaspes' pearly shore.
    Dear ghost, forgive these our untimely tears,
By which our loving mind, though weak, appears;
Our loss, not thine, when we complain, we weep,
For thee the glist'ring walls of heaven do keep
Beyond the planets' wheels, above that source
Of spheres, that turns the lower in its course,

Where sun doth never set, nor ugly night
Ever appears in mourning garments dight;   150
Where Boreas' stormy trumpet doth not sound,
Nor clouds, in lightnings bursting, minds astound;
From care's cold climates far, and hot desire,
Where time is banish'd, ages ne'er expire;
Amongst pure sprights environed with beams,
Thou think'st all things below to be but dreams,
And joy'st to look down to the azur'd bars
Of heaven, indented all with streaming stars;
And in their turning temples to behold,
In silver robe the moon, the sun in gold,   160
Like young eye-speaking lovers in a dance,
With majesty by turns retire, advance.
Thou wond'rest earth to see hang like a ball,
Clos'd in the ghastly cloister of this All;
And that poor men should prove so madly fond,
To toss themselves for a small foot of ground,
Nay, that they even dare brave the powers above,
From this base stage of change that cannot move.
All worldly pomp and pride thou seest arise
Like smoke, that scatt'reth in the empty skies.   170
Other hills and forests, other sumptuous towers,
Amaz'd thou find'st, excelling our poor bowers;
Courts void of flattery, of malice minds,
Pleasure which lasts, not such as reason blinds:
Far sweeter songs thou hear'st and carollings,
Whilst heavens do dance, and quire of angels sings,
Than mouldy minds could feign: even our annoy,
If it approach that place, is chang'd in joy.
  Rest, blessed spright, rest satiate with the sight
Of him whose beams both dazzle and delight,   180
Life of all lives, cause of each other cause,
The sphere and centre where the mind doth pause;
Narcissus of himself, himself the well,
Lover, and beauty, that doth all excel.
Rest, happy ghost, and wonder in that glass
Where seen is all that shall be, is, or was,

While shall be, is, or was do pass away,
And nought remain but an eternal day:
For ever rest; thy praise fame may enrol
In golden annals, whilst about the pole   190
The slow Boötes turns, or sun doth rise
With scarlet scarf, to cheer the mourning skies:
The virgins to thy tomb may garlands bear
Of flowers, and on each flower let fall a tear.
Moeliades sweet courtly nymphs deplore,
From Thule to Hydaspes' pearly shore.

[ALCON]

A PASTORAL ELEGY

ON THE DEATH OF SIR ANTHONY ALEXANDER

In sweetest prime and blooming of his age,
Dear Alcon ravish'd from this mortal stage,
The shepherds mourn'd as they him lov'd before:
Among the rout him Idmon did deplore,
Idmon, who, whether sun in east did rise
Or dive in west, pour'd torrents from his eyes
Of liquid crystal, under hawthorn shade;
At last to trees and rocks this plaint he made:
Alcon, delight of heaven, desire of earth,
Offspring of Phoebus, and the Muses' birth,   10
The Graces' darling, Adon of our plains,
Flame of the fairest nymphs the earth sustains,
What power of thee hath us bereft? what fate
By thy untimely fall would ruinate
Our hopes? O Death! what treasure in one hour
Hast thou dispersed! how dost thou devour
What we on earth hold dearest! All things good,
Too envious heavens, how blast ye in the bud!
The corn the greedy reapers cut not down
Before the fields with golden ears it crown,   20
Nor doth the verdant fruits the gardener pull,
But thou art cropt before thy years were full.

With thee, sweet youth, the glories of our fields
Vanish away, and what contentments yields;
The lakes their silver look, the woods their shades,
The springs their crystal want, their verdure meads,
The years their early seasons, cheerful days;
Hills gloomy stand now desolate of rays;
Their amorous whispers zephyrs not us bring,
Nor do air's quiristers salute the spring;   30
The freezing winds our gardens do deflow'r.
Ah, Destinies! and you whom skies empow'r,
To his fair spoils his spright again yet give,
And like another phoenix make him live.
The herbs, though cut, sprout fragrant from their stems,
And make with crimson blush our anadems;
The sun, when in the west he doth decline,
Heaven's brightest tapers at his funerals shine;
His face, when wash'd in the Atlantic seas,
Revives, and cheers the welkin with new rays: 40
Why should not he, since of more pure a frame,
Return to us again, and be the same?
But wretch, what wish I? To the winds I send
These plaints and prayers. Destines cannot lend
Thee more of time, nor heavens consent will thus
Thou leave their starry world to dwell with us;
Yet shall they not thee keep amidst their spheres
Without these lamentations and tears.
    Thou wast all virtue, courtesy, and worth,
And as sun's light is in the moon set forth,   50
World's supreme excellence in thee did shine;
Nor, though eclipsed now, shalt thou decline,
But in our memories live, while dolphins streams
Shall haunt, whilst eaglets stare on Titan's beams,
Whilst swans upon their crystal tombs shall sing,
Whilst violets with purple paint the spring.
A gentler shepherd flocks did never feed
On Albion's hills, nor sung to oaten reed:
While what she found in thee my muse would blaze,
Grief doth distract her, and cut short thy praise.   60

How oft have we, environ'd by the throng
Of tedious swains, the cooler shades among,
Contemn'd earth's glow-worm greatness, and the chase
Of fortune scorned, deeming it disgrace
To court inconstancy! How oft have we
Some Chloris' name grav'n in each virgin tree,
And, finding favours fading, the next day
What we had carv'd we did deface away!
Woful remembrance! Nor time nor place
Of thy abodement shadows any trace,   70
But there to me thou shin'st: late glad desires,
And ye once roses, how are ye turned briers!
Contentments passed, and of pleasures chief,
Now are ye frightful horrors, hells of grief.
  When from thy native soil love had thee driven,
Thy safe return prefigurating, a heaven
Of flattering hopes did in my fancy move,
Then little dreaming it should atoms prove.
These groves preserve will I, these loved woods,
These orchards rich with fruits, with fish these floods;   80
My Alcon will return, and once again
His chosen exiles he will entertain;
The populous city holds him, amongst harms
Of some fierce Cyclops, Circe's stronger charms.
These banks, said I, he visit will, and streams,
These silent shades ne'er kiss'd by courting beams;
Far, far off I will meet him, and I first
Shall him approaching know, and first be blest
With his aspect; I first shall hear his voice,
Him find the same he parted, and rejoice   90
To learn his passed perils, know the sports
Of foreign shepherds, fauns, and fairy courts.
No pleasure to the fields; an happy state
The swains enjoy, secure from what they hate:
Free of proud cares they innocently spend
The day, nor do black thoughts their ease offend;
Wise nature's darlings they live in the world,
Perplexing not themselves how it is hurl'd.

These hillocks Phoebus loves, Ceres these plains,
These shades the Sylvans, and here Pales strains   100
Milk in the pails, the maids which haunt the springs
Dance on these pastures, here Amintas sings;
Hesperian gardens, Tempe's shades are here,
Or what the eastern Ind and west hold dear.
Come then, dear youth, the wood-nymphs twine thee boughs
With rose and lily, to impale thy brows.
Thus ignorant, I mus'd, not conscious yet
Of what by death was done, and ruthless fate:
Amidst these trances, Fame thy loss doth sound,
And through my ears gives to my heart a wound;   110
With stretch'd-out arms I sought thee to embrace,
But clasp'd, amaz'd, a coffin in thy place;
A coffin! of our joys which had the trust,
Which told that thou wast come, but chang'd in dust.
Scarce, even when felt, could I believe this wrack,
Nor that thy time and glory Heavens would break.
Now since I cannot see my Alcon's face,
And find nor vows nor prayers to have place
With guilty stars, this mountain shall become
To me a sacred altar, and a tomb   120
To famous Alcon; here, as days, months, years
Do circling glide, I sacrifice will tears,
Here spend my remnant time, exil'd from mirth,
Till death in end turn monarch of my earth.
  Shepherds on Forth, and ye by Doven rocks
Which use to sing and sport, and keep your flocks,
Pay tribute here of tears; ye never had
To aggravate your moans a cause more sad;
And to their sorrows hither bring your maunds
Charged with sweetest flowers, and with pure hands,   130
Fair nymphs, the blushing hyacinth and rose
Spread on the place his relics doth enclose;
Weave garlands to his memory, and put
Over his hearse a verse in cypress cut:

"Virtue did die, goodness but harm did give
After the noble Alcon left to live;
Friendship an earthquake suffer'd; losing him,
Love's brightest constellation turned dim."

JOHN MILTON

LYCIDAS

In this Monody the Author bewails a learned Friend, unfortunately drowned in his passage from Chester on the Irish Seas, 1637; and, by occasion, foretells the ruin of our corrupted Clergy, then in their height.

Yet once more, O ye Laurels, and once more,
Ye Myrtles brown, with ivy never sere,
I come to pluck your berries harsh and crude,
And with forced fingers rude
Shatter your leaves before the mellowing year.
Bitter constraint and sad occasion dear
Compels me to disturb your season due;
For Lycidas is dead, dead ere his prime,
Young Lycidas, and hath not left his peer.
Who would not sing for Lycidas? he knew   10
Himself to sing, and build the lofty rhyme.
He must not float upon his watery bier
Unwept, and welter to the parching wind,
Without the meed of some melodious tear.
   Begin, then, Sisters of the sacred well
That from beneath the seat of Jove doth spring;
Begin, and somewhat loudly sweep the string.
Hence with denial vain and coy excuse:
So may some gentle Muse
With lucky words favour *my* destined urn,   20
And as he passes turn,
And bid fair peace be to my sable shroud!
For we were nursed upon the self-same hill,
Fed the same flock, by fountain, shade, and rill.
   Together both, ere the high lawns appeared
Under the opening eyelids of the Morn,
We drove a-field, and both together heard
What time the grey-fly winds her sultry horn,
Battening our flocks with the fresh dews of night,
Oft till the star that rose at evening bright   30

Toward heaven's descent had sloped his westering wheel.
Meanwhile the rural ditties were not mute;
Tempered to the oaten flute
Rough Satyrs danced, and Fauns with cloven heel
From the glad sound would not be absent long;
And old Damoetas loved to hear our song.

But, oh! the heavy change, now thou art gone,
Now thou art gone and never must return!
Thee, Shepherd, thee the woods and desert caves,
With wild thyme and the gadding vine o'ergrown,   40
And all their echoes, mourn.
The willows, and the hazel copses green,
Shall now no more be seen
Fanning their joyous leaves to thy soft lays.
As killing as the canker to the rose,
Or taint-worm to the weanling herds that graze,
Or frost to flowers, that their gay wardrobe wear,
When first the white-thorn blows;
Such, Lycidas, thy loss to shepherd's ear.

Where were ye, Nymphs, when the remorseless deep   50
Closed o'er the head of your loved Lycidas?
For neither were ye playing on the steep
Where your old Bards, the famous Druids, lie,
Nor on the shaggy top of Mona high,
Nor yet where Deva spreads her wisard stream.
Ay me! I fondly dream
"Had ye been there," . . . for what could that have done?
What could the Muse herself that Orpheus bore,
The Muse herself, for her inchanting son,
Whom universal nature did lament,   60
When, by the rout that made the hideous roar,
His gory visage down the stream was sent,
Down the swift Hebrus to the Lesbian shore?

Alas! what boots it with uncessant care
To tend the homely, slighted, Shepherd's trade,
And strictly meditate the thankless Muse?
Were it not better done, as others use,
To sport with Amaryllis in the shade,

Or with the tangles of Neaera's hair?
Fame is the spur that the clear spirit doth raise   70
(That last infirmity of noble mind)
To scorn delights and live laborious days;
But the fair guerdon when we hope to find,
And think to burst out into sudden blaze,
Comes the blind Fury with the abhorrèd shears,
And slits the thin-spun life. "But not the praise,"
Phoebus replied, and touched my trembling ears:
"Fame is no plant that grows on mortal soil,
Nor in the glistering foil
Set off to the world, nor in broad rumour lies,   80
But lives and spreads aloft by those pure eyes
And perfet witness of all-judging Jove;
As he pronounces lastly on each deed,
Of so much fame in heaven expect thy meed."
   O fountain Arethuse, and thou honoured flood,
Smooth-sliding Mincius, crowned with vocal reeds,
That strain I heard was of a higher mood.
But now my oat proceeds,
And listens to the Herald of the Sea,
That came in Neptune's plea.   90
He asked the waves, and asked the felon winds,
What hard mishap hath doomed this gentle swain?
And questioned every gust of rugged wings
That blows from off each beakèd promontory.
They knew not of his story;
And sage Hippotades their answer brings,
That not a blast was from his dungeon strayed:
The air was calm, and on the level brine
Sleek Panope with all her sisters played.
It was that fatal and perfidious bark,   100
Built in the eclipse, and rigged with curses dark,
That sunk so low that sacred head of thine.
   Next, Camus, reverend Sire, went footing slow,
His mantle hairy, and his bonnet sedge,
Inwrought with figures dim, and on the edge
Like to that sanguine flower inscribed with woe.

"Ah! who hath reft," quoth he, "my dearest pledge?"
Last came, and last did go,
The Pilot of the Galilean Lake;
Two massy keys he bore of metals twain   110
(The golden opes, the iron shuts amain).
He shook his mitred locks, and stern bespake:—
"How well could I have spared for thee, young swain,
Anow of such as, for their bellies' sake,
Creep, and intrude, and climb into the fold!
Of other care they little reckoning make
Than how to scramble at the shearers' feast,
And shove away the worthy bidden guest.
Blind mouths! that scarce themselves know how to hold
A sheep-hook, or have learnt aught else the least   120
That to the faithful Herdman's art belongs!
What recks it them? What need they? They are sped;
And, when they list, their lean and flashy songs
Grate on their scrannel pipes of wretched straw;
The hungry sheep look up, and are not fed,
But, swoln with wind and the rank mist they draw,
Rot inwardly, and foul contagion spread;
Besides what the grim Wolf with privy paw
Daily devours apace, and nothing said.
But that two-handed engine at the door   130
Stands ready to smite once, and smite no more."
    Return, Alpheus; the dread voice is past
That shrunk thy streams; return, Sicilian Muse,
And call the vales, and bid them hither cast
Their bells and flowerets of a thousand hues.
Ye valleys low, where the mild whispers use
Of shades, and wanton winds, and gushing brooks,
On whose fresh lap the swart star sparely looks,
Throw hither all your quaint enamelled eyes,
That on the green turf suck the honeyed showers,   140
And purple all the ground with vernal flowers.
Bring the rathe primrose that forsaken dies,
The tufted crow-toe, and pale gessamine,
The white pink, and the pansy freaked with jet,

The glowing violet,
The musk-rose, and the well-attired woodbine,
With cowslips wan that hang the pensive head,
And every flower that sad embroidery wears;
Bid amaranthus all his beauty shed,
And daffadillies fill their cups with tears,   150
To strew the laureate hearse where Lycid lies.
For so, to interpose a little ease,
Let our frail thoughts dally with false surmise.
Ay me! whilst thee the shores and sounding seas
Wash far away, where'er thy bones are hurled;
Whether beyond the stormy Hebrides,
Where thou perhaps under the whelming tide
Visit'st the bottom of the monstrous world;
Or whether thou, to our moist vows denied,
Sleep'st by the fable of Bellerus old,   160
Where the great Vision of the guarded mount
Looks toward Namancos and Bayona's hold.
Look homeward, Angel, now, and melt with ruth:
And, O ye dolphins, waft the hapless youth.

　　Weep no more, woeful shepherds, weep no more,
For Lycidas, your sorrow, is not dead,
Sunk though he be beneath the watery floor.
So sinks the day-star in the ocean bed,
And yet anon repairs his drooping head,
And tricks his beams, and with new-spangled ore   170
Flames in the forehead of the morning sky:
So Lycidas sunk low, but mounted high,
Through the dear might of Him that walked the waves,
Where, other groves and other streams along,
With nectar pure his oozy locks he laves,
And hears the unexpressive nuptial song,
In the blest kingdoms meek of joy and love.
There entertain him all the Saints above,
In solemn troops, and sweet societies,
That sing, and singing in their glory move,   180

And wipe the tears for ever from his eyes.
Now, Lycidas, the shepherds weep no more;
Henceforth thou art the Genius of the shore,
In thy large recompense, and shalt be good
To all that wander in that perilous flood.

Thus sang the uncouth Swain to the oaks and rills,
While the still Morn went out with sandals grey:
He touched the tender stops of various quills,
With eager thought warbling his Doric lay:
And now the sun had stretched out all the hills,   190
And now was dropt into the western bay.
At last he rose, and twitched his mantle blue:
To-morrow to fresh woods, and pastures new.

THE LAMENT FOR DAMON

Argument

Thyrsis and Damon, who were shepherds of the same region and had followed the same studies, were the closest possible friends from boyhood.
Thyrsis, while on a pleasure trip abroad, received news of Damon's death.
Later, on returning home and learning that this is the fact, he bewails himself and his loneliness in this poem. By the person of Damon we are to
understand here Charles Diodati, whose family on his father's side came
from the Tuscan city of Lucca, but who otherwise was an Englishman, a
youth outstanding, while he lived, for ability, scholarship, and all other
splendid virtues.

Nymphs of Himera (for you recall Daphnis and Hylas and the
long-bewailed fate of Bion), sing a Sicilian lay among the towns

EPITAPHIUM DAMONIS

Argumentum

Thyrsis et Damon, eiusdem viciniae pastores, eadem studia sequuti, a pueritia
amici erant, ut qui plurimum. Thyrsis, animi causa profectus, peregre de
obitu Damonis nuncium accepit. Domum postea reversus, et rem ita esse
comperto, se suamque solitudinem hoc carmine deplorat. Damonis autem
sub persona hic intelligitur Carolus Deodatus, ex urbe Hetruriae Luca paterno
genere oriundus, caetera Anglus; ingenio, doctrina, clarissimisque caeteris
virtutibus, dum viveret, iuvenis egregius.

Himerides Nymphae (nam vos et Daphnin et Hylan,
Et plorata diu meministis fata Bionis),

of the Thames: the cries, the groans which unhappy Thyrsis poured
forth, and the unceasing lamentations with which he disturbed the
caves and the rivers and the restless springs and the seclusion of
the groves, while lamenting that Damon had been torn untimely
from him; nor did he exclude the deep night from his grief as he
wandered through lonely places. Already the stalk was rising a
second time with its green ear of wheat and as many times did the
granaries number the yellow harvests, since the final day had
carried Damon beneath the shades; but Thyrsis had not yet come,
for sweet love of the Muse held that shepherd in the Tuscan city.
But when his mind was sated and care for the flock he had left
recalled him home, as soon as he sat beneath the accustomed elm,
then, then at last he truly felt the loss of his friend, and began
thus to unburden his limitless grief:

> *"Go home, unfed, my lambs,*
> *Your master has time for you no more.*

Ah me! what gods shall I say are on the earth, what gods in the
heaven, now that they have torn thee away, Damon, in cruel death?
Dost thou leave us so; shall thy virtues thus pass on unnamed
and be numbered in the company of the obscure shades? But he

10

20

Dicite Sicelicum Thamesina per oppida carmen:
Quas miser effudit voces, quae murmura Thyrsis,
Et quibus assiduis exercuit antra querelis.
Fluminaque, fontesque vagos, nemorumque recessus,
Dum sibi praereptum queritur Damona, neque altam
Luctibus exemit noctem, loca sola pererrans.
Et iam bis viridi surgebat culmus arista,
Et totidem flavas numerabant horrea messes,
Ex quo summa dies tulerat Damona sub umbras,
Nec dum aderat Thyrsis; pastorem scilicet illum
Dulcis amor Musae Thusca retinebat in urbe.
Ast ubi mens expleta domum pecorisque relicti
Cura vocat, simul assueta seditque sub ulmo,
Tum vero amissum, tum denique, sentit amicum,
Coepit et immensum sic exonerare dolorem:—
  "Ite domum impasti; domino iam non vacat, agni.
Hei mihi! quae terris, quae dicam numina coelo,
Postquam te immiti rapuerunt funere, Damon?
Siccine nos linquis? tua sic sine nomine virtus
Ibit, et obscuris numero sociabitur umbris?

10

20

who divides the souls with golden wand would not wish this; rather would he lead thee to a host worthy of thyself and would keep afar all the mean flock of the silent dead.

> "Go home, unfed, my lambs,
> Your master has time for you no more.

30 Whatever shall be, surely, unless a wolf beholds me first, thou shalt not crumble away in an unwept tomb, but thy fame shall endure and long flourish among the shepherds. They shall delight to pay thee their vows second after Daphnis, after Daphnis to sing thy praises, as long as Pales, as long as Faunus shall love the countryside, if it avails one aught to have kept the faith of old and righteousness and the arts of Pallas and to have had a singer as a friend.

> "Go home, unfed, my lambs,
> Your master has time for you no more.

40 These sure rewards await thee, these shall be thine, Damon; but what, pray, will now become of me? Who will be my faithful comrade, clinging near to my side, as often thou wast wont in harsh cold and in places choked with frost, or under the scorching sun

At non ille animas virga qui dividit aurea
Ista velit, dignumque tui te ducat in agmen,
Ignavumque procul pecus arceat omne silentum.
  "Ite domum impasti; domino iam non vacat, agni.
Quicquid erit, certe, nisi me lupus ante videbit,
Indeplorato non comminuere sepulchro,
Constabitque tuus tibi honos, longumque vigebit
Inter pastores. Illi tibi vota secundo   30
Solvere post Daphnin, post Daphnin dicere laudes,
Gaudebunt, dum rura Pales, dum Faunus amabit;
Si quid id est, priscamque fidem coluisse, piumque,
Palladiasque artes, sociumque habuisse canorum.
  "Ite domum impasti; domino iam non vacat, agni.
Haec tibi certa manent, tibi erunt haec praemia, Damon.
At mihi quid tandem fiet modo? Quis mihi fidus
Haerebit lateri comes, ut tu saepe solebas,
Frigoribus duris, et por loca foeta pruinis,
Aut rapido sub sole, siti morientibus herbis,   40

when the herbage was dying of thirst or if there was need to join combat with mighty lions or to frighten greedy wolves from the high folds? Who will now soothe each day with speech and with song?

"Go home, unfed, my lambs,
Your master has time for you no more.

To whom shall I trust my heart? Who will teach me to quiet gnawing cares, to beguile the long nights with sweet conversation, when the mellow pear hisses on the cheerful fire and the hearth crackles with nuts, while the harmful south wind confuses all outdoors and roars down through the elm?

"Go home, unfed, my lambs,   50
Your master has time for you no more.

Or in the summer when the wheel of day is turning in mid-heaven, when Pan takes his slumber sheltered by the oak tree's shade, and the nymphs return to their familiar haunts beneath the waters, and the shepherds hide, and the farmer snores beneath the hedge, who will then bring back to me thy soothing presence, thy laughter, thy Cecropian wit, thy graceful charm?

"Go home, unfed, my lambs,
Your master has time for you no more.

Sive opus in magnos fuit eminus ire leones,
Aut avidos terrere lupos praesepibus altis?
Quis fando sopire diem cantuque solebit?
"Ite domum impasti; domino iam non vacat, agni.
Pectora cui credam? Quis me lenire docebit
Mordaces curas, quis longam fallere noctem
Dulcibus alloquiis, grato cum sibilat igni
Molle pirum, et nucibus strepitat focus, at malus Auster
Miscet cuncta foris, et desuper intonat ulmo?
"Ite domum impasti; domino iam non vacat, agni.   50
Aut aestate, dies medio dum vertitur axe,
Cum Pan aesculea somnum capit abditus umbra,
Et repetunt sub aquis sibi nota sedilia Nymphae,
Pastoresque latent, stertit sub sepe colonus,
Quis mihi blanditiasque tuas, quis tum mihi risus,
Cecropiosque sales referet, cultosque lepores?
"Ite domum impasti; domino iam non vacat, agni.

But now I wander alone through the fields, alone through the
meadows; where the branching shadows grow deeper in the valleys,
60   here I await the evening; above my head the storm cloud and the
east wind sigh mournfully and the twilight flickers in the tossing
forest.

> *"Go home, unfed, my lambs,*
> *Your master has time for you no more.*

Ah, how my fields, well tended of yore, are choked with insolent
weeds, and even the tall grain cracks with blight; the unwed grape
is withering with neglected cluster, and I have no joy in the
myrtles; even of the sheep am I weary, while they grieve and turn
their eyes to their keeper.

> *"Go home, unfed, my lambs,*
> *Your master has time for you no more.*

Tityrus is calling me to the hazels, Alphesiboeus to the ash trees,
70   Aegon to the willows, lovely Amyntas to the rivers: 'Here are cool
springs, here are grasses dotted with moss, here are zephyrs, here
the arbutus rustles amid peaceful waters.' But they sing this to
one unhearing; I found me a bush and went from them.

> *"Go home, unfed, my lambs,*
> *Your master has time for you no more.*

At iam solus agros, iam pascua solus oberro;
Sicubi ramosae densantur vallibus umbrae,
Hic serum expecto; supra caput imber et Eurus   60
Triste sonant, fractaeque agitata crepuscula silvae.
    "Ite domum impasti; domino iam non vacat, agni.
Heu! quam culta mihi prius arva procacibus herbis
Involvuntur, et ipsa situ seges alta fatiscit!
Innuba neglecto marcescit et uva racemo,
Nec myrteta iuvant; ovium quoque taedet, at illae
Moerent, inque suum convertunt ora magistrum.
    "Ite domum impasti; domino iam non vacat, agni.
Tityrus ad corylos vocat, Alphesiboeus ad ornos,
Ad salices Aegon, ad flumina pulcher Amyntas: 70
'Hic gelidi fontes, hic illita gramina musco,
Hic Zephyri, hic placidas interstrepit arbutus undas.'
Ista canunt surdo; frutices ego nactus abibam.
    "Ite domum impasti; domino iam non vacat, agni.

Thereat Mopsus, as by chance he had espied me returning (and skilled in the tongue of birds and in the stars was Mopsus), exclaimed, 'Thyrsis, what is this? What unseemly bile disquiets you? Either love destroys you or a star casts an evil spell upon you. The star of Saturn has often been grievous to shepherds and with glancing lead pierces deep within the heart.'   80

> *"Go home, unfed, my lambs,*
> *Your master has time for you no more.*

The nymphs wonder and say, 'What is to become of you, Thyrsis? What is it you desire? Not the wont of youth are a clouded brow, wild eyes, grim looks. 'Tis dances, merry sport, and love that youth ever seeks, and rightly; twice wretched is he who loves too late.'

> *"Go home, unfed, my lambs,*
> *Your master has time for you no more.*

Hyas came, and Dryope and Aegle, daughter of Baucis, a maid trained in music, skilled with the lyre, but ruinously proud; Chloris came, neighbor of the Idumanian river; but no blandishments, no   90 words of comfort, naught that is at hand moves me, nor do I have hope of the future.

> *"Go home, unfed, my lambs,*
> *Your master has time for you no more.*

Mopsus ad haec, nam me redeuntem forte notarat
(Et callebat avium linguas et sidera Mopsus),
'Thyrsi, quid hoc?' dixit; 'quae te coquit improba bilis?
Aut te perdit amor, aut te male fascinat astrum;
Saturni grave saepe fuit pastoribus astrum,
Intimaque obliquo figit praecordia plumbo.'   80
    "Ite domum impasti; domino iam non vacat, agni.
Mirantur nymphae, et 'Quid te, Thyrsi, futurum est?
Quid tibi vis?' aiunt: 'non haec solet esse iuventae
Nubila frons, oculique truces, vultusque severi:
Illa choros, lususque leves, et semper amorem
Iure petit; bis ille miser qui serus amavit.'
    "Ite domum impasti; domino iam non vacat, agni.
Venit Hyas, Dryopeque, et filia Baucidis Aegle,
Docta modos, citharaeque sciens, sed perdita fastu;
Venit Idumanii Chloris vicina fluenti: 90
Nil me blanditiae, nil me solantia verba,
Nil me si quid adest movet, aut spes ulla futuri.
    "Ite domum impasti; domino iam non vacat, agni.

Ah, me! how like are the bullocks that sport in the meadows, all congenial comrades together by nature's law, and none separates one from the herd as his friend before another. So the jackals come in crowds to their pastures, and the shaggy wild asses join equally with their fellows. The same is the law of the sea: on **100** an abandoned shore Proteus numbers his hosts of seals. Even the meanest of birds, the sparrow, always has his friend to be with, and with him he gladly flies about all the stores of grain, returning late to his home; but if chance gives this friend over to death, whether a kite with curved beak causes his doom or a digger brings him down with his reed, straightway he flies off and seeks him another for his friend. But we are a stern tribe, and the race of men, harassed by dread fates, alien to one another in spirit and discordant in heart, can scarce find each for himself one equal **110** friend out of the thousands; or if fortune, not unkind to our prayers at last, grants us one, an unexpected day, at an unlooked-for hour steals him from us, leaving an undying hurt for all time.

"Go home, unfed, my lambs,
Your master has time for you no more.

Hei mihi! quam similes ludunt per prata iuvenci,
Omnes unanimi secum sibi lege sodales!
Nec magis hunc alio quisquam secernit amicum
De grege; sic densi veniunt ad pabula thoes,
Inque vicem hirsuti paribus iunguntur onagri:
Lex eadem pelagi: deserto in littore Proteus
Agmina phocarum numerat: vilisque volucrum   100
Passer habet semper quicum sit, et omnia circum
Farra libens volitet, sero sua tecta revisens;
Quem si sors letho obiecit, seu milvus adunco
Fata tulit rostro, seu stravit arundine fossor,
Protinus ille alium socio petit inde volatu.
Nos durum genus, et diris exercita fatis
Gens, homines, aliena animis, et pectore discors;
Vix sibi quisque parem de millibus invenit unum;
Aut, si sors dederit tandem non aspera votis,
Illum inopina dies, qua non speraveris hora   110
Surripit, aeternum linquens in saecula damnum.
    "Ite domum impasti; domino iam non vacat, agni.

Alas! what aimless wandering drew me to go to unknown shores
across towering cliffs and the snow-clad Alps?   Was it worth so
much to see buried Rome—though it were such as when of yore
Tityrus himself to visit it left his sheep and his fields—that
I could deprive myself of thee, so sweet a comrade, could place
between us so many deep seas, so many mountains, so many forests   120
and rocks and roaring rivers?   Oh that I might at least have
touched thy hand at the last, and thy carefully closed eyes as thou
didst die in peace, and could have said to thee, 'Farewell! Remembering me thou shalt rise to the stars.'

> "Go home, unfed, my lambs,
> Your master has time for you no more.

Yet, never shall I regret remembering you also, Tuscan shepherds,
youths busied with the Muses—here was Charis and Lepos; and
thou also, Damon, wast a Tuscan from that ancient city of Lucumo
whence thou dost derive thy race.   Oh, how great was I when,
reclining by the cool Arno's murmuring stream and the poplar   130
grove, where the grass was softest, I could pluck now violets,
now myrtle tips, and could hear Menalcas striving with Lycidas.

Heu: quis me ignotas traxit vagus error in oras
Ire per aëreas rupes, Alpemque nivosam?
Ecquid erat tanti Romam vidisse sepultam
(Quamvis illa foret, qualem dum viseret olim
Tityrus ipse suas et oves et rura reliquit),
Ut te tam dulci possem caruisse sodale,
Possem tot maria alta, tot interponere montes,
Tot silvas, tot saxa tibi, fluviosque sonantes?   120
Ah! certe extremum licuisset tangere dextram,
Et bene compositos placide morientis ocellos,
Et dixisse 'Vale! nostri memor ibis ad astra.'
    "Ite domum impasti; domino iam non vacat, agni.
Quamquam etiam vestri nunquam meminisse pigebit,
Pastores Thusci, Musis operata iuventus,
Hic Charis, atque Lepos; et Thuscus tu quoque Damon,
Antiqua genus unde petis Lucumonis ab urbe.
O ego quantus eram, gelidi cum stratus ad Arni
Murmura populeumque nemus, qua mollior herba,   130
Carpere nunc violas, nunc summas carpere myrtos,
Et potui Lycidae certantem audire Menalcam!

Even I myself dared to contend, nor do I think I displeased you much, for here also with me are your gifts, baskets of rushes and of wicker and the waxen bonds of hemlock, and my name also have Dati and Francini taught their beech trees, and both of these were known for their singing and their studies, both of the blood of the Lydians.

> *"Go home, unfed, my lambs,*
> *Your master has time for you no more.*

140   These words the dewy moon then suggested to me in my joy, when all alone I enclosed the tender kids within the pens. Ah! how often I said, when the black ashes already possessed thee: 'Now Damon is singing or now he is stretching nets for the hare; now he is weaving osiers, that they may serve for his varied needs'; and what then with unworried thought I hoped would be, I lightly seized upon in my prayer and imagined it as present. 'Now, my good friend, hast thou nothing else to do? Unless perhaps some task detains thee, shall we go and lie down a bit in the rustling shade, either by the waters of the Colne or among the acres of

150   Cassibelaunus? Thou wilt run over tales of doctors, of thy grasses,

Ipse etiam tentare ausus sum; nec puto multum
Displicui; nam sunt et apud me munera vestra,
Fiscellae, calathique, et cerea vincla cicutae:
Quin et nostra suas docuerunt nomina fagos
Et Datis et Francinus; erant et vocibus ambo
Et studiis noti, Lydorum sanguinis ambo.
  "Ite domum impasti; domino iam non vacat, agni.
Haec mihi tum laeto dictabat roscida luna,   140
Dum solus teneros claudebam cratibus haedos.
Ah! quoties dixi, cum te cinis ater habebat,
'Nunc canit, aut lepori nunc tendit retia Damon;
Vimina nunc texit varios sibi quod sit in usus';
Et quae tum facili sperabam mente futura
Arripui voto levis, et praesentia finxi.
'Heus bone! numquid agis? nisi te quid forte retardat,
Imus, et arguta paulum recubamus in umbra,
Aut ad aquas Colni, aut ubi iugera Cassibelauni?
Tu mihi percurres medicos, tua gramina, succos,   150

juices, and hellebore, and the lowly crocus and leaf of the hyacinth, and the herbs which yonder marsh contains, and the arts of healers.' Ah! curse on their herbs, curse on the arts of healers, their grasses, since they gave no help to the master himself. Even I myself— for somehow an exalted strain was sounding from my pipe—it is now the second day following the eleventh night—and then as it chanced I had placed my lip on the new hemlock stalks, but they sprang asunder, bursting their fastening, nor could they there- after endure the weighty sounds. Perhaps I may be arrogant, but still I will tell it. Withdraw, you forests.   160

> "Go home, unfed, my lambs,
> Your master has time for you no more.

I myself will sing of Dardanian ships in the Rutupian waters, and the ancient kingdom of Imogene, daughter of Pandrasus, and of Brennus and Arviragus, the leaders, and ancient Belinus, and the settlers of Armorica, at last brought under the Briton's law; then of Igraine, pregnant with Arthur through fatal guile, of deceptive features, and the taking up of the arms of Gorlois, the deceit of Merlin. Oh, if life should but remain with me, you, my pipe, shall hang far away, on an aged pine, quite forgotten by me, or else   170

Helleborumque, humilesque crocos, foliumque hyacinthi,
Quasque habet ista palus herbas, artesque medentum.'
Ah! pereant herbae, pereant artesque medentum,
Gramina, postquam ipsi nil profecere magistro!
Ipse etiam—nam nescio quid mihi grande sonabat
Fistula—ab undecima iam lux est altera nocte—
Et tum forte novis admoram labra cicutis:
Dissiluere tamen, rupta compage, nec ultra
Ferre graves potuere sonos: dubito quoque ne sim
Turgidulus; tamen et referam; vos cedite, sylvae.   160
    "Ite domum impasti; domino iam non vacat, agni.
Ipse ego Dardanias Rutupina per aequora puppes
Dicam, et Pandrasidos regnum vetus Inogeniae,
Brennumque Arviragumque duces, priscumque Belinum,
Et tandem Armoricos Britonum sub lege colonos;
Tum gravidam Arturo fatali fraude Iögernen;
Mendaces vultus, assumptaque Gorlöis arma,
Merlini dolus. O, mihi tum si vita supersit,
Tu procul annosa pendebis, fistula, pinu
Multum oblita mihi, aut patriis mutata Camoenis   170

transformed with the native Muses, you shall utter a British strain. But how so? All things are not given to one man; it is not given to one man to hope for all things. It will be a rich enough reward for me, great honor for me (though I be unknown forever, and quite without fame in the outer world) if the yellow-tressed Ouse should read me, and he who drinks of the Alan, and the Humber with its many whirlpools, and all the grove of Trent, and my own Thames beyond all, and Tamar dark with metals, and the Orkneys in their remote waves should learn me.

> "Go home, unfed, my lambs,
> Your master has time for you no more.

180 All this was I saving for thee under the tough bark of a laurel tree, this and much more with it, as also the cups which Manso gave me, Manso, not the least glory of the shore of Chalcidice, a pair of cups, a wondrous masterpiece of art, and he himself was wondrous, and he had carved their sides with a two-fold tale: In the center is the wave of the Red Sea and the fragrant springtime, the long shores of Arabia and balsam-dripping forests; amid these the Phoenix, divine bird, unique on earth, of resplendent green with many-colored wings, looks toward the dawn which rises over the 190 glassy waves. On another side is the all-spreading sky and great

Brittonicum strides! Quid enim? omnia non licet uni,
Non sperasse uni licet omnia; mi satis ampla
Merces, et mihi grande decus (sim ignotus in aevum
Tum licet, externo penitusque inglorius orbi),
Si me flava comas legat Usa, et potor Alauni,
Vorticibusque frequens Abra, et nemus omne Treantae,
Et Thamesis meus ante omnes, et fusca metallis
Tamara, et extremis me discant Orcades undis.
    "Ite domum impasti; domino iam non vacat, agni.
Haec tibi servabam lenta sub cortice lauri,   180
Haec, et plura simul; tum quae mihi pocula Mansus,
Mansus, Chalcidicae non ultima gloria ripae,
Bina dedit, mirum artis opus, mirandus et ipse,
Et circum gemino caelaverat argumento.
In medio Rubri Maris unda, et odoriferum ver,
Littora longa Arabum, et sudantes balsama sylvae;
Has inter Phoenix, divina avis, unica terris,
Caeruleum fulgens diversicoloribus alis,
Auroram vitreis surgentem respicit undis;
Parte alia polus omnipatens, et magnus Olympus: 190

Olympus, and—who would think it?—Love also is here, and
his quiver painted in a cloud, and his flashing arms, his torches,
and darts dipped in fiery bronze. Nor does he smite weak souls
from here, nor the ignoble hearts of the crowd, but turning about
his blazing eyes, he is ever scattering his shafts upward through
the spheres, ever active, and he never looks aside to shoot downward; hence are set on fire the holy minds and the shapes of the
gods.

"Thou too art among them—nor does a deceptive hope mislead
me, Damon—thou too art surely among them, for where else would
thy sweet and sacred innocence have gone, where else thy pure   200
virtue? It is not right to seek thee in Lethean Orcus; no tears are
suited for thee, nor shall I weep more. Go hence, you tears:
Damon lives in the pure heavens; he possesses heaven, himself
pure. He has thrust away the rainbow with his foot. Among the
souls of heroes and everliving gods he quaffs heavenly waters and
drinks joys with sacred lips. So, now that thou hast received the
rights of heaven, stand graciously by me and serenely favor me,
whatever the name by which thou art called, whether thou wilt be
my Damon or art more pleased with the name of Diodotus, by   210

Quis putet? hic quoque Amor, pictaeque in nube pharetrae,
Arma corusca, faces, et spicula tincta pyropo;
Nec tenues animas, pectusque ignobile vulgi,
Hinc ferit; at circum flammantia lumina torquens,
Semper in erectum spargit sua tela per orbes
Impiger, et pronos nunquam collimat ad ictus;
Hinc mentes ardere sacrae, formaeque deorum.
   "Tu quoque in his—nec me fallit spes lubrica, Damon—
Tu quoque in his certe es; nam quo tua dulcis abiret
Sanctaque simplicitas? nam quo tua candida virtus?   200
Nec te Lethaeo fas quaesivisse sub Orco;
Nec tibi conveniunt lacrymae, nec flebimus ultra.
Ite procul, lacrymae; purum colit aethera Damon,
Aethera purus habet, pluvium pede reppulit arcum;
Heroumque animas inter, divosque perennes,
Aethereos haurit latices et gaudia potat
Ore sacro. Quin tu, caeli post iura recepta,
Dexter ades, placidusque fave, quicunque vocaris;
Seu tu noster eris Damon, sive aequior audis
DIODOTUS, quo te divino nomine cuncti   210

which divine name all the dwellers in heaven know thee, but thou wilt still be called Damon in the woodlands.   Because crimson modesty and youth without stain were thy choice, because thou never didst taste the joys of wedlock, lo, virginal honors are in store for thee.   With thy radiant head garlanded in a ruddy crown, and bearing the joyous shade of the leafy palm, thou wilt eternally enjoy immortal nuptials; where there is song and the lyre revels, mingled with blissful dances, and gay festal orgies are rife with the thyrsus of Zion."

Caelicolae norint, sylvisque vocabere Damon.
Quod tibi purpureus pudor, et sine labe iuventus
Grata fuit, quod nulla tori libata voluptas,
En! etiam tibi virginei servantur honores!
Ipse, caput nitidum cinctus rutilante corona,
Laetaque frondentis gestans umbracula palmae
Aeternum perages immortales hymenaeos,
Cantus ubi, choreisque furit lyra mista beatis,
Festa Sionaeo bacchantur et Orgia thyrso."

ALEXANDER POPE

PASTORAL 4

WINTER; OR, DAPHNE

TO THE MEMORY OF MRS. TEMPEST

Lycidas.   Thyrsis.

Lyc. Thyrsis! the music of that murm'ring spring
Is not so mournful as the strains you sing;
Nor rivers winding thro' the vales below
So sweetly warble, or so smoothly flow.
Now sleeping flocks on their soft fleeces lie,
The moon, serene in glory, mounts the sky;
While silent birds forget their tuneful lays,
O sing of Daphne's fate, and Daphne's praise!
Thyr. Behold the groves that shine with silver frost,
Their beauty wither'd, and their verdure lost.   10
Here shall I try the sweet Alexis' strain,
That call'd the list'ning Dryads to the plain?
Thames heard the numbers as he flow'd along,
And bade his willows learn the moving song.
Lyc. So may kind rains their vital moisture yield,
And swell the future harvest of the field.
Begin: this charge the dying Daphne gave,
And said, 'Ye shepherds, sing around my grave!'
Sing, while beside the shaded tomb I mourn,
And with fresh bays her rural shrine adorn.   20
Thyr. Ye gentle Muses, leave your crystal spring,
Let Nymphs and Sylvans cypress garlands bring:
Ye weeping Loves, the stream with myrtles hide,
And break your bows, as when Adonis died!
And with your golden darts, now useless grown,
Inscribe a verse on this relenting stone:
'Let Nature change, let Heav'n and Earth deplore,
Fair Daphne's dead, and Love is now no more!'
  'Tis done; and Nature's various charms decay,
See gloomy clouds obscure the cheerful day!   30

Now hung with pearls the dropping trees appear,
Their faded honours scatter'd on her bier.
See, where on earth the flow'ry glories lie,
With her they flourish'd, and with her they die.
Ah, what avail the beauties Nature wore?
Fair Daphne's dead, and Beauty is no more!

   For her the flocks refuse their verdant food,
The thirsty heifers shun the gliding flood;
The silver swans her hapless fate bemoan,
In notes more sad than when they sing their own;   40
In hollow caves sweet Echo silent lies,
Silent, or only to her name replies;
Her name with pleasure once she taught the shore;
Now Daphne's dead, and Pleasure is no more!

   No grateful dews descend from ev'ning skies,
Nor morning odours from the flowers arise;
No rich perfumes refresh the fruitful field,
Nor fragrant herbs their native incense yield.
The balmy zephyrs, silent since her death,
Lament the ceasing of a sweeter breath;   50
Th' industrious bees neglect their golden store:
Fair Daphne's dead, and sweetness is no more!

   No more the mountain larks, while Daphne sings,
Shall, list'ning in mid-air, suspend their wings;
No more the birds shall imitate her lays,
Or, hush'd with wonder, hearken from the sprays;
No more the streams their murmurs shall forbear,
A sweeter music than their own to hear;
But tell the reeds, and tell the vocal shore,
Fair Daphne's dead, and music is no more!   60
Her fate is whisper'd by the gentle breeze,
And told in sighs to all the trembling trees;
The trembling trees, in every plain and wood,
Her fate remurmur to the silver flood;
The silver flood, so lately calm, appears
Swell'd with new passion, and o'erflows with tears;
The winds and trees and floods her death deplore,
Daphne, our Grief, our Glory now no more!

But see! where Daphne wond'ring mounts on high
Above the clouds, above the starry sky!   70
Eternal beauties grace the shining scene,
Fields ever fresh, and groves for ever green!
There while you rest in amaranthine bowers,
Or from those meads select unfading flowers,
Behold us kindly, who your name implore,
Daphne, our Goddess, and our Grief no more!
Lyc. How all things listen, while thy Muse complains!
Such silence waits on Philomela's strains,
In some still ev'ning, when the whisp'ring breeze
Pants on the leaves, and dies upon the trees.   80
To thee, bright Goddess, oft a lamb shall bleed,
If teeming ewes increase my fleecy breed.
While plants their shade, or flowers their odours give,
Thy name, thy honour, and thy praise shall live!
Thyr. But see, Orion sheds unwholesome dews;
Arise, the pines a noxious shade diffuse;
Sharp Boreas blows, and Nature feels decay,
Time conquers all, and we must Time obey.
Adieu, ye vales, ye mountains, streams, and groves;
Adieu, ye shepherds' rural lays and loves;   90
Adieu, my flocks; farewell, ye sylvan crew;
Daphne, farewell; and all the world adieu!

AMBROSE PHILIPS

PASTORAL 3

ALBINO

Angelot. Palin.

When Virgil thought no shame the Dorick reed
To tune, and flocks on Mantuan plains to feed,
With young Augustus' name he grac'd his song:
And Spenser, when amid the rural throng
He carol'd sweet, and graz'd along the flood
Of gentle Thames, made every sounding wood
With good Eliza's name to ring around;
Eliza's name on every tree was found:
Since then, through Anna's cares at ease. we live,
And see our cattle unmolested thrive,   10
While from our Albion her victorious arms
Drive wasteful warfare, loud in dire alarms,
Like them will I my slender musick raise,
And teach the vocal valleys Anna's praise.
Mean-time, on oaten pipe a lowly lay,
As my kids browse, obscure in shades I play:
Yet, not obscure, while Dorset thinks no scorn
To visit woods, and swains ignobly born.
   Two valley swains, both musical, both young,
In friendship mutual, and united long,   20
Retire within a mossy cave, to shun
The crowd of shepherds, and the noon-day sun.
A gloom of sadness overcasts their mind:
Revolving now, the solemn day they find,
When young Albino died. His image dear
Bedews their cheeks with many a trickling tear:
To tears they add the tribute of their verse;
These Angelot, those Palin, did rehearse.
Ang. Thus, yearly circling, by-past times return;
And yearly, thus, Albino's death we mourn.   30

Sent into life, alas! how short thy stay:
How sweet the rose! how speedy to decay!
Can we forget, Albino dear, thy knell,
Sad-sounding wide from every village-bell?
Can we forget how sorely Albion moan'd,
That hills, and dales, and rocks, in echo groan'd,
Presaging future woe, when, for our crimes,
We lost Albino, pledge of peaceful times,
Fair boast of this fair Island, darling joy
Of Nobles high, and every shepherd-boy?   40
No joyous pipe was hear'd, no flocks were seen,
Nor shepherd found upon the grassy green,
No cattle graz'd the field, nor drank the flood,
No birds were hear'd to warble through the wood.
In yonder gloomy grove out-stretch'd he lay,
His lovely limbs upon the dampy clay;
On his cold cheek the rosy hue decay'd,
And, o'er his lips, the deadly blue display'd:
Bleating around him ly his plaintive sheep;
And mourning shepherds come, in crowds, to weep.   50
Young Buckhurst comes: and, is there no redress?
As if the grave regarded our distress!
The tender virgins come, to tears yet new,
And give, aloud, the lamentations due.
The pious mother comes, with grief opprest:
Ye trees, and conscious fountains, can attest
With what sad accents, and what piercing cries,
She fill'd the grove, and importun'd the skies,
And every star upbraided with his death,
When, in her widowed arms, devoid of breath,   60
She clasp'd her son: nor did the Nymph, for this,
Place in her dearling's welfare all her bliss,
Him teaching, young, the harmless crook to wield,
And rule the peaceful empire of the field.
As milk-white swans on streams of silver show,
And silvery streams to grace the meadows flow,
As corn the vales, and trees the hills adorn,
So thou, to thine, an ornament wast born.

Since thou, delicious youth, didst quit the plains,
Th' ungrateful ground we till with fruitless pains,   70
In labour'd furrows sow the choice of wheat,
And, over empty sheaves, in harvest sweat,
A thin increase our fleecy cattle yield;
And thorns, and thistles, overspread the field.
How all our hope is fled, like morning-dew!
And scarce did we thy dawn of manhood view.
Who, now, shall teach the pointed spear to throw,
To whirl the sling, and bend the stubborn bow,
To toss the quoit with steady aim, and far,
With sinewy force, to pitch the massy bar?   80
Nor dost thou live to bless thy mother's days,
To share her triumphs, and to feel her praise,
In foreign realms to purchase early fame,
And add new glories to the British name:
O, peaceful may thy gentle spirit rest!
The flowery turf ly light upon thy breast;
Nor shrieking owl, nor bat, thy tomb fly round,
Nor midnight goblins revel o'er the ground.
Pal. No more, mistaken Angelot, complain:
Albino lives; and all our tears are vain: 90
Albino lives, and will, for ever live
With Myriads mixt, who never know to grieve,
Who welcome every stranger-guest, nor fear
Ever to mourn his absence with a tear,
Where cold, nor heat, nor irksome toil annoy,
Nor age, nor sickness, comes to damp their joy:
And now the royal Nymph, who bore him, deigns
The land to rule, and shield the simple swains,
While, from above, propitious he looks down:
For this, the welkin does no longer frown,   100
Each planet shines, indulgent, from his sphere,
And we renew our pastimes with the year.
Hills, dales, and woods, with shrilling pipes resound;
The boys and virgins dance, with chaplets crown'd,
And hail Albino blest: the valleys ring
Albino blest!   O now, if ever, bring

The laurel green, the smelling eglantine,
And tender branches from the mantling vine,
The dewy cowslip, which in meadow grows,
The fountain-violet, and the garden-rose,   110
Marsh-lillies sweet, and tufts of daffadil,
With what ye cull from wood, or verdant hill,
Whether in open sun, or shade, they blow,
More early some, and some unfolding slow,
Bring, in heap'd canisters, of every kind,
As if the summer had with spring combin'd,
And nature, forward to assist your care,
Did no profusion for Albino spare.
Your hamlets strew, and every publick way;
And consecrate to mirth Albino's day: 120
Myself will lavish all my little store,
And deal about the goblet flowing o'er:
Old Moulin there shall harp, young Myco sing,
And Cuddy dance the round amid the ring,
And Hobbinol his antick gambols play:
To thee these honours, yearly, will we pay;
Nor fail to mention thee in all our chear,
And teach our children the remembrance dear,
When we or shearing-feast, or harvest, keep,
To speed the plow, and bless our thriving sheep.   130
While willow kids, and herbage lambs, pursue,
While bees love thyme, and locusts sip the dew,
While birds delight in woods their notes to strain,
Thy name and sweet memorial shall remain.

JOHN GAY

FRIDAY;

OR, THE DIRGE

Bumkinet. Grubbinol.

Bum. Why, Grubbinol, dost thou so wistful seem?
There's sorrow in thy look, if right I deem.
'Tis true, yon oaks with yellow tops appear,
And chilly blasts begin to nip the year;
From the tall elm, a shower of leaves is borne,
And their lost beauty riven beeches mourn.
Yet e'en this season pleasance blithe affords,
Now the squeezed press foams with our apple hoards.
Come, let us hie, and quaff a cheery bowl,
Let cyder new wash sorrow from thy soul.   10
Grub. Ah Bumkinet! since thou from hence wert gone,
From these sad plains all merriment is flown;
Should I reveal my grief 'twould spoil thy cheer,
And make thine eye o'erflow with many a tear.
Bum. Hang sorrow! Let's to yonder hut repair,
And with trim sonnets cast away our care.
'Gillian of Croydon' well thy pipe can play,
Thou sing'st most sweet, 'O'er hills and far away,'
Of 'Patient Grissel' I devise to sing,
And catches quaint shall make the valleys ring,   20
Come, Grubbinol, beneath this shelter come,
From hence we view our flocks securely roam.
Grub. Yes, blithesome lad, a tale I mean to sing,
But with my woe shall distant valleys ring,
The tale shall make our kidlings droop their head,
For woe is me!—our Blouzelind is dead.
Bum. Is Blouzelinda dead? farewell my glee!
No happiness is now reserved for me.
As the wood-pigeon coos without his mate,
So shall my doleful dirge bewail her fate.   30

Of Blouzelinda fair I mean to tell,
The peerless maid that did all maids excel.

   Henceforth the morn shall dewy sorrow shed,
And ev'ning tears upon the grass be spread;
The rolling streams with wat'ry grief shall flow,
And winds shall moan aloud—when loud they blow.
Henceforth, as oft as autumn shall return,
The drooping trees, whene'er it rains, shall mourn;
This season quite shall strip the country's pride,
For 'twas in autumn Blouzelinda died.   40

   Where-e'er I gad, I Blouzelind shall view,
Woods, dairy, barn and mows our passion knew.
When I direct my eyes to yonder wood,
Fresh rising sorrow curdles in my blood.
Thither I've often been the damsel's guide,
When rotten sticks our fuel have supplied;
There I remember how her faggots large,
Were frequently these happy shoulders' charge.
Sometimes this crook drew hazel boughs adown,
And stuff'd her apron wide with nuts so brown;   50
Or when her feeding hogs had miss'd their way,
Or wallowing 'mid a feast of acorns lay;
Th' untoward creatures to the sty I drove,
And whistled all the way—or told my love.

   If by the dairy's hatch I chance to hie,
I shall her goodly countenance espy,
For there her goodly countenance I've seen,
Set off with kerchief starch'd and pinners clean.
Sometimes, like wax, she rolls the butter round,
Or with the wooden lily prints the pound.   60
Whilome I've seen her skim the clouted cream,
And press from spongy curds the milky stream.
But now, alas! these ears shall hear no more
The whining swine surround the dairy door,
No more her care shall fill the hollow tray,
To fat the guzzling hogs with floods of whey.
Lament, ye swine, in gruntings spend your grief,
For you, like me, have lost your sole relief.

When in the barn the sounding flail I ply,
Where from her sieve the chaff was wont to fly,   70
The poultry there will seem around to stand,
Waiting upon her charitable hand.
No succour meet the poultry now can find,
For they, like me, have lost their Blouzelind.

   Whenever by yon barley mow I pass,
Before my eyes will trip the tidy lass.
I pitch'd the sheaves (oh could I do so now)
Which she in rows piled on the growing mow.
There every deal my heart by love was gain'd.
There the sweet kiss my courtship has explain'd.   80
Ah Blouzelind! that mow I ne'er shall see,
But thy memorial will revive in me.

   Lament, ye fields, and rueful symptoms show,
Henceforth let not the smelling primrose grow;
Let weeds instead of butter-flowers appear,
And meads, instead of daisies, hemlock bear;
For cowslips sweet let dandelions spread,
For Blouzelinda, blithesome maid, is dead!
Lament ye swains, and o'er her grave bemoan,
And spell ye right this verse upon her stone.   90
Here Blouzelinda lies—Alas, alas!
Weep, shepherds,—and remember flesh is grass.
Grub. Albeit thy songs are sweeter to mine ear,
Than to the thirsty cattle rivers clear;
Or winter porridge to the lab'ring youth,
Or buns and sugar to the damsel's tooth;
Yet Blouzelinda's name shall tune my lay,
Of her I'll sing for ever and for aye.

   When Blouzelind expired, the wether's bell
Before the drooping flock toll'd forth her knell;   100
The solemn death-watch click'd the hour she died,
And shrilling crickets in the chimney cried;
The boding raven on her cottage sate,
And with hoarse croaking warn'd us of her fate;
The lambkin, which her wonted tendance bred,
Dropp'd on the plains that fatal instant dead;

Swarm'd on a rotten stick the bees I spied,
Which erst I saw when goody Dobson dy'd.

How shall I, void of tears, her death relate,
While on her darling's bed her mother sate!   110
These words the dying Blouzelinda spoke,
And of the dead let none the will revoke:

Mother, quoth she, let not the poultry need,
And give the goose wherewith to raise her breed,
Be these my sister's care—and ev'ry morn
Amid the ducklings let her scatter corn;
The sickly calf that's housed, be sure to tend,
Feed him with milk, and from bleak colds defend.
Yet e'er I die—see, mother, yonder shelf,
There secretly I've hid my worldly pelf.   120
Twenty good shillings in a rag I laid,
Be ten the Parson's, for my sermon paid.
The rest is yours—my spinning-wheel and rake,
Let Susan keep for her dear sister's sake;
My new straw hat that's trimly lined with green,
Let Peggy wear, for she's a damsel clean.
My leathern bottle, long in harvests tried,
Be Grubbinol's—this silver ring beside;
Three silver pennies, and a nine-pence bent,
A token kind, to Bumkinet is sent.   130
Thus spoke the maiden, while her mother cried,
And peaceful, like the harmless lamb, she died.

To show their love, the neighbours far and near,
Follow'd with wistful look the damsel's bier.
Sprigg'd rosemary the lads and lasses bore,
While dismally the parson walk'd before.
Upon her grave the rosemary they threw,
The daisy, butter-flower, and endive blue.

After the good man warn'd us from his text,
That none could tell whose turn would be the next;   140
He said, that heaven would take her soul, no doubt,
And spoke the hour-glass in her praise—quite out.

To her sweet mem'ry flowery garlands strung,
O'er her now empty seat aloft were hung.

With wicker rods we fenced her tomb around,
To ward from men and beast the hallow'd ground,
Lest her new grave the parson's cattle raze,
For both his horse and cow the church-yard graze.
   Now we trudged homeward to her mother's farm,
To drink new cider mull'd, with ginger warm.   150
For gaffer Treadwell told us by the bye,
Excessive sorrow is exceeding dry.
   While bulls bear horns upon their curled brow,
Or lasses with soft strokings milk the cow;
While paddling ducks the standing lake desire,
Or batt'ning hogs roll in the sinking mire;
While moles the crumbled earth in hillocks raise,
So long shall swains tell Blouzelinda's praise.
   Thus wail'd the louts in melancholy strain,
Till bonny Susan sped across the plain;   160
They seized the lass in apron clean array'd,
And to the ale-house forced the willing maid;
In ale and kisses they forget their cares,
And Susan Blouzelinda's loss repairs.

PERCY BYSSHE SHELLEY

ADONAIS

AN ELEGY ON THE DEATH OF JOHN KEATS

'Αστὴρ πρὶν μὲν ἔλαμπες ἐνὶ ζώοισιν ἐῶος.
Νῦν δὲ θανὼν, λάμπεις ἕσπερος ἐν φθιμένοις.

PLATO.

Φάρμακον ἦλθε, Βίων, ποτὶ σὸν στόμα, φάρμακον εἶδες.
Τοιούτοις χείλεσσι ποτέδραμε, κοὐκ ἐγλυκάνθη;
Τίς δὲ βροτὸς τοσσοῦτον ἀνάμερος, ἢ κεράσαι τοι
Ἢ δοῦναι χατέοντι τὸ φάρμακον ἔκφυλεν ἆδαν;

MOSCHUS.

i

I weep for Adonais—he is dead!
Oh, weep for Adonais! though our tears
Thaw not the frost which binds so dear a head!
And thou, sad Hour, selected from all years
To mourn our loss, rouse thy obscure compeers,
And teach them thine own sorrow! Say: 'With me
Died Adonais; till the Future dares
Forget the Past, his fate and fame shall be
An echo and a light unto eternity!'

ii

Where wert thou, mighty Mother, when he lay,   10
When thy Son lay, pierced by the shaft which flies
In darkness? where was lorn Urania
When Adonais died?   With veilèd eyes,
'Mid listening Echoes, in her Paradise
She sate, while one, with soft enamoured breath,
Rekindled all the fading melodies,
With which, like flowers that mock the corse beneath,
He had adorned and hid the coming bulk of death.

iii

O, weep for Adonais—he is dead!
Wake, melancholy Mother, wake and weep!   20
Yet wherefore? Quench within their burning bed
Thy fiery tears, and let thy loud heart keep
Like his a mute and uncomplaining sleep;
For he is gone, where all things wise and fair
Descend. Oh, dream not that the amorous Deep
Will yet restore him to the vital air;
Death feeds on his mute voice, and laughs at our despair.

iv

Most musical of mourners, weep again!
Lament anew, Urania!—He died,
Who was the sire of an immortal strain,   30
Blind, old, and lonely, when his country's pride
The priest, the slave, and the liberticide
Trampled and mocked with many a loathèd rite
Of lust and blood; he went, unterrified,
Into the gulf of death; but his clear Sprite
Yet reigns o'er earth, the third among the sons of light.

v

Most musical of mourners, weep anew!
Not all to that bright station dared to climb;
And happier they their happiness who knew,
Whose tapers yet burn through that night of time   40
In which suns perished; others more sublime,
Struck by the envious wrath of man or God,
Have sunk, extinct in their refulgent prime;
And some yet live, treading the thorny road,
Which leads, through toil and hate, to Fame's serene abode.

vi

But now, thy youngest, dearest one has perished,
The nursling of thy widowhood, who grew,
Like a pale flower by some sad maiden cherished
And fed with true-love tears instead of dew;

Most musical of mourners, weep anew!   50
Thy extreme hope, the loveliest and the last,
The bloom, whose petals, nipped before they blew,
Died on the promise of the fruit, is waste;
The broken lily lies—the storm is overpast.

vii

To that high Capital, where kingly Death
Keeps his pale court in beauty and decay,
He came; and bought, with price of purest breath,
A grave among the eternal.—Come away!
Haste, while the vault of blue Italian day
Is yet his fitting charnel-roof! while still   60
He lies, as if in dewy sleep he lay;
Awake him not! surely he takes his fill
Of deep and liquid rest, forgetful of all ill.

viii

He will awake no more, oh, never more!
Within the twilight chamber spreads apace
The shadow of white Death, and at the door
Invisible Corruption waits to trace
His extreme way to her dim dwelling-place;
The eternal Hunger sits, but pity and awe
Soothe her pale rage, nor dares she to deface   70
So fair a prey, till darkness, and the law
Of change, shall o'er his sleep the mortal curtain draw.

ix

Oh, weep for Adonais!—The quick Dreams,
The passion-wingèd Ministers of thought,
Who were his flocks, whom near the living streams
Of his young spirit he fed, and whom he taught
The love which was its music, wander not,—
Wander no more, from kindling brain to brain,
But droop there, whence they sprung; and mourn their lot
Round the cold heart, where, after their sweet pain,   80
They ne'er will gather strength, or find a home again.

x

And one with trembling hand clasps his cold head,
And fans him with her moonlight wings, and cries,
'Our love, our hope, our sorrow, is not dead;
See, on the silken fringe of his faint eyes,
Like dew upon a sleeping flower, there lies
A tear some Dream has loosened from his brain.'
Lost Angel of a ruined Paradise!
She knew not 'twas her own; as with no stain
She faded, like a cloud which had outwept its rain.   90

xi

One from a lucid urn of starry dew
Washed his light limbs, as if embalming them;
Another clipped her profuse locks, and threw
The wreath upon him, like an anadem,
Which frozen tears instead of pearls begem;
Another in her wilful grief would break
Her bow and wingèd reeds, as if to stem
A greater loss with one which was more weak;
And dull the barbèd fire against his frozen cheek.

xii

Another Splendor on his mouth alit,   100
That mouth whence it was wont to draw the breath
Which gave it strength to pierce the guarded wit,
And pass into the panting heart beneath
With lightning and with music; the damp death
Quenched its caress upon his icy lips;
And, as a dying meteor stains a wreath
Of moonlight vapor, which the cold night clips,
It flushed through his pale limbs, and passed to its eclipse.

xiii

And others came—Desires and Adorations,
Wingèd Persuasions and veiled Destinies,   110
Splendors, and Glooms, and glimmering Incarnations

Of hopes and fears, and twilight Fantasies;
And Sorrow, with her family of Sighs,
And Pleasure, blind with tears, led by the gleam
Of her own dying smile instead of eyes,
Came in slow pomp;—the moving pomp might seem
Like pageantry of mist on an autumnal stream.

xiv

All he had loved, and moulded into thought
From shape, and hue, and odor, and sweet sound,
Lamented Adonais. Morning sought   120
Her eastern watch tower, and her hair unbound,
Wet with the tears which should adorn the ground,
Dimmed the aërial eyes that kindle day;
Afar the melancholy thunder moaned,
Pale Ocean in unquiet slumber lay,
And the wild winds flew round, sobbing in their dismay.

xv

Lost Echo sits amid the voiceless mountains,
And feeds her grief with his remembered lay,
And will no more reply to winds or fountains,
Or amorous birds perched on the young green spray,   130
Or herdsman's horn, or bell at closing day;
Since she can mimic not his lips, more dear
Than those for whose disdain she pined away
Into a shadow of all sounds:—a drear
Murmur, between their songs, is all the woodmen hear.

xvi

Grief made the young Spring wild, and she threw down
Her kindling buds, as if she Autumn were,
Or they dead leaves; since her delight is flown,
For whom should she have waked the sullen year?
To Phoebus was not Hyacinth so dear,   140
Nor to himself Narcissus, as to both
Thou, Adonais; wan they stand and sere

Amid the faint companions of their youth,
With dew all turned to tears; odor, to sighing ruth.

xvii

Thy spirit's sister, the lorn nightingale,
Mourns not her mate with such melodious pain;
Not so the eagle, who like thee could scale
Heaven, and could nourish in the sun's domain
Her mighty youth with morning, doth complain,
Soaring and screaming round her empty nest,   150
As Albion wails for thee: the curse of Cain
Light on his head who pierced thy innocent breast,
And scared the angel soul that was its earthly guest!

xviii

Ah woe is me! Winter is come and gone,
But grief returns with the revolving year;
The airs and streams renew their joyous tone;
The ants, the bees, the swallows reappear;
Fresh leaves and flowers deck the dead Seasons' bier;
The amorous birds now pair in every brake,
And build their mossy homes in field and brere;   160
And the green lizard and the golden snake,
Like unimprisoned flames, out of their trance awake.

xix

Through wood and stream and field and hill and Ocean,
A quickening life from the Earth's heart has burst,
As it has ever done, with change and motion,
From the great morning of the world when first
God dawned on Chaos; in its stream immersed,
The lamps of Heaven flash with a softer light;
All baser things pant with life's sacred thirst,
Diffuse themselves, and spend in love's delight   170
The beauty and the joy of their renewèd might.

XX

The leprous corpse, touched by this spirit tender,
Exhales itself in flowers of gentle breath;
Like incarnations of the stars, when splendor
Is changed to fragrance, they illumine death
And mock the merry worm that wakes beneath.
Nought we know, dies. Shall that alone which knows
Be as a sword consumed before the sheath
By sightless lightning? the intense atom glows
A moment, then is quenched in a most cold repose.   180

xxi

Alas! that all we loved of him should be,
But for our grief, as if it had not been,
And grief itself be mortal! Woe is me!
Whence are we, and why are we? of what scene
The actors or spectators?   Great and mean
Meet massed in death, who lends what life must borrow.
As long as skies are blue and fields are green,
Evening must usher night, night urge the morrow,
Month follow month with woe, and year wake year to sorrow.

xxii

He will awake no more, oh, never more!   190
'Wake thou,' cried Misery, 'childless Mother, rise
Out of thy sleep, and slake, in thy heart's core,
A wound more fierce than his with tears and sighs.'
And all the Dreams that watched Urania's eyes,
And all the Echoes whom their sister's song
Had held in holy silence, cried, 'Arise!'
Swift as a Thought by the snake Memory stung,
From her ambrosial rest the fading Splendor sprung.

xxiii

She rose like an autumnal Night, that springs
Out of the East, and follows wild and drear   200
The golden Day, which, on eternal wings,

Even as a ghost abandoning a bier,
Had left the Earth a corpse;—sorrow and fear
So struck, so roused, so rapt Urania;
So saddened round her like an atmosphere
Of stormy mist; so swept her on her way
Even to the mournful place where Adonais lay.

xxiv

Out of her secret Paradise she sped,
Through camps and cities rough with stone, and steel,
And human hearts, which to her airy tread   210
Yielding not, wounded the invisible
Palms of her tender feet where'er they fell;
And barbèd tongues, and thoughts more sharp than they,
Rent the soft Form they never could repel,
Whose sacred blood, like the young tears of May,
Paved with eternal flowers that undeserving way.

xxv

In the death-chamber for a moment Death,
Shamed by the presence of that living Might,
Blushed to annihilation, and the breath
Revisited those lips, and life's pale light   220
Flashed through those limbs, so late her dear delight.
'Leave me not wild and drear and comfortless,
As silent lightning leaves the starless night!
Leave me not!' cried Urania; her distress
Roused Death; Death rose and smiled, and met her vain caress.

xxvi

'Stay yet awhile! speak to me once again;
Kiss me, so long but as a kiss may live;
And in my heartless breast and burning brain
That word, that kiss shall all thoughts else survive,
With food of saddest memory kept alive,   230
Now thou art dead, as if it were a part
O thee, my Adonais! I would give
All that I am to be as thou now art!
But I am chained to Time, and cannot thence depart!

xxvii

'O gentle child, beautiful as thou wert,
Why didst thou leave the trodden paths of men
Too soon, and with weak hands though mighty heart
Dare the unpastured dragon in his den?
Defenceless as thou wert, oh, where was then
Wisdom the mirrored shield, or scorn the spear?   240
Or hadst thou waited the full cycle, when
Thy spirit should have filled its crescent sphere,
The monsters of life's waste had fled from thee like deer.

xxviii

'The herded wolves, bold only to pursue;
The obscene ravens, clamorous o'er the dead;
The vultures, to the conqueror's banner true,
Who feed where Desolation first has fed,
And whose wings rain contagion;—how they fled,
When, like Apollo, from his golden bow,
The Pythian of the age one arrow sped   250
And smiled!—The spoilers tempt no second blow,
They fawn on the proud feet that spurn them lying low.

xxix

'The sun comes forth, and many reptiles spawn;
He sets, and each ephemeral insect then
Is gathered into death without a dawn,
And the immortal stars awake again;
So is it in the world of living men:
A godlike mind soars forth, in its delight
Making earth bare and veiling heaven, and when
It sinks, the swarms that dimmed or shared its light   260
Leave to its kindred lamps the spirit's awful night.'

xxx

Thus ceased she; and the mountain shepherds came,
Their garlands sere, their magic mantles rent;
The Pilgrim of Eternity, whose fame

Over his living head like Heaven is bent,
An early but enduring monument,
Came, veiling all the lightnings of his song
In sorrow; from her wilds Ierne sent
The sweetest lyrist of her saddest wrong,
And love taught grief to fall like music from his tongue.   270

xxxi

'Midst others of less note, came one frail Form,
A phantom among men; companionless
As the last cloud of an expiring storm
Whose thunder is its knell; he, as I guess,
Had gazed on Nature's naked loveliness,
Actaeon-like, and now he fled astray
With feeble steps o'er the world's wilderness,
And his own thoughts, along that rugged way,
Pursued, like raging hounds, their father and their prey.

xxxii

A pard-like Spirit beautiful and swift—   280
A love in desolation masked;—a Power
Girt round with weakness;—it can scarce uplift
The weight of the superincumbent hour;
It is a dying lamp, a falling shower,
A breaking billow;—even whilst we speak
Is it not broken?   On the withering flower
The killing sun smiles brightly; on a cheek
The life can burn in blood, even while the heart may break.

xxxiii

His head was bound with pansies over-blown,
And faded violets, white, and pied, and blue;   290
And a light spear topped with a cypress cone,
Round whose rude shaft dark ivy-tresses grew
Yet dripping with the forest's noonday dew,
Vibrated, as the ever-beating heart
Shook the weak hand that grasped it; of that crew
He came the last, neglected and apart;
A herd-abandoned deer struck by the hunter's dart.

xxxiv

All stood aloof, and at his partial moan
Smiled through their tears; well knew that gentle band
Who in another's fate now wept his own,   300
As in the accents of an unknown land
He sung new sorrow; sad Urania scanned
The Stranger's mien, and murmured, 'Who art thou?'
He answered not, but with a sudden hand
Made bare his branded and ensanguined brow,
Which was like Cain's or Christ's—oh! that it should be so!

xxxv

What softer voice is hushed over the dead?
Athwart what brow is that dark mantle thrown?
What form leans sadly o'er the white death-bed,
In mockery of monumental stone,   310
The heavy heart heaving without a moan?
If it be He, who, gentlest of the wise,
Taught, soothed, loved, honoured the departed one,
Let me not vex with inharmonious sighs
The silence of that heart's accepted sacrifice.

xxxvi

Our Adonais has drunk poison—oh,
What deaf and viperous murderer could crown
Life's early cup with such a draught of woe?
The nameless worm would now itself disown;
It felt, yet could escape the magic tone   320
Whose prelude held all envy, hate and wrong
But what was howling in one breast alone,
Silent with expectation of the song,
Whose master's hand is cold, whose silver lyre unstrung.

xxxvii

Live thou, whose infamy is not thy fame!
Live! fear no heavier chastisement from me,
Thou noteless blot on a remembered name!
But be thyself, and know thyself to be!

And ever at thy season be thou free
To spill the venom when thy fangs o'erflow;   330
Remorse and Self-contempt shall cling to thee;
Hot Shame shall burn upon thy secret brow,
And like a beaten hound tremble thou shalt—as now.

xxxviii

Nor let us weep that our delight is fled
Far from these carrion kites that scream below;
He wakes or sleeps with the enduring dead;
Thou canst not soar where he is sitting now.
Dust to the dust! but the pure spirit shall flow
Back to the burning fountain whence it came,
A portion of the Eternal, which must glow   340
Through time and change, unquenchably the same,
Whilst thy cold embers choke the sordid hearth of shame.

xxxix

Peace, peace! he is not dead, he doth not sleep—
He hath awakened from the dream of life—
'Tis we, who lost in stormy visions, keep
With phantoms an unprofitable strife,
And in made trance strike with our spirit's knife
Invulnerable nothings. *We* decay
Like corpses in a charnel; fear and grief
Convulse us and consume us day by day,   350
And cold hopes swarm like worms within our living clay.

xl

He has outsoared the shadow of our night;
Envy and calumny and hate and pain,
And that unrest which men miscall delight,
Can touch him not and torture not again;
From the contagion of the world's slow stain
He is secure, and now can never mourn
A heart grown cold, a head grown grey in vain;
Nor, when the spirit's self has ceased to burn,
With sparkless ashes load an unlamented urn.   360

xli

He lives, he wakes—'tis Death is dead, not he;
Mourn not for Adonais. —Thou young Dawn,
Turn all thy dew to splendor, for from thee
The spirit thou lamentest is not gone;
Ye caverns and ye forests, cease to moan!
Cease, ye faint flowers and fountains, and thou Air
Which like a mourning veil thy scarf hadst thrown
O'er the abandoned Earth, now leave it bare
Even to the joyous stars which smile on its despair!

xlii

He is made one with Nature: there is heard   370
His voice in all her music, from the moan
Of thunder, to the song of night's sweet bird;
He is a presence to be felt and known
In darkness and in light, from herb and stone,
Spreading itself where'er that Power may move
Which has withdrawn his being to its own;
Which wields the world with never-wearied love,
Sustains it from beneath, and kindles it above.

xliii

He is a portion of the loveliness
Which once he made more lovely; he doth bear   380
His part, while the one Spirit's plastic stress
Sweeps through the dull dense world, compelling there
All new successions to the forms they wear,
Torturing the unwilling dross that checks its flight
To its own likeness, as each mass may bear,
And bursting in its beauty and its might
From trees and beasts and men into the Heaven's light.

xliv

The splendors of the firmament of time
May be eclipsed, but are extinguished not;
Like stars to their appointed height they climb,   390
And death is a low mist which cannot blot

The brightness it may veil. When lofty thought
Lifts a young heart above its mortal lair,
And love and life contend in it for what
Shall be its earthly doom, the dead live there
And move like winds of light on dark and stormy air.

xlv

The inheritors of unfulfilled renown
Rose from their thrones, built beyond mortal thought,
Far in the Unapparent. Chatterton
Rose pale, —his solemn agony had not   400
Yet faded from him; Sidney, as he fought
And as he fell, and as he lived and loved
Sublimely mild, a Spirit without spot,
Arose; and Lucan, by his death approved;
Oblivion as they rose shrank like a thing reproved.

xlvi

And many more, whose names on Earth are dark,
But whose transmitted effluence cannot die
So long as fire outlives the parent spark,
Rose, robed in dazzling immortality.
'Thou are become as one of us,' they cry;   410
'It was for thee yon kingless sphere has long
Swung blind in unascended majesty,
Silent alone amid an Heaven of song.
Assume thy wingèd throne, thou Vesper of our throng!'

xlvii

Who mourns for Adonais? Oh, come forth,
Fond wretch! and know thyself and him aright.
Clasp with thy panting soul the pendulous Earth;
As from a centre, dart thy spirit's light
Beyond all worlds, until its spacious might
Satiate the void circumference: then shrink   420
Even to a point within our day and night;
And keep thy heart light lest it make thee sink
When hope has kindled hope, and lured thee to the brink.

xlviii

Or go to Rome, which is the sepulchre,
Oh, not of him, but of our joy; 'tis nought
That ages, empires, and religions, there
Lie buried in the ravage they have wrought;
For such as he can lend,—they borrow not
Glory from those who made the world their prey;
And he is gathered to the kings of thought   430
Who waged contention with their time's decay,
And of the past are all that cannot pass away.

xlix

Go thou to Rome, —at once the Paradise,
The grave, the city, and the wilderness;
And where its wrecks like shattered mountains rise,
And flowering weeds and fragrant copses dress
The bones of Desolation's nakedness,
Pass, till the Spirit of the spot shall lead
Thy footsteps to a slope of green access,   440
Where, like an infant's smile, over the dead
A light of laughing flowers along the grass is spread.

l

And grey walls moulder round, on which dull Time
Feeds, like slow fire upon a hoary brand;
And one keen pyramid with wedge sublime,
Pavilioning the dust of him who planned
This refuge for his memory, doth stand
Like flame transformed to marble; and beneath,
A field is spread, on which a newer band
Have pitched in Heaven's smile their camp of death,
Welcoming him we lose with scarce extinguished breath.   450

li

Here pause: these graves are all too young as yet
To have outgrown the sorrow which consigned
Its charge to each; and if the seal is set,
Here, on one fountain of a mourning mind,

Break it not thou! too surely shalt thou find
Thine own well full, if thou returnest home,
Of tears and gall. From the world's bitter wind
Seek shelter in the shadow of the tomb.
What Adonais is, why fear we to become?

lii

The One remains, the many change and pass;   460
Heaven's light forever shines, Earth's shadows fly;
Life, like a dome of many-coloured glass,
Stains the white radiance of Eternity,
Until Death tramples it to fragments. —Die,
If thou wouldst be with that which thou dost seek!
Follow where all is fled! —Rome's azure sky,
Flowers, ruins, statues, music, words, are weak
The glory they transfuse with fitting truth to speak.

liii

Why linger, why turn back, why shrink, my Heart?
Thy hopes are gone before; from all things here   470
They have departed; thou shouldst now depart!
A light is passed from the revolving year,
And man, and woman; and what still is dear
Attracts to crush, repels to make thee wither.
The soft sky smiles, —the low wind whispers near;
'Tis Adonais calls! oh, hasten thither,
No more let Life divide what Death can join together.

liv

That Light whose smile kindles the Universe,
That Beauty in which all things work and move,
That Benediction which the eclipsing Curse   480
Of birth can quench not, that sustaining Love
Which through the web of being blindly wove
By man and beast and earth and air and sea,
Burns bright or dim, as each are mirrors of
The fire for which all thirst, now beams on me,
Consuming the last clouds of cold mortality.

lv

The breath whose might I have invoked in song
Descends on me; my spirit's bark is driven
Far from the shore, far from the trembling throng
Whose sails were never to the tempest given;   490
The massy earth and spherèd skies are riven!
I am borne darkly, fearfully, afar;
Whilst, burning through the inmost veil of Heaven,
The soul of Adonais, like a star,
Beacons from the abode where the Eternal are.

MATTHEW ARNOLD

THYRSIS

A MONODY, TO COMMEMORATE THE AUTHOR'S FRIEND,
ARTHUR HUGH CLOUGH, WHO DIED AT FLORENCE, 1861.

How changed is here each spot man makes or fills!
  In the two Hinkseys nothing keeps the same;
    The village street its haunted mansion lacks,
  And from the sign is gone Sibylla's name,
    And from the roofs the twisted chimney-stacks—
      Are ye too changed, ye hills?
  See, 'tis no foot of unfamiliar men
    To-night from Oxford up your pathway strays!
    Here came I often, often, in old days—
Thyrsis and I; we still had Thyrsis then.   10

Runs it not here, the track by Childsworth Farm,
  Past the high wood, to where the elm-tree crowns
    The hill behind whose ridge the sunset flames?
  The signal-elm, that looks on Ilsley Downs,
    The Vale, the three lone weirs, the youthful Thames?—
      This winter-eve is warm,
  Humid the air! leafless, yet soft as spring,
    The tender purple spray on copse and briers!
    And that sweet city with her dreaming spires,
She needs not June for beauty's heightening.   20

Lovely all times she lies, lovely to-night!—
  Only, methinks, some loss of habit's power
    Befalls me wandering through this upland dim.
  Once pass'd I blindfold here, at any hour;
    Now seldom come I, since I came with him.
      That single elm-tree bright
  Against the west—I miss it! is it gone?
    We prized it dearly; while it stood, we said,
    Our friend, the Gipsy-Scholar, was not dead;
While the tree lived, he in these fields lived on.   30

Too rare, too rare, grow now my visits here,
   But once I knew each field, each flower, each stick;
     And with the country-folk acquaintance made
By barn in threshing-time, by new-built rick.
     Here, too, our shepherd-pipes we first assay'd.
       Ah me! this many a year
My pipe is lost, my shepherd's holiday!
     Needs must I lose them, needs with heavy heart
     Into the world and wave of men depart;
But Thyrsis of his own will went away.   40

It irk'd him to be here, he could not rest.
   He loved each simple joy the country yields,
     He loved his mates; but yet he could not keep
For that a shadow lour'd on the fields,
     Here with the shepherds and the silly sheep.
       Some life of men unblest
He knew, which made him droop, and fill'd his head.
     He went; his piping took a troubled sound
     Of storms that rage outside our happy ground;
He could not wait their passing, he is dead.   50

So, some tempestuous morn in early June,
     When the year's primal burst of bloom is o'er,
     Before the roses and the longest day—
When garden-walks and all the grassy floor
     With blossoms red and white of fallen May
       And chestnut-flowers are strewn—
So have I heard the cuckoo's parting cry,
     From the wet field, through the vext garden-trees,
     Come with the volleying rain and tossing breeze:
The bloom is gone, and with the bloom go I!   60

Too quick despairer, wherefore wilt thou go?
   Soon will the high Midsummer pomps come on,
     Soon will the musk carnations break and swell,
Soon shall we have gold-dusted snapdragon,
     Sweet-William with his homely cottage-smell,
       And stocks in fragrant blow;

Roses that down the alleys shine afar,
  And open, jasmine-muffled lattices,
    And groups under the dreaming garden-trees,
  And the full moon, and the white evening-star.   70

He hearkens not! light comer, he is flown!
  What matters it? next year he will return,
    And we shall have him in the sweet spring-days,
  With whitening hedges, and uncrumpling fern,
    And blue-bells trembling by the forest-ways,
      And scent of hay new-mown.
  But Thyrsis never more we swains shall see;
    See him come back, and cut a smoother reed,
    And blow a strain the world at last shall heed—
  For Time, not Corydon, hath conquer'd thee!   80

Alack, for Corydon no rival now!—
  But when Sicilian shepherds lost a mate,
    Some good survivor with his flute would go,
  Piping a ditty sad for Bion's fate;
    And cross the unpermitted ferry's flow,
      And relax Pluto's brow,
  And make leap up with joy the beauteous head
    Of Proserpine, among whose crowned hair
    Are flowers first open'd on Sicilian air,
  And flute his friend, like Orpheus, from the dead.   90

O easy access to the hearer's grace
  When Dorian shepherds sang to Proserpine!
    For she herself had trod Sicilian fields,
  She knew the Dorian water's gush divine,
    She knew each lily white which Enna yields,
      Each rose with blushing face;
  She loved the Dorian pipe, the Dorian strain.
    But ah, of our poor Thames she never heard!
    Her foot the Cumner cowslips never stirr'd;
  And we should tease her with our plaint in vain!   100

Well! wind-dispersed and vain the words will be,
 Yet, Thyrsis, let me give my grief its hour
  In the old haunt, and find our tree-topp'd hill!
 Who, if not I, for questing here hath power?
  I know the wood which hides the daffodil,
   I know the Fyfield tree,
 I know what white, what purple fritillaries
  The grassy harvest of the river-fields,
  Above by Ensham, down by Sandford, yields,
And what sedged brooks are Thames's tributaries;   110

I know these slopes; who knows them if not I?—
 But many a dingle on the loved hill-side,
  With thorns once studded, old, white-blossom'd trees,
 Where thick the cowslips grew, and far descried
  High tower'd the spikes of purple orchises,
   Hath since our day put by
 The coronals of that forgotten time;
  Down each green bank hath gone the ploughboy's team,
  And only in the hidden brookside gleam
Primroses, orphans of the flowery prime.   120

Where is the girl, who by the boatman's door,
 Above the locks, above the boating throng,
  Unmoor'd our skiff when through the Wytham flats,
 Red loosestrife and blond meadow-sweet among
  And darting swallows and light water-gnats,
   We track'd the shy Thames shore?
 Where are the mowers, who, as the tiny swell
  Of our boat passing heaved the river-grass,
  Stood with suspended scythe to see us pass?—
They are all gone, and thou art gone as well!   130

Yes, thou art gone! and round me too the night
 In ever-nearing circle weaves her shade.
 I see her veil draw soft across the day,
 I feel her slowly chilling breath invade
  The cheek grown thin, the brown hair sprent with grey;
  I feel her finger light

Laid pausefully upon life's headlong train;—
  The foot less prompt to meet the morning dew,
  The heart less bounding at emotion new,
And hope, once crush'd, less quick to spring again.   140

And long the way appears, which seem'd so short
  To the less practised eye of sanguine youth;
    And high the mountain-tops, in cloudy air,
The mountain-tops where is the throne of Truth,
  Tops in life's morning-sun so bright and bare!
    Unbreachable the fort
Of the long-batter'd world uplifts its wall;
  And strange and vain the earthly turmoil grows,
  And near and real the charm of thy repose,
And night as welcome as a friend would fall.   150

But hush! the upland hath a sudden loss
  Of quiet!—Look, adown the dusk hill-side,
    A troop of Oxford hunters going home,
As in old days, jovial and talking, ride!
  From hunting with the Berkshire hounds they come.
    Quick! let me fly, and cross
Into yon farther field!—'Tis done; and see,
  Back'd by the sunset, which doth glorify
  The orange and pale violet evening-sky,
Bare on its lonely ridge, the Tree! the Tree!   160

I take the omen! Eve lets down her veil,
  The white fog creeps from bush to bush about,
    The west unflushes, the high stars grow bright,
And in the scatter'd farms the lights come out.
  I cannot reach the signal-tree to-night,
    Yet, happy omen, hail!
Hear it from thy broad lucent Arno-vale
  (For there thine earth-forgetting eyelids keep
  The morningless and unawakening sleep
Under the flowery oleanders pale),   170

Hear it, O Thyrsis, still our tree is there!—
  Ah, vain! These English fields, this upland dim,
    These brambles pale with mist engarlanded,
  That lone, sky-pointing tree, are not for him;
      To a boon southern country he is fled,
        And now in happier air,
Wandering with the great Mother's train divine
      (And purer or more subtle soul than thee,
      I trow, the mighty Mother doth not see)
Within a folding of the Apennine,   180

Thou hearest the immortal chants of old!—
  Putting his sickle to the perilous grain
    In the hot cornfield of the Phrygian king,
  For thee the Lityerses-song again
      Young Daphnis with his silver voice doth sing;
        Sings his Sicilian fold,
His sheep, his hapless love, his blinded eyes—
      And how a call celestial round him rang,
      And heavenward from the fountain-brink he sprang,
And all the marvel of the golden skies.   190

There thou art gone, and me thou leavest here
  Sole in these fields! yet will I not despair.
    Despair I will not, while I yet descry
  'Neath the mild canopy of English air
      That lonely tree against the western sky.
        Still, still these slopes, 'tis clear,
Our Gipsy-Scholar haunts, outliving thee!
      Fields where soft sheep from cages pull the hay,
      Woods with anemonies in flower till May,
Know him a wanderer still; then why not me?   200

A fugitive and gracious light he seeks,
  Shy to illumine; and I seek it too.
    This does not come with houses or with gold,
  With place, with honour, and a flattering crew;
      'Tis not in the world's market bought and sold—
        But the smooth-slipping weeks

Drop by, and leave its seeker still untired;
  Out of the heed of mortals he is gone,
    He wends unfollow'd, he must house alone;
Yet on he fares, by his own heart inspired.   210

Thou too, O Thyrsis, on like quest wast bound;
  Thou wanderedst with me for a little hour!
    Men gave thee nothing; but this happy quest,
If men esteem'd thee feeble, gave thee power,
    If men procured thee trouble, gave thee rest.
      And this rude Cumner ground,
Its fir-topped Hurst, its farms, its quiet fields,
  Here cam'st thou in thy jocund youthful time,
  Here was thine height of strength, thy golden prime!
And still the haunt beloved a virtue yields.   220

What though the music of thy rustic flute
  Kept not for long its happy, country tone;
    Lost it too soon, and learnt a stormy note
Of men contention-tost, of men who groan,
    Which task'd thy pipe too sore, and tired thy throat—
      It fail'd, and thou wast mute!
Yet hadst thou alway visions of our light,
  And long with men of care thou couldst not stay,
  And soon thy foot resumed its wandering way,
Left human haunt, and on alone till night.   230

Too rare, too rare, grow now my visits here!
  'Mid city-noise, not, as with thee of yore,
    Thyrsis! in reach of sheep-bells is my home.
—Then through the great town's harsh, heart-wearying roar,
  Let in thy voice a whisper often come,
    To chase fatigue and fear:
Why faintest thou? I wander'd till I died.
  Roam on! The light we sought is shining still.
  Dost thou ask proof? Our tree yet crowns the hill,
Our Scholar travels yet the loved hill-side.   240

COMMENTARY AND NOTES

THEOCRITUS

(fl. 270 B.C.)

Theocritus was born in Syracuse, about 310 B.C., a son of Praxagoras and Philina. For students of his true bucolics the most important period of his life is marked by his sojourn in the island of Cos, about 290–283. Here he studied under Philetas, known as an elegiac poet and a critic, joined a sort of literary club, and began writing pastorals. To this period belong both the first and seventh idyls. It is from the latter, filled as it is with biographical information, that we learn of the poet's friends, associates in the club (see notes for Idyl 7). Theocritus probably returned to Sicily for a short time before departing for Alexandria (c. 274 B.C.). In Idyl 17 he bids for the patronage of the young ruler, Ptolemy Philadelphus, possibly a friend of his Coan days. Idyl 15 finely illustrates the dramatic powers of the erstwhile pastoralist, yet shows the extent to which he has succumbed to the urban charm and oriental taste of the Egyptian court; the theme of the *Women at the Adonis Festival* (translated by Matthew Arnold) was later to become accepted as pastoral through Bion's treatment of it and through the association of Adonis with shepherd life. Perhaps repelled by the corruptions at Ptolemy's court, perhaps as a result of a rupture with the ruler, about the year 270 Theocritus left Alexandria to return to Cos. Probably the famous second idyl belongs to this last period of his activity. A visit to Miletus is the final bit of evidence about the life of Theocritus. This is contained in Idyl 28, which his biographers place after the poet's retirement to Cos.

IDYL 1

DAPHNIS

As the parent of all succeeding elegies in framework and literary devices as well as theme, Idyl 1 is all-important. The dialogue form of the poem, closely akin to that of the singing-match, provides a dramatic introduction and conclusion, and permits the poet to sketch an appropriate setting for the song. After the exchange of compliment, the goatherd begs a song for which he promises Thyrsis a finely wrought cup. The elaborate description of this gift is imitated by all elegists who adopt the Theocritean dialogue frame. The song itself has many features which, almost accidental in the Greek, in time become inevitably associated with the elegy: (1) the recurrent refrain, which changing near the close gives earnest of the later consolation, (2) the address to the nymphs, (3) the visits of the various deities, and (4) the prayer that Nature reverse her course. Mention of these familiar devices leaves out of account innumerable phrases and turns of thought which were caught up and woven into later elegies. (See further *supra*, p. 4.)

[The editor has freely abbreviated references: for example, Vir., 5.45–47 stands for Virgil, Eclogue 5, lines 45–47; in cross references to authors represented in the book by a single poem, eclogue titles are omitted: for example, Marot, 1–24 refers to this passage in *De Madame Loyse*. Line numbers of the glossed passages appear in heavier type throughout.]

1–11. This is the language of compliment characteristic of elegies in which dialogue precedes the song itself. For literal imitations cf., for example, Mos., 55–57; Vir., 5.45–47; Marot, 1–24.

12–14. In Idyl 3.1–5 Tityrus, probably a servant, is called upon to tend the herds. The device becomes conventional from Vir., 5.12.

25–60. The elaborate description of the rewards, which in singing matches are wagers, became conventional through Virgil's adaptation in 3.36–47. Marot's adaptation, 33–48, is followed by Spenser, "November," 41–48. **52.** Virgil's imitation, 10.71, popularized for the later pastoral such employments. In Theocritus the trap was to catch locusts; in Virgil it is a basket for pressing curds or cheese.

64 ff. The Song of Thyrsis was a set piece, the form of the Daphnis legend here followed being probably well known to his auditors. It falls naturally into four parts: (1) the introductory excursus including the address to the nymphs and the mourning of Nature, (2) the visits of the deities and friends of Daphnis, (3) the coming of Aphrodite, her proud taunt, and Daphnis' reproach, and (4) the farewell of Daphnis and his death. The refrain, said to be characteristic of Sicilian poetry, is common to all ages and all languages. Its use here, in Idyl 2, and in Bion and Moschus established it, happily, as a stock feature in pastoral elegy.

65–69. The nymphs would be the natural associates of Daphnis if, as is sometimes understood, he was married to a nymph; according to another tradition his parents were Hermes and a nymph (see further note for Arnold, 171–190). This appeal to the nymphs or other companions becomes familiar: Vir., 10.9–12; Alamanni, 1.64–71; Baïf, 2.25–36; Spenser, *Astrophel*, 127–132; Milton, *Lycidas*, 50–55; Shelley, 10–13.

71–75. Such passages popularized the "pathetic fallacy": Mos., 32–49; Vir., 5.27–28, and 10.8, 13–15; Sannazaro, 5.42–49; Marot, 97–128; Spenser, "November," 67–69, 125–139. Virgil (5.27) repeats the incongruous reference in Theocritus to lions, which are hardly native to Sicily. After commenting upon the absence of lions in Sicily, the Scholiast adds, "The lion *would* have wept had he been there." Professor Rand remarks (*The Magic Art of Virgil*, p. 92, n. 1), "This fidelity to geography, alas, does not correct the Greek poet's lamentable infidelity to biology." In Vir., 10.13–15 laurels, tamarisks, and rocks replace the Greek beasts.

77–94. Deities, shepherds, and others visit the afflicted shepherd: Vir., 10.19–30; Marot, 133–154; Spenser, *Astrophel*, 199–210; Milton, *Lycidas*, 88–131, and *Epitaphium Damonis*, 69–92; Shelley, 262–315.

115–131. In 5.43–44, Virgil makes Daphnis announce his own epitaph, a variation from the lines of the Greek Daphnis, who has refused to communicate with his fellows. The variation in the refrain (127) denotes the approaching death of Daphnis. This change perhaps contributes to the later elegy's joyful close; see Vir., 5.56–80 and notes.

132–136. The prayer that Nature reverse her course in sympathy is repeated in Vir., 5.36–39.

140–141. *the stream:* usually understood as "the stream of death." Cholmeley (ed. *Theocritus,* p. 384) believes the legend may reflect the folk belief in the fatal consequences of inconstancy in the love of a mortal for a nymph. Thus Daphnis "approached the stream," which was a water-sprite; she "drew him under and swept him away" as a consequence of his passion for a mortal woman. Cf. *Lycidas,* 51 and note.

143–145. Marot, 253–260. **146–148.** Vir., 5.45–49 and 81–84; Sannazaro, *Phyllis,* 106–111; Marot, 261–272.

IDYL 7

THE HARVEST FESTIVAL

In outline Idyl 7 is simple, spontaneous, and natural. The Coan setting is described incidentally as the poet tells of his journey with two friends to the scene of the harvest celebration. On the way they encounter Lycidas, a famous singer in disguise. They agree to a singing-match, Lycidas in good fellowship promising to award a staff. The two songs follow: Lycidas sings the voyage of Ageanax to Mitylene, Simichidas (see note for 21) answers by extolling the love of Aratus. After mutual compliment Lycidas parts company, and Simichidas and his friends proceed to the festival, which he describes in all its luxuriance and beauty. This poem resembles the earlier idyl in its Coan setting—more distinct, of course, here—, in its characteristically happy mood, and in its inclusion of songs, set pieces, which are skilfully introduced by narrative leading naturally to the singing, but which here occur incidentally during the activities of the day.

"We have here," writes Cholmeley (ed. *Theocritus,* p. 13), "clearly a description of a day actually spent by the poet with his friends, while they were still young and full of enjoyment, linked in common pursuits and poetic rivalry in Cos, amusing themselves by exercises in pastoral poetry." Probably the poem was written as a sort of "pseudo-bucolic joke," in which the poet, masquerading as the shepherd Simichidas, good-humoredly enters into rural life and into the fellowship of his friends, who are disguised in name only. This idyl, Cholmeley continues, is "modeled on the rural ditties which were to be heard then, as now, in Greek country-sides and villages, but differing in tone and content; and differing consciously as much as Milton's *Lycidas* differs from the *Masque of Pyramus and Thisbe.*" As Idyl 1 established for later centuries the conventions to be associated with elegy, so Idyl 7 gave precedent for the personal, allegorical element in all pastoral. (See further, *supra,* p. 4.)

4. *Phrasidamus and Antigenes:* Like Eucritus, these are probably real names. **12.** *Lycidas:* This masquerading goatherd is probably Leonidas of Tarentum. **21.** *Simichidas:* This name for Theocritus is said to be a nickname, a diminutive of σιμός (snub-nosed). Thus the poet assumes the name by which he was perhaps known because of a flat nose.

39–41. Here Theocritus as the shepherd-poet Simichidas, declining comparison with two professed poets, acknowledges that he is himself a poet. In

Moschus and Virgil this autobiographical element becomes fully and permanently established. **40.** *I do not yet surpass* . . . It has been suggested that Theocritus had at this time already achieved fame. *Sicelidas:* identified by the Scholiast as Asclepiades of Samos, an epigrammatist; the name may be a patronymic or a *nom de plume*. *Philetas:* a native Coan, a great teacher and writer of elegies.

71–72. Vir., 5.72. Here Theocritus refers to two of his Coan fellow students or fellow poets. *Tityrus:* possibly Alexander of Aetolia, author of a poem dealing with the Daphnis legend. **74.** Bion, 31; Mos., 1; Vir., 10.13. **98.** *Aratus:* a real name. *Aristis:* "doubtless a real person, a thinly disguised friend of Aratus" (Cholmeley). **111–114.** Vir., 10.65.

135 ff. The rest of the poem is given over to a description of summer delights. For this Idyl 7 is more justly famous than for its allegory, which marks its importance for this volume. **148.** The Nymphs as well as the Muses were patronesses of song: Vir., 7.21.

(Bibliography follows notes for Moschus.)

BION

(Second Century, B.C.)

Practically nothing is known about the life of Bion, author of the *Lament for Adonis*. Scattered bits of information occur in the *Anthology*, in Suidas, and in two poems on his death—one by Moschus, the other by a pupil. Apparently he was a native of Smyrna, the city associated also with Homer, though his pupil connects his name with Syracuse and Sicilian Muses. Moschus implies that Bion died by poison. Suidas states that he was younger than Moschus.

IDYL 1

THE LAMENT FOR ADONIS

Though Bion's pupil reckons his master a leading bucolic poet of his day, none of the poems or fragments is a true pastoral. The *Lament for Adonis*, ascribed to Bion solely on the evidence of Moschus, was caught up in the pastoral stream for three reasons: Moschus' poem, the tradition that Adonis once tended sheep (see Theocr., 1.109, and Vir., 10.18), and the inclusion of both Bion and Moschus in early editions of Theocritus—the Aldine (1495), the Juntine (1515), and other sixteenth century editions. The *Lament for Adonis* contains no pastoral features, for as partly in Idyl 15 of Theocritus, here the poet endeavors solely to imitate the dirge sung for the dead Adonis during the festival in his honor. Bion's piece lacks the drama and the humor of Theocritus, but in some particulars it resembles the other poem. And naturally the popularity of the Adonis legend was enhanced by Ovid's extensive treatment, *Met*. 10.519 ff.

The *Lament for Adonis* was intended apparently to be sung or recited by one person. Thus, although it lacks many features common to the dialogue form, the piece exhibits such typical elegiac devices as the refrain, the pathetic fallacy, and the flower motif. Moreover, two contributions to the later consolation are added. The quenching of the Hymeneal torches suggests that the dirge followed the celebration of the first day, given to joy in the resurrection of the dead Adonis (see 89 and 99–100). And finally, the prayer near the close of the poem, that Venus refrain from her lamentation, parallels the change in the refrain in Theocritus' Idyl 1. These aspects of the poem bear directly upon the formal separation of the two moods, sorrow and joy, which Virgil was to effect in Eclogue 5. This book includes adaptations of Bion by Ronsard, Spenser, and Shelley; for detailed references see notes for *Adonis*, *Astrophel*, and *Adonais*, respectively.

33. Mos., 2. **35.** *Ibid.*, 5. **39.** Vir., 10.3.

76. The fading flowers, closely linked with the earlier Adonis tradition, contributed to the later pathetic fallacy; see further *supra*, pp. 2–3.

89. Here reference is to the past hymeneal; in Theocr., 15, the wedding song anticipates the dirge of the next day. The festival began apparently on the first day of the six-months period of Adonis' sojourn upon earth (the rest of the year was spent with Persephone).

99–100. Theocr., 15.143–144: "Dear to us has thine advent been, Adonis, and dear shall it be when thou comest again" (tr. Lang); Ovid, *Met.* 10.725–727: "My grief, Adonis, shall have an enduring monument, and each passing year in memory of your death shall give an imitation of my grief" (tr. Miller).

(Bibliography follows notes for Moschus.)

MOSCHUS

(Date uncertain)

Like Bion, Moschus, too, is an obscure figure. Comparing the styles of the two poets, Edmonds and others have concluded that Moschus is the earlier writer and cannot have been the author of *The Lament for Bion*; it has been suggested that the poem was written by a pupil of Bion. But Suidas states that Moschus was the pupil of Aristarchus, who taught at Alexandria from 180–144 B.C. Suidas and the author of a note appended to Moschus' *Love the Runaway* in the *Anthology* agree that Moschus was a Syracusan, a grammarian, and that he was accounted the second bucolic poet after Theocritus. In the *Lament* Moschus refers to his "Ausonian" song, possibly to distinguish himself from the Syracusan Theocritus. This poem is the only true pastoral of Moschus, who is better known for his *Love the Runaway* and *Europa and the Bull*, both pieces translated and adapted many times during the Renaissance.

IDYL 3

THE LAMENT FOR BION

In spite of its affectation and extravagance the *Lament for Bion* marks several important advances. Adopting and emphasizing devices in Theocritus' Idyls 1 and 7 and following the lyric form of Bion's dirge, Moschus introduced two motives which are significant additions: the association of the dead shepherd with poetic attainment, and the pastoral intimacy with the poet-singer, upon whom falls the poetic mantle, or as later expressed, to whom the dead singer bequeaths the gift of song. Moreover, the first pastoral elegy honoring a real person instead of a mythical Daphnis or symbolic Adonis, the *Lament for Bion* is the first of the class in which the poet himself enters, as in the *Harvest Festival* of Theocritus. This facilitates the poet-shepherd's account of his intimacy with the dead shepherd, as it also affords a natural means of digression upon such themes as poetic ambition or, later, church and state. Yet for these allegorical innovations Idyl 7 of Theocritus provided ultimate suggestion. As the poem was included in early editions of Theocritus, it was accepted as part of the classical tradition and imitated generously. As Bion's *Lament for Adonis* was to gain unparalleled popularity as a lyric theme, so Moschus introduced new motives which assisted the development and perpetuation of elegy. The *Lament for Bion* is closely followed by Sannazaro, Eclogue 11, and Alamanni, Eclogue 2 (see notes for these poems).

1–2. The introduction of rivers (cf. Bion, 33–34) reappears in 70–71 and becomes a stock device. **6–7.** The hyacinth is traditionally identified with pastoral elegy: Sannazaro, 11.31–33; Milton, *Lycidas*, 106.

11–12. Bion is associated with shepherd life as in Theocritus' elegy Daphnis the herdsman was also famed as a singer. Moschus invents the fiction that with the passing of Bion not only song but all good things have died.

50–84. This passage sets forth the poetic attainments of Bion, the poet-shepherd, who sings and tends his flocks at the same time. "By thus applying the imagery of the pastoral to a real person," writes Hanford (*P.M.L.A.*, XXV), "the author of the *Lament* had transformed what was previously a *genre* of erotic verse into the more serviceable type of the personal elegy in pastoral form." **55–57.** Theocr., 1.1–11 and note.

93–97. These lines introduce the fiction that the singer inherits the poetic gifts of the dead shepherd: Vir., 5.49; Milton, *Lycidas*, 64 and note.

99–104. For comment upon this sentiment see *supra*, p. 3. It reappears variously: Sannazaro, 11.58–63; Castiglione, 54–66; Alamanni, 2.115–124; Marot, 177–180; Spenser, "November," 83–89; Shelley, 154 ff.; Arnold, 62 ff.

111–114. This stands as a motto for *Adonais*, when Shelley "dipped his pen in consuming fire for Keats' destroyers."

115–126. Sannazaro, 11.64–66, 70–75; Arnold, 82–100.

Text: *Bucolici Graeci*, ed. U. Wilamowitz-Moellendorff, Oxford, 1905.

Other editions: *The Idylls of Theocritus with Bion and Moschus*, ed. the Reverend J. Banks, London, 1911; *The Idyls of Theocritus*, ed. R. J. Cholmeley, London, 1919; *The Greek Bucolic Poets*, ed. J. M. Edmonds, *Loeb Classical Library*, London, 1912; *The Idylls and Epigrams commonly attributed to Theocritus*, ed. Herbert Kynaston, Oxford, 1892; *Theocritus, Bion, and Moschus*, translated by Andrew Lang, London, 1928.

Comment: Sir James G. Frazer, *The Golden Bough*, 2 vols., New York, 1929, I; Frank R. Hamblin, *The Development of Allegory in the Classical Pastoral*, Abstract of Thesis, the University of Chicago, 1922; J. H. Hanford, "The Pastoral Elegy and Milton's *Lycidas*," *P.M.L.A.*, XXV (1910), 403–447;

W. P. Mustard, *Classical Echoes in Tennyson*, New York, 1904; *idem*, "Later Echoes of the Greek Bucolic Poets," *American Journal of Philology*, XXX (1909), 245–283.

VIRGIL
(70–19 B.C.)

Virgil was born October 15, 70 B.C., at Andes, the modern Pietole, in the Mantuan plain. His father, a poor man, gained wealth from his purchase of woodland tracts and from bee-keeping. Virgil's early rural surroundings fostered in him a love and understanding of the country which later found varied expression in the *Eclogues* and *Georgics*. But the poet's interests were not centered in home. Early in life he left his father's roof to attend school at Cremona, where at the age of fifteen he assumed the *toga virilis*; and, possibly never again returning to Mantua, he proceeded to Milan and thence to Rome to complete his studies in medicine, astrology, and philosophy. In youth Virgil began a history of Rome in verse, abandoning the task only as he became convinced of his immaturity. Jerram remarks the coincidence that John Milton, too, early contemplated an epic dealing with British history, which years later he wrote in prose. In Eclogue 6.3–5 Virgil announces that Apollo warned him against the epic undertaking and urged him to turn to rural themes. Political events more than native rural inspiration were to prompt Virgil's pastoral Muse, and the *Eclogues* themselves, as well as the minor poems, often sound the note of epic for which the poet was from the beginning so eminently fitted. With the exception of Eclogue 5, the compliment to Julius Caesar, all the poems are directly and indirectly concerned with the four friends—Varus, Pollio, Gallus, and Maecenas. Occupying some three years in the writing, and being arranged, rearranged, and polished, Virgil's ten eclogues were published in Naples, probably in 37 B.C. The poet died in 19 B.C.

ECLOGUE 5

DAPHNIS

Like Book 1 of the *Georgics*, Eclogue 5 pays tribute to Julius Caesar, whom Virgil regarded, in Conington's phrase, "as the saviour of his country," the hero of his boyhood days. As Virgil's theme is Roman, so the form of the poem is Theocritean. The first idyl provides the Daphnis theme as well as the exchange of courtesies at the beginning and end. Otherwise the form of the poem is that of the singing-match, as in Eclogue 3, with the absence, however, of wagers and the substitution of two longer strains of twenty-five lines for the short "amoebean" answers. (Virgil reserves for Eclogue 10 the Greek theme of Daphnis' erotic sorrow.) After Mopsus sings the dead Daphnis (ll. 20–44), Menalcas celebrates his deification (ll. 56–80), Virgil thus resuming the theme where Theocritus had left off. In this joyful motif lies the poem's most important contribution to elegy; for later pastoralists it remained only to substitute the joys of a Christian heaven. And though both Theocritus and Bion provided suggestions, the formal separation of these elements was first effected in the present poem.

Daphnis: The individual titles, like the collective one "Eclogae," were supplied by commentators. For the allegory of the two singers see notes for 48–49 and 86–87.

2. As in Theocritus' Idyl 1, one singer is skilled in piping, the other in singing.

8. Amyntas is a jealous shepherd in 2.38. But, like the later pastoralists, Virgil represents different individuals under the same names in different eclogues.

12. Tityrus, probably a servant here, is the name under which erroneously Virgil was thought to have shadowed himself, particularly in Eclogue 1. The line, from Theocr., 3.1–5 (see note for Theocr., 1.14), often reappears with variations: Vir., 10.7; Sannazaro, *Phyllis*, 31–32; Marot, 25–28; Spenser, "November," 7–8.

20. The nymphs weep (cf. Theocr., 1.65–69 and note), for Daphnis was the son of Hermes and a nymph, who now appears in the story for the first time. Virgil, remembering Venus' mourning for Adonis, identifies *mater* with Venus, from whom descended the Julian line. "Virgil, then, is mingling the legends of Daphnis and Adonis in the interests of a purpose different from either" (Rand, *The Magical Art of Virgil*, p. 92).

24–28. Theocr., 1.71–75 and note. Virgil conveys the impression of the herdsmen's neglect occasioned by their grief. The refusal of the cattle to eat or drink—the later pathetic fallacy—is possibly reminiscent of a story told by Suetonius in his *Life of Caesar*. The horses which Caesar had consecrated to the gods at the passage of the Rubicon and left at large, shed tears and refused to feed; the incident was accepted as an omen of Caesar's approaching death.

36–39. Theocr., 1.132–136, where the dying Daphnis prays that nature's course be changed; here, in the absence of the rural deities, a general blight has fallen.

40–42. This provided a suggestion for the later flower motif: Castiglione, 142–150; Marot, 225–240; Milton, *Lycidas*, 139–151. **43–44.** Theocr., 1.120–122; Sannazaro, *Phyllis*, 101–105; Castiglione, 151–154.

45–47. Together with 82–84, cf. Theocr., 1.7–8, and 8.83: "Better is it to listen to thy singing, than to taste the honeycomb" (tr. Lang). Cf. also Sannazaro, *Phyllis*, 106–108; Marot, 17–20, 261–272.

48–49. If "your teacher" *(magistrum)* be taken as referring to Daphnis, famed for his singing, the line repeats Moschus (97), who speaks of himself as Bion's poetical successor. Servius identifies Menalcas with Theocritus, and the younger man Mopsus with Virgil; that is, Virgil has surpassed his master (see further note for 86–87).

56–80. The apotheosis with its joyful theme forms the counterpart of the song of mourning.

60–64. The peace and amity include the animal world as in the Golden Age, pictured in Virgil's fourth eclogue. Conington observes parallels with the Hebraic prophecies: e.g., Isaiah, 11.6, 14.8, and 42.11. Virgil here attributes joy to the mountains, as in 1.28 and 10.15 sorrow, but he implies secondarily that these emotions proceed from the persons frequenting the mountains. Cf. Radbert, 94–99 and note. **65.** Sannazaro, *Phyllis*, 97–98; Milton, *Lycidas*, 183–185, and *Epitaphium Damonis*, 208. **76–78.** "An appeal to the uniformity of nature, as in 1.59, not altogether consistent with the language in which (1.60) he makes a breach in this uniformity a mark of the golden age just beginning" (Conington). **79–80.** Sannazaro, *Phyllis*, 99–100; Milton *Epitaphium Damonis*, 29–32.

81–84. Theocr., 1.7–8, which is genuinely Sicilian.

86–87. By thus quoting the first lines of Eclogues 2 and 3, Virgil seems to identify himself with Menalcas as the author not only of the two previous eclogues but also of this one. Virgil is, then, not only the Menalcas who sings the apotheosis, but he is the spokesman of the entire piece.

ECLOGUE 10

GALLUS

This poem, the last of the series, is Virgil's tribute to a fellow-poet and friend of his Neapolitan school days, C. Cornelius Gallus. Here again Virgil follows Greek precedent: like Gallus, the mythical Daphnis of the first idyl was famed as a singer, and in the seventh Theocritus the poet masquerades as a shepherd; and even Moschus does not deny himself a rôle in singing the praises of the poet Bion. Thus the allegory of the poet-shepherd was well established. In celebrating the shepherd Gallus Virgil does not neglect the martial theme, for it appears that Gallus was at the time serving in a military campaign, presumably under Octavian against Sextus Pompeius. The poem thus involves a discrepancy in presenting at once the soldier in active service and yet also the jilted lover languishing in Arcadia (ll. 16 and 31–36). But Virgil's poem is, in Sellar's phrase, "the idealised expression of unfortunate love," a theme by which he honors his unfortunate friend Gallus as soldier as well as erotic poet. The seeming incongruities of the poem prepared the way for a new elasticity and freedom in the pastoral, and the romantic sentiment greatly enhanced its attraction for later ages. Together with the famous fourth, which pictures the Golden Age about to begin, the tenth voices the innate and universal longing for escape. The influence of the poem has not been confined to pastoral poetry.

In one important particular the framework presents a novelty: in eight introductory lines the poet invokes the Muse and announces his theme; then having sung his song he gracefully concludes in an equal number of lines. To many later poets, including Milton, this manner and method held a stronger appeal than did the dialogue form of Eclogue 5. With the loss of the dramatic setting and approach, the subjective element enters more freely as the poet speaks outright in his own person. Hence the later introduction of matter alien to the major theme, as personal digression or church satire, becomes more easily integrated with pastoral elegy.

9–12. Theocr., 1.65–69, where the Sicilian nymphs are the natural companions of Daphnis; here they represent the Muses, whose haunts are not Arcadia, the scene of Gallus' suffering, but Parnassus, Pindus, and Aganippe.

Thus the subjective mood of the poem is enhanced as the Muses are connected not only with Gallus but with Virgil himself, who has just addressed Arethusa. Most later poets, following Theocritus, allude to the scenes associated with the dead shepherd's fate: Baïf, 2.25–33; *Lycidas,* 50–55. (Baïf's poem throughout closely follows Virgil; see notes.)

13–15. Theocr., 1.71–75 and note.

16–18. As in Theocr., 1.109, where Daphnis defends "the homely shepherd's trade" by alluding to Adonis, so here Virgil seems to apologize to Gallus for introducing him in a pastoral.

19–30. Theocr., 1.77–94 and note. **19.** *Ibid.,* 80. **21–22.** *Ibid.,* 81–82, Virgil substituting Apollo as the god of shepherds (5.35) and of poets (7.22).

26–27. Usually the woodland deities were accounted dangerous to see (Theocr., 1.16–18); the sight of Pan was supposed to produce madness, or "panic."

31–36. Theocr., 1.92–93. Here, instead of directly answering his visitors, Gallus turns to the consoling thought that the Arcadians will eternize his love in their songs. Soldier that he is, he half wishes himself an Arcadian, a shepherd with a vineyard. But Virgil seems to have already represented Gallus as a shepherd, his sheep about him (16). The confusion results possibly from Virgil's imaginary picture of Gallus which conflicts with the real Gallus, a soldier.

53–54. The carving of love verses in the bark of trees, as in 5.13, becomes commonplace in pastoral: e.g., Sannazaro, 11.103–106.

77. Throughout the homely conclusion (70–77) Virgil maintains the shepherd rôle, as here he indicates that he is to write no more pastorals; cf. the concluding line of *Lycidas.*

Text: *P. Vergili Maronis Opera,* ed. John Conington, 3 vols., London, 1881, I.

Other editions: *Virgil's Bucolics,* ed. C. S. Jerram, Oxford, 1887; *P. Vergili Maronis Opera,* ed. T. L. Papillon and A. E. Haigh, 2 vols., Oxford, 1902, II.

Comment: Tenney Frank, *Virgil: A Biography,* New York, 1922; Edward K. Rand, *The Magical Art of Virgil,* Harvard University Press, 1931; W. Y. Sellar, *The Roman Poets of the Augustan Age,* Oxford, 1883; *Servii Grammatici qui feruntur in Vergilii Bucolica et Georgica Commentarii,* ed. G. Thilo and H. Hagen, 3 vols., Leipzig, 1887.

NEMESIAN

(fl. 290 A.D.)

M. Aurelius Olympius Nemesianus, a native of Africa, lived in Rome during the time of the Emperor Carus and his sons (282–284). Petrarch shows his acquaintance with Nemesian by an allusion in Eclogue 10.199–201:

> Hinc procul, et Latio et Musis carissimus afris,
> Fluctivagos alius numerans sub gurgite pisces,
> Aurea plectra, apio cinctus viridante movebat.

The eclogues of Nemesian, as printed first in Rome, 1471, then in Venice, 1472, appeared as the last four in a group of eleven all attributed to

Calpurnius Siculus (first century). The Parma edition of Angelus Ugoletus (1500) first separated the respective eclogues, and recent scholarship has added more evidence of Nemesian's authorship of the poems in question. Four further editions appeared during the sixteenth century.

ECLOGUE 1

MELIBOEUS

This poem commemorates the death and noble character of Meliboeus, doubtless such a patron as in the eulogistic first eclogue of Calpurnius. With Nemesian personal allegory is less obtrusive than with Calpurnius. Nemesian once (2.84) refers to Virgil as Tityrus; here either of the interlocutors may stand for the author. Possibly, as in Virgil's first eclogue, the poet represents himself in both speakers. Nemesian's elegy follows generally the structural outline of Virgil's fifth eclogue, and it pervasively reflects the imagery of Virgil. Yet in the graceful picture of old age the poem claims real distinction. This theme is new to pastoral elegy, which is usually associated with premature death; and through Sannazaro the new motif received classical sanction (see notes for Prose 5 and Eclogue 5 from the *Arcadia*).

1–8. A typical Virgilian mosaic including suggestions from 10.71; 2.12–13, "raucis . . . resonant arbusta cicadis"; 3.52, "Quin age, si quid habes"; 9.32, "Incipe, si quid habes"; 5.2 and 2.34, "calamo trivisse labellum"; 2.32–33, "Pan primum calamos cera coniungere plures/ instituit"; 1.77–78, "non me pascente, capellae,/ florentem cytisum et salices carpetis amaras"; and *Geor.* 3.325 ff., "dum mane novum . . ./ et ros in tenera pecori gratissimus herba," from a passage concerning the management of flocks during summer. **27–29.** Vir., 5.13–15.

35. Here the lament proper begins, the preceding dialogue merging with it. **48–63.** This passage is conspicuous for its originality. **64–71.** With the flower passage are combined the visits of rural deities. **86.** Vir., 2.67, "et sol crescentes decedens duplicat umbras"; Castiglione, 56–59.

Text: *Minor Latin Poets*, ed. J. Wight Duff and Arnold M. Duff, *Loeb Classical Library*, London and Cambridge, 1934.

Comment: John Conington, "On the Later Bucolic Poets of Rome," *P. Vergili Maronis Opera*, London, 1881, I, 121–129; H. E. Butler, *Post-Augustan Poetry*, Oxford, 1909; J. Wight Duff, *A Literary History of Rome in the Silver Age*, London, 1927.

RADBERT

(c. 790–c. 865)

Paschasius Radbertus was born about 790 in or near the Gallic city of Soissons. Here as a boy he entered the convent of the Blessed Mary, where he was educated by the Benedictine nuns. After a brief period of secular life, before the year 812 he entered the Corvie (Corbie or Corvey) monastery, on the Somme, near Amiens, of which Adalhardus was founder and abbot (see notes for ll. 26 and 109). As a monk Radbert now gave himself not only to Scriptural exegesis and the writings of the Fathers, but to the study of profane letters, which so distinguished the age of Charles the Great. During this period Radbert left the monastery on many legations and journeys. In 822, he accompanied Louis the Pious, son of Charles the Great, on an expedition into Saxony for the purpose of founding a new monastery, the New Corbie, constructed on the banks of the Weser, in Westphalia. On the death of Adalhard, who it is to be gathered was instrumental in the founding of New Corbie, Radbert was dispatched on a mission to Louis to obtain consent for the election of the old abbot's successor at the Gallic Corbie, namely, Wala, whose life Radbert later chronicled. In 844 Radbert himself succeeded to this post, becoming the fourth abbot after Adalhard; but about 851 he resigned to devote himself entirely to his philosophical and theological studies. He died in 865 or thereabouts.

ECLOGUE BY TWO NUNS

This poem concludes the *De Vita S. Adalhardi,* which was written between the time of Adalhard's death (826) and just before or soon after the succession of Wala. The long prose *Vita* is filled with adulation, much of which the concluding *Egloga* repeats. Extensive analogues with the prose appear throughout the poem; and illustrative passages are quoted in the notes. The *Egloga* constitutes a kind of *l'envoi* to the life of Adalhard, celebrating in highly allegorized verse the chief work of the old abbot: his usefulness at Old Corbie and his foresight in establishing the New Corbie in a barbarous land. (See further *supra,* pp. 6–7.)

The prefatory gloss, by Radbert or another, explains the allegory of the poem. Its addition would, in the eyes of Petrarch, confirm that poet's convictions about the allegorical nature of pastoral. *Unam:* that is, Phyllis or Gallic Corbie, referred to in the poem as the spouse of Adalhard; *aliam:* Galatea or Saxon Corbie. Hers is the chief rôle as the elegist who mourns the death of Adalhard and greets his successor. The device of giving to pastoral personages names which in Greek or Latin signify their characteristics or features is adopted by both Petrarch and Boccaccio.

1. Radbert's *Vita S. Adalhardi,* section 83 (Migne): "Quapropter, quaeso, attendite, viri, et videte, universi populi, matrem Corbeiam flentem (quod est alvearium monachorum) flentem, inquam, ac dicentem: Ablatus est magnificus meus mihi, et nullus est qui consoletur me ex omnibus charis."

3. Vir., 5.40. **9–10.** *maximus ille:* that is, Virgil, who is often referred to or quoted; cf. *V.A.* 42, "ut quidam poetarum eximius ait," followed by two lines from the *Georgics.* Here the line quoted is Ecl. 5.42. **16.** From the pastoral epitaph of Virgil's Daphnis, 5.44. **20.** Vir., 5.54, "cantari dignus," and 89, "dignus amari."

25–35. Cf. 62–72. The contemplation of death, though a prelude to that of Heaven, is pervasive. **26.** *Prosapies augustorum:* Adalhard was the son of Bernardus, uncle of Charlemagne; cf. *V.A.* 7, "Qui cum esset regali prosapia, Pippini magni regis nepos, Caroli consobrinus Augusti, . . ."

35. *ille choro laetatur:* a suggestion of the consolation theme yet to be elaborated. **37.** *V.A.* 85, "salsis lacrimarum rigant fontibus."

46–55. This self-praise is explained by Galatea's identification of herself, the "happy offspring" (46), with New Corbie, "the sacred monastery filled with monks" (55). **48.** Vir., 5.49. **53.** *Vertit aras:* that is, Adalhard. The implicit figure of the pastor and his flock is later to become in Petrarch an effective weapon for church satire.

61. A reference to the parable of the talents, Matthew, 25.14 ff.

76. *virgo ferox, multis sanguinea bellis:* allusion to the uncivilized state of Saxony and the wars waged there by Charles the Great. New Corbie and Hervordia, a nunnery nearby, were supposed to have been founded as a memorial of these wars. **82.** Compare the description of Galatea in the prose key.

88. *Misce favos:* This is possibly reminiscent of the pagan libation of milk, honey, and wine, as in Vir., Geor. 1.344.

89. *V.A.* 85: "Unde interim quando aliud non valemus, iura sepulcri tui flentes circumsedemus, et superadspergimus orationum flores . . . Nam nostrum alii pallentes violas tibi et candentia lilia carpunt, alii narcissum et florentes rosas, alii serpillum bene olentem spargunt, isti colocasia et mollibus illud vaciniis pingunt: quidam et suaves intermiscent odores. . . ." Cf. Vir., 2.45–50; 4.18–20.

94–99. Isaiah, 55.12-13: "Quia in laetitia egrediemini, et in pace deducemini; montes et colles cantabunt coram vobis laudem, et omnia ligna regionis plaudent manu. Pro saliunca ascendet abies, et pro urtica crescet myrtus. . . ." Cf. Vir., 5.60-64 and notes, for similar description of joy attending the apotheosis of Daphnis; and with 97–99 cf. Vir., 4.18-20, as if New Corbie fulfills Virgil's prophesy. Thus Virgil is combined with Isaiah, whom some authorities accept as one of his sources.

98. *V.A.* 9: "hortus autem deliciarum eo vocatus est paradisus, quod intelligitur mens hominis, quia Eden *hortus deliciarum* interpretatur." The implied identification of Paradise with Eden was to persist and to exercise considerable influence upon the pastoral elegy; cf. 159-174, the description of Paradise.

100–101. Galatea is still spoken of as a place. **103–104.** The text is here corrupt.

109. Adalhard died in 826 at about the age of seventy-five, for in 771 he became a monk at twenty.

110. That is, as the monastery was but newly established at this time, the days of her fruitful maturity were yet to come.

111. Ecclesiastes, 12.6: "Antequam rumpatur funiculus argenteus, et recurrat vitta aurea, et conteratur hydria super fontem, et confringatur rota super cisternam."

114. Here, as in ll. 142 and 175, Galatea assumes the rôle of comforter. Compare the change of mood in the later elegy: e.g., Petrarch, 11. **119–122.** With this medieval commonplace cf. Spenser, "November," 183-186.

126–132. Having praised his great work in establishing a new monastery, the poet turns to the personal qualities of Adalhard.

133–134. Compare the identification of Phyllis in the prose key.

135. Vir., 10.73–74. **139.** *Ibid.*, 60. **142.** *Ibid.*, 6.

143–144. This illustrates a favorite habit in the later pastoral: e.g., Spenser, "June" 57–61, where Calliope "wyth Muses moe" leave their song to hear that of Colin Clout.

149–174. Here the joyful mood is elaborate and significant for the later elegy. The mingling of Virgilian imagery (from the fifth eclogue and *Aeneid* 6.637 ff.) and a pastoralized Paradise clothed like Eden are to find full expression in such poems as Boccaccio's *Olympia.* **152.** The Virgilian name Menalcas (cf. 5.64–65) is here applied to Adalhard.

175. *V.A.* 86, "Absterge, quaeso, lacrymas," for Wala succeeds Adalhard. Cf. Vir., 9.66–67:

> Desine plura, puer, et quod nunc instat agamus.
> Carmina tum melius, cum venerit ipse, canemus.

Text: *Monumenta Germaniae Historica: Poetae Latini Aevi Carolini,* ed. L. Traube, Berlin, 1896, III.

Another edition: *Patrologiae: Sancti Paschasii Radberti Opera Omnia,* ed. J. P. Migne, Paris, 1879, CXX.

Comment: Enrico Carrara, *La Poesia Pastorale,* Milan, 1909; M. L. W. Laistner, *Thought and Letters in Western Europe: A.D. 500 to 900,* New York, 1931; J. E. Sandys, *A History of Classical Scholarship,* 3 vols., Cambridge, 1908–21, I; H. O. Taylor, *The Medieval Mind,* 2 vols., London, 1911, I.

PETRARCH

(1304–1374)

BUCOLICUM CARMEN

In the summer of 1346, when Petrarch was enjoying the solitude of Vaucluse, he began his pastorals, the *Bucolicum Carmen.* According to Tatham, the idea of writing in this vein occurred to the poet during the previous year, when a friend showed him the pastoral epistles of Dante and del Virgilio; later Petrarch declared that his own eclogues had been planned years before. To the year 1346 belong the first four eclogues and the twelfth. The remaining seven occupied Petrarch's leisure during the next few years, the group of twelve, Carrara states, being complete in 1361. The *editio princeps* of Petrarch's works was issued at Cologne in 1473; and before the close of the century the *Bucolicum Carmen* had appeared in eight separate editions. Nine more editions were published in the course of the sixteenth century.

ARGUS

A key for this poem was written as a postscript in a letter Petrarch addressed to his friends Barbato and Barili, in Naples (*Epistolae Variae,* 49—translated by Tatham, II, 393–394). The poem mourns Petrarch's great patron, Robert of Naples, who died on January 19, 1343, and expresses the poet's concern and sorrow over the subsequent political turmoil. The King had arranged that the succession fall to Joan, daughter of his son Charles, Duke of Calabria (d. 1328), and Andrew, son of Robert's nephew, Carobert,

King of Hungary. The two heirs apparent, Joan seventeen and her fiancé sixteen, were married in 1342. Petrarch's fears were justified, for soon after at Avignon he received from Barbato news of the murder of Andrew, September 18, 1345, two days before he was to be crowned king. *Argus* was written shortly after this date. In intricacy of allegory, which can be understood only by reference to the various glosses, *Argus* well exemplifies Petrarch's pastoral manner. In great part original as the poem is, Petrarch yet follows generally the great classical model, Virgil's fifth eclogue, though he neglects the consolation.

1–7. These lines describe the peace and security of the recent reign of King Robert: the setting sun represents the period before the tumult occasioned by the murder of Andrew, the cypress. The allegory is characteristically explained by a commentator, Francesco Piendibeni da Montepulciano: "Aureus: In hoc laudat virtutes et gloriam Roberti regis cuius tempore et opere laureatus fuit autor. In hoc enim et introducit Ideum pastorem laudantem primo vitam Roberti, secundo ostendit mala post obitum subsecuta in Regno; unde dicit; iam sol aureus ab effectu tendebat ad occasum.— Allegorice per solem intelligit Regem Robertum qui claritate sua omnes reges mundi excellebat. Preterea sol excellentissimos doctores facit, sicut Robertus fuit rex omni genere scientiarum clarus."

20–23. Many persons went into voluntary exile after Andrew's death and the subsequent attempts to fix the guilt.

24 ff. Barili (Ideus) in Naples is represented as hearing and narrating the laments of his two friends, Petrarch (Silvius) and Barbato (Pythias), one in Avignon, the other away.

29 ff. Reference to Christ and the Virgin, according to Imola. **34.** *Ubera:* another commentator, possibly Donato, notes: "virginis marie, que humana fuit, te moveant ad reconciliandum omnes, ubera, signata (dico) tuis teneris labellis."

47 ff. Imola comments: "Vidimus nebulones procul surgere qui venerunt a Provincia, quae est sterilis terra (i.e., adventurers come into Italy from Provence). Grus est avis pacifica, unde grues, idest homines pacificos et sapientes quaerentes pacem; tunc isti erant expulsi de civitate. Mergi enim nesciunt aliud facere nisi capere pisces, et nihil convertunt in suam utilitatem. Mergi intelliguntur nebulones qui omnia vorabant. Corvos idest malos homines alte garulantes. Fulices vagas, quae sunt viles aves; unde fulices idest homines viles et loquaces" (i.e., plebeians).

51. The moon covered by clouds Imola rightly interprets as Robert's queen, who on his death "facta est monacha et sumpsit habitum sanctae Chatarinae eo quod noluit videre tot mala." Queen Sancia of Aragon, Robert's second wife, was married to him in 1302.

58–68. The usual exchange, as in Vir., 5.1–19. **63.** Allusion to Virgil's praise of Caesar in Eclogue 5; he (Petrarch) should so praise Robert.

74 ff. Nemesian, 51–63, where the pastoral accomplishments of Meliboeus are told.

76. Milton, *Epitaphium Damonis*, 46–47. The succeeding passage bears intimate comparison with the elegy upon Diodati. **103–106.** Vir., 5.45–55. **115.** Boccaccio, 152.

117–118. Vir., 5.56–57. This is the only hint of the usual consolation.

122–123. *arva Sulmonis:* those of Barbato; *silvas Etruscas:* those of Petrarch.

ECLOGUE 11

GALATEA

The movement of this eclogue is simple and suggestive. Two mournful sisters, Niobe and Fusca, take their way to the tomb of Galatea. On the path they see approaching Fulgida, who reproving them for excessive sorrow, offers consolation in the thought of immortality. Apparently this theme is drawn from the Biblical story of the three Marys met by the angel who comforts their sorrow with the announcement of the resurrection. From Imola's commentary it is learned that the poet's professed subject is Laura, the setting the Franciscan chapel at Avignon, but that grief itself is the major subject of the poem. Fusca stands for reason confused with passion and earthly thought, Fulgida for reason illuminated by faith beyond the grave. Niobe, standing midway between, signifies uncontrollable sorrow; later she assumes the rôle of mediator. Containing fewer Virgilian echoes than Radbert's elegy, with which Petrarch's elegy invites comparison, *Galatea* exhibits a balance and compression which are wanting in the medieval poem. In general the allegorical figures of the two mourning sisters correspond to the sisters in Radbert's poem. The name Galatea appears in both in its literal sense of "resplendent" (see prefatory gloss for Radbert's poem). Moreover, each poem includes an elaborate and closely similar disquisition on Death; and consolation is found only in longing to join the blest. The completeness in this union of new and old, seldom recognized, here gains significant illustration.

2–6. Radbert, 114. Niobe here resembles Phyllis, who yearns for an ample expression of grief. **9.** Radbert, 41 and 139–140.

10–12. Laura is said to have been a native of Avignon, where she was buried in the chapel of the church of Franciscans, Minor Conventuals (Cordéliers).

28–30. With this anticipation of the consolation cf. Radbert, 34–35.

35–41. Niobe promises pagan rites for the dead, as in Vir., 5.65 ff.

64–66. Such reflections are not uncommon: Spenser, "November," 183–186, and *Lay*, 91–96; Shelley, 300, 334–335, 345–346, 348–350, and 352–355.

67–68. Radbert, 142 and 149–150.

69. Here the allegorical Fusca appears as "animus concupiscibilis" (Imola). Cf. Boccaccio, 272–274, where Silvius is unconverted. **75–77.** Niobe assumes the rôle of mediator. **79–80.** Petrarch does not dilate upon the joys of heaven, as does Radbert, 160–174. Here the consolation is dampened by thoughts of the futility of life and of high desert. **79.** *tonantis:* This classical epithet for God occurs in Mantuan (e.g., 7.37) and other Renaissance poets.

98–102. Vir., 5.76–78.

Texts: *Il Bucolicum Carmen e i suoi Commenti Inediti,* ed. Antonio Avena, Padova, 1906; *Poemata Minora,* ed. D. Rossetti, 3 vols., Milan, 1829–1834, I. (The present text was prepared from a collation of Avena and Rossetti.)

Comment: E. Carrara, "I Commenti Antichi e la Cronologia delle Ecloghe Petrarchesche," *Giornale Storico della Lett. Ital.,* XXVIII (1896), 123–153; *idem, Poesia Pastorale,* Milan, 1909; *Epistolae de Rebus Familiaribus,* ed. G. Fracassetti, 3 vols., Florence, 1859; W. P. Ker, *The Dark Ages,* Edinburgh and London, 1923; Pierre de Nolhac, *Petrarque et l'Humanisme,* 2 vols., Paris, 1907; Edward H. R. Tatham, *Francesco Petrarca His Life and Correspondence,* 2 vols., London, 1926.

BOCCACCIO

(1313–1375)

ECLOGUE 14

OLYMPIA

Sixteen poems comprise the *Bucolicum Carmen* of Boccaccio. Directly inspired by Petrarch, Boccaccio's pastoral effort did not enjoy the early publication or the popularity of his master's. The series appeared first from the press of Giunta, 1504, and again in 1546 in the collection of Oporinus. (See further *supra,* pp. 8–9.)

The key, written by the poet as a letter to Martino da Signa (see Massèra, pp. 216 ff.), follows the practice of Petrarch. The name Terapon, which has eluded his memory, is the Greek θεράπων (servant).

1 ff. The picture of the refulgent wood echoing with song derives from Dante: *Paradiso,* 30.46–50; *Purgatorio,* 29.16–18 and especially 34–36. **12–17.** Vir., 5.76–78; Petrarch, 11.98–102. **25 ff.** With 25–26 cf. *Purg.* 29.21; with 31–32 cf. *ibid.,* 55–57; with 35–38 cf. *ibid.,* 28.30–60, 29.82–90, and 30.10–33 (Dante's meeting with Matilda and Beatrice).

47. *Sine numine divum:* a characteristic incongruity, for Olympia is a citizen in a Christian heaven. **48.** *huc veni lacrimas . . .:* In accordance with medieval belief Olympia appears matured in mind and teaches the heavenly lessons of resignation and solace. **51.** *Fusca:* probably the child's mother, the name from Petrarch, 11. **60.** The yellow marriage garments symbolize Olympia's union with Christ.

91–111. For this hymn, with its even cadence and refrain, *Olympia* is famous. In the attempt to pastoralize Christ's life, Boccaccio gains a fine lyric effect. The identification of the delights of the Elysian Fields with those of heaven, medieval in manner as it is, is further elaborated in Olympia's later account of her abode. Carrara cites parallels with the *Inferno.* Codrus descends to the vales of Pluto ("Plutarci"), as Christ goes to Limbo.

170–196. This account of Heaven is largely from Dante's Earthly Paradise, described by Matilda as on a mountain in Purgatory (*Purg.* 28.91–144 and adjacent passages).

201. *Archesilas:* as in 10.154, the poet's name for God. Christ, now as a white Lamb, and the Holy Ghost, as a Fire, complete the Godhead.

213–226. The four orders of the blest in their proximity to the Godhead are arranged, like Dante's, according to virtue.

231–248. Olympia's account of her reception in Heaven reflects both Dante and Virgil.

249–261. *Parthenos:* the Virgin. **250.** *Par.* 33.1. **272–274.** Petrarch, 11.69.

275–279. The teachings of Olympia comprise the acts enjoined by Christ (Matthew, 25.35–36).

284–285. The Virgilian close emphasizes the contrast between the pseudo-classical background of the poem and the central Christian theme. In the later elegy classical pastoral elements are to merge with church satire, but never again are the two traditions to be brought together with such startling inconsistency.

Text: *Boccaccio: Opere Latine Minori,* ed. A. F. Massèra, *Scrittori d'Italia* series, Bari, 1928.

Comment: E. Carrara, *La Poesia Pastorale,* Milan, 1909; *idem, Un Oltre-tomba Bucolico,* Bologna, 1899; A. Dobelli, "Il Culto del Boccaccio per Dante," *Giornale Dantesco,* V (1898), 193–221, 241–269, 289–320; I. Gollancz, *Boccaccio's Olympia with English Rendering,* London, 1913; T. P. Harrison, Jr., "Spenser and Boccaccio's *Olympia,*" *Texas Studies in English,* XIV (1934), 5–30; H. Hauvette, "Sulla cronologia delle Ecloghe Latine del Boccaccio," *Giornale Storico della Lett. Ital.,* XXVIII (1896), 154–175; Edward Hutton, *Giovanni Boccaccio,* London and New York, 1910; *idem, Some Aspects of the Genius of Giovanni Boccaccio, Proceedings of the British Academy,* Oxford, 1922; W. P. Ker, "Boccaccio," *Essays on Medieval Literature,* London and New York, 1905; W. H. Schofield, "The Nature and Fabric of the Pearl," *P.M.L.A.* XII (1904), 154–215; B. Zumbini, "Le Ecloghe del Boccaccio," *Giornale Storico della Lett. Ital.,* VII (1886), 94–152.

SANNAZARO

(1458–1530)

Jacopo Sannazaro was born in Naples, 1458, and though much of his life was spent outside of Italy, recollections of his beloved Naples pervade not only his later Piscatory Eclogues but the *Arcadia* itself. In youth he became a devoted friend of Gioviano Pontano, the well known Neapolitan poet whose works he edited in 1505, two years after Pontano's death. As a member of the Accademia Pontaniana, Sannazaro acquired the nickname Actius Sincerus, under which he shadows himself in the *Arcadia.* To his youth belongs also his love for Carmosina Bonifacio, celebrated possibly in the first of the Piscatory Eclogues. In 1504 Sannazaro returned to Naples, where he died in 1530.

ARCADIA

The *Arcadia* was partly complete in 1481, when there is evidence that it was first imitated. A Naples MS. of the year 1489 contains the first ten

Prose and *Egloghe.* A piratical edition of this in 1502 (Venice) prompted the author to issue the complete work in 1504 (Naples), with the help of his friend Pietro Summonte (the "Summontio" of the last eclogue). The *Arcadia* saw many editions before the close of the century, some with elaborate commentaries. An elegant edition appeared in 1514 from the press of Aldus. The two verse elegies which occur in the *Arcadia* comprise Eclogues 5 and 11. Preceding the fifth and introducing it appears a prose elegy which also honors the poet's father, "Androgeo." Relative to the growth of pastoral elegy the prose and verse here reprinted gain additional significance in their direct reflection of the elegy of Nemesian. (See further *supra,* pp. 9–10.)

PROSE 5

[ANDROGEO]

The first lines derive from Catullus, 96, and Boccaccio, *Filocolo;* the rest is from Nemesian, 37–41. **28–30.** Nem., 51–55. **30–34.** Vir., 9.17–20. **37–43.** Vir., 5.34–41. **44–55.** Nem., 64–74. **56–60.** Vir., 5.24–28, 69–75. **61–63.** Nem., 75–80.

The singer of the lament now, Ergasto, is the poet himself, who elsewhere appears as Sincerus.

ECLOGUE 5

This song was frequently imitated and generally admired by Renaissance pastoralists. In his romance *Galatea* Cervantes translated a great part of it; in France Marot and, more evidently, Ronsard knew the poem; and Milton drew from it as well as from *Phyllis,* the piscatory elegy. Sannazaro's poem, modeled upon Virgil, 5, is reminiscent also of Petrarch (*Sonetti* and *Canzoni*) and, among the elegiac pastoralists, Moschus and Bion. The poem begins in the spirit of the apotheosis.

6–16. Vir., 5.56–57. **27–31.** *Ibid.,* 32–34. **40–49.** *Ibid.,* 20–28. **54–65.** *Ibid.,* 72–80.

ECLOGUE 11

[MAMILLIA]

The last two *Prose* and *Egloghe* were written probably much later than the rest of the *Arcadia,* for they were not included in the pirated edition of 1502. The Aldine edition of Theocritus (Venice, 1495) included Moschus' poem, which was possibly unknown to Sannazaro before 1502; hence the present imitation of Moschus. The poem is Sannazaro's memorial to his mother, the pseudonym Massilia being suggested by her real name Massella (see Scherillo, pp. ccii–cciii).

3–10. Mos., 3. **13–15.** *Ibid.,* 30. **31–40.** *Ibid.,* 5–7. **46–48.** *Ibid.,* 9–12. **55–63.** *Ibid.,* 99–104 and note. **64–75.** *Ibid.,* 115 ff.

88–93. *Ibid.,* 70–75, where the river Meles is called upon to mourn Bion, her second sorrow. The river addressed in the present passage is possibly the Sebeto, as in *Phyllis,* 105. **103–106.** Vir., 10.53–54. (With the entire passage,

101–108, cf. the piscatory equivalent in *Phyllis*, 121–125.) **107–108.** Vir., 5.76–78. **112–116.** Vir., 4.1.

141. Theocr., 1.125. The change in key with "Ponete fine" corresponds to the earlier "Ricominciate." **157–160.** The poet combines the idea of the eternizing power of verse with that of due rites to the dead. **158.** Mos., 104.

PISCATORY ECLOGUE 1

PHYLLIS

According to Hall, the Phyllis of this poem is possibly Sannazaro's early love, Carmosina Bonifacio, a lady celebrated in the last eclogue of the *Arcadia*. In this case, Lycidas is the poet himself and Mycon is his friend Basilius Zanchius. Scherillo, however, believes that in both piscatory and pastoral Phyllis stands for Adriana Saxon (d. 1491), the wife of Sannazaro's friend Pontano. (She is mourned as Ariadne by her husband in an elegy, *Meliseus*, which Sannazaro imitates closely in Eclogue 12 of the *Arcadia*.) In *Phyllis*, then, Lycidas would stand for Pontano. Professor Mustard concludes that it is "hardly necessary to refer this purely conventional lament to the death of any real person—whether Carmosina Bonifacio or another." The poem, modeled after Virgil's fifth eclogue, enjoyed widespread popularity. The chief interest of *Phyllis* lies in its influence upon Milton's *Lycidas*. "What must have attracted Milton to this poem, if he did indeed know it," states Hanford (*P.M.L.A.*, XXV, 433), "is its felicity of style, and the circumstance that the lament is for one who had met death by drowning." (See further, *supra*, pp. 10–11.)

1. The name Mycon appears in Theocr., 5.112; Lycidas is more common: e.g., Theocr., 7.

3–7. Petrarch, 2.49–50, Marot, 181–188, Milton, *Lycidas*, 100–101, and *Epitaphium Damonis*, 79–80: all allude to various ill omens.

12–14. Mycon's night fishing "and the melancholy and loneliness of the entire piece show the author's indebtedness to Theocritus as indisputably as imitation of particular passages in the Latin poems proves indebtedness to Virgil" (Hall, p. 41). Sannazaro's love of Posilipo, the island of Nisida, and other localities near Mergellina finds constant expression in the *Arcadia*.

24–28. This passage was imitated by Phineas Fletcher, in *Myrtillus*, 27–29, one of two Latin piscatories written about 1610 and issued in 1633 (see further note for 72–75).

29–32. The poem now turns to the elegiac theme: Vir., 5.10–13; 3.52 and 55–57. **33–36.** Vir., 5.13 and 9.26. **42–43.** Vir., 5.12; Nem., 6–8.

45–50. Glaucus is the piscatory equivalent of the pastoral Apollo. Ovid, *Met.*, 13.919 ff., tells the story of his transformation.

72–75. Fletcher, *Myrtillus*, 37–40; Milton, *Lycidas*, 157–158.

79–90. The honors for Phyllis answer generally to those for Daphnis in Vir., 5.65–73. **91–98.** Vir., 5.56–65, the apotheosis of Daphnis. **94–96.** Vir., 2.45–50. **101–105.** Adding 123–125 cf. Vir., 5.42–44; Theocr., 21.41–44 (Hall). **106–108.** Vir., 5.45–47, 81–84. (The halcyon is praised in Theocr., 7.57–60). **109–113.** Theocr., 1.146–148; Vir., 9.30–32.

Texts: *Arcadia di Jacobo Sannazaro*, ed. M. Scherillo, Torino, 1888; *The Piscatory Eclogues of Jacobo Sannazaro*, ed. W. P. Mustard, Baltimore, 1914.

Comment: W. W. Greg, *Pastoral Poetry and Pastoral Drama*, London, 1906; "Sannazaro and *Arcadia*," *L.T.L.S.*, September 4, 1930, 689–690; H. M. Hall, *Idylls of Fishermen*, New York, 1914; J. H. Hanford, "The Pastoral Elegy and Milton's *Lycidas*," *P.M.L.A.*, XXV (1910), 403–447; W. P. Mustard, "Later Echoes of the Greek Bucolic Poets," *American Journal of Philology*, XXX (1909), 245–283; J. A. Symonds, *The Renaissance in Italy*, Pt. II, New York, 1882; F. Torraca, *Gl' Imitatori Stranieri di Jacopo Sannazaro*, Rome, 1882.

CASTIGLIONE
(1478–1529)

ALCON

During the period, 1492–1499, when Baldassare Castiglione was a student in Milan, he became acquainted with youthful Matteo Falcone, whom later he engaged as tutor to Jeronimo, a younger brother. In honor of Falcone, who died in 1505, Castiglione composed *Alcon*. The elegy follows the form popular with Renaissance pastoralists: that of Virgil's tenth eclogue. In *Alcon* the introduction (1–23) without invocation states the theme and setting. And throughout the rest, lacking in the formal Virgilian conclusion, the point of view of the singer is maintained. The poem proper falls into three parts: part one (24–82) exploits freely the pathetic fallacy, its major theme; part two (83–129) concerns Iolas' absence in Rome; part three (130–154) concludes the poem, as Iolas invokes the shade of his friend and declares that he will raise an empty tomb on the banks of the Anio, deck it with flowers, and append an epitaph. A comparison with the *Epitaphium Damonis* discloses marked similarities pointing to Milton's acquaintance with the Italian poem. (See further, *supra*, p. 11.)

3–5. Castiglione throughout extols his subject as a poet; hence the weeping of all Nature and the woodland deities. **5.** Iolas, from Vir., 2.57, stands for the poet himself; Alcon, named in Vir., 5.11, represents Falcone. **11–15.** Vir., *Geor.*, 4.511–515. **15–23.** Milton, *Epitaphium Damonis*, 5–8. **18–20.** Vir., 5.24–26. Cf. refrain in Milton. **21.** Vir., *Geor.* 4.465. **23.** *Epit. Dam.*, 73 and note.

27–33. Execration against death becomes in Milton a reflection upon life itself: *Epit. Dam.* 19–22. **54–66.** Mos., 99–104; Milton, *Lycidas*, 30–31, 168–171. **68–82.** In its emphasis upon the intimacy of the singer and his dead friend, *Alcon* extends the scope of the pastoral elegy: *Epit. Dam.* 37–43, 51–52, 55–56; *Lycidas*, 23–31.

83–129. For this passage the traditional elegy provides no suggestions. **83.** *Epit. Dam.* 113 and note. **84–86.** Spenser, *Astrophel*, 137–138; *Epit. Dam.* 121–122. **101–102.** *Epit. Dam.* 28; *Lycidas*, 12–14. **103–130.** In *Epit. Dam.* 155–178, Milton digresses by telling his own poetical ambitions. **122–124.** Vir., 10.42–43. Both Gallus and Iolas imagine they are sharing these pleasures with their beloved. Cf. *Epit. Dam.* 71–72; the Italian's delight in Rome (123) parallels Milton's regret that he yielded to the impulse to visit the city (115). **125.** Vir., 2.1, and 5.86.

130–131. *Epit. Dam.* 142 and 180. **136–137.** *Lycidas*, 163. **139–140.** *Ibid.*, 152–153. "So the singer in *Lycidas*, 'to interpose a little ease,' fancies that he is decking the tomb of Lycidas" (Hanford). **142–154.** Vir., 2.45–50; 5.40.

Text: *Selecta Poemata Italorum*, ed. Alexander Pope, 2 vols., London, 1740, II.

Comment: J. Cartwright, *Baldassare Castiglione*, London, 1908; J. H. Hanford, "The Pastoral Elegy and Milton's *Lycidas*," *P.M.L.A.*, XXV (1910), 403–447; C. Hare, *Courts and Camps of the Italian Renaissance*, New York, 1908; T. P. Harrison, Jr., "The Latin Pastorals of Milton and Castiglione," *P.M.L.A.*, L (1935), 480–943; P. A. Serassi, *Delle Lettere del Conte Baldassare Castiglione*, 2 vols., Padova, 1769–1771; G. Saintsbury, *The Earlier Renaissance*, London, 1901; J. A. Symonds, *The Renaissance in Italy: the Revival of Learning*, New York, 1883.

ALAMANNI

(1495–1556)

Luigi Alamanni, born October 3, 1495, attended the University of Florence, where he studied under Francesco da Diacceto, a disciple of the famous Platonist, M. Ficino. A formative influence in Alamanni's early years lay in his associations at the house of Bernardo Rucellai, for the Rucellai gardens, Orti Oricellari, became a modern Platonic Academy. Here Alamanni came to know and to love young Cosimo Rucellai, Bernardo's grandson, whose premature death from the plague in 1518 he mourned in pastorals. In 1522 Alamanni was implicated in a conspiracy against the life of Cardinal Giulio dei Medici, and thereafter difficulties beset the young rebel from every side. The succeeding years find him engaged in various missions, including efforts to secure the aid of King Francis. A turn of affairs in Italy, with the Pope's effort to apprehend his old enemies, resulted in Alamanni's decision to remain in France. The year 1530 marks the beginning of a new life as the young Florentine now set out to win personal favor from the King. In 1532–1533 Alamanni dedicated to King Francis his two volumes, *Opere Toscane*, and the King recognized Alamanni with various gifts which brought him considerable wealth. In 1539 Alamanni again visited his native Italy. In the service of the Cardinal Ippolito II d' Este, he traveled now as a considerable figure in the world. Again at the court of Francis in 1540, he was made ambassador to Venice, accepting many other dignities. The remainder of his life was spent in France, where after Francis' death he enjoyed the favor of Catherine de Medici as well as that of Henry II. On August 18, 1556, Alamanni died at Amboise. He was buried in Paris, and the celebrated Italian historian Benedetto Varchi composed an epitaph. (See further, *supra*, p. 12.)

ECLOGUE 1
[COSMO]

The plan of this poem, the first of four commemorating Cosimo Rucellai, follows that in Idyl 1 of Theocritus, the chief variation being the substitution of Fortune (98 ff.) for the Venus of Thyrsis' song. In detail the poet exercises much freedom in condensation. Alamanni's editors offer no suggestion concerning the identities of the speakers, Thyrsis and Melibeus.

1–20. Theocr., 1.1–18. **24.** For "Chromis of Libya" is substituted "tosco Aiolle," or Aiolle Francesco, an Italian musician. **33–56.** Theocr., 1.25–61: the two gifts of the goatherd. **63 ff.** Thyrsis addresses, not the nymphs of Sicily, but the Muses (Vir., 10.9–12), the Graces, and Virtues, like the Dreams and Splendors of Shelley's *Adonais* (73 ff.). **73–76.** Theocr., 1.71–75. **78 ff.** Apollo and Pan (Vir., 10.21 and 26) mourn the dead youth; Fortune, "con dolor falso" (100), replaces Cypris. **106 ff.** The commonplace execration against Fortune replaces Daphnis' reproach of Cypris, 100 ff. The poet returns to his model in the usual concluding civilities.

ECLOGUE 2
[COSMO]

In this imitation of Moschus Alamanni freely applies the Greek elegy to Italy and his own countrymen, but more closely follows his original. Cosmo, "il nuovo tosco Orfeo" (19), replaces the Dorian Orpheus with conventional fulsomeness. The Arno, "il tosco fiume" (87), supplants the Greek Meles. Dante (92), Petrarch (96), and Boccaccio (101–106) supplant Pindar, Hesiod, Sappho, and others in Moschus. **115–125.** Mos., 99–104 and note.

Text: *Versi e Prose di Luigi Alamanni*, ed. Pietro Raffaelli, 2 vols., Florence, 1859, I.

Comment: John M. Berdan, *Early Tudor Poetry*, New York, 1920; Henri Hauvette, *Luigi Alamanni: Sa Vie et Son Oeuvre*, Paris, 1903; Sir Sidney Lee, *The French Renaissance in England*, New York, 1910.

MAROT
(1496–1544)

Clément Marot was born at Cahors, in Quercy, late in 1496 or early in the next year. First as page in the house of a French nobleman, then as pensioner at the court of Margaret of Navarre, young Marot acquired a knowledge of the arts of war and of letters. To his youth belongs his attachment to Diane de Poitiers, celebrated in his verse. In 1523 he entered the service of King Francis, to whom he had already presented verse, and in the next year he joined the expedition into Italy during which he was wounded and captured. In 1525, at the court of Margaret, he expressed too freely his religious beliefs, with resulting imprisonment for heresy. Freed through the influence of Margaret, he enjoyed for a time the patronage of the King and leisure for his literary talents. Although Marot's religious imprudence was to exact heavy penalties, in 1536 he obtained more favor than ever at the court of King Francis. A vernacular rendering of some fifty of the Psalms met with such tremendous popular success that the Sorbonne was again impelled to condemn the poet. Marot fled to Geneva, to Italy, wherever he might find the protection of his king. He died in the autumn of 1544. (See further, *supra*, pp. 12–13.)

LOUISE OF SAVOY

In the last edition of Marot's works (1538) the pastoral elegy in honor of the King's mother, Louise of Savoy, stands as *Complainte 4*. This poem, first issued in 1531, gained the immediate applause of King and court; and even later, as Guiffrey (I, 178) testifies, "Au temps de la Pléiade, cette pièce aurait pu soutenir la comparaison avec les meilleures de Ronsard." The beloved Queen-mother Louise of Savoy (1476–1531) had been celebrated by Alamanni in canzone and sonnet. Marot's elegy, based generally upon the plan of Theocritus' *Daphnis*, reflects also the influence of Moschus and, among moderns, of Boccaccio and Sannazaro. More than the work of Baïf and Ronsard, the poem is marked by a homeliness which is not inconsistent with its scholarship. (See "November" and notes for the imitation by Edmund Spenser.)

1–24. Theocr., 1, 1–11; Mos., 55–57. **25–28.** Theocr., 1.12–14; Vir., 5.12. The usual Tityrus, who looks after the flocks, is replaced here by the dog.

35–48. Thenot's homely gifts have little to suggest those elaborately described in Theocr., 1.24–61. Marot's Michau replaces the Calydnian ferry-man (57), and his double pipe supplants the Greek cup.

50. This refrain undergoes the usual variation in 216 and 260.

65–92. This intimate picture, having no traditional counterpart, is suggested by its subject. "Louise de Savoie, imitant en cela l'exemple d'Anne de Bretagne, avait groupé à la cour les filles de tous les grands du royaume; elle les dirigeait, les conseillait, présidait à leur travaux" (Guiffrey, I, 177–178).

97–128. The details in this elaboration of the pathetic fallacy point mainly to Moschus and Sannazaro, 5. **133–134.** Theocr., 1.80 ff.; Mos., 25–29; Vir., 10.19–30. **139–140.** Sannazaro, 5.32–34 (Torraca). **141–152.** Mos., 82–84. **157–160.** *Ibid.*, 86–92. **177–180.** *Ibid.*, 99–104. **181–188.** Petrarch, 2.42–53; Sannazaro, *Phyllis*, 3–7 and note. **190–215.** Boccaccio, 176–196.

225–240. Marot brings back to pastoral elegy the classical catalogue of flowers.

245–248. Theocr., 1.123–126, the appeal to Pan. **253–260.** *Ibid.*, 143–145. **261–272.** This passage combines Theocr., 1.146–148, and Vir., 5.45–49 and 81–84.

Text: *Oeuvres Complètes de Clément Marot, avec Préface, Notes, et Glossaire*, ed. M. Pierre Jannet, 4 vols., Paris, 1868–72, II.

Other editions: *Oeuvres de Clément Marot*, ed. G. Guiffrey, 3 vols., Paris, 1875–1881, I; *Chefs-d'Oeuvre Poétiques de Marot, Ronsard, J. du Bellay, d'Aubigné et Regnier*, ed. A. P. Lemercier, Paris, n.d.

Comment: T. P. Harrison, Jr., "Spenser and the Earlier Pastoral Elegy," *Texas Studies in English*, XIII (1933), 36–53; *idem*, "Spenser and Boccaccio's Olympia," *ibid.*, XIV (1934), 5–30; C. d'Héricault, Biography and Glossary, Jannet's edition, IV; W. P. Mustard, "Later Echoes of the Greek Bucolic Poets," *American Journal of Philology*, XXX (1909), 245–283; Sir Sidney Lee, *The French Renaissance in England*, New York, 1910; George Saintsbury, *A Short History of French Literature*, Oxford, 1901; F. Torraca, *Gl' Imitatori Stranieri di Jacopo Sannazaro*, Rome, 1882.

BAIF

(1532–1589)

Ian Antoine de Baïf was born February, 1532, in Venice, the natural son by an Italian woman of Lazare de Baïf, ambassador to the Venetian state. The father, a man of scholarly tastes, provided for his son a thorough training in both Greek and Latin, and on his death, in 1545, left young Antoine a competency which permanently relieved him of pecuniary burden. Like Ronsard, Baïf developed early in life a passion for poetry and versifying, so that in 1549, the year of du Bellay's famous manifesto, he entered enthusiastically into the projected reforms of the group which, under the guidance of Jean Dorat, was later known as La Pléiade. At the Collège Coqueret he was thrown with Ronsard, du Bellay, Belleau, and Jodelle. Of the group, with the exception of their master Dorat, Baïf was probably the best Greek scholar. It was he who tutored Ronsard in the language. (See further, *supra*, pp. 13–14.)

ECLOGUE 2

BRINON

Jean Brinon played Maecenas to the young Parisian group, La Pléiade. In the early days of his residence in Paris, Baïf was a frequent guest at Brinon's villa "de Medan," and to him he addressed many poetical compliments. It is said that by his gifts and entertainment of *littérateurs* Brinon completely impoverished himself; and when he died, March, 1555, "les poètes prodiguèrent les fleurs sur son tombeau et l'immortalisèrent" (Laumonier, *Ronsard Poète Lyrique*, p. 134). The eclogue honoring Brinon freely paraphrases Virgil's famous tribute to Gallus. For a few lines (121–128) the poet follows Sannazaro's piscatory *Galatea* (65–72), this passage itself being imitated from Virgil, 10.64–69. Like its classic original, the poem honors the unsuccessful lover.

13–16. Vir., 10.4–5. **25–36.** *Ibid.*, 9–12. The allusion to the Seine (33) localizes the scene. **43–46.** *Ibid.*, 10.19–21. **54 ff.** Mercury approaches, as in Theocr., 1.77; but in l. 61 Baïf returns generally to Vir., 10.21 ff. **141–152.** Vir., 10.70–78. Baïf cannot resist the hope that his lines may be agreeable to "Francine," possibly a mistress.

Text: *Oeuvres de Ian-Antoine de Baïf avec une Notice biographique et des notes*, ed. Ch. Marty-Laveaux, 5 vols., Paris, 1886, III.

Comment: Mathieu Augé-Chiquet, *La Vie, Les Idées et l'Oeuvre de Jean-Antoine de Baïf*, Paris, 1909; Sir Sidney Lee, *The French Renaissance in England*, New York, 1910; George Saintsbury, *A Short History of French Literature*, Oxford, 1901.

RONSARD

(1524–1585)

Pierre de Ronsard, son of a maitre d'hôtel of Francis I, was born on September 1, 1524, near Vendôme, in the Loire valley. When ten years old, he entered the service of the court, and he lived an active, vivid life in connection with various embassies until an illness which caused permanent deafness forced him to turn to letters. With other enthusiasts under Dorat at the Collège Coqueret Ronsard led the movement for literary reform, his own *Odes* (1550) illustrating the principles set forth in du Bellay's *La Deffence*. Under Charles IX Ronsard enjoyed even greater royal favor, which continued undiminished on the accession of Henry III. On the death of Charles (1574), however, the poet sought the retirement of his abbeys, Saint-Côme-lez-Tours and Croix-Val, where during his last years he accomplished some of his best work. On his death, December, 1585, France united in mourning her greatest poet. (See further, *supra*, pp. 14–15.)

BERGERIE

ECLOGUE 1

ANGELOT

1–14. In this liberal use of the pathetic fallacy Ronsard depends upon Virgil, 5, Sannazaro, 5, and Marot. **19–40.** Vir., 5.32–44. (With 39–40 cf. Sann., 5.67–68.) **41–64.** Sann., 5.1–16 (Torraca). But with 50–51 and 56 cf. Marot, 202–204 and 192; and with 57–60 cf. Boccaccio, 190–196. **65–69.** Vir., 5.62–75. **69–78.** Ronsard depends here upon the Venetian Navagero (1483–1529), author of the Latin *Iolas* and *Damon* (see Kuhn). **79–82.** Vir., 5.76–78; Sann., 5.59–62. **83–92.** Vir., 5.65–75; Sann., Prose 5.53–55, 58–60.

ADONIS

Following Alamanni's version (Eclogue 10), Bion's *Lament for Adonis* was popularized in France by Mellin de Saint-Gelais, in *Élégie ou chanson lamentable de Vénus sur la mort du bel Adonis* (1547), by Baïf in Eclogue 9, and by Belleau in *La Bergerie*. Among other names is that of Gabriel le Breton, who published in 1579 *Adonis*, a play allegorizing the death of Charles IX: Adonis is the dead king, Venus is France. Ronsard's *Adonis*, first published in 1563, is included in the second book of *Nouvelles Poesies*; in the collected edition of 1567 it appeared among the *Élégies*. The first half of the poem depends upon Ovid, the second upon Bion. *Adonis* is especially interesting as a model for Spenser's *Astrophel*.

5–8. Ovid (*Met.* 10.535 ff.) states that Cupid accidentally grazed his mother with an arrow. **9.** Theocr., 1.109; Vir., 10.18. **10 ff.** Ovid, 10.523. **29 ff.** *Ibid.*, 529 ff. **53–64.** *Ibid.*, 555–559. **65–69.** *Ibid.*, 537–539. Ronsard pastoralizes the earlier story of the lovers' hunting. **78.** Vir., 10.71. **101–114.** Ovid, 10.543–552 and 705–709. **107.** Sir Sidney Lee compares Shakespeare's *Venus and Adonis*, 615–618. Little evidence points to Shakespeare's dependence upon Ronsard; unlike Shakespeare, the French poet draws also from Bion. **115–174.** The motive of Mars' jealousy and plan for revenge is lacking in both Bion and Ovid. **175–194.** Ovid, 10.710–716. **195–204.** *Ibid.*, 720–723; Bion, 8 ff. **211–212.** Bion, 60–61. **213–214.** *Ibid.*, 11–12. **217–218.** Cf. the refrain in Bion (15, *passim*) and Mos., 65–67. **220–221.** Bion, 13. **234–236.** *Ibid.*, 53. **239–240.** *Ibid.*, 29. **251–256.** *Ibid.*, 32–36. **264–267.** *Ibid.*, 20–22. **298–302.** *Ibid.*, 64–66; Ovid, 10.727–739. **308–309.** Bion, 71. **319–328.** *Ibid.*, 81–87. **331.** *Ibid.*, 57. **334–346.** *Ibid.*, 42–54. **359 ff.** Ronsard produces an original conclusion.

Text: *Oeuvres Complètes de Pierre de Ronsard*, ed. P. Laumonier, 5 vols., Paris, 1914–1919; vol. III contains *Bergerie*, vol. IV *Adonis*.

Comment: T. P. Harrison, Jr., "Spenser, Ronsard, and Bion," *M. L. N.*, XLIX (1934), 139–145; P. Kuhn, "L'Influence Neo-Latine dans les Églogues de Ronsard," *Revue d'Histoire Litt.* (1914), 309–325; W. P. Mustard, "Later Echoes of the Greek Bucolic Poets," *American Journal of Philology*, XXX (1909), 245–283; Sir Sidney Lee, *The French Renaissance in England*, New York, 1910; idem, *Shakespeare's Venus and Adonis*, Oxford, 1905; P. Laumonier, *Ronsard Poète Lyrique*, Paris, 1923; F. Torraca, *Gl' Imitatori Stranieri di Jacopo Sannazaro*, Rome, 1882; George Wyndham, "Ronsard and La Pléiade," *Essays in Romantic Literature*, London, 1919.

EDMUND SPENSER
(1552–1599)

THE SHEPHEARDES CALENDER

This collection of twelve pastoral poems was probably begun as early as Spenser's residence at Pembroke Hall, Cambridge (1569–1576); it was completed late in 1578, when the book was entered in the Stationers' Register. The following year found the poet in the service of the Earl of Leicester and "in some use of familiarity" with such courtiers as Philip Sidney and Edward Dyer. Then it was that the young poet gathered together his pastoral compositions, arranged and rearranged them artistically and tactfully, secured Edward Kirke as commentator, and, finally deciding to dedicate the work to Sidney and signing himself only as "Immerito," sent the little volume to the press. (See further, *supra*, pp. 15–16.)

NOVEMBER
[DIDO]

There is no certain evidence as to the identity of Dido, mourned in this poem, which closely follows the French *De Madame Loyse*. That she died by drowning (l. 37) is the only specific information disclosed, and for this Marot's poem contains no suggestion. An old theory still obtains that Dido is Ambrosia Sidney, Sir Philip's sister (d. 1575), and another that she is a daughter of Spenser's patron, the Earl of Leicester, by Lady Sheffield. Recently Professor A. C. Judson has suggested (*A Biographical Sketch of John Young*, p. 24) that Spenser's Dido is Susan Watts, stepdaughter of John Young, Bishop of Rochester. W. L. Renwick, (ed. *S.C.*, p. 221) dismisses the question: "E. K. says Spenser would not tell him who the lady was: perhaps he was telling the truth—though commentators always assume he was lying when his statements do not suit their preconceptions; we may be excused ignorance on a point which Spenser was careful to conceal."

5–8. Marot, 25–28. The entire passage, 1–8, bears comparison with the opening of Virgil, 5; with 7–8 cf. especially 5.10–11.

9–20. "Of the three poets, Spenser displays the greatest dramatic imagination, since in Virgil's and Marot's poems the theme is merely announced. Spenser leads up to it more carefully" (Renwick, ed. *S.C.*).

13. The definition of "welked" by E. K. as "shortned or empayred" is clearly wrong. As Herford suggests, the word means "withered up," the reference being to "the gloom of winter, rather than its shorter day." E. K.'s inaccuracies are fully recorded by Herford (ed. *S.C.*).

16. The sun is in Pisces in February, not November, as E. K. declares. The engraving at the head of the "November" eclogue rightly represents the Centaur in the heavens (see frontispiece), and Pisces over "February." Renwick suggests that Spenser transposed the two poems for artistic reasons, "November" being originally written for second place in the *Calender*.

21–24. Marot, 17–20. **25–26.** *Ibid.*, 29–30; in England the titmouse, not Marot's woodpecker, was proverbially contrasted with the nightingale. **27–48.** *Ibid.*, 31–48. **49.** *Ibid.*, 49. **53–57.** *Ibid.*, 50–52 and 265–266—for the allusion to Melpomene. The song itself now follows Marot less closely.

60–62. *Ibid.*, 50 and note. Spenser's refrain, leading each stanza to a close, greatly enhances the lyric effectiveness alien to Marot's homely style.

63–67. "Spenser picks up a word here and there: Marot, 57, 53–54" (Renwick). **63.** *Ibid.*, 218; each poet localizes the setting. **67–69.** *Ibid.*, 102–104. **71.** *Ibid.*, 105. **77–79.** *Ibid.*, 91–95.

83–92. *Ibid.*, 177–180, which follow Mos., 99–104. Herford believes that Spenser follows Moschus; Renwick notes the analogue in Job, 14.7–10.

93–99. Marot, 65–92. Spenser's attempted rusticity hardly equals the intimate picture of the Queen-mother's household. **103–112.** *Ibid.*, 93–98. **114–121.** *Ibid.*, 87–92, reference to the royal maids of honor.

125–129. *Ibid.*, 101–104, 113–114. **133–134.** *Ibid.*, 107–108, or Vir., 5.25–26. **135–137.** Marot, 117–120. **138–141.** *Ibid.*, 125, 127–128. **143–147.** *Ibid.*, 225–236. The flower passage in "April," 136–144, offers readier comparison with Marot.

153–157. For this, a frequent theme in Spenser, Marot includes no suggestion except perhaps ll. 139–140.

163 ff. Marot, 189–192. With the consolation passage in Spenser, Herford compares *Lycidas*, 165, and *Adonais*, xxxix: "The transition is less beautiful in Spenser, chiefly because it is less sudden. He gives the reason first, and the appeal based upon it afterwards, a procedure which has logic but not poetry on its side." Shelley apparently follows Spenser. **187–189.** Marot, 193–200. **191.** *Ibid.*, 203–204. **194–196.** *Ibid.*, 197, 206–207. **201.** *Ibid.*, 216.

203–208. *Ibid.*, 261–264, and 269–276. Colin's emblem, upon which E. K. moralizes, appears with most of Marot's prefaces. Here it serves as Spenser's label acknowledging his discipleship.

ASTROPHEL

On October 17, 1586, Sir Philip Sidney died of a wound received in battle near Zutphen, in the Netherlands. His body was returned to England and interred with elaborate ceremony and eulogy equalled only in the next reign, at the untimely passing of Prince Henry. In 1591 appeared a volume of Spenser's minor poems under the title *Complaints*. One of the poems, *The Ruines of Time*, honors Sidney and other of the Dudleys. Possibly before leaving England to return to Ireland Spenser wrote a second elegy to the memory of Sidney, a poem even more formal than the lines in *The Ruines of Time*. *Astrophel* heads a group of elegies to Sidney: two by Bryskett, possibly the fulfillment of earlier intentions; others are by Matthew Roydon and Walter Ralegh. All are included in the volume devoted chiefly to *Colin Clouts Come Home Again* (1595).

Spenser chose as his model the pseudo-pastoral myth of Venus and Adonis, not directly from Bion but from an adaptation by Ronsard from Bion and Ovid. In Ronsard's *Adonis* Spenser recognized a fairly close correspondence with the actual circumstances of Sidney's life and death; accordingly, with a measure of independence, he modified the French poem to fit the actual facts. Sidney was young and universally admired for his accomplishments. Spenser's story of Astrophel's hunting and fatal encounter with the boar represents the final chapter in Sidney's life: his martial exploits in the Netherlands and his death. As Lady Sidney attended her husband during his last illness, so Stella reached the side of the dying Astrophel (see note for 55). Finally, where Ronsard's poem remained true to the legend, Spenser respectfully if untruthfully departs from the accepted versions of the Adonis myth: Stella follows her lover in death. The *Lay of Clorinda*, so-called in *Astrophel*, seems also to be Spenser's. The device by which the poet attributed the piece to the Countess of Pembroke appears to be a means only of denoting the conclusion of the Astrophel-Adonis theme as Spenser now again pays his respects to Sidney's illustrious sister.

The three introductory stanzas serve not only as a statement of theme but as heading for all the poems on Sidney.

15–48. This description of Sidney suggests Sir Calidore in the *Faerie Queene*, 6, and "the brave courtier" in *Mother Hubberds Tale*. Sidney, the poet of the *Arcadia*, answers well the traditional equation of shepherd and poet: Mos., 51–56, 82–84; Ronsard, *Adonis*, 9–28.

55. Sidney married Frances Walsingham in 1583; in 1590 she married Robert Devereux, second Earl of Essex and brother of Lady Rich, traditionally accepted as the Stella of Sidney's *Astrophel and Stella.* But like Spenser, Bryskett identifies Stella with Lady Sidney: *The Mourning Muse of Thestylis,* 93 ff. (See further Friedrich, *E.L.H.,* III, 114–139.)

67–88. "The mingling of chivalric characteristics with the pastoral is quite after Sidney's own manner. See *Mother Hubberds Tale,* 739–762" (Renwick, ed. *Daphnaïda and Other Poems*).

79. Here begins the Adonis theme: Ronsard, 9. **89–90.** *Ibid.,* 101–102.

91 ff. Spenser now applies the account of Adonis' hunting (Ronsard, 175 ff.) to Sidney's exploits in the Lowlands. **97.** Ronsard, 279, "toiles & filets." **108.** *borespear: ibid.,* 190, "espieu." **115–124.** *Ibid.,* 189–194; Spenser omits the name of the beast.

127–132. Ronsard offers no suggestion for this conventional interrogative pattern: Baïf, 2.25 ff.; Vir., 10.9–10; Theocr., 1.66–69. **137–138.** Castiglione, 84–86.

147. Lady Sidney attended her husband during his fatal illness. **151–168.** Ronsard, 195–204; Ovid, *Met.* 10.720–723; Bion, 19–31, 40–49. (The same scene in a tapestry is described in *F.Q.,* 3.1.38.) Bion and Ronsard elaborate the theme of Venus' grief, here subordinated (169–172). **173–174.** Ronsard, 355–358. In other versions of the myth the boar's attack is immediately fatal to Adonis.

175–198. Unlike Venus, who mourns that she cannot follow her lover to Hades (Bion, 51–53), Stella dies immediately.

199. With the coming of the shepherds, whom Spenser introduces to sing their elegies, cf. Shelley, 262 ff., where actual persons, "mountain shepherds," visit the bier of Keats.

[THE LAY OF CLORINDA]

1–60. This entirely conventional passage links the poem with *Astrophel* and prepares for the consolation, for which the Adonis theme provided no place. **61 ff.** The Platonism here seems to be echoed in *Adonais,* e.g., 338–340. **67.** Compare the change of key in "November," 163 ff.; the rest of the poem strongly suggests the consolation there.

Text: *The Complete Poetical Works of Edmund Spenser,* ed. R. E. N. Dodge, Student's Cambridge Edition, New York, 1908.

Other editions: *The Shepherd's Calendar,* ed. C. H. Herford, London, 1895; *The Shepherd's Calendar,* ed. W. L. Renwick, London, 1930; *Daphnaïda and Other Poems,* ed. W. L. Renwick, London, 1929.

Comment: Walter G. Friedrich, "The Stella of Astrophel," *E.L.H.,* III (1936), 114–139; T. P. Harrison, Jr., "Spenser and the Earlier Pastoral Elegy," *Texas Studies in English,* XIII (1933), 36–53; *idem,* "Spenser, Ronsard, and Bion," *M.L.N.,* XLIX (1934), 139–145; J. J. Higginson, *The Shepherd's Calendar,* New York, 1912; Hoyt H. Hudson, "Penelope Devereux as Sidney's Stella," *Huntington Lib. Bull.,* 7 (1935), 89–129; M. Y. Hughes, "Spenser and the Greek Pastoral Triad," *S.P.,* XX (1923), 184–215; *idem.,*

Virgil and Spenser, Berkeley, California, 1929; H. S. V. Jones, *A Spenser Handbook*, New York, 1930; A. C. Judson, *A Biographical Sketch of John Young, Bishop of Rochester*, Bloomington, Indiana, 1933; F. Kluge, "Spenser's Shepherd's Calendar Und Mantuan's Eclogen," *Anglia*, III (1880), 266–274; P. W. Long, "Spenseriana," *M.L.N.*, XXXI (1916), 79–82; C. G. Osgood, "The Doleful Lay of Clorinda," *M.L.N.*, XXXV (1920), 90–96; James M. Purcell, *Sidney's Stella*, New York, 1934; O. Reissert, "Bemerkungen über Spenser's Shepheards Calendar und die frühere Bukolik," *Anglia*, IX (1886), 205–224; W. L. Renwick, *Edmund Spenser*, London, 1925; R. Shafer, "Spenser's Astrophel," *M.L.N.*, XXVIII (1913), 224–226.

WILLIAM DRUMMOND
(1585–1649)

William Drummond was born at Hawthornden, near Edinburgh, December 13, 1585. Destined to succeed as the second laird of Hawthornden, he was reared in the atmosphere of the Scottish court. After graduating at the University of Edinburgh in July, 1605, he proceeded to the Continent to study law. His years in France, however, were devoted more to letters, and there he cultivated for French and Italian poets tastes later manifest in his work. In 1610, on the death of his father, young Drummond settled down at Hawthornden to a life of ease and studious pursuit. He died on December 4, 1649. Belated recognition of Drummond's pastoral Muse is evidenced in a poem by one G. Lauder published in 1711, *Damon: or a Pastoral Elegy on the Death of his Honoured friend William Drummond of Hawthornden*. Damon was the name by which Drummond was generally known among his fellow poets; his bosom friend Sir William Alexander, Earl of Stirling, was known as Alexis.

TEARS ON THE DEATH OF MOELIADES

The death of Prince Henry in his nineteenth year (1612) occasioned Drummond's first appearance as a poet. *Tears on the Death of Moeliades* was twice issued in 1613 and again the next year; and amid floods of other tears called forth at the death of the young Prince of Wales Drummond's contribution earned a general acclaim which is shared by modern critics. Borrowing generously from Sidney, Drummond's *Tears* rings the changes upon the familiar imagery of pastoral elegy: inexorable Death visits high and low, young and old; with darkened earth and weeping heaven Nature reverses her usual courses; rivers, deities, flowers—all betoken their grief. Yet three paragraphs of the seven—the second (ll. 35–70) and the concluding ones (ll. 143–196)—show independence and originality. The poem concludes with a distinctly Spenserian consolation which is memorable for its sincerity, its easy diction, and its vivid Platonism. Blended with more Christian feeling, the Platonic consolation—not from Drummond, however—was to gain magnificent expression in the closing lines of Milton's tribute to Diodati.

3. *Moeliades:* "The name which in these verses is given to Prince Henry is that which he himself, in the challenges of his martial sports and masquerades was wont to use, MOELIADES, PRINCE OF THE ISLES, which, in anagram, maketh MILES A DEO"—Drummond's note.

9–12. Spenser, "November," 87–89; Sidney, *Arcadia,* "a song of Lamentation" at the death of Basilius (ed. Feuillerat, I, 501) :

> Thus, thus the mindes, which over all doo clime,
>> When they by yeares experience get best graces,
>> Must finish then by deaths detested crime.
> We last short while, and build long lasting places.

Clearer dependence upon this song appears in ll. 69–70 and 119–142.

18. Bion, 89–91, where the sense is literal.

69–70. With the double refrain cf. Ronsard, *Adonis,* 217–218, *passim;* and Sidney, *Arcadia,*

> Your dolefull tunes sweet Muses now applie.

107–110. Bion, 83. **119–142.** Sidney, *Arcadia* (Feuillerat, I, 499–500).

143 ff. In combining Platonic thought and Ptolemaic astronomy the consolation perhaps evidences Drummond's reading in Spenser, the *Hymne of Heavenly Beautie;* cf. also "November," 173 ff., and the *Lay,* 79 ff.

ALCON

Appearing in 1638, the elegy on the death of Sir Anthony Alexander was the last of the poems published in Drummond's lifetime. Its subject was the son of Sir William Alexander, Drummond's dear friend. This youth died in London, September 17, 1637, and his body, brought home by sea, was interred in the church at Stirling. What merits appear in *Alcon* the poet seems to owe to his model, Castiglione's *Alcon.* Unlike his more common method of adaptation, Drummond considerably condenses his original. His labored couplets have lost the grace and sincerity of Castiglione. Ward (II, 300) agrees that *Alcon* is Drummond's worst performance, that "its sentiment is forced, and the artificiality of the plan is nowhere redeemed by happy images or memorable lines. One conjectures that Drummond was but slightly acquainted with young Alexander, and that he laboured this memorial as a duty imposed by his long friendship with the father."

1–8. Castiglione, 1–23. **9–34.** *Ibid.,* 24–53. Drummond both omits and expands. **35–42.** *Ibid.,* 54–66. **43–60.** This passage is mostly original. **53–56.** Vir., 5.76–78. **61–69.** Castiglione, 68–77, the account of athletic prowess and love songs. (Ll. 78–82 from the Italian, overlooked by Drummond, are recalled by Milton, *Lycidas,* 23–31.) **69–74.** Drummond's invention. **75–106.** Castiglione, 103–129. Love has driven Drummond's Alcon from home; Idmon awaits his return. This replaces Castiglione's account of his absence from Alcon and his hope of Alcon's coming to Rome. **107.** *Ibid.,* 130. **109–116.** Again invention. **117–138.** Roughly from Castiglione, 132–154. The "Shepherds on Forth, and ye by Doven rocks" replace the Italian nymphs and boys.

Text: *The Poems of William Drummond of Hawthornden,* ed. William C. Ward, 2 vols., *The Muses Library,* London, n.d.

Another edition: *The Poetical Works of William Drummond of Hawthornden,* ed. L. E. Kastner, 2 vols., London, 1913.

Comment: Sir H. J. C. Grierson, *The First Half of the Seventeenth Century,* Edinburgh and London, 1906.

JOHN MILTON
(1608–1674)

LYCIDAS

Edward King was the son of Sir John King, Secretary to the English government in Ireland. At Christ's College, Cambridge, he was both tutor and fellow. Though with Milton it is evident that King had only slight acquaintance, the general esteem in which he was held is attested by the volume of elegiac verse occasioned by his death. On August 10, 1637, the vessel bearing King to Ireland for a vacation visit foundered upon a rock off the Welsh coast and sank; the young Cambridge student was lost. In due course Milton, at Horton, was asked to contribute to a verse collection. In November, 1637, *Lycidas* was written, and in the following year it appeared as the last poem in the volume comprising thirteen elegies—*Obsequies to the Memory of Edward King.*

Considered as the last great elegy in a tradition beginning in Theocritus, *Lycidas* in outline betrays nearest kinship with Virgil's tenth eclogue: invocation, procession of mourners, and eight-line conclusion. One difference appears in that there is no mention of the poet-shepherd in *Lycidas* until the close, when Milton introduces "the uncouth swain." Here the pastoral disguise is consistently maintained except in the famous passage on the clergy, the theme of which was suggested to the poet by his recollection of King's clerical ambition. To this passage Milton gave emphasis by adding, for the 1645 edition, the lines in the heading. Yet the pastoral metaphor, representing Milton and King as shepherds in the fields, keeps within the bounds of accepted conventions. "The allegory proper," observes Jerram (ed. *Lyc. and Epit. Dam.*), "extends only to King's life and to Milton's connection with him, while the catastrophe is given as it actually occurred." Virgil had similarly represented Gallus as soldier and shepherd at the same time. Milton gains naturalness in the allusion to the shipwreck by drawing upon the imagery and language of the piscatory eclogue, and thus he is not compelled to alter the facts of King's death at sea. (See further *supra,* pp. 17–18. Limited space prevents inclusion in the notes of innumerable echoes from classical and Renaissance poets.)

1–2. Vir., 2.54–55:

> et vos, o lauri, carpam et te, proxima myrte,
> sic positae quoniam suaves miscetis odores.

"The bay and the myrtle were usually combined, perhaps for the reason given here" (Jerram).

8–9. Lycidas is a common shepherd name from the time of Theocritus. In Idyl 7 and in *Lycidas*, Sandys remarks, "the two principal personages are the poet and his friend, and, in both, that friend is named Lycidas." (See also Strathmann, *M.L.N.*, LII, 398–400.)

10–14. Even had King not been a poet, Milton might still have reckoned him as such: Mos., 50-84 and note. *Who would not. . . .* Vir., 10.3, "neget quis. . . ." *build:* used in the Latin sense of *condere* (to put together); in Vir., 2.4 *incondita* means unstudied, artless. Horace, *Ars Poet.*, 436, uses "condere carmen" in the sense of "to compose a poem."

15–16. "The customary invocation of the Muses is studied from the opening lines in Hesiod's Theogony" (Jerram). Milton may refer, as Sandys also agrees, "not to Olympus, but to Helicon, the 'Aonian mount,' above which he 'intends to soar,' in 'Paradise Lost' (1.15). . . . In the context [of Hesiod], the Muses are described as 'dancing around the altar of the mighty Zeus,'" possibly to be identified with Milton's "seat of Jove," though it seems natural to identify this with Olympus and the "sacred well" with Pieria.

17. *somewhat loudly:* Vir., 4.1,

> Sicilides Musae, paulo maiora canamus.

(See note for 87.) The "somewhat louder chord" of Virgil, higher than pastoral, was the theme of Pollio's child.

19–22. Vir., 10.4–5.

23–24. Patterson corrects the usual error of beginning the paragraph with l. 23 (for evidence favoring the correction see Tillyard, *Milton*, Appendix E).

25–31. The poem now passes into the pastoral mood. "The hill is Cambridge, the joint feeding of the flocks is companionship in study, the rural ditties are academic iambics and elegiacs. . . ." (Masson). **25–27.** Theocr., 7.35; Castiglione, 78–80. **30.** *the star that rose:* Hesperus, the "star that bids the shepherd fold" (*Comus*, 93). Jerram compares Virgil's use of *venit* in 10.77 and 5.82, adding that other classical writers use the same word of a wind rising or coming up. The word *surgere* is often used similarly (see Hanford, *M.L.N.* XXXVII, 444–445).

34–36. Alluding first to miscellaneous Cambridge friends, the poet probably remembers Damoetas as a particular friend: Chappell, Milton's old tutor, or Bambridge, Master of Christ's, or more probably Joseph Mead, fellow of Christ's (see Nicolson, *M.L.N.*, XLI, 293–300). Cf. Vir., 6.27–28:

> Tum vero in numerum Faunosque ferasque videres
> ludere, tum rigidas motare cacumina quercus.

Hanford adds Vir., 8.4,

> et mutata suos requierunt flumina cursus.

37–38. Iteration, as in 8–9 and 39, is a classical usage.

39–49. Milton "does not dwell on the fiction that the natural objects express grief; he is taken up with the beauty of the things themselves. It is the description that we remember, not the conceit" (Hanford). Contrast is afforded in Bion, 32–34; Mos., 28–32; Vir., 1.38–39 and 5.27–28. In Vir., 5.3

hazels are mentioned, in 10.40 are willows. *gadding:* as in Vir., 4.19, "errantes hederas."

50–55. Theocr., 1.66–69; Vir., 10.9–12. But, as Hanford adds, "Whereas Milton, like Theocritus, mentions places near the region where his shepherd met his fate, Virgil declares that the nymphs were absent, not from Arcady, where the scene of his eclogue is laid, but from their accustomed haunts in Sicily." *Closed o'er:* Hanford notices the peculiar application of Theocritus' phrase "washed over" (1.141) and its context to the circumstances of King's death, in giving Milton the idea of employing the pastoral form. For the entire passage, including 58–60, cf. also Propertius, III, 7, "On the Drowning of Paetus" (Godolphin, *M.L.N.,* XLIX, 162–166).

56. This recollection "marks by a rhetorical device, repeated in 1. 152, the abandonment of a false surmise" (Tuckwell). Cf. Vir., 10.60; Arnold, 172 ff.

58–63. The story of Orpheus often appears in pastoral elegy: Mos., 115–126; Vir., 10.65; Radbert, 145; Sannazaro, 11.64–66; Arnold, 82–100.

64 ff. "This sense of personal relation as a poet to the subject of his song justifies the writer in allowing himself digressions concerning his own poetic achievements and aspirations" (Hanford). The precedent is ancient (Mos., 97); Milton's achievement lies in the naturalness with which the thought of King's tragedy leads him to questions about life itself (cf. *Epit. Dam.* 161 ff.). Jerram remarks that the pastoral landscape disappears as the shepherd is merged with the poet. Not finally until 1. 132 is the rural Muse recalled.

64–84. With 19–22 these lines perhaps voice the poet's fear of premature death (Tillyard, pp. 81–85). *meditate the thankless Muse;* Vir., 1.2,

> silvestrem tenui musam meditaris avena.

and 6.8,

> Agrestem tenui meditabor harundine musam.

To sport with Amaryllis . . . the tangles of Neaera's hair: Amaryllis and Neaera are imaginary mistresses; Amaryllis appears in Theocr., 3.1, Vir., 1.5, and 2.14; Neaera appears in Vir., 3.3. **73–76.** *Epit. Dam.* 109–111. **77–84.** "What Milton had been saying about poetic fame might be understood, he saw, as applicable to himself" (Masson). **77.** Vir., 6.3–5:

> Cum canerem reges et proelia, Cynthius aurem
> vellit et admonuit: 'Pastorem, Tityre, pingues
> pascere oportet oves, deductum dicere carmen.'

Virgil thus apologizes to Varus for addressing to him a pastoral instead of an heroic poem. But as Masson and Sandys remark, the point of the two passages is different.

85. The digression past, the poem now returns with apology to the pastoral mood with the address to Arethusa: Theocr., 1.117; Mos., 10, 77; Vir., 10.1. **86.** As Arethusa suggests Theocritus, so Mincius is the river honored by Virgil. **87.** *Epit. Dam.* 160, "vos cedite, sylvae," *That strain:* reference to 76–84; *higher:* like "maiora" in Vir., 4.1 (cf. "loudly" in 17); *mood:* L. *modus,* character, as in the musical scale. **88 ff.** The various deities approach, as in Theocr., 1.80 ff., and Vir., 10.19 ff. **90–91.** Baïf, 15 (*Damet*), a translation of the pseudo-Virgilian *Dirae*:

> Ces gros monstres, Neptune, amene avec la mer
> Faisant *de vents felons* les vagues ecumer.

99. Panope, a Nereid, is mentioned in Sannazaro, *Phyllis*, 86. **100–102.** Portents are not infrequent: Petrarch, 2.42–53; Sannazaro, *Phyllis*, 3–7; Marot, 181–188. (On Milton and Sannazaro, see further notes for 157–159, 163, and 183–185.) **103–105.** In Bryskett, *Pastorall Aeglogue*, the Thames, the Humber, the Severn, and other rivers mourn the death of Sidney. The description of Camus (termed reedy Cam, "arundineum camum," in Elegy 1.11) derives from Vir., 10.24–25.

113–131. These scathing reflections are prompted by the thought that King had intended to take church orders. The ninth century *Egloga* of Radbert illustrates the manner in which church matters found place in elegies for departed monks; and obviously familiar with this poem, Petrarch was first to use the eclogue to scourge abuses in Rome (cf. especially Eclogue 6, in which St. Peter rebukes Pope Clement). Mantuan further developed the church eclogue separately (see note for *Lyc.*, 128–129); and Spenser in "September" takes Mantuan as his model. But a striking passage of satire from "May," 39 ff., should especially be compared with Milton's lines here. (On John Skelton, Spenser, and Milton, see Baskervill, *Nation*, XCI, 546–547). **123–124.** Vir., 3.26–27:

> non tu in triviis, indocte, solebas
> stridenti miserum stipula disperdere carmen?

(on *indocte*, see note for 186–193). Virgil's lines follow Theocr., 5.5–8, lighthearted banter preceding a singing match; Milton's studied contempt denotes a different mood. Sandys quotes Calpurnius, 3.60, "acerbae stridor avenae." **128–129.** Mantuan, 9.141–147:

> mille lupi, totidem vulpes in vallibus istis
> lustra tenent, . . .
>   factum vicinia ridet
> nec scelus exhorret nec talibus obviat ausis.

(see further note for 193).

132–133. "As the return from the former digression (1.85) was marked by the invocation of Arethusa, so now the poet addresses Alpheus, her legendary lover" (Jerram). As Masson remarks, both are now united in the fountain Arethusa, "jointly the 'Sicilian Muse.'" And the return of a pagan divinity is more natural in view of the passing of the voice of Peter, which is like that of Christ himself; cf. Boccaccio, 122, where the nymphs flee at the approach of the heavenly visitant.

134–151. Suggestions of the familiar catalogue of flowers appear in Theocr., 11.54–59; Bion, 75; Mos., 1–7; Vir., 2.45–55, 4.19 ff., and 5.36–40; Castiglione, 142 ff.; Marot, 225–240; Spenser, who in "April," 136 ff., includes many flowers here named. Milton's list mentions three kinds of berries and eleven kinds of flowers; but on August 11, the date of King's death, none of the berries would have appeared and nine of the eleven flowers would not be blooming. Shakespeare (*The Winter's Tale*, 4.4.122 ff.), it is often remarked, is careful to distinguish the flowers of summer and winter. And long before, Theocritus (11.54–59) naming lilies and poppies, adds that as these belong to different seasons they could not be fetched the same day. Virgil, in 2.45–55, disregards the seasons.

152–154. "Milton has been speaking of the 'hearse' of Lycidas, and the flowers fit to be strewn upon it in mourning, when he suddenly reminds himself that all that is but fond fancy, inasmuch as Lycidas had perished at sea, and his body had never been recovered" (Masson). Hanford cites Castiglione, 140, where Iolas erects a tomb "nostri solatia luctus."

157–158. Sannazaro, *Phyllis*, 72–76.

160 ff. "Can anyone who reads Milton doubt that the mere sound of the stately names of classic history and mythology exercised a real influence on the poet's fancy?" (Conington, ed. *Virgil*, I, 8). With the present passage and 54–55, cf. Vir., 2.24 and 8.44 (Sandys). **163.** Sannazaro, *Phyllis*, 91–98, where as here the spirit of the departed is addressed. Hence the sudden transition from the idea of the spirit looking down to that of the body wafted by dolphins. The supplication to the departed soul to "look down" is a commonplace: e.g., Vir., 5.56–57 (see further 183–185 and note).

165 ff. The traditional note of joy gains effect by its suddenness. Masson observes the "close resemblance, even to identity of expression, to the closing part of the *Epitaphium Damonis*." **166.** *Your sorrow:* Lat. *tua cura* (cf. Vir., 1.57). **168–171.** Castiglione, 57–60, where the sun's course is contrasted with death. **174–175.** Sannazaro, 5.14–16, or the adaptation of it in Ronsard, 1.61–64. **176.** A similar idea of Christ's reunion with his Church appears in *Epit. Dam.* 217. **183 ff.** "Here, after a contemplation of the state of the dead Lycidas which is purely Christian and Biblical, there is a relapse into the classic manner, and Lycidas is converted into a *numen*" (Masson). **183–185.** Sannazaro, *Phyllis*, 97–98, which follows Vir., 5.65. Milton literally renders Virgil's "bonus," Sannazaro's "laetum omen" (compare 163, where the spirit of King is invoked).

186–193. These lines, a stanza in *ottava rima*, correspond in length and manner with the close of Vir., 10. *uncouth:* rude, untaught (cf. "indocte," Vir., 3.26). *the tender stops of various quills:* varied strains (76, 88, 113, 132, 165) and varied metre of the poem. *Doric:* after the Greek pastoral, written in the Doric Greek. **190–191.** Vir., 1.83, and 2.67. **193.** Like Virgil (10.70), Milton means that he will write no more pastorals.

EPITAPHIUM DAMONIS

Charles Diodati was the son of Theodore Diodati, an Italian physician, and his English wife. The father's family originated during the fourteenth century in Lucca, which Milton later visited when on his Italian tour. Almost of the same age, Milton became deeply attached to Diodati at St. Paul's School; and though young Charles left for Trinity College, Oxford, in February, 1621–1622, three years before Milton went up to Cambridge, the two friends did not permit separation to destroy their intimacy. During Milton's absence in Italy Diodati died in August, 1638.

Like many Renaissance pastorals which modify the pattern of Virgil's tenth eclogue, Castiglione's *Alcon* and Milton's *Epitaphium* contain an introduction separate from the lament proper. The lament in Milton falls into three distinct parts, and the refrain marks its successive moods. What may be called part one (18–111) precedes the account of the Italian journey and is thoroughly conventional. Part two (112–197) includes, first (112–160) the poet's memories of Damon and his grief in being absent when Damon died; second (161–178) plans for a British epic; and third (180–197) a description of the cups, gifts of Manso. The poem ends briefly (198–219) with an account of the heavenly joys of Damon, Milton's adaptation of Virgil's deification of Caesar being colored with Platonism. (See further *supra*, pp. 18–19.)

The introductory argument provides a key to the allegory, as in Radbert and Petrarch. Observe the freedom with which pastoral convention merges with actuality: the two friends are shepherds, yet Damon travels to foreign lands for pleasure.

1–3. Vir., 4.1 and 6.1; *Lycidas*, 133. Milton invokes the Sicilian Muses, though direct reminiscences of Theocritus and Moschus are lacking. *Himera:* the river of Theocritus is associated with Daphnis in Idyl 7.73–75. The story of Hylas is told in Theocr., 13, which is neither pastoral nor elegy. **4.** The stock name Thyrsis occurs in Theocr., 1, and Vir., 7; Damon (7) is a singer in Vir., 8. **5–6.** Castiglione, 15 (with the phrase "antra querelis" cf. *Alcon*, 138, "antra querelas"). Verbal parallels with Castiglione are less common than those of organization, idea, and figure. **9–10.** These lines give the exact date of Diodati's death, August, 1638. Thus the elegy was composed in the late spring or early summer of 1640, and published immediately (see Bradner). **12–13.** Diodati had died when Milton was in Florence. **15.** Theocr., 1.21; by "the accustomed elm" Milton has in mind his father's house at Horton. **18.** With the refrain cf. *Alcon*, 18–20; Vir., 5.24–26, and 7.44,

Ite domum pasti, si quis pudor, ite iuvenci.

19–22. *Alcon*, 27–33. **27.** An ancient superstition existed that if one met a wolf without first catching its eye, he would be struck dumb: Vir., 9.53–54. **29–32.** Vir., 5.78–80. **37–43.** *Lyc.*, 23–31. *morientibus herbis: Alcon*, 38. For other details cf. Vir., 5.27, 9.52, and 10.55–58. **46–47.** Petrarch, 2.76. **52.** Theocr., 1.16–18 and note. **55–56.** *Alcon*, 71–72. **63–67.** *Ibid.*, 38–42: the meadows, the corn, the sheep. The shepherd's possessions suffer through neglect: *Lyc.*, 39 ff.

69–92. The personal note dropped for the moment, Milton now turns to the traditional visits of deities and friends: Theocr., 1.77–91. Unlike Shelley, 262 ff., probably Milton has in mind no real persons in the common classical names, Tityrus, etc. **71.** *Alcon*, 124 and its original in Vir., 10.42–43. **73.** Vir., 10.8, "non canimus surdis." In Milton the singer, like Daphnis in Theocr., 1.93, is deaf to the various appeals. **75 ff.** Baïf, 2.54 ff. In Theocr., 1 Hermes is first to approach the afflicted Daphnis; in Vir., 5, Mopsus is the first singer. **79–80.** Petrarch, 2.42–53. **82–86.** Theocr., 1.82–91, the nymphs in Milton replacing Priapus in the Greek poem. **88 ff.** Vir., 10.19 ff. **100–105.** *Alcon*, 8–15, where, however, the point of comparison is directly opposite. *seu stravit arundine fossor: Alcon*, 11. **109–111.** *Lycidas*, 73–76. **113.** *Alcon*, 83. Each poet mourns his absence from his friend at the final hour, and each proceeds to an account of foreign travel. **115–117.** *Ibid.*, 122–123 and 125; Vir., 1.26,

> Et quae tanta fuit Romam tibi causa videndi?

Milton in Rome deplores his absence from England, Castiglione in Rome dreams of his friend's coming. **121–122.** *Alcon*, 84–86; Spenser, *Astrophel*, 137–138. **132.** Allusion to academic discussions and debates which Milton had witnessed in Florence. **133–135.** Among Milton's poems written in Italy Masson names *Ad Leonoram, Ad Salsillum, Mansus*, and the five Italian sonnets and canzone. To the gifts mentioned in 135 the poet later adds elaborately (181–197) the "cups" presented to him by Manso. *fiscellae . . .:* Vir., 10.71. Masson believes these are doubtless "poetical names for little presents actually received from Florentine friends." **136–138.** With the real names Carlo Dati and Antonio Francini, compare the fictitious ones, Lycidas and Menalcas (132)—another instance of momentary abandonment of the pastoral allegory.

142–178. *Alcon*, 103–129, as each poet tells of his dreams of the absent friend. **144.** Vir., 2.71–72, and 10.71. **145–146.** *Alcon*, 103–104. **150–154.** Allusion to Diodati's medical studies and botanical knowledge. **155–160.** With 155 ("grande") cf. *Lyc.*, 87 (the "strain of higher mood"). With 160 ("vos cedite, sylvae") cf. Vir., 10.63, "ipsae rursus concedite silvae." Thus the recognition, as in *Lycidas*, of digression (162–178) from the elegiac pastoral theme.

162–168. Milton's project would trace the history of the Britons from the coming of the Trojan Brutus down to the reign of Arthur. **168–171.** The second important announcement is that he will abandon the pastoral and substitute English for Latin. **169.** Vir., 7.24. *omnia non licet uni:* Vir., 8.63. **172–178.** With the references to the English rivers—Ouse, Alan, Humber, Trent, Thames, and Tamar—cf. Mos., 71 ff.; Marot, 161 ff.; *Lycidas*, 103–106. **180.** *Alcon*, 130; Castiglione concludes his foreign meditations.

181–197. Theocr., 1.27–63. Milton had received from Manso, not an actual pair of cups, but two books (see de Filippis, *P.M.L.A.*, LI, 745–756). **191–197.** Both Ovid, *Met.* 1.455–476, and Moschus, Idyl 1, allude to Cupid's activity among the gods. The picture is allegorical, for Milton is describing heavenly love after Plato and Spenser. The poet thus prepares for the transition to the account of Damon's heavenly joys, the concluding theme.

198–219. Like the corresponding passage in *Lycidas*, 165–185, this owes much to Virgil's fifth eclogue; but unlike *Lycidas*, here classical imagery predominates (see Hanford, "The Youth of Milton"). **203–204.** Vir., 5.56–57; Sannazaro, 5.9–10. **205–208.** *Lyc.*, 184–185; Vir., 5.65; Sannazaro, 11.148–149, and *Phyllis*, 97–98; Spenser, "November," 195–196. **217.** *Lyc.*, 176–177.

Text: *The Complete Poetical Works of John Milton*, Student's Cambridge Edition, ed. William Vaughan Moody, Boston, 1899. New edition, E. K. Rand, 1924.

Other editions: *The Lycidas and Epitaphium Damonis*, ed. C. S. Jerram, London, 1874; *Seventeenth Century Lyrics*, ed. A. C. Judson, University of Chicago Press, 1927; *The Latin Poems of John Milton*, ed. W. MacKellar, Yale University Press, 1930; *The Poetical Works of John Milton*, ed. David Masson, 3 vols., London, 1903; *The Student's Milton*, ed. F. A. Patterson, New York, 1936; Milton's *Lycidas*, ed. C. A. Patrides, New York, 1961.

Comment: E. C. Baldwin, "Milton and *Ezekiel*," *M.L.N.*, XXXIII (1918) 211–215; C. R. Baskervill, "Two Parallels to 'Lycidas,'" *Nation*, XCI (1910), 546–547; Leicester Bradner, "Milton's 'Epitaphium Damonis,'" *L.T.L.S.*, August 18, 1932; John S. Diekhoff, "*Lycidas*, line 10," *P.Q.*, XVI (1937), 408–410; G. R. Coffman, "The Parable of the Good Shepherd, 'De Contemptu Mundi,' and 'Lycidas': Excerpts for a Chapter on Literary History and Culture," *E.L.H.*, III (1936), 101–113; A. S. Cook, "Two Notes on Milton," *M.L.R.*, II (1907) 121–128; *idem*, "Four Notes," *S.P.*, XVI (1919), 177–186; D. C. Dorian, "Milton's 'Two-handed Engine,'" *P.M.L.A.*, XLV (1930), 204–215; Oliver F. Emerson, "The Shepherd's Star in English Poetry," *Anglia*, XXXIX (1916), 495–516; Michele De Filippis, "Milton and Manso: Cups or Books," *P.M.L.A.*, LI (1936), 745–756; L. S. Friedland, "Milton's *Lycidas* and Spenser's *Ruines of Time*," *M.L.N.*, XXVII (1912), 246–250; A. H. Gilbert, *A Geographical Dictionary of Milton*, Yale University Press, 1919; F. R. B. Godolphin, "Milton, *Lycidas* and Propertius, Elegies, III, 7," *M.L.N.*, XLIX (1934), 162–166; Rudolf Gottfried, "Milton, Lactantius, Claudian, and Tasso," *S.P.*, XXX (1933), 497–503; J. W. Hales, "Milton's 'Lycidas,'" *Athenaeum*, August 1, 1891; H. F. Hamilton, "The Sources of Milton's 'Lycidas,'" *Sewanee Review*, XVII (1909), 235–240; J. H. Hanford, "The Pastoral Elegy and Milton's Lycidas," *P.M.L.A.*, XXV (1910), 403–447; *idem*, "The Youth of Milton," *Studies in Shakespeare, Milton, and Donne*, University of Michigan, 1925; *idem*, "The Evening Star in Milton," *M.L.N.*, XXXVII (1922), 444–445; *idem*, "Haemony (*Comus* 616–648)," *L.T.L.S.*, November 3, 1932, 815; R. D. Havens, *The Influence of Milton on English Poetry*, Harvard University Press, 1922; Deborah Jones, "Lodowick Bryskett and his Family," *Thomas Lodge and Other Elizabethans*, ed. Chas. J. Sisson, Harvard University Press, 1933; Laura E. Lockwood, "Milton's Corrections to the Minor Poems," *M.L.N.*, XXV (1910), 201–205; Grant McColley, "Lycidas and Lycaeus," *N. & Q.*, CLXXIII (1937), 159; Thomas O. Mabbott,, "Lycidas and Lycaeus," *N. & Q.*, CLXXII (1937), 352, 447, 462; David Masson, *Life of John Milton*, 7 vols., London, 1859–1894, I; Marjorie Nicolson, "Old Damoetas," *M.L.N.*, XLI (1926), 293–300; C. S. Osgood, "*Lycidas* 130, 131," *R.E.S.*, I (1925), 339–341; E. K. Rand, "Milton in Rustication," *S.P.*, XIX (1922), 109–135; Sir John E. Sandys, "The Literary Sources of Milton's 'Lycidas,'" *Transactions of the Royal Society of Literature*, XXXII, Second Series (1914), 233–264; Thomas K. Sidey, "*The Uncouth Swain* in Milton's 'Lycidas,'" *M.L.N.*, XXIII (1908), 92; Donald A. Stauffer, "Milton's 'Two-handed Engine,'"

M.L.R., XXXI (1936), 57–60; Ernest A. Strathmann, "*Lycidas* and the Translation of 'May,'" *M.L.N.*, LII (1937), 398–400; Marian H. Studley, "That Two-handed Engine," *Eng. Jour.*, College ed., XXVI (1937), 148–151; E. M. W. Tillyard, *Milton*, London, 1930; Rev. W. Tuckwell, *Lycidas: a Monograph*, London, 1911.

ALEXANDER POPE
(1688–1744)

PASTORAL 4

WINTER

Mrs. Tempest: "This lady was of an ancient family in Yorkshire, and particularly admired by the author's friend Mr. Walsh, who, having celebrated her in a pastoral elegy, desired his friend to do the same, as appears from one of his letters, dated Sept. 9, 1706: 'Your last eclogue being on the same subject with mine on Mrs. Tempest's death, I should take it very kindly in you to give it a little turn as if it were to the memory of the same lady.' Her death having happened on the night of the great storm in 1703, gave a propriety to this eclogue, which in its general turn alludes to it. The scene of this pastoral lies in a grove, the time at midnight."—Pope. The names Thyrsis and Lycidas Pope remembered from Virgil, 7 and 9, respectively; Thyrsis here sings the lament, as in Theocritus 1. (See further, *supra*, pp. 20–21.)

1–4. Theocr., 1.7–8; Vir., 5.45–47 and 82–84. The careful balancing of lines follows the Greek idyl. **11.** Alexis is the youth celebrated in Vir., 2. **13.** Vir., 6.83. **17.** Vir., 5.41. **23–28.** Bion, 80–82; Vir., 5.42–44. The refrain appears as in Vir., 8. **37–38.** Vir., 5.25–26. **39–42.** Mos., 14–16 (the Strymonian swans), and 30–31 (Echo). **49–50.** "I wish that his fondness had not overlooked a line in which the zephyrs are made to lament in silence" (Samuel Johnson). **51.** Mos., 33–35. **69–70.** Vir., 5.56–57. **72.** Spenser, "November," 189. **75–76.** Vir., 5.65. **77–80.** *Ibid.*, 45–47 and 82. **81–84.** *Ibid.*, 74–78. (With 81 cf. Vir., 1.7–8.) **86.** Vir., 10.75–76; for juniper Pope substitutes pines. **88.** *Ibid.*, 69; for Love Pope writes Time. **89–92.** Spenser, "December," 151–155.

(Bibliography follows notes for Gay)

AMBROSE PHILIPS
(1675–1749)

PASTORAL 3

ALBINO

This is an anniversary poem honoring the young Duke of Gloucester, only child of Anne to survive infancy, who died on July 29, 1700, at the age of eleven. The Act of Settlement had designated him for the throne. Virgil's fifth and tenth eclogues are Philips' models. The introduction of subject and setting in the first 28 lines is the manner of Virgil's tenth eclogue, and the

formal division of the lament—Angelot singing the lament proper, Palin celebrating the apotheosis—follows Virgil's fifth. The names are suggested from
the French pastoral (Angelot appears in Ronsard's first eclogue). In the
1708 edition Philips' chief model is acknowledged in a quotation from Virgil's
Daphnis.

1–8. Here Philips proclaims his discipleship. **16.** Vir., 5.12. **21.** *Ibid.*,
6–7. **43.** *Ibid.*, 25–26 (cf. Pope, 37–38). **45–48.** Bion, 7–12. **49–50.** Vir.,
10.16–20 (the sheep, the allusion to Adonis, the visitors). **51.** *Ibid.*, 10.28, the
interrogation of Gallus. **55–64.** Vir., 5.22–23; a nymph was the fabled
mother of Daphnis (see l. 97). **65–74.** *Ibid.*, 32–39. **77–80.** *Ibid.*, 29–31
(the account of Caesar's accomplishments). **89–134.** Palin's consolation
depends less upon Vir., 5, than does Angelot's lament. **97–98.** *the royal
Nymph, who bore him:* Queen Anne. **99–106.** Vir., 5.56–64 (the general
rejoicing of man and nature). Philips' lines attempt a more homely effect.
116. Philips apologizes for the collection of flowers which defy the season
(see note for *Lycidas*, 134–151). **121–134.** Vir., 5.67–78.

(Bibliography follows notes for Gay)

JOHN GAY
(1685–1732)

THE SHEPHERD'S WEEK

FRIDAY, OR THE DIRGE

"Dirge, or Dyrge, a mournful ditty, or song of lamentation over the dead,
not a contraction of the Latin Dirige in the popish hymn Dirige Gressus
meos, as some pretend. But from the Teutonick Dyrke, Laudare, to praise
and extol. Whence it is possible their Dyrke and our Dirge, was a laudatory
song to commemorate and applaud the dead. Cowell's interpreter"—Gay.
The first suggestion is correct, for the word derives from the Latin *dirige*,
which opens the Latin antiphon referred to.

1 ff. Goldsmith (*The Citizen of the World*, 1760–1761, Letter CVI) describes the manner of commencing funeral elegies: "But the most usual
manner is this: Damon meets Menalcas, who has got a most gloomy
countenance. The shepherd asks his friend, whence that look of distress?
To which the other replies, that Pollio is no more. 'If that be the case, then,'
cries Damon," etc., etc. **15–20.** Vir., 5.10–11. **26.** The charms of Blouzelind
are sung by Lobbin Clout in "Monday." **29–30.** This is a playful variation
of the conventional simile deriving from Virgil: see Castiglione, 8–15. **33–40.**
Gay thus burlesques the usual pathetic fallacy. **43–80.** This homely account
of rural courtship vies with Touchstone's fanciful recollections, *A.Y.L.I.*
2.4.49 ff. **84–87.** Vir., 5.38–39 (Gay). **90–91.** *Ibid.*, 5.42 (Gay). **93–98.**
Ibid., 5.45–47, 50–51 (Gay). **96.** Gay cites Theocr., 8.83 (quoted in note for
Vir., 5.45–47). **109–132.** Gay here abandons burlesque. **133–138.** Only
simple flowers are named; see Gay's Proem for ridicule of Philips' catalogue
(106–118). **153–158.** Vir., 5.76–78 (Gay).

Texts: *The Poetical Works of Alexander Pope*, ed. Henry W. Boynton, Student's Cambridge Edition, New York, 1903; "A Variorum Text of Four Pastorals by Ambrose Philips," ed. R. H. Griffith, *Texas Studies in English*, XII (1932)—text of the 1748 edition; *The Poetical Works of John Gay*, ed. John Underhill, 2 vols., *The Muses Library*, London and New York, 1893.

Comment: Marion K. Bragg, *The Formal Eclogue in the Eighteenth Century*, *University of Maine Studies*, Oronto, 1926; Richard F. Jones, "Eclogue Types in English Poetry of the Eighteenth Century" *Journal of English and Germanic Philology*, XXIV (1925), 33–60; E. C. Knowlton, "The Pastoral in the Eighteenth Century," *M.L.N.*, XXXII (1917), 471–474; H. E. Mantz, "Non-Dramatic Pastoral in Europe in the Eighteenth Century," *P.M.L.A.*, XXXI (1916), 421–427.

SHELLEY

(1792–1822)

ADONAIS

Shelley's genius was a peculiarly assimilative and scholarly one, and many of his debts are unconsciously incurred, as he himself recognized. Writing to the Gisbornes, July 21, 1821, he inquires as to whether *Adonais* betrays his reading in Goethe, and he adds: "Poets—the best of them, are a very cameleonic race; they take the colour not only of what they feed on, but of the very leaves under which they pass." (See further, *supra*, pp. 21–22.)

Mottoes: Shelley's translation of the Platonic lines is later elaborated in stanza xlvi. As the second motto appear ll.111–114 of Moschus' *Lament for Bion*, later developed in stanza xxxvi. **1–9(i).** Bion, 1–5; Mos., 1–2, 7, 17–18. The refrain, repeated with variations through the first stanzas (i, iii, iv, v, vi, x), is from Bion, 1–2. *Most musical, most melancholy:* Mos., 70. **10–12.** *Lycidas*, 50–51. The address to Urania prepares for her important rôle. She is the "mighty Mother," the heavenly counterpart of Bion's Venus; she represents "spiritual or intellectual aspiration, the love of abstract beauty, the divine element in song" (Rossetti). **16.** Mos., 53–54. **24–27.** Bion, 55–56. **28–36(iv).** Adding 46–54, cf. Mos., 71–76, the allusion to Homer (Norlin).

61. Bion, 71. From this point as far as stanza xxxviii (l.333), Shelley follows chiefly the *Lament for Adonis*. **73–99.** *Dreams . . . who were his flocks:* that is, Keats' poems. In Bion (75–86) those who ministered to the dead Adonis were, not Dreams, but Loves. **109–117(xiii).** Mos., 26–29, where the Satyrs, the Priapi, the Pans, and the fountain nymphs mourn for Bion. **127–135(xv).** *Ibid.*, 30–31. **136–138.** *Ibid.*, 32. "Probably Shelley supposed Keats to have died in the spring" (Rossetti). **140.** *Ibid.*, 26 (Apollo). **143.** Bion, 35; Mos., 4 (flowers). **145–151.** Mos., 9, 37–44, 87–93. Shelley remembers also Vir., *Geor.* 4.511–515 (cf. Castiglione, 8–15). **154–180(xviii–xx).** Mos., 99–104 (with 177–180 cf. Spenser, "November," 83–91). **191.** This appeal parallels that to Cypris in Bion, 4, as Shelley now returns to the Greek theme. **193.** Bion, 17. **198.** *Ibid.*, 3.

208–216(xxiv). The coming of Urania suggests Plato, *Symposium*, 195 (concerning the softness and delicacy of Love), and Bion (with 208–212 cf. Bion, 21–22; with 215–216 cf. Bion, 64–66).

217–261(xxv–xxix). Bion, 40–61. **226–234(xxvi).** *Ibid.*, 43–53. "In line 9 the turn given to the thought of Bion is singular, and in fact the words sound like an anticipation of the closing mood of the poem, and a direct expression of Shelley's own sadness" (Woodberry). **235–252(xxvii–xxviii).** *Ibid.*, 60–61; Spenser, *Astrophel*, 91–101 (Sidney's exploits in the Netherlands). *the unpastured dragon:* the boar in the Greek poem; here the world.

244–248. With "herded wolves" and "contagion" cf. Milton's "grim wolf" and "foul contagion" (*Lyc.* 127–128). **262–315(xxx–xxxv).** Vir., 10.19 ff.; Spenser, *Astrophel*, 200 ff. **271–307(xxxi–xxxiv).** With this personal motive cf. Milton, *Lycidas*, 64–84, and *Epitaphium Damonis*, 37 ff. **316–333 (xxxvi–xxxvii).** Before the final change of key the poem now returns to the earlier theme of Keats' murderers. The first stanza elaborates the motto, Mos., 111–114.

334–342(xxxviii). "November," 163–171, where Spenser effects a similar transition to the concluding mood. With 338–342 cf. the *Lay*, 77–84. The succeeding stanzas also bear comparison with Spenser. **361–369(xli).** Virgil, 5.56–64, represents Nature rejoicing; here Shelley appeals to Nature to cease the mourning which he had described in 118–144. Through the remainder of the poem he abandons all pastoral conventions. **411–414.** Shelley varies the Platonic motto of the poem.

Text: *The Complete Poetical Works of Percy Bysshe Shelley*, ed. George E. Woodberry, Student's Cambridge Edition, New York, 1901.

Other editions: *Shelley's Epipsychidion und Adonais*, ed. Richard Ackermann, Berlin, 1900; *The Poems of Percy Bysshe Shelley*, ed. C. D. Locock, 2 vols., London, 1911; *Complete Poetical Works*, ed. W. M. Rossetti, 3 vols., London, 1881; *Adonais*, ed. T. J. Wise, Shelley Soc. Pub., London, 1886.

Comment: Richard Ackermann, *Quellen, Vorbilder, Stoffe zu Shelley's Poetischen Werken*, Erlangen and Leipzig, 1890; T. Böhme, *Spensers Literarisches Nachleben bis zu Shelley*, Berlin, 1911; Lane Cooper, "Notes on Byron and Shelley," *M.L.N.*, XXIII (1908), 118–119; A. Droop, *Die Belesenheit Percy Bysshe Shelley's*, Weimar, 1906; Sir Oliver Elton, *Shelley*, London, 1924; T. P. Harrison, Jr., "Spenser and Shelley's 'Adonais,'" *Texas Studies in English*, XIII (1933), 54–63; Fred L. Jones, "Adonais: The Source of XXVII–XXVIII," *M.L.N.*, XLVI (1931), 236–239; George Norlin, "Greek Sources of Shelley's 'Adonais,'" *University of Colorado Studies*, I (1902–3); Walter E. Peck, "The Source-Book of Shelley's 'Adonais,'" *L.T.L.S.*, April 7, 1921, 228–229.

MATTHEW ARNOLD
(1822–1888)

THYRSIS

The academic sequence of Arthur Hugh Clough—Rugby, Balliol, and Oriel—was repeated by Matthew Arnold, who from his father's school proceeded to Oxford in 1841, five years after the entrance of his friend. Both men earned Oriel fellowships and to both came the chance of remaining at Oxford. But in 1847 Arnold departed to accept a secretarial post, and the next year Clough resigned his tutorship, tortured by religious doubts. Enduring an unsettled, nomadic life—England, America, the Continent, the Near East—, Clough died in his forty-second year, on November 13, 1861, in Florence, near which he was laid to rest in the "broad lucent Arno-vale." (See further, *supra*, pp. 22–24.)

1–10. The poet stands in imagination upon a hill overlooking the Thames and the village of Oxford. "The Oxford country is treated in that holiday spirit which gives Clough's Long Vacation Pastoral also its charm" (Houghton).
29. Here and in 197 ff. the poet alludes to *The Scholar Gypsy*, a companion to *Thyrsis* not only in its stanzaic form and Oxford setting but in its realistic pastoral manner. **36–37.** This is the traditional way of saying that he has not written poetry for a long time: *Lycidas*, 1–5. **40–50.** Clough's religious doubts finally impelled him to resign from Oriel, in 1848; Arnold here implies that this spiritual conflict caused his death.
62–77. Moschus, 99–104; but here Arnold, like Milton (*Lycidas*, 133–151), is preoccupied with the beauty of the things described. **80–81.** In Virgil, 7, Corydon vanquishes Thyrsis in a singing match. **82–100.** Moschus, 115–126 (Orpheus' successful journey to Hades). With 98–100, cf. *Lycidas*, 103, and *Epitaphium Damonis*, 177 (river allusions).
121–130. The poet here alludes to river expeditions in company with Clough; cf. *Lycidas*, 25–36, where the pastoral fiction continues unbroken. With the recurring thought in 130–131, cf. *Lycidas*, 37–38. **131–150.** The simplicity of this passage is in marked contrast to the usual digressive, self-conscious disquisition on death.
171–190. Without the emphasis ordinarily secured by its position at the close, the theme of immortality here is lightly touched. **184.** The name Lityerses is found in Theocr., 10.41, where it is connected with the earliest accounts of reaping and reapers' songs. Arnold combines two traditions about Daphnis explained by Servius in comment upon Vir., 5.20 and 8.68. This comment has been summarized: "Daphnis, the ideal Sicilian shepherd of Greek pastoral poetry, was said to have followed into Phrygia his mistress Piplea, who had been carried off by robbers, and to have found her in the power of the king of Phrygia, Lityerses. Lityerses used to make strangers try a contest with him in reaping corn, and to put them to death if he overcame them. Hercules arrived in time to save Daphnis, took upon himself the

reaping-contest with Lityerses, overcame him and slew him. The Lityerses-song connected with this tradition was, like the Linus-song, one of the early plaintive strains of Greek popular poetry, and used to be sung by corn-reapers. Other traditions represented Daphnis as beloved by a nymph who exacted from him an oath to love no one else. He fell in love with a princess, and was struck blind by the jealous nymph. Mercury, who was his father, raised him to heaven, and made a fountain spring up in the place from which he ascended. At this fountain the Sicilians offered yearly sacrifices."—note from text.

Text: *Poems by Matthew Arnold*, The Macmillan Company, New York, 1923.

Comment: H. W. Garrod, "The Poetry of Matthew Arnold," *Poetry and the Criticism of Life*, Harvard University Press, 1931; Ralph E. C. Houghton, *The Influence of the Classics on the Poetry of Matthew Arnold*, Oxford, 1923; *The Letters of Matthew Arnold to Arthur Hugh Clough*, ed. Howard F. Lowry, Oxford University Press, 1932; *The Letters of Matthew Arnold*, collected and arranged by George W. E. Russell, 2 vols., London and New York, 1895.

A SELECTIVE CATALOGUE OF PROPER NAMES

ACHARNAE, a place near Athens. Theocr., 7.71.

ACIS, a river in Sicily. Theocr., 1.69.

ADONIS, young shepherd and hunter, loved by Venus, killed by a boar (see further *supra*, pp. 1–2). Theocr., 1.109; Mos., 70; Vir., 10.18; Drummond, *Tears*, 110, and *Alcon*, 11; Pope, 24. Subject of poems by Bion and Ronsard.

ADONAIS, John Keats (1795–1821), subject of the poem by Shelley.

AEGILUS, a town in Attica famous for its figs. Theocr., 1.147.

AEGIPAN, a goat-shaped god often identified with Pan, worshiped in the fields. Ronsard, 1.84.

AEGLE, probably the Naiad, daughter of Zeus and Neaera, called by Virgil (6.20) "Naiadum pulcherrima." Milton, *Epit. Dam.* 88.

AEGON, a shepherd. Vir., 5.72; Milton, *Epit. Dam.* 70.

AEGEANAX, subject of the song of Lycidas. Theocr., 7.52.

AIOLLE Francesco, an Italian musician. He appears in a del Sarto fresco representing the Magi in the church S. S. Annunziata, and he is mentioned by Vasari, *Lives of the Painters.* Alamanni, 1.24, 26.

ALAN, the English river formed by the Stour and the Avon and flowing into the Solent, Hampshire. Milton, *Epit. Dam.* 175.

ALBINO, the Duke of Gloucester, only child of Queen Anne to survive infancy; died in 1700 at the age of eleven; subject of the poem by Philips.

ALCAEUS, lyric poet of Lesbos (fl. 590 B.C.). Mos., 90.

ALCON: (1) a shepherd, Vir., 5.11; (2) Matteo Falcone, subject of the poem by Castiglione; (3) Sir Anthony Alexander (d. 1637), subject of Drummond's *Alcon*.

ALCYONE, wife of Ceyx. Both were changed into halcyons, a species of Mediterranean tern. Theocr., 7.57; Mos., 40; Alamanni, 2.51.

ALEXIS: (1) a fair youth celebrated in Virgil's second eclogue: Vir., 5.86; Boccaccio, 71; Castiglione, 125; Pope, 11; (2) Sir William Alexander, Earl of Stirling, father of young Anthony, celebrated in Drummond's *Alcon*, and author of *Elegie on the Death of Prince Henrie* (1612): Drummond, *Tears*, 93.

ALPHESIBOEUS, a shepherd. Vir., 5.73; Milton, *Epit. Dam.* 69.

ALPHEUS, a river-god enamored of the nymph Arethusa and united with her in the fountain bearing her name (see ARETHUSA). Milton, *Lycidas*, 132.

AMARYLLIS, an imaginary mistress. Milton, *Lycidas*, 68.

AMATHUS, an ancient city in Cyprus with a temple of Adonis and Aphrodite (Venus Amathusia). Ronsard, *Adonis*, 34.

AMBOISE, a French city near Tours on the left bank of the Loire. Marot, 161.

AMPHRYSUS, a small river in Thessaly near which Apollo fed the flocks of Admetus. Baïf, 2.72.

AMYNTAS: (1) perhaps a real name, Theocr., 7.2, 131; (2) a fictitious shepherd: Vir., 5.8, 15, 18, and 10.37, 41; Sannazaro, *Phyllis*, 26; Drummond, *Alcon*, 102; Milton, *Epit. Dam.* 70.

ANAPUS, a river in Sicily. Theocr., 1.68, and 7.151.

ANDROGEO, father of Sannazaro. *Arcadia*, Prose 5 and Eclogue 5.

ANGELOT: (1) Francis, Duke of Alençon and later of Anjou, one of those to whom *Bergerie* was dedicated (see ANJOU), the singer in Ronsard, 1; (2) a singer in Philips.

ANGOULÊME, a town in southwest France on the Charente, northeast of Bordeaux. Marot, 160.

ANIO, a river flowing into the Tiber near Rome. Castiglione, 139.

ANJOU, a duchy in western France, held as an appanage by Louise of Savoy until her death (1531), when it was given to Francis, Duke of Alençon. Marot, 160.

ANNA, Queen Anne of England (1702–1714). Phillips, 9.

ANTIGENES: (1) a real name, Theocr., 7.4; (2) a fictitious name, Vir., 5.89.

ARATUS, the real name of a friend of the poet, who sings his unrequited love. Theocr., 7.98.

ARCHESILAS, Gr. "chieftain," God. Boccaccio, 201.

ARCHILOCHUS, a poet born on the island of Paros (fl. 670 B.C.). Mos., 92.

ARETHUSA, a nymph pursued by the river-god Alpheus, changed by Artemis into a stream which flowed beneath the sea and rose again in Syracuse, in Sicily. This fountain bearing her name became synonymous with the Greek pastoral (see DORIS). Theocr., 1.117; Mos., 10, 78; Vir., 10.1; Milton, Lycidas, 85.

ARGUS, King Robert of Naples (1275–1343), subject in Petrarch, 2.

ARISTIS, probably a real name. Theocr., 7.99.

ARIUSIA, a town in Chios, famed for its sweet wines. Vir., 5.71.

ARLO, Aherlo, a forest valley in the Irish Galty Mts. near Kilcolman, the poet's home. Spenser, Astrophel, 96.

ARMORICA, the peninsula on the west coast of Gaul, roughly Brittany. Milton, Epit. Dam. 165.

ARVIRAGUS, son of the British King Cymbeline. Milton, Epit. Dam. 164.

ASCRA, a town of Boeotia, birthplace of Hesiod. Mos., 88.

ASTROPHEL, Sir Philip Sidney, subject of the poem by Spenser; see notes.

ASYLAS, father of Boccaccio. Olympia, 225.

ATHOS, a mountain on the Strymonian Gulf in Macedonia. Theocr., 7.77.

ATREUS, son of Pelops and brother of Thyestes. Mos., 80.

AUSONIAN, pertaining to Ausonia, part of Magna Graecia, in southern Italy. Moschus thus distinguishes himself from the Syracusan Theocritus by naming the land of his birth. Mos., 101.

BAIAE, a famous ancient city ten miles west of Naples. Sannazaro, Phyllis, 42.

BAUCIS, wife of Philemon, both honored by metamorphosis for their hospitality to Jupiter and Mercury. Milton, Epit. Dam. 88.

BAYONA, a seaport in southwestern Galicia; it is "south of Cape Finisterre, which interrupts direct vision from 'the guarded Mount' to Bayona" (Gilbert). Milton, Lycidas, 162.

BERECINTIA. See CYBELE. Boccaccio, 139.

BELINUS, a Briton prince who marched with his brother Brennus through Gaul and was said to have captured Rome. Milton, Epit. Dam. 164.

BELLERUS, Roman Bellerium, near Land's End, in Cornwall. Milton, Lycidas, 160.

BISTONIAN, Thracian. Mos., 18.

BLEMYES, a people who lived near the source of the Nile. Theocr., 7.114.

BOURBON, Constable de Bourbon (1490–1527), remembered chiefly for his military exploits against his own country. Drummond, Tears, 47.

BRASILAS, said to be another name for Poseidon, whom mythology connects with Cos. Theocr., 7.11.

BRENNUS. See BELINUS. Milton, *Epit. Dam.* 164.

BRINON, Jean (d. 1555), a patron of the Pléiade, subject of Eclogue 2, by Baïf; see notes.

BUCKHURST, the courtesy title of Lionel C. Sackville (1688–1765), who succeeded to Earl of Dorset in 1706 and later became Duke. Philips had thought of dedicating his pastorals to him, but had been dissuaded by Swift. Philips, 51.

BURINA. See CHALCON. Theocr., 7.6.

BYBLIS, a spring at Miletus. Theocr., 7.115.

CALYDNIAN, pertaining to the group of islands near Cos, the probable setting of Idyl 1. (Cholmeley reads *Calydonian,* reference being to "a coaster from Calydon to Sicily," which he takes as the setting.) Theocr., 1.57.

CAMALUS, a servant speaker in Boccaccio (see prefatory Letter).

CAMUS, the genius of the river Cam (or Granta) and of Cambridge. Milton, *Lycidas,* 103.

CASSIBELAUNUS, either the neighborhood of St. Albans in Hertfordshire, headquarters of the British king Cassivellaunus (Masson), or the Horton district, for the realm of Cassivellaunus, extending north of the Thames, included Buckinghamshire (Gilbert). Milton, *Epit. Dam.* 149.

CECROPIAN wit, Attic or genuine wit. Cecrops, first king of Attica, was said to have introduced many usages of civilization. Milton, *Epit. Dam.* 56.

CERYLUS, a fabulous sea bird (probably not a proper name). Mos., 41.

CEYX. See ALCYONE. Mos., 40; Alamanni, 2.51.

CHALCIDIAN: (1) pertaining to Chalcis, in Euboea, home of Euphorion (third century B.C.), some of whose poems were translated by Gallus: Vir., 10.50; (2) the region of Cumae, founded by colonists from Chalcis: Boccaccio, 52; Milton, *Epit. Dam.* 182.

CHALCON, son of Clytia and Eurypylus, a legendary Coan king. Chalcon discovered a fountain by applying his knee to the spot beneath which he was told was water. Over the fountain, Burina (modern Vourina), a statue to him was erected. Theocr., 7.6.

CHARIS, a pseudonym for a Florentine wit known by the poet. Milton, *Epit. Dam.* 127.

CHIAN, pertaining to Chios, an island in the Aegean, famous for its wine. Theocr., 7.47.

CHIRON, a centaur renowned for wisdom, friend of Heracles (see PHOLUS). Theocr., 7.150.

CHLORIS: (1) a nymph, personification of spring, identified by the Romans with Flora: Drummond, *Alcon,* 66; (2) possibly a real person because of the local allusion to the Chelmer (see IDUMANIAN): Milton, *Epit. Dam.* 90.

CHROMIS, a rival singer conquered by Thyrsis. Theocr., 1.24.

CISSAETHA, name of a goat, the milking of which had been promised to Thyrsis. Theocr., 1.151.

CLORINDA, Lady Mary Sidney, Countess of Pembroke, brother of Sir Philip Sidney, the fancied author of the *Lay* (see notes). Spenser, *Astrophel,* 211.

CODRUS: (1) possibly a poet hostile to the author: Vir., 5.11; (2) a name for Christ, suggested perhaps from Codrus, the Athenian king who died for his country: Boccaccio, 91, *passim.*

COGNAC, a town in southwestern France on the left bank of the Charente. Marot, 158.

COLIN, the shepherd singer in Marot and in Spenser, "November."

COLNE, an English river flowing near Horton and dividing Buckinghamshire and Middlesex. Milton, *Epit. Dam.* 149.

COMATAS, probably Sotades, author of love poems and friend of Theocritus. He was imprisoned for denouncing the incestuous marriage of Ptolemy. Theocr., 7.83.

CORYDON: (1) a shepherd in Virgil's second eclogue: Vir., 5.86; Castiglione, 125; (2) a master-singer in Virgil's seventh eclogue: Arnold, 80, 81.

COSMO Rucellai, young Florentine (d. 1518), celebrated by Alamanni; see notes for the two poems here included.

CUDDY, a rustic, his name from Spenser's *Calender*. Philips, 124.

CUMNER, Cumnor, a hill west of Oxford overlooking the city. Arnold, 99, 216.

CYBELE, or Berecintia, the Oriental, Greek, and Roman mother of all living, goddess of field, forest, and mountain. Petrarch, 2.79; Boccaccio, 53; Arnold, 177 ("the great Mother").

CYCLADES, Aegean islands circling Delos, the most important of the group. Drummond, *Tears*, 77.

CYDONIA, a town in Crete; Cretan reeds were good for arrows. Theocr., 7.12; Vir., 10.59.

CYMODOCE, a Nereid. Sannazaro, *Phyllis*, 85.

CYTHERA, an island off southern Greece, birthplace of Venus. Bion, 35.

DAMOETAS: (1) a shepherd: Vir., 5.72; Alamanni, 1.30; (2) probably Joseph Mead (see note), Milton, *Lycidas*, 36.

DAMON, Charles Diodati, subject of Milton, *Epitaphium Damonis*; see notes.

DAPHNE, Mrs. Tempest, subject of Pope, "Winter"; see note.

DAPHNIS: (1) son of Hermes and a nymph and subject of Thyrsis' song: Theocr., 1.19 and 65 ff.; his love for Xenea: Theocr., 7.73; (2) name for Julius Caesar, subject of Vir., 5; (3) synonym for the Theocritean pastoral: Petrarch, 2.63; Boccaccio, 70; Sannazaro, 5.22; Milton, *Epit. Dam.* 1, 31; Arnold, 185.

DATI, Carlo, Italian poet and friend of Milton. *Epit. Dam.* 137.

DEO, another name for Demeter, or Ceres; her festival is the chief theme of the poem. Theocr., 7.3.

DELIA, Artemis, twin sister of Apollo, born on Delos. Boccaccio, 13.

DEVA, Roman form for the Dee, which flows into the Irish Sea near Chester, from which King sailed; the poet alludes to the supposed magical powers of this river. Milton, *Lycidas*, 55.

DIDO, probably Susan Watts, subject of Spenser, "November"; see notes.

DIONE, Aphrodite or her mother. Theocr., 7.116.

DORIAN, Sicilian, a reference to Theocritus as a Dorian. Mos., 1, 12, 18, 95, 122; Arnold, 92, 94, 97.

DORIC. See DORIAN. Milton, *Lycidas*, 189; Philips, 1.

DORIS, the wife of Nereus; she represents generally the sea, through which Arethusa fled from Alpheus. Vir., 10.5.

DORSET. (See BUCKHURST). Philips, 17.

DOVEN, the Devon, which flows near Menstrie, home of Sir William Alexander. Drummond, *Tears*, 94; *Alcon*, 125.

DRYOPE, daughter of Dryops, loved by Apollo and later lured by the Dryads, who changed her into a nymph. Another myth states that she was changed into a tree because she injured the Dryad Lotis. Milton, *Epit. Dam.* 88.

EBRO, a river in northeastern Spain emptying into the Mediterranean. Boccaccio, 12.

EDONIANS, Thracians. Theocr., 7.11.

EGERIA, Roman nymph and a goddess of prophesy and childbirth; noted for wisdom, she advised King Numa. Sannazaro, 11.19.

ELISA, possibly a dead mistress. Alamanni, 1.140.

ELIZA, a reference to Spenser's panegyric to Queen Elizabeth in "April" of the *Calender*. Philips, 7.

ELSA, a river flowing near Certaldo, home of Boccaccio. Alamanni, 2.101.

ENNA, a town in Sicily near which Pluto found Prosperine and carried her away to Hades. Arnold, 95.

EOS. (See MEMNON.) Mos., 43.

ERGASTO, the poet as singer. Sannazaro, 5 and 11.

ERYX, a mountain in Sicily associated with the worship of Venus. Ronsard, *Adonis*, 34.

EUCRITUS, probably a pseudonym. Theocr., 7.1.

FIAMMETTA, mistress of Boccaccio and theme of his novel with this title. Alamanni, 2.104.

FICTES, a patron to whom the poet addresses this piece. Ronsard, *Adonis*, 1.

FRANCINE, the poet's mistress, real or imagined. Baïf, 2.145.

FRANCINI, Antonio, Italian poet and friend of Milton. *Epit. Dam.* 137.

FULGIDA, a speaker in Petrarch, 11; see notes.

FUSCA: (1) a speaker in Petrarch, 11 (see notes); (2) the mother of Olympia, Boccaccio, 51.

GALATEA: (1) daughter of Nereus and Doris. The unrequited love of the Cyclops Polyphemus for her is the theme of Bion's fragmentary Idyl 14 and of Theocritus' Idyl 11; hence her association with the pastoral: Mos., 59, 62; Sannazaro, *Phyllis*, 86; Alamanni, 2.65; (2) a speaker in Radbert (see Argument); (3) Laura, subject of Petrarch, 11; (4) an imaginary mistress in Castiglione, 76.

GALLUS, C. Cornelius, Roman poet (d. 26 B.C.), subject in Vir., 10; see notes.

GILLIAN of Croydon, a song the air to which was commonly known as "Moll Peatly." Gay, 17.

GLAUCUS, a fisherman who was transformed into an inhabitant of the sea and endowed by sea divinities with powers of prophesy and song. As pastoral Apollo pursued Daphne, so Glaucus, his piscatory equivalent, pursued the nymph Scylla. Sannazaro, *Phyllis*, 47.

GORGONIAN cave, apparently on Mt. Helicon near the spring of Hippocrene, which was produced by a blow from the hoof of Pegasus, the winged horse created from the blood of Gorgon Medusa. The place was a favorite haunt of the Muses, Apollo their leader. Boccaccio, 121.

HAEMONY, Haemonia, a poetical name for Thessaly. Spenser, *Astrophel*, 3.

HAEMUS, a mountain range in Thrace. Theocr., 7.76.

HALES, probably the river in Cos entering the sea at the town of Alice. Theocr., 7.1.

HEBRUS, a Thracian river near Mt. Rhodope; Orpheus was born nearby. Theocr., 7.112; Vir., 10.65 (see SITHONIAN); Milton, *Lycidas*, 63.

HELICE, Callisto, daughter of King Lycaon of Arcadia, where were her tomb and that of her son Arcas. Arcas was thus a grandson, not a son, of Lycaon. Theocr., 1.126.

HENRIOT, Henry II of France (1503–1555), subject of Ronsard, 1.

HIMERA, a river in northern Sicily. Theocr., 7.75; Milton, *Epit. Dam.* 1.

HINKSEYS, two villages, North H. and South H., near Oxford. Arnold, 2.

HIPPOTADES, Aeolus, god of winds, son of Hippotes. Milton, *Lycidas*, 96.

HOBBINOL, Spenser's name for Gabriel Harvey; a rustic in Philips, 125.

HOMOLE, a mountain in Thessaly. Theocr., 7.103.

HUMBER, an estuary on the east cost of England separating Yorkshire and Lincolnshire. Milton, *Epit. Dam.* 176.

HURST, a hill southwest of Oxford. Arnold, 217.

HYAS, son of Atlas and Aethra, brother of the Hyades and Pleiades. Milton, *Epit. Dam.* 88.

HYDASPES, a river of India; scene of one of Alexander's great victories, 326 B.C. Drummond, *Tears*, 70, *passim*.

HYETIS, a spring at Miletus. Theocr., 7.115.

HYLAS, a beautiful youth whom Heracles took with him on the Argonautic expedition; water nymphs fell in love with him and drew him beneath the water (Theocritus, 13). Milton, *Epit. Dam.* 1.

IDMON, the poet as singer. Drummond, *Tears*.

IDEUS, Barili, a speaker in Petrarch, 2; see notes.

IDUMANIAN river, the Chelmer in Essex, which flows into Blackwater Bay, called by Ptolemy *Portus Idumanius*. Milton, *Epit. Dam.* 90.

IOLAS, the poet as singer. Castiglione.

ISCHIRUS, a shepherd. Boccaccio, 129.

ISTER, an old name for the Danube. Drummond, *Tears*, 39.

JANOT, Ian Antoine de Baïf, the poet. Ronsard, 1.75.

JULIUS, a brother of Olympia. Boccaccio, 72.

LAURA, the mistress of Petrarch. Alamanni, 2.97.

LEPOS, pseudonym for a Florentine wit known by the poet. Milton, *Epit. Dam.* 127.

LEUCIPPUS, Castiglione's brother Jeronimo (d. 1506). *Alcon*, 87.

LYNCEAN, pertaining to Lynceus, son of Aphareus, famous for an extraordinarily keen vision; the adjective is applied to Argus, mythically the hundred-eyed guardian of Io. Petrarch, 2.108.

LINUS, the famous shepherd-singer who died in youth; see *supra*, pp. 1–2. Nemesian, 25.

LITYERSES, a Phrygian king. Arnold, 184; see note.

LOBBIN, the father of Dido. Spenser, "November," 167.

LOUISE of Savoy (1476–1531), mother of King Francis, subject in Marot.

LOUISET, pseudonym for a teacher of Brinon. Baïf, 2.47.

LUCUMO, Etruscan king, founder of Lucca, on the river Serchio. Milton visited this city, possibly on account of Diodati, whose family originated there; see Argument. Milton, *Epit. Dam.* 128.

LYAEUS, a surname of Bacchus. Boccaccio, 81.

LYCAEUS, a mountain in Arcadia. Theocr., 1.123; Vir., 10.15; Boccaccio, 114.

LYCAON. See HELICE. Theocr., 1.127.

LYCIDAS: (1) a shepherd singer, probably Leonidas of Tarentum: Theocr., 7; (2) a speaker: Sannazaro, *Phyllis*; Pope; (3) Edward King, subject in Milton, *Lycidas*; (4) pseudonym for a Florentine wit: Milton, *Epit. Dam.* 132.

LYCOPE, a city of Aetolia. Theocr., 7.72.

LYCORIS: (1) Cytheris, mistress of Gallus, formerly a mistress of Antony: Vir., 10.2, 22; (2) an imaginary mistress: Castiglione, 75.

LYCOTAS, a rival lover. Sannazaro, *Phyllis*, 25.

LYCTUS, a town in Crete. Vir., 5.72.

MAENALUS, a mountain in Arcadia. Theocr., 1.124; Vir., 10.55; Boccaccio, 114; Baïf, 2.73.

MAINE, an old French province to the south of Normandy. Marot, 162.

MANSO, Giambattista (1560–1645), Marquis of Villa, Florentine friend of Tasso and subject of a Latin elegy written in compliment by Milton. Milton, *Epit. Dam.* 181.

MANTO, a prophetess, mother of Ocnus, founder of Mantua, to which he gave his mother's name. Sannazaro, 11.19.

MARGOT, Margaret of Navarre (1492–1549), sister of Francis I, patroness of letters, author of the *Heptaméron.* Marot, 59, 109.

MARGUERITE, Margaret of Valois (1523–1574), daughter of Francis I, sister of Henry II, patroness of La Pléiade. Ronsard, 1.31.

MARIUS, a brother of Olympia. Boccaccio, 72.

MEGAERA, one of the Furies. Sannazaro, 11.67.

MEGARIA, a small island near Naples, now occupied by the Castel dell'Ovo. Sannazaro, *Phyllis*, 109.

MELES, a river near Smyrna, supposed birthplace of Bion and Homer. Mos., 72.

MELIBOEUS: (1) a shepherd named in Virgil's third eclogue: Vir., 5.87; (2) subject in Nemesian; (3) a name for Virgil: Sannazaro, 5.22; (4) a speaker: Alamanni, 1.

MEMNON, king of Aethiopia, son of Tithonus and Eos. When he was slain by Achilles at Troy, his mother obtained for him immortality. From his ashes came forth birds called after him Memnonides, which fought over his pyre and each year returned to the encounter. Mos., 44.

MENALCAS: (1) a singer: Vir. 5; (2) a shepherd: Vir., 10.20; (3) a name for Adalhard: Radbert, 152; (4) a pseudonym for a Florentine wit: Milton, *Epit. Dam.* 132.

MERGELLINA, site of the poet's home, at the east end of Posilipo, near Naples. Sannazaro, *Phyllis*, 110.

MICHAU, possibly a pseudonym. Marot, 44.

MILCON, a fisherman. Sannazaro, *Phyllis*, 42.

MINCIUS, tributary to the Po, almost encircling Mantua, Virgil's city. The river stands for Virgil. Milton, *Lycidas*, 85.

MINCIADES, Virgil. Boccaccio, 167.

MISENUM, the famous Italian promontory, three miles south of Baiae. Sannazaro, *Phyllis*, 122.

MITYLENE, a city on the island of Lesbos, which claimed Sappho. Theocr., 7.52; Mos., 93.

MOELIADES, Henry, Prince of Wales (1593–1612), subject in Drummond, *Tears* (see note for 3).

MOLOSSIAN, the mastiff, noted for its size and strength. Petrarch, 11.12.

MONA, classical name for the island of Anglesey, a northern county of Wales; it was a retreat of the Druids. Milton, *Lycidas*, 54.

MOPSUS: (1) a singer: Vir., 5 (see notes for 48–49 and 86–87); (2) a name possibly for Homer: Boccaccio, 126; (3) a shepherd: Milton, *Epit. Dam.* 75, 76.

MYRTO, a shepherdess. Theocr., 7.97.

NAMANCOS, error for Nemancos, name of one of the archpresbyteries into which the archbishopric of Santiago de Compostella is divided; the district is "the most western part of the country, terminating in Cape Finisterre" (Gilbert). (See BAYONA.)   Milton, *Lycidas*, 162.

NEAERA, an imaginary mistress.   Milton, *Lycidas*, 69.

NISIDA, a small island beyond Posilipo.   Sannazaro, *Phyllis*, 14.

NISAEE, a Nereid.   Sannazaro, *Phyllis*, 84.

OEAGRIAN, Thracian, or pertaining to the myth of Orpheus, son of Oeagrus, a Thracian king (see STRYMONIAN).   Mos., 17; Nemesian, 25.

OECUS, a town near Miletus; there was a shrine of Aphrodite here.   Theocr., 7.116.

OLYMPIA, the poet's daughter Violante, a speaker (see prefatory Letter).   Boccaccio, 241.

ORCUS, a god of the underworld, the name being often used of the underworld itself.   Milton, *Epit. Dam.* 201.

OUSE, of two English rivers of this name, probably that rising in Oxfordshire and flowing through Buckinghamshire, Bedford, Huntington, Cambridge, and Norfolk into the Wash.   Milton, *Epit. Dam.* 175.

PALAEMON, a sea-god, on earth called Melicertes, son of Leucothea, who before her transformation was named Ino (see PANOPE).   Sannazaro, *Phyllis*, 85.

PALES, an Italian deity of flocks.   Vir., 5.35; Baïf, 2.63.

PANOPE, a Nereid by whose aid Melicertes and Ino were changed into deities.   Sannazaro, *Phyllis*, 86; Milton, *Lycidas*, 99.

PAROS, one of the Cyclades (see ARCHILOCHUS).   Mos., 92.

PARRHASIAN, pertaining to Parrhasia, a city in Arcadia.   Boccaccio, 127.

PARTHENIUS, a mountain in Arcadia.   Vir., 10.57.

PENEUS, a river in Thessaly rising on Mt. Pindus.   Theocr., 1.67.

PERMESSUS, a river in Boeotia rising on Mt. Helicon, sacred to Apollo and the Muses.   Baïf, 2.30.

PERROT, the poet himself.   Ronsard, 1.86.

PHILINUS, a real or unreal name of a friend of the poet.   Theocr., 7.105, 118, 121.

PHILETAS, a Coan teacher and writer of elegies.   Theocr., 7.40.

PHOLUS, a centaur who entertained Heracles in his cave on Mt. Pholoe with wine given to him by Bacchus.   The other centaurs flocked to the treat and were killed by the arrows of Heracles.   Both Pholus and Chiron accidentally met death in this encounter.   Theocr., 7.149.

PHRASIDEMUS, a real name.   Theocr., 7.3.

PHYLLIS: (1) an imaginary mistress: Vir. 5.10 and 10.37, 41; (2) one of the singers in Radbert (see prefatory Argument); (3) subject in Sannazaro, *Phyllis* (see notes).

PINDUS, the Thessalian mountain on the borders of Macedonia and Epirus, seat of the Muses.   Theocr., 1.67; Vir., 10.11.

POSILIPO, a promontory northwest of Naples.   Sannazaro, *Phyllis*, 13.

PRIAPUS, a rustic god of fertility, or his effigy.   Theocr., 1.21, 81; Mos., 27.

PROCIDA, an island southwest of Naples.   Sannazaro, *Phyllis*, 122.

PTELEA, probably a place in Cos.   Theocr., 7.65.

PUNIC, Carthaginian, African.   Vir., 5.27.

PYLEMON, a fictitious name.   Sannazaro, *Phyllis*, 11.

PYTHIAS, Barbato, friend of the poet, a speaker in Petrarch, 2; see notes.

PYXA, a Coan town. Theocr., 7.130.

RAFFY of Lyons, a shepherd artisan, real or imaginary. Marot, 42.

RHADAMANTHUS, son of Jupiter and Europa, brother of Minos, and on earth a wise lawgiver; after death he was made a judge in the lower world. Sannazaro, 11.67.

RHODOPE, a mountain range in Thrace, a part of the Haemus. Theocr., 7.77.

ROMORANTIN, a small town near Blois, in central France, at the confluence of the Sauldre and the Morantin. Marot, 159.

ROSALIND, Colin's mistress. Spenser, "November," 44.

RUTUPIAN, called by Ptolemy *Rhutupiae*, an ancient city in Kent standing at the southern mouth of the Wantsum. Milton, *Epit. Dam.* 162.

SABAEAN, pertaining to the Biblical Sheba, in southern Arabia, noted for its fragrant gums and spices. Boccaccio, 36.

SAMOS, an island off the coast of Asia Minor. Theocr., 7.40.

SEBETO, a small stream entering the sea at Naples. Sannazaro, *Phyllis*, 105.

SICANIAN, Sicilian; the Sicani were the oldest inhabitants of the island. Vir., 10.4.

SICELIDAS, a patronymic or *nom de plume* of Asclepiades of Samos, an epigrammatist. Theocr., 7.40.

SIDERE, a pseudonym for Brinon's mistress. Baïf, 2.6, *passim*.

SILVANUS, Roman god of woods and fields. Vir., 10.24; Boccaccio, 78.

SILVIUS, name for the two poets as speakers: Petrarch, 2; Boccaccio, *Olympia* (see prefatory Letter).

SIMICHIDAS, the poet as speaker and singer; see note. Theocr., 7.21.

SIREN: (1) the marvelous singers who attempted to entice Odysseus: Mos., 37; (2) one of their group, Parthenope, who threw herself into the sea and whose body was washed ashore near Naples, first named for her: Sannazaro, 11.91; *Phyllis*, 104.

SITHONIAN. Thracian. "The Thracian Hebrus and 'Sithonian snows' mark extremes of cold, as Aethiopia does of heat. . . . Sithone is the middle promontory of the three which extend from Chalcidice into the Aegean Sea" (Jerram). Vir., 10.66.

STELLA, Frances Walsingham, wife of Sir Philip Sidney; four years after his death, in 1586, she married Robert Devereux, second Earl of Essex. Spenser, *Astrophel*, 189.

STIMICHON, a fictitious name. Vir., 5.55.

STRYMONIAN, pertaining to Strymon, a river in Thrace, home of Orpheus. Mos., 14.

SULMO, modern Sulmona, the native city of Barbato (and of Ovid). Petrarch, 2.122.

SYRINX, the Arcadian Hamadryad who escaped the embraces of Pan and was changed into a reed—the syrinx or Pan's pipe. Marot, 247.

TAGUS, the longest river of Spain. Drummond, *Tears*, 117.

TAMAR, a river in southwestern England emptying into the Channel. Milton, *Epit. Dam.* 178.

TEIAN, pertaining to Teos, city in Ionia, birthplace of Anacreon. Mos., 91.

TERAPON, a servant speaker. Boccaccio (see prefatory Letter).

THENOT, a speaker. Marot; Spenser, "November."

THULE, an island in the extreme north of Europe regarded by the ancients as the most northerly point on earth, possibly Iceland. Drummond, *Tears*, 70, *passim*.

THYMBRIS, a place in Sicily, either a mountain or a valley. Theocr., 1.118.

THYRSIS: (1) the singer: Theocr., 1; Milton, *Epit. Dam.*; Pope; Alamanni, 1; (2) Arthur Hugh Clough (1819–1861), subject in Arnold.

TIMETAS, the singer in Nemesian.

TIRYNTHIAN, Hercules, who was reared at Tiryns, a town of Argolis. Alamanni, 2.130.

TITYRUS: (1) pseudonym for Alexander of Aetolia, author of a poem dealing with the Daphnis legend. He was a son of Satyros, and *Tityrus* is said to be the Doric equivalent of *Satyrus:* Theocr., 7.72; (2) a servant: Vir., 5.12; (3) a speaker: Nemesian; (4) a name for Virgil: Boccaccio, 125; Milton, *Epit. Dam.* 117; (5) an imaginary shepherd: Milton, *Epit. Dam.* 69.

TOUVRE, a river in southwestern France flowing into the Charente. Marot, 163.

TRENT, a river rising in northern Staffordshire and uniting with the Ouse to form the Humber. Milton, *Epit. Dam.* 176.

TRIVIA, surname of Hecate as goddess of ghosts. Boccaccio, 83.

TYNDAREUS, a Spartan king, supposed father of Helen of Troy, though Zeus was more generally accounted her sire. Mos., 79.

WYTHAM flats, northwest of Oxford, on the Thames. Arnold, 123.

XENEA, a maiden, possibly a nymph, associated with one of the forms of the Daphnis legend (see notes). Theocr., 7.73.